An Incurable Past

UNIVERSITY PRESS OF FLORIDA

Florida A&M University, Tallahassee
Florida Atlantic University, Boca Raton
Florida Gulf Coast University, Ft. Myers
Florida International University, Miami
Florida State University, Tallahassee
New College of Florida, Sarasota
University of Central Florida, Orlando
University of Florida, Gainesville
University of North Florida, Jacksonville
University of South Florida, Tampa
University of West Florida, Pensacola

An Incurable Past

Nasser's Egypt Then and Now

Mériam N. Belli

UNIVERSITY PRESS OF FLORIDA

Gainesville | Tallahassee | Tampa | Boca Raton
Pensacola | Orlando | Miami | Jacksonville | Ft. Myers | Sarasota

Copyright 2013 by Mériam N. Belli
All rights reserved
Printed in the United States of America on acid-free paper

This book may be available in an electronic edition.

22 21 20 19 18 17 16 6 5 4 3 2 1

First cloth printing, 2013
First paperback printing, 2017

A record of cataloging-in-publication data is available from the Library of Congress.
ISBN 978-0-8130-4404-0 (cloth)
ISBN 978-0-8130-5409-4 (pbk.)

The University Press of Florida is the scholarly publishing agency for the State University System of Florida, comprising Florida A&M University, Florida Atlantic University, Florida Gulf Coast University, Florida International University, Florida State University, New College of Florida, University of Central Florida, University of Florida, University of North Florida, University of South Florida, and University of West Florida.

University Press of Florida
15 Northwest 15th Street
Gainesville, FL 32611-2079
http://www.upf.com

Aux âmes soeurs et rebelles

The sea is angry, the sea does not laugh
For it's not a laughing matter
The sea has a wound that does not heal
And our wound has no cure
Poor us, we laugh of misery

Fu'ad Nigm and Najib Surur, "Why does the sea laugh?"

Contents

List of Figures viii
List of Tables ix
Acknowledgments xi

Introduction: This Incurable Otherness 1

Part I. Retelling Salah al-Din: The Future Is Everything 15

Chapter 1. Farouk Is Gone, Long Live the Revolution 19

Chapter 2. The New Order 49

Part II. Burn, Edmund, Burn: The Present Is Everything 75

Chapter 3. When Edmund Allenby Became al-Limby 85

Chapter 4. Port Said, Martyr City 105

Chapter 5. The End of History 136

Part III. St. Mary, Mother of Egypt: The Past Is Everything 163

Chapter 6. The Science of Miracles 167

Chapter 7. Globalizing the Virgin, Nationalizing Religion 192

Conclusion: "What Revolution?!" 216

List of Abbreviations 225
Notes 227
Bibliography 265
Index 285

Figures

1.1. Women and education. Bronze mural, 1969 35
1.2. *Falaqa* punishment at the kuttab. Watercolor, ca. 1937 37
1.3. Schoolgirls in uniform. Sculpture, ca. 1937 40
4.1. Female combatant, Port Said, 2007 125
6.1. 1968 Mariophany in Zaytun 169
6.2. Devotional image of Pope Kyrillus VI and St. Menas 180
6.3. Devotional image of the 1986 apparition of the Virgin at St. Damiana Church, Papadouplo 186
7.1. Marian apparition of 2000 reported in *Akhir Sa'a* 194
7.2. Immaculata of Zaytun keychain 205
C.1. Graffiti of Nasser on the side of a building in Qena, 2012 217

Tables

1.1. Educational levels for history instruction and course content during the Mubarak years, 1996–2000   22
1.2. Student enrollment (in thousands), 1952–2009   29
2.1. The Nasser years in primary, preparatory, and secondary level textbooks, 1995–2000   60
2.2. Historical themes, primary to secondary school, 1995–2000   62
2.3. Events and places cited in fourth-grade 1998 history curriculum   65
2.4. Fourth grade 1998 history curriculum   66
7.1. Mariophanies in the national press, 1968–2000   202

Acknowledgments

A series of thanks reads curiously like a eulogy. But then, here it is. Over the years, from the beginning through the numerous revisions of this manuscript, I have become indebted to many people. A book is in innumerable ways a collective creation. I owe a debt of gratitude to the troubled family of the Centre d'Études et de Documentation Économique Juridique et Sociale (CEDEJ)—an amazing center of pluridisciplinary academic encounter, unlike any other, with a remarkable collection of dossiers and eclectic, passionate minds. I owe most to those people, too many to be named, who shared with a foreigner and a stranger bits and pieces of their lives and thoughts in the midst of much distrust. Thus, the testimonies that seem to so naturally belong to the pages of this manuscript were more often than not a struggle to gather. I am grateful for the generosity of the people who received me into their homes even while they did not know me, like the Masri family in Ismailia and the 'Awad family in Port Said. May Ra'uf 'Abbas, 'Amm 'Awad, 'Abd al-Rahim al-Banna, and 'Amm 'Uthman rest in peace. These were rare and noble hearts.

Many helped with the little, big, and grueling tasks of book writing and editing. Some read parts or all of my manuscript. Others provided insightful professional and technical advice. Others gave me needed encouragement and professional and academic support. Others corrected my Frenglish. At both ends of my journey, I am most indebted to James B. Collins, my unrelenting mentor and first editor. Our intellectual exchange, while I was doing research in Egypt, was crucial to the existence of this book. I am equally grateful to Walter Armbrust, a man whose knowledge and humility have inspired me as a teacher and as a scholar. He much informed the theoretical direction of this work. At the other end of the journey I am grateful to Israel Gershoni for his sagacity. He welcomed a stranger to his table and gave me invaluable recommendations. I am thankful to many of my colleagues and to diverse institutions for their support during the different stages of this work: to Eve Troutt-Powell and Pillarisetti Sudhir when I was at the American Historical Association (AHA); to Philip Khoury at the welcoming Massachusetts Institute of Technology (MIT); and in my new home, to the indispensable Patricia Goodwin, to Michaela Hoenicke-Moore, Dean Raul Curto, Lisa Heineman, Colin Gordon, Stephen Vlastos, Shel Stromquist, Michael Moore, Paul Greenough, Jeffrey Cox, and to the resourceful John Hammond. For his help over the years, too, I extend heartfelt thanks to Dr. John Voll. At the University Press of Florida, for their work bringing my manuscript to press, my sincere thanks to Amy Gorelick and most especially to Nevil Parker and Patti Bower for their exemplary scrutiny, their professionalism, and their compassion.

Many organizations and institutions supported the research for this book. In Cairo, I thank Mahmoud Salah, chief editor at *Akhir Sa'a*. In Port Said, I salute Colonel Salah al-Din al-Sukri, director of the Museum of War. While obscurantism and politics plagued many of my bureaucratic endeavors in Egypt this year, these individuals received my project with intellectual interest, respect, and professionalism. In Washington, D.C., the Library of Congress was my home away from home for years, and it hosted me again for a fruitful summer in 2007, thanks to the National History Center and Wm. Roger Louis, as well as the American Historical Association. At the University of Iowa Library, I thank the bibliographer of the Middle East and Africa collection, Dr. Edward Miner, who is simply amazing. I thank the many institutions that have supported this work financially. I am most grateful to the Fulbright Commission, as well as to MIT and the University of Iowa, which provided me with research funds for the completion of this project and the beginning of a new one.

In Cairo, still and always my love to Shohdy Muhammad and his inspiring creative historical fabrications that glow like the ends of his ever-burning cigarettes. Thanks to Mahmud al-Wardani, voice of many untold tales. In Boston, I thank for their encouragement and friendship the mad Paul Saba and the wise Abu Ahmad. I am honored to know them. They brought me warmth and an irreplaceable sense of place and self. In Iowa City, that sense of place I owe in equal measure to Lisa, Michaela, and Michael, to Ted Redding at the Crowded Closet, to the tribe of Ronalds Street, and to the Bike Library folks. With few words but profound feeling, I thank my partner in suffering, joy, Bourgogne, and mischief, along with my second mother, for their loving support over these past few years. But I owe everything to my sister, who will never read this book yet brags about how I tell stories.

Introduction: This Incurable Otherness

> Identity = reality, as if, in the end, everything must necessarily and absolutely be one and the same. But the other refuses to disappear; it subsists; it persists; it is the hard bone on which reason breaks its teeth. Abel Martín, with a poetic faith as human as rational faith, believed in the other, in "the essential Heterogeneity of being," in what might be called the incurable otherness from which oneness must always suffer.
>
> Antonio Machado Ruiz, *Juan de Mairena*

Cairo, 2003

So spoke Taha Sa'ad 'Uthman:

To start with, [I am] Taha Sa'ad 'Uthman. ... I live ... in Shubra al-Khayma. ... Ms. Mériam Belli ... asked to meet me for her [study] on the Egyptian [working] people, that is the life of ordinary people, unlike the life written in the books on the beys and the pashas and the ministers and the parties and the political developments. She wants on the contrary to apply the method followed by al-Jabarti in his recording of the life of the Egyptian people, from fact and from nature, and she has chosen the life of Taha Sa'ad 'Uthman ... that is me ... as an example of the life of the poor Egyptian people. ... This meeting took place in my domicile, on Tuesday, December 10th 2002. ... [1]

Prior to granting me an interview, 'Uthman, retired worker, political activist, and amateur historian, had me give my word of honor that I would provide him with a copy of the tapes and transcripts of our conversations. His home office displayed his own abundant publications on the labor movement; he wanted me to publicize his name and work. He was not new to interviews. Reputable labor historians had preceded me. He was aware of contributing to a bottom-up history, but he simultaneously acknowledged disciplinary authority (al-Jabarti, doctorate). He shared his recollections with marked self-awareness, methodically, without irony, as one does a precious material object. Giving, yet retaining.

Port Said, 2000

For reasons of public safety, state authorities banned a street festival commemorating the popular resistance against British presence on the Suez Canal. I look in vain, all evening, for the elusive "al-Limby." I finally find him at the end of the night, on the way back to my hotel . . . its large corpse, rather, which police agents are dragging in the street. And then throw into a truck. Meanwhile, government authorities announced without irony their decision to honor the soon-to-be-defunct Limby effigy-burning festival with a documentary film and a commemorative museum. If ever built, this museum would add to the existing museum of war, and to military monuments and murals that the tourist industry has not yet drowned in the shadow of its gaudy hotels.

These two anecdotes illustrate the primary focus of this work: vernacular agencies, be they the likes of 'Uthman in Shubra al-Khayma or the many anonymous actors of the Limby Spring festival in Port Said. Contemporary scholarship and media often cast their attention on political leadership and organized movements. However, recent events in the Middle East have reasserted the momentous role of vernacular, unregulated agencies in shaping history.

These anecdotes also bring forward the core questions of this book. What are the processes involved in history-making? What is the interplay between a historical experience and its telling? By the act of telling, we strive to make sense of yet thereby ineluctably alter, order, and homogenize the past. The past is thus an incurable otherness. But the idea that one might be able to preserve and resurrect the *reality* of things past is a potent chimera. Individuals and collectivities alike often perform this task with confidence. In our society of spectacle, sophisticated bloggers, social media platform, and self-advertisement, the idea that the present is already history we can *show* as it is might never be stronger. In 2011–12, during demonstrations on "the Square," men and women used cameras and cell phones to encapsulate what they saw as history as it was happening. The present is thus immediately memorialized. And the image substitutes for the text. News is made of those images in addition to those (sometimes contradictory) of the mass media, which populism has its precedent in the 1950s–60s. Newspapers, television, and transistors transformed the political field and established its tone. They also shaped today's popular demand for social justice and a virtuous state.

This book examines Egyptian vernacular politics, agencies, and historical perceptions through both a history of the 1950s–60s and later cultural productions. I study historical utterances of the 1950s–60s, by which I signify both the intimate and the public expressions of social experiences unequally shared and produced by heterogeneous groups, simultaneously in the past and in the present. Like the "history of memory" (sites/realms of memory) of Pierre Nora that inspired this work, a study of historical utterances requires confronting historical evidence as well as the simultaneous "material, symbolic, and functional" realities of historical representations.[2] Thus, I similarly examine "the evolution of different social practices, their form and content, *having for object or for effect*, explicitly or not, the representation of the past and the maintenance of remembrance."[3] Yet I seek to develop an alternative study of history, which promotes noninstitutional, nonelite sources, as well as a dialogic and dynamic understanding of history-making. Thus, I posit that historical utterances are relational and referential projections about human experience. I premise that the form and content of such projections are unstable and often contradictory. For what we imagine, say, sing, and write about the past is in "continuous and constant interaction," in interactive dialogue with other individual and collective, endogenous and extraneous instances—such as what others saw, heard, wrote, and read.

The conceptual framework of this book builds upon the works of historian Alessandro Portelli, sociologist Maurice Halbwachs, and literary critic Mikhail Bakhtin.[4] This book simultaneously weaves together textually based empirical accounts, oral and written testimonies, historiographical reflection, and official history, such as "the life written in the books on the beys and pashas." I thus conceived of this history anthropologically as a "subjectification of the object" of history.[5] A multilateral, nonlinear history is best explored through materials that give us insights into some of the subjective and emotional dimensions of culture and politics and through conventional material artifacts. In addition, as in any work of anthropological history, a study of historical utterances consciously integrates specialized and vernacular media. It treats equally these different genres within the realm of social and cultural productions. This book thus includes oral accounts, memoirs, songs, art works, films, television, exhibits, archives, newspapers, literature, textbooks, and so on. Such sources offer *intimate* and vernacular (oral testimonies) and *communal* and official (historiography, commemorations, exhibits) accounts.

An Incurable Past?

The initial observation that prompted this study was the conservancy of the 1950s–60s in Egyptian intimate and communal narratives, down to the iconography that sprang up after the January 2011 events. Their overwhelming political weight and the sharp disagreements they spawned intrigued me. To its detractors, this was a period of oppression and betrayed aspirations. To its advocates, this was an age of promises derailed by reactionary forces. The evocative power of Jamal 'Abd al-Nasser in the present, some forty years after his death, is matched only in the United States and France by such quasi-mythical figures as John F. Kennedy and Charles de Gaulle. Yet American and French shopkeepers do not commonly adorn their shops with pictures of the dead presidents.

As conveyed by sociologist Maurice Halbwachs, "the past, in reality, does not re-appear as is"; rather, "we reconstruct it from the vantage point of the present."[6] What use, then, have utterances of the 1950s–60s served in the many presents in which they have been articulated since Nasser's death in 1970? How do they refract ways of thinking past and present? What do they teach about past and present? Why would Egyptians negotiate their present by reference to Nasserian policies (revolution) and to those policies that the republic rebutted (constitutional monarchy)? On a political level, the 1950s–60s generally recall decolonization, pan-Arabism, the nonalignment movement, and Egyptian autonomy. On an individual level, though, the 1950s–60s evoke a more complex and contradictory spectrum of experiences, where the historical is evaluated in the light of the personal. Yet post–World War II Middle East historiography, and even more so the historiography of the past thirty years, generally adopts the former conventional political tropes.[7] It thus recounts political leaders, ideologies, military strategies, and the Arab-Israeli conflict.[8] This sharply contrasts with a premodern and modern Middle East historiography, and the historiography found in other fields—such as American, European, and South American historiography, which are concerned with everyday life.[9] By contributing to a social and cultural history of the 1950s–60s and developing new tropes, I thus intend to partake of the historiographical "process of cultural decolonization."[10]

One means to do so is a study of historical utterances that does not discriminate between historical sources.[11] Books, television, radio, and cinema all feed personal representations of the past.[12] Conversely, personal experiences weave the fabric of public media, professional history, and political rationalities. As Marc Bloch wrote, "In truth, consciously or not, it is always from our everyday life experiences that . . . we borrow in last analysis the elements we need to reconstruct the past."[13] Moreover, the historian who tries to capture the past does so with the interpretive constraints of the present.[14] Thus, no record of the past truly and objectively reflects "things as they really happened," in the famous words of Leopold von Ranke. Historians who have been intimate with the most factual consulate and embassy records know that their objectivity is largely artificial.

Fortunately, historical truth is not the object, per se, of this work.[15] Historical utterances certainly point to material realities. But they most especially illuminate the "workings of culture," "moral life," and subjective realities.[16] Like these realities, the present account is thus made of disparate, heterogeneous elements that are in dialogue with one another, in the past and in the present. As a result, the polyphony of historical utterances is constantly renegotiated. In addition, utterances are situated in a specific time and place (*chronotopia*, or time-place), and one cannot assume their validity in another *chronotopia*.

Memory and Collectivity

I have proceeded on the assumption that singular events and accounts of the past (such as a life story) enable us to peek into larger historical moments.[17] I hence espouse "a nonessentialist definition of event as a cultural construction based on the context created by memory though selection and connection among a multiplicity of happenings and by the form in which the story is told. I will then go on to interpret the 'meaning' of these events, that is, what they tell us about the culture that experiences and remembered them."[18] The accent here is on the present tense of the experience, the past tense of remembering, and the interconnectedness of both past and present. There is a multiplicity of potential storytelling, for the form and content of an utterance is contextual. Furthermore, historical reconstruction, Portelli reminds us, is an individually active and complex process informed by both reason and emotion.

Studying historical experiences and their representations naturally brings about similar questions and requires similar methodologies as those of the scholarship on memory. Yet, along the line of Richard Handler and James Clifford, who wrote about identity, we need another language than the discourse of memory in order to comment creatively upon the object of that discourse. Admittedly, though, no matter how deeply compromised memory is, one can hardly do without this term.[19] While including it in this work, I thus attempt to restrict its usage to intimate utterances. I favor an alternative terminology that invites self-consciousness. "Historical utterance" thus more adequately characterizes conceptually the dynamic ways by which individuals and collectivities summon a particular past, in a time-place. This best describes the constant reappraisal of the past, this movement of narratives between now and then. Also, historical utterances convey the fragility and ephemerality of those representations often construed as solid truths.

Similarly, we need to develop a language other than "collective memory" to discuss historical experiences and representations unequally shared.[20] The notion of collective memory has become overloaded. It has often been crystallized and adopted without sufficient appraisal.[21] Like "memory" and "identity," the term commonly eludes debate. It simply is.[22] I have hence retained from Halbwachs' *Cadres de la mémoire* its essential contributions. I embrace the idea that individuals transmit historical utterances through various media (remembrances, commemorative ceremonies, etc.) and within dynamic, plural, and overlapping social environments (family, religion, class, etc.).[23] I thus apply to historical utterances Halbwachs' cultural understanding of memory as developed in the revised 1997 edition of *La mémoire collective*, in which memory is a common language acquired by the group.[24] Halbwachs likens it to a code of musical notations in the case of musicians: "These complex combinations [of sound] can be broken down into simpler combinations, the simpler combinations are certainly more abundant than the notes, but they are often reproduced in a same piece, or from one piece to another.... That which must retain the attention is the combination of elementary motifs, the assembly of notes or words already known. Thus is reduced and simplified the task of memory."[25] Time-space thus unifies the disparate elements of memory, like musical measures and phrases unify notations. Memory is thus language (music, rhetoric) composed of "complex combinations" (arrangements and variations, grammar), which can be dismantled into smaller elements (notes, motifs). I understand historical utterances as such and structured this book accordingly. While the combinations and assembling of elementary motifs are almost infinite, these motifs themselves are finite. Like an orchestra's musical motifs and speech genres, historical utterances are simultaneously heterogeneous, boundless, and limited. They are circumscribed but leave space for original improvisations.[26]

The early scholarship on representations of the past, however, built on the social framework of *Les cadres* rather than the semantic notion articulated in

La mémoire collective. As a result, the notion of "collective identity" prevails in the history of memory scholarship. It crystallizes around the idea of a collective narrative, or shared oblivion, or both, to which the group owes its social coherence.[27] However, as Jocelyn Dakhlia has argued, "oblivion is real only if the body is real."[28] The notion of shared memory/oblivion thus postulates the group. It rigidifies the collectivity and erroneously equates group with collectivity. It grants permanence to a historically transient body of individuals. *Les lieux de mémoire*, along with *Les cadres*, helped diffuse such equation between group and collectivity, and, further, between collectivity and nation.[29] Much of the scholarship on nationalism, remembrance, and identity hence centers on the national collectivity. It thus operates, explicitly or not, in relation to the nation-state. Equating collectivity, community, nation, and state leads to neglecting utterances that coexist along with the historiography of the nation-state and that are not necessarily exceptional, marginal, or subsumed by national institutions.[30]

The scholarship on nationalism, remembrance, and identity nonetheless provides powerful analytical tools and insights into the articulation between modern nation-building and history-making. I retain the notion, developed by Eric Hobsbawm and Terence Ranger in *The Invention of Tradition* (1983), that modern societies creatively reinvent and reframe tradition and the sacred.[31] Hobsbawm and Ranger show that societies root modern, novel political rituals and cultural artifacts in the far mythical past as a means of achieving social cohesion by creating a sense of temporal continuity. A transient body of individuals thus imagines itself permanent or ancient.

I also borrow another aspect of remembrance and identity from Nora's *Lieux*: the *historiographical* death of memory and the sacred *as we knew it*.[32] Not that totemic and critical narratives are so very distinct from one another, as Nora argues. Yet our modern societies differentiate between positivist historical science and discipline and mythical, ontological, and epic narrative— thus reinventing the sacred.[33] 'Uthman appraises differently the Hilalian epic from Jabarti's account of Napoleon's invasion. Some certainly question the authority of positivist science. They use religious scriptures, for example, as factual evidence to explain the creation of the universe, homophobia, cataclysmic beliefs, and so on. But as Jeanne Favret-Saada has shown, positivist modes of explanation today supersede and frame supernatural ones, even in ecclesiastical milieus.[34] Likewise, as shown in this book, religious authorities, at the apparition of the Virgin Mary at Zaytun in 1968, legitimated the supernatural within a positivist framework of analysis.

This book also adopts from the literature on nation (alism), memory, and history its interest in memory-politics. Yet the scholarship on memory routinely supports the idea that political institutions and organizations effectively impress historical narratives on credulous populations. Such manipulation would ineluctably condition predesigned ideological attitudes and mentalities.[35] This book, however, questions Mnemosyne's power. To what extent, we must ask, can we presume the almightiness of memory-politics? Can we surmise the ability of a group, an organization, and institutions to impress a specific historical projection? Do particular conditions, tools, and strategies secure such indoctrination? And for how long do realms of memory remain potent? Indeed, as ostentatious as they might be, history books, patriotic hymns, military parades, and monuments do not infallibly determine any specific effect on their targets. Landmarks, cenotaphs, and street names certainly inform us of the politics of memory of a civic association, a municipal council, or a ministry. Yet how shall we account for these sites' influence on vernacular historical imagination and political action? Who among the French thinks of *À la recherche du temps perdu* when savoring a little madeleine? Without an evaluation of their reception by their intended audience, objects of memory only point to the ideological design or to the emotional makeup of those who generated them. Design, however, proves neither instrumentality nor effect. It does not indicate whether objects of memory achieved their calculated goal. For instance, news of the Zaytun Mariophany served an ideological purpose in 1968. But was this premeditated? And even so, didn't crowds see the Virgin? However, how many of these seers believed the apparition to be heaven's blessing of Arab nationalism? The ontological apparition and following Mariophanies remain polysemic. Some utterances targeted a national audience. They had an ideological intent. Others had an intimate meaning. They were intended for the Coptic community. Furthermore, commemorative events and monuments that celebrate a particular rule, government, and ideologues, and that are the product of narcissistic performances, are most evanescent. Who can identify the many equestrian statues of Buenos Aires outside Plaza de Mayo? This holds all the more true when physical and immaterial monuments were not the product of a consensus and a dialogue between civil society and public institutions.

Thus, apprehending the workings of historical utterances without being limited to their public and institutional forms, and without presupposing their impact, demands the association of historical, anthropological, and sociological methods of inquiry. Only then can we account for vernacular agencies, ways individuals reflexively receive and act upon historical utterances, make history, and position themselves politically.

Historical Utterances

The notion of historical utterance I advance, based upon Bakhtin's concept of speech genre and experience, eludes the metaphoric and phenomenological associations attached to memory/remembrance and benefits vernacular history. What historians commonly define as memory by opposition to history, in account of the subjectivity of the former and the objectivity of the latter, can thus be defined as a "speech genre" within the larger sphere of cultural instances that "speak of the past." Historical utterance avoids the dialectic relationship of the object and its image. It is rather an inclusive notion that embraces the wide sphere of "human communication and activity" that takes history for object.

Bakhtin defined literary utterances as referentially semantic elements defined by their field.[36] Correspondingly, historical utterances are above anything else relational, codependent, and situated. Historical imaginations, interpretations, and narratives borrow their constitutive elements from past and coeval utterances to which they respond. Also, in the same way that we articulate our personal identity by opposition to a presumed otherness, we also articulate the past in *response* to what we presume it was not. In the words of Bakhtin, the process involved is one of "*assimilation*—more or less creative—of others' words (and not the words of a language). Our speech, that is, all our utterances (including creative works), is filled with others' words, varying degrees of otherness or varying degrees of 'our-own-ness,' varying degrees of awareness and detachment. These words of others carry with them their own expression, their own evaluative tone, which we assimilate, rework, and reaccentuate."[37] Thus, the ways we define ourselves and name others in turn (identification) are narrowly bound to the presentation and projection (image) of ourselves in time. The historian utters her narrative in the present and thus recounts the self and the other in the past and in the present.[38] Historical utterances hence share in a society's dialogue among its various constituents. For example, education is a familiar theme in the reminiscence and historiography of 1950s–60s things past. Yet interpretations as to the benefits and development of education under Nasser vary. Individuals thus produce "polyphonic" and "polysemic" narratives that are "called continually into question."[39]

Polymorphism does not mean relativism. The polymorphy of historical utterances does not mean that history, as a result, becomes aleatory, incoherent, and meaningless. Time-space provides coherence. In addition, historical utterances are organized around a set of vast yet limited chronotopic motifs. Coherence tolerates dissonance.[40] For contradiction is the very essence of humanness. Narrative incoherencies provoke reevaluation, which potentially generates motion. Thus, dissonance is the essence of a society's dynamism. Dissonance conduces to confrontation and, eventually, to a society's acceptance of its contradictory past.

Performances

"We produce histories by performing them and we live by being critics of their theatre," Greg Dening wrote. Against the distinction between history as past perfect and memory as present, Dening argues that "in history, past and present are . . . indivisible. Performances about the past in HISTORY *are* present. . . . But both the past, and the Other are more than present. They are *presented*—they are *presented* in the dramaturgies of our inventions."[41] This book studies the "indivisible" past and present performances of Nasserian times past by merging conventional and alternative historical objects and tools. I examine nation-state building and the institutional formulation of national identity. I study institutional discourses about the national community in the light of vernacular formulations and actions. I study power relations as manifested by competitive historical narratives.[42] I weigh up elite and institutional constructions of history, myths, and symbols,[43] along with and against vernacular accounts.[44] To that end, I conducted extensive interviews, for oral history helps us capture the experiences of subaltern groups. As Portelli writes, "oral history is more intrinsically itself when it listens to speakers who are not already recognized protagonists in the public sphere" because such protagonists adopt "established genres of historical writing."[45]

Recording interviewees happened to be an arduous task. Outside of public actors (politicians, intellectuals), most ordinary people were reluctant and often fearful to speak to a recorder, despite guarantees of anonymity. People were most unguarded and comfortable outside formal settings. I thus used both formal interviews and informal conversations in the fabric of these chapters. My interviewees were protagonists situated both inside and outside the public sphere: historians, lawyers, writers, artists, students, housewives, teachers, and workers.

The Nasser Years

There is but one history monograph on vernacular experiences in Nasserian Egypt, Reem Saad's social anthropology of Upper Egypt. Saad's pioneering work examines rural historical perceptions and how these define a "collective image of a moral and political order." Saad stresses two crucial experiences: war and agrarian reform. More recently, the collective history of memory edited by Elie Podeh and Onn Winckler offers a first venture into a sociocultural history of the 1950s–60s, even though this book focuses on defining the political and ideological movement called Nasserism.[46]

I chose three windows to the 1950s–60s—three motifs, time and again encountered during fieldwork: schooling, conflict, and national unity. In the words of Bakhtin, I tackle each of these "individual areas" by investigating their "boundaries."[47] Such boundaries are thus partially subjective, if only because I selected the objects of this inquiry on the basis of what I perceived was their narrative predominance—many instances would be forgotten if it were not for historians' grave-digging and artificial conservation, a dubious enterprise this book ineluctably joins in.[48] The areas under study here are polysemic, discrete, yet bound. They represent three levels of community, experience, and narration—national, regional, and religious. These individual areas owe their cohesion to three elements: time-space, elementary motif, and context. Narratively, they all belong to one time-space: the 1950s–60s, Egyptian things past. Thematically, they all evoke the same elementary motif, the republican utopia of egalitarianism or social justice. Historically, they point to diverse facets of the sociocultural homogenization that has taken place since the 1950s at both a regional and global level and that has accompanied nation-state building in the age of mass media. They are also all entries into vernacular experiences in relation to institutions (educational, political, religious). Although not directly recounted, the 1967 War also binds these sections, as it appears repeatedly in both intimate and public utterances. President Jamal 'Abd al-Nasser also surfaces throughout the book, the political commonly framing the personal.

Each section of the book called for methods, theory, and sources corresponding to its object. In the first section, "Retelling Salah al-Din," I mostly relied on literacy, education policy, and pedagogy works. I used textbooks, newspapers, illustrations, paintings, exhibits, literature, and films. In the second section, "Burn, Edmund, Burn," I mainly relied on historical and anthropological works about carnival and performance, rituals of resistance, and popular culture. I drew on periodicals, films, exhibits, songs, novels, and American, French, and British archival sources. In the last section, "St. Mary, Mother of Egypt," I relied on works about religious ritual and spirituality and about the politics of religion. I used periodicals, religious pamphlets, illustrations, and material artifacts. Throughout the book, together with the aforementioned sources gathered between 1999 and 2012, I interweave interviews mainly collected during a two-year research period (1999–2002); earlier interviews collected in the mid-1990s; and archival sources from the Egyptian Ministry of Education, the U.S. Department of State, the French Ministère des Affaires Etrangères, the Archives du Monde du Travail, and British Foreign Affairs.[49]

The first part, "Retelling Salah al-Din," discusses universal schooling because it is a prominent motif in recollections of the 1950s–60s and in critiques of their legacy. This part is first and foremost a means of introduction to the historical approach I develop in the following sections. It analyzes the mechanisms by which myth replaces history. First, monarchic reforms in matters of education are commonly attributed to the Free Officers. I argue that governmental outreach, through the mass media, and female education contributed to this historical misrepresentation. Second, I agree that the politics of oblivion in regard to the Nasser years might have "for purpose to impose the oblivion of politics."[50] Yet I argue that the mediocrity of historical learning in Egyptian education (including the Nasser years) overall owes to material and structural deficiencies rather than political design. I finally question the relevance of a site of predilection in the history of memory: the idea that school, in our modern societies, is the matrix of the nation and that schoolbooks are its catechism. I show that textbooks in Egypt failed to inculcate a substantial national narrative and civic ethos. This failure has less to do with the politics of oblivion than with shortsighted educational policies and a lack of investment in public welfare.

The second part, "Burn, Edmund, Burn," explores vernacular and institutional politics through experiences and representations of conflict in the Suez Canal. War and social and nationalistic resistance deeply marked both the colonial and postcolonial periods in this region more than anywhere else in Egypt. I recount its history through an effigy-burning festival that took place during the spring festivities of Shamm al-Nasim in the Suez Canal cities. This festival originally celebrated the departure of British general and high commissioner Edmund Allenby at the end of World War I.

In the 1950s, it turned into a nationalist celebration of liberation. In the 1970s, festivities glorified the free market economy. Yet the festival always retained its initial vernacular manifestation of social resistance. State authorities banned "the Limby" in the late 1990s. But effigies and bonfires shyly reappeared in 2011 and 2012 after President Mubarak's dislodging. One has yet to see whether the festival might fully reemerge someday. This section follows the chronology of the festival (haraq al-Limbi) in Port Said and secondarily in Ismailia. It evinces how historical utterances become arts of resistance. Through the festival, I reflect upon the interface between national, local, communal, intimate, institutional, and vernacular cultural and political manifestations. Canal dwellers' discrete experience of World War I, World War II, the 1956 War, and the 1967 War show the mobilization of political, social, economic, and emotional factors in the fashioning of historical utterances. This section also displays the dissonance between national and regional experiences. It illustrates as well the active and performative political creativity of vernacular actors over institutional attempts to subdue refractory social bodies.

The last part, "St. Mary, Mother of Egypt," examines communal belonging, interconfessional relationships, and modern spirituality. It evokes the last chapter of the Nasserian dramaturgy by recounting the story of the apparition of the Virgin Mary in 1968, in the wake of the June War. I consider the 1968 event, its recollections, and later stories of Marian apparitions from the 1980s to the present. These stories illustrate the modernist reconceptualization of the sacred in which the religious is subsumed under scientific epistemology. The Marian dramaturgy also conveys the influence of scripturalism on spiritual practices and theological beliefs. I argue that the resulting severance of social performances (such as festivals, rituals, and healing practices) that facilitate interconfessional intimacy has contributed to new forms of social exclusion and distinction—and new forms of solidarity—independently from faith-based political activism. Furthermore, this section shows that religious performances and reenactments, like secular ones, creatively serve as arts of resistance and self-reinvention. Finally, it shows that the mass media, new technologies, and capitalistic mass-market commodities have had for function to affirm the distinction of the Coptic Church, but also for contradictory effect to level such distinction by inserting it within a larger global Christianity.

"The Revolution Will Be Televised"

Historical utterances of the 1950s–60s have to do as much with the indeterminate past as with the dithering present. Most of all, they capture how citizens integrated the republican idea that the state ought to be the steward of egalitarianism, owing its existence to, and embodying the will of the nation. The Free Officers publicly and ideologically supported a democratic, classless society. Social equality was to transcend gender and religious boundaries. Such ideas clashed with prerevolutionary, dominant concepts of gender, class, and religious privileges. The Nasserian state, however, betrayed its promises. Its offshoot continued to deny citizens their right to fashion their polity. Schooling stories summon the *utopia* (no-place) of equal opportunity. They also call forth the *uchronia* (no-event) of the downfall of social privileges. Limby stories invoke the utopia of a society of justice and equal rights. They also evoke the uchronia of the demise of arbitrariness and socioeconomic segregation. Marian stories conjure the utopia of national solidarity and spiritual unity and the uchronia of civic equality. In the 1960s, the infamous Mujamma' on Tahrir [Liberation] Square in Cairo, the bureaucratic state-center, became the emblem of this failure. In 2011 Egyptian demonstrators historically reinvested this site. The "Arab Spring" thus manifested the integration of republican ideals and expectations such as egalitarianism and social justice. It also reaffirmed the enterprise and inventiveness of vernacular agencies as well as their disagreements and disparities, which this book explores.

Part I

Retelling Salah al-Din

The Future Is Everything

In the summer of 1925 'Abd al-Hamid al-'Ajati, director of the secondary school of Mansura, gravely warned, in front of foreign and national teachers, pedagogues, and public officials at the Congress of Compulsory Instruction, that education "denatured" the lower classes and endangered the patriarchal social order:[1] "This ignorant and weak-willed *fellah* sends his son to a school that changes his milieu, his disposition and his costume . . . so that when he leaves school, he finds it difficult to come back to this milieu. . . . As he leaves school, the student must still have the age of a malleable being who will not revolt against his father's authority."[2] The bey had recognized the ineluctable tension between disciplining and enlightening and between instruction and education. Instruction is a functionalist concept. Accordingly, school produces subjects loyal to the state and workers who fit the demands of the economy. Instruction is the basic knowledge that permits future subjects/citizens to function in society without "changing their costume." Education, however, translates a more idealistic and humanistic approach whereby school is a place of learning and emancipation. In a nationalist perspective, which befits both concepts, school is what one might call the "matrix of the nation." While disciplining and enlightening the youth, the educational matrix also inculcates an emotional fusion between the future citizens and the nation-state. As al-'Ajati rightly perceived, education is conducive to social rebellion and to the erosion of class differentiations.[3] In Egypt over the last sixty years, recurring youth rebellion against state authority owes much to the success of mass education—including the 2011–12 demonstrations. Such success is matched only by the failure of the state to provide school graduates with means of subsistence.[4] Tahrir Square has been filled daily with a youth that had nothing to lose.

•

In 1923, a couple of years before al-'Ajati's speech, Article 19 of the Egyptian Constitution had established the right to compulsory (*ilzami*) and tuition-free "elementary" (*awwali*) instruction.[5] Boys and girls would now be taught in governmental (*amiriyya*) schools (*maktab*, pl. *makatib*). Elementary schools were created in parallel to the selective-entrance and paying primary (*ibtida'i*) schools. The offspring of the masses, on the one hand, and the social elites, on the other, were thus spatially and institutionally segregated. Unlike primary education, the open-access, tuition-free basic instruction did not grant access to secondary school. By the 1930s, however, the idea of a national one and unique universal public education was gaining ground. Between 1943 and 1947, *awwali* and *ibtida'i* schools merged into a unified, free, and compulsory basic primary (*ibtida'i*) level.[6] Today most of the literature interchangeably uses the terms "elementary," "primary," and "basic" education. For example, "elementary" might refer both to primary schools and *ilzami* (compulsory) education, hence including the preparatory cycle.[7] After 1953 a preparatory (*i'dadi*) level was created that "prepared" the child for either the technical or the academic secondary (*thanawi*) level. I will use these terms as they appear in the literature with the understanding that after 1947 "elementary" designates the first level of schooling within a unified primary school system.

In 1950–51, on the eve of the July Revolution, the Faruq monarchy extended tuition-free education to the secondary level. Thus, Wafdist ministries undertook the reform of primary and secondary levels.[8] All the same, the idea that the Free Officers established free universal schooling is a central historical utterance of 1950s–60s things past.[9] How are we to understand this historical misrepresentation, which colors uneducated and specialist discourses alike, from laypeople to historians and political scientists (John Waterbury, Ahmad Abdalla), education specialists (Judith Cochran, Saad Zaki), and sociologists (Shahida al-Baz)?[10]

The specialized literature contains inaccuracies because it blurs the definitions of "primary" and "basic" schooling, variably studying legal and/or constitutional events, and legislative implementation or promulgation. It also oftentimes indulges in self-referential statements.[11] In addition, political and ideological rivalries have led to misrepresentations.[12] Memory-politics clouds both the prerevolutionary and the revolutionary past. Educational debates are a veneer for contesting the authority of rival political factions. Conservative Wafdists and other proponents of a return to an elitist educational system have an interest in forgetting their own prerevolutionary inclusive policies.[13] Others, such as neo-Nasserists and the Left, capitalize on Wafdist strategies. They appropriate prerevolutionary reforms and are keen on recalling prerevolutionary social elitism.

Historical distortions further testify to the authority of individual experiences and to their projection onto the national collectivity. Political masquerades incidentally helped maintain, rather than create, this particular historical fallacy.[14] This section analyzes present historical utterances that obliterate pre-1952 history through an exploration of the construction of the Nasserian myth of universal and free education. Historiographically, this study shows that the practice of everyday life belies the republican ideals of the schoolhouse. The nonobservance of national holidays; the social studies curriculum, especially after 1981; and people's forgetting of their history lessons all dispute the omnipotence of the schoolhouse.[15] Schoolbooks do, however, inculcate a broad historical ethos and narrative time. These merge both prerevolutionary and revolutionary nationalist motifs. Nonetheless, republican curricula show little preoccupation today with historical instruction, as if they obeyed Jacobinist or Bolshevik precepts according to which "in revolution one should never look back" and in which "the future is everything, the present not much, and the past nothing." Yet, as Michel Edmé-Petit indignantly asked when he challenged Jacobins during the French Revolution, and whom Egyptian intellectual Taha Husayn echoed in the 1930s, what "human force ... in revolution could separate from the other the past, the present, and the future?"[16]

1

Farouk Is Gone, Long Live the Revolution

The brilliant thinker, writer, and civil administrator Taha Husayn served as technical adviser to the Ministry of Education (1942–44) during one of the many brief returns of the Wafd to government. During his term, he set out to democratize and secularize education. He developed higher learning facilities, he founded the University of Alexandria, and he established one-track, universal, free compulsory primary education. Minister of education from 1950 until a few months prior to the 1952 coup, Husayn furthered what liberal nationalists had been advocating for decades. He thus instituted tuition-free secondary education. He created the University of 'Ayn al-Shams, and he laid the foundations of the University of Asyut as well as the financial grounds for the University of Mansura.[1] Like other liberals, he upheld education as a keystone of national emancipation. Despite his competence, though, in the words of Egyptian intellectual Luwis 'Awad, Husayn received "honorary posts but no power at all" after the '52 Revolution.[2] The Free Officers faced an uneasy situation. They could not repudiate a man of Husayn's stature. Yet they could not embrace a former royal minister or his liberalism. This led to an incongruous situation in which a proponent of restrictive policies and Husayn's former opponent, Isma'il al-Qabbani, received the portfolio of the first republican ministry of education. 'Awad suggests that this effectively severed Husayn's expansive educational policy.[3]

However, Husayn was not immediately cast out. He collaborated in 1955 on one of the earliest new textbooks of the Nasserian schoolhouse.[4] Moreover, the republic elevated him into a sort of Jules Ferry of the Egyptian educational system.[5] Husayn thus maintains an honorific place in today's schoolbooks. He sits among the founding fathers of the modern nation, along with patriots Mustafa Kamil and Muhammad Farid.[6] In addition, the republic espoused many of the policies advocated by Husayn and other liberal nationalists,[7] such as greater state intervention, Arabic and Islamic teaching, curricular uniformity, secularization and institutional supervision of the venerable

Islamic university of al-Azhar, open-access to university, and expanding free education.[8]

Despite these continuities, the republic also departed from earlier policies. Governmental institutions promoted and at times imposed measures of social inclusion, as in al-Azhar. They worked at fashioning the schoolhouse as the matrix of the new political order. They officially and ideologically championed education (knowledge) over instruction (literacy). The ministry was renamed and textbooks proclaimed the Cultural Revolution.[9] In 1954 the newly edited preparatory-level history textbook mentioned that "one of the goals of the revolution was to realize social justice and to bridge the gap between the nation's [social] classes."[10] In contrast, the monarchy had a history of timid reforms. Political speeches and contemporaneous artifacts alike reflect this caution. The commercially successful 1939 film *Al-'Azima* (Determination) is indicative of royalist politics concerning education and social promotion.[11] As Walter Armbrust has pointed out, the film's main protagonist resembles an aspiring Tal'at Harb, the renowned Egyptian capitalist who promoted nationalist industrialism between the early 1920s and the late 1930s. This film was held in vast esteem after 1952 because of its explicitly nationalistic and optimistic language.[12] Possibly limited by political and commercial pressures, director Kamal Salim stripped his film of social critique as he recounts a man's honorable social ascension. He depicts an idyllic and picturesque *hara* (alley), where poverty is a virtue.[13] In a prototypical narrative of self-achievement, the young Muhammad Hanafi toils while displaying infallible ethics. He undergoes the countless trials endemic to a world of artisans and shopkeepers, the prejudices of the bourgeoisie, and the Great Depression. Thanks to a capitalist system that prizes outstanding, hardworking individuals and fate—which rewards moral virtue—he overcomes such adversities. The patronage of the upper class is, however, indispensable. It appears in the guise of an honest pasha, Salih bey, who rewards morality, talent, and determination. At the end, Hanafi achieves the petit-bourgeois dream of material success. His rise to fortune is an ode to the middle class, and to education, which allows the transcendence of one's birth. Hanafi's education thus improves his material condition without alienating him. Indeed, Hanafi does not forsake his origins, and he marries his poor neighbor.

In 1930s Egypt Hanafi would have enjoyed a free basic education with restrictions. The two-tiered educational system—a constitutional paragraph much ignored by the literature—"promised free education [but] only on the 'lower elementary education' track," and rural educational facilities were rare.¹⁴ Primary school tuition was prohibitive. Thus, Hanafi's father begs for his master's financial support.¹⁵ Only a minority among the lower classes thus joined primary schools. Entrance was conditional upon passing selective exams, obtaining private or state scholarships, and having a sponsor. Such was the case of the young Taha Sa'ad 'Uthman, who transferred from the *kuttab* (religious instruction) to primary school in the 1920s. His account points to the social homogeneity of spaces of learning. Primary schools provided to the social elite because of expensive tuition and selective entrance. A state scholarship covered the six-pound tuition, which included school supplies:

> *When I took the exams and entered in primary school and the expenses were 6 pounds, I entered for free. The school . . . gave us a pencil and a . . . blotting pad and a quill with a large nib to use for big calligraphy and an English nib for writing. And we started learning English in the first year. And we had very extensive lessons. . . . You know, when I see the level of children today, my son and the son of my son . . . , I wonder how we were able to assimilate all that quantity of knowledge in the sciences and health and in history and geography, and in the Arabic language and English language. . . . School was really teaching for teaching, and teachers were very devoted to the extent that . . . at the end of the year by about a month, the teachers [decided] to give us supplementary lessons to explain the questions, one before the course and another class after the course, and this was free, without any extra charge. And at the exam at the end of the year, I can't recall any attempt to cheat, and any other attempt, on our part or that of the teachers. And those who attended school were all the sons of the notables, because the poor could not afford paying 6 pounds.*¹⁶

One might easily read this passage as a nostalgic and hyperbolical endorsement. However, a close examination of elementary-level textbooks from 1948 to 1999 supports 'Uthman's claim. It shows that historical narratives from the 1940s to the 1960s were qualitatively superior to those that followed. Textual substance and material quality markedly dropped in 1971. The last generation of civics textbooks (2010–11) shows distinct improvements in visual and pedagogical quality compared to a decade earlier (1999) but not so much so in narrative substance (see table 1.1).¹⁷

In contrast to primary schools, elementary schools were open-access and tuition free. But these "practical schools created for the poor"¹⁸ did not and "should not" grant access to secondary school, let alone university.¹⁹ To be sure, this two-tiered educational system had precedents and equivalents.

Table 1.1. Educational levels for history instruction and course content (history pages/**total pages of textbook**) during the Mubarak years,* 1996–2000

High School, General, Secondary Level, History	3rd year: No history
	2nd year: From Islamic history to the 1952 revolution and the Israeli-Arab conflict (265/**265**)
	1st year: Pharaonic history and civilization (232/**232**)**
Preparatory School, Secondary Level, Social Studies	3rd year: From the 'Urabi Revolution to 1952 revolution; Arab-Israeli war (34/**77**); world societies and geography
	2nd year: Islamic history (48/**76**) and social sciences (economy, development, industry)
	1st year: Pharaonic history (50/**89**) and natural sciences
	5th year: Pharaonic, Islamic, and contemporary history (34/**86**); geography, environment, and natural resources
	4th year: Dates, events, and names (4/**44**); geography, civil education, natural environment and resources
Elementary School,* Primary Level, Social Studies	3rd year: No history
	2nd year: No history
	1st year: No history

*The sixth-year primary level was abolished between 1988 and 1999. The history curriculum for 2009–10 is similar to the 1999 one. Compulsory education varied under President Mubarak. It was six years in 1982, nine years in 1990, five years in 1996, and eight years in 1999. Such changes have altered enrollment statistics. There is only one national standard textbook for each grade level since the 1950s, and textbooks are produced and controlled by the state.

**History curriculum eliminated for this grade level between 1969 and 1985; date of reinstatement not known.

Sources: (all United Arab Republic, Ministry of Education) fourth- and fifth-year elementary: *Al-Dirasat al-Ijtima'iyya* (1998–99 and 1996–97); first- and second-year preparatory: *Al-Dirasat al-Ijtima'iyya* (1999–2000); third-year preparatory: *Al-Dirasat al-Ijtima'iyya* (1998–99); first- and second-year secondary: *Al-Ta'rikh li-al-thanawiyya al-'amma*, 1997–98.

In other countries, the division it established was also racial.[20] Until 1933 in Egypt, elementary secular and religious curricula were similar.[21] Even when elementary schools had theoretically disappeared, the level of instruction was much lower than in primary schools, as indicated by 1949 textbooks.[22] While elementary and "general" primary educations formally merged in 1944 into a unique free "basic primary level," disparities between formerly divided establishments subsided. As a result, in 1951 the government promulgated a law that aimed at equalizing teaching and education. At the same time, it extended free tuition to secondary school.[23] A couple of years and one revolution later, the Muhammad Najib government issued Law No. 210 of 1953. As in 1951, this law stipulated the reorganization of primary schools and the redistribution of material and human resources among establishments. Legal decrees and textbooks point to the temporal gap between political reform and social change. On the one hand, they indicate an institutional continuity before and after the 1952 Revolution. On the other hand, they offer another instance of historical utterances at the service of a creative past. As noted earlier, Law No. 210 of the 1953 Act is commonly conflated with the 1951 law, while the democratization of monarchic education has been largely forgotten.

The intellectual contradictions of reformists explain in part this inaccuracy. The insightful Taha Husayn himself, as adviser and minister, upheld politics that some viewed as radical. Yet he sided with elitists, aristocrats, and the Liberal Constitutional Party between the early 1920s and the early 1940s, although he did not believe in immanent social privileges. He defended the idea of a wholesome, intellectual, moral, and physical education that would generate fulfilled, patriotic, and responsible citizens. Considering that the "sons of the [common] people" sacrificed their lives for the homeland, the state owed them the benefits of an elementary instruction.[24] Schooling, Husayn remarkably insisted, was a "democratic" right.[25] Poorly educated citizens, he argued, were more likely to threaten state authority and instigate "social upheavals, which beginning we well know, which end we cannot predict, and which know no bounds."[26]

Husayn boldly exposed his views in *The Future of Education*, first published in 1938. He advocated the "advancement of the poor" in the 1920s–30s. He defended a universal, "reading-writing-and-counting" public instruction modeled after Western European policies. Since the mid-nineteenth century, the elite particularly emulated the French.[27] But Husayn upheld a cautious version of Ferrist republican education: he opposed the imposition of a one-track "general education." He believed that the dual-track system best suited pupils' unequal abilities and needs.[28] "Most [common] people," he wrote, "can live a peaceful daily life without all [the] knowledge [provided in primary school]," such as chemistry or foreign languages and history.[29] It also befitted the ministry's limited budget. Within a context of economic depression and warmongering nations, Husayn opted for realism, pragmatism, and rationalism against egalitarianism and idealism.[30] General education, Husayn noted, was more expensive than basic instruction. It thus required citizens' financial participation.[31] The state could therefore provide full or partial state financial support, but "only to those among the needy who would prove in earnest their preparation for this education by passing examinations, during elementary school or such, while competitions should be most scrupulous, and free of nonsense and favoritism."[32]

Born in 1916 in Upper Egypt to a modest family—his father was a landless peasant who worked occasionally as a gardener—'Uthman was one of these select and fortunate children.

> T.S.U. *Basic and compulsory education both led to the same result, which was the teaching of reading and writing and calculation and sciences and history and these kinds of things. . . . If you could complete your education further, at a higher degree, there was an education called the [elementary] education . . . and within [elementary] education, there was a part that was led by charitable organizations, in particular the Islamic Charitable Association. . . . They opened many elementary and secondary schools in some of the existing head districts. And that's a sort of education that taught at a very high level and, from the first year of [primary] school, they taught English and Arabic, and history and geography, and sciences and many things, and it was four years long. Those who got in there were the sons of middle-class families . . . who completed their education and could pay for expenses. . . . Because the studies lasted four years at six pounds for tuition per year . . .*
>
> M. B. *Was six pounds a lot?*
>
> T.S.U. *It was enormous compared to the income . . .*
>
> M. B. *For example, how much did a peasant make?*
>
> T.S.U. *No. . . . It was hard. . . . For example, to give you an idea . . . a normal guard in the government, his salary was 97 piasters and a half, that is less than a pound a month, so it was hard . . . and regarding peasants, for example I told you that my father was working in gardens for two piasters and a half a day. So it was very hard for him to pay six pounds . . . and be-*

cause of that, as I said, when I entered elementary school with a scholarship and the [Administration Council] cancelled teaching scholarships, I stayed home until a decree was issued again in favor of scholarship grantees, so I went until the elementary examinations . . .
M. B.   *Who got a scholarship?*
T.S.U.   *Who were those who obtained a scholarship? It was a limited number of outstanding [pupils].*[33]

According to 'Uthmans' account, the annual primary school fee (LE6) was the equivalent of six to eight months of a working-class salary (at 2.5 to 3.25 piasters a day, 100 piasters = LE1) in the 1920s. Add to this exorbitant six-pound school fee the need to sustain a large family, the absence of savings among the poor, selective entry exams, the irregular allocation of state scholarships, and the unreliability of private funding and one might safely conclude that the educational system institutionally and financially maintained social disparities and hierarchies. Personal connections proved instrumental to 'Uthman's ability to overcome his social handicap.

During the 1950s–60s, the mass media insisted on such elitism and disparities. The republic used periodicals, cinema, radio, and, after 1960, the television as an "instrument of popular education and propaganda" to discredit the monarchy.[34] The state co-opted some filmmakers. But a number of independent artists were inspired by promises of social justice and reform. Television nourished generations of viewers with the rich Egyptian "Golden Age," especially in the 1970s–80s. Incidentally, the low rental cost of these state-owned films has facilitated their mass diffusion.[35] The economy of culture thus helped the economics of remembrance. The multiplication of television sets further stimulated a historical imagination of the 1950s–60s based on cinematic images. Although few families in rural areas outside large cities owned a television in the 1970s, there were sets in cafés, some of which were designated for patrons.[36] By the late 1980s, though, TV sets became a common household commodity throughout Egypt.[37] Television thus fueled a "prosthetic past," that is, a past projected by images. And individuals appropriated a past they did not personally experience. A prosthetic televised or screened past lasts as long as persist both the language in which its associated images emerged and the social environment that gave them meaning. People commonly describe years past through the lens of movies. We use visual artifacts more than any other utterances to refer to "the way things were." Photographs and films thus "remind" us of past sexual and sartorial mores in the 1960s, how short our mothers' skirts were, how deep their cleavage. Spellbound, we bypass the difference between costumes and clothing. We overlook the distance between performance and experience. At times, the prosthetic past instrumentally serves to disclaim present social and cultural conditions as deviations.[38] Optimistically, historical prostheses affirm the revocability of the present state of society. Pessimistically, they lament the irreparable loss of the past. Morally, they point to the historical sources of present social illnesses. Nostalgically, they fashion times of certitude past. They serve as a prosthetic past through which people are able to voluntarily reconstitute a sense of self that their environment might not bestow.[39]

"Not for us or our children"

In the 1950s–60s, cinema dwelled on the injustices suffered under the monarchy and trumpeted the nation's liberation. The monarchy had its reformists and revolutionaries in the arts, but it did not encourage them. In 1948 film censors forbade and hindered the distribution of films that either explicitly or subtly contested the sociopolitical order.[40] The fine arts operated within a world financed by private patrons, the royal family, and other elites. Cinema was a private industry too. Prerevolutionary movies about the lower classes were rare. Those that existed were paternalistic, and their imagery was exotic and folkloric.[41] In contrast, melodrama and social realism set in popular classes flourished in the 1950s–60s. These films became edifying instruments through which the new elite portrayed "itself as a social vanguard."[42] The hardships of common folk thus served state populism and nationalism. Films could escape censorship as long as they recounted the anterevolution.[43] Thus, they abundantly described social discrimination under the pre-1952 ancien régime. They idealized the sacrifices that the underprivileged went through in order to educate their progeny. They recounted the trials of getting a high school diploma and the collective pride when graduating. They narrated the scarcity of professional venues for graduates of modest origin. But three realms circumvented the cinematic cliché of prerevolutionary exclusion. Indeed, public administration, the police, and above all the military figured as paths of social mobility.

The latter is the setting of *Rudd qalbi* (My Heart's Return),[44] produced in 1957, which begins its story in 1930 and ends in 1952. According to Walter Armbrust, this is *the* film of the revolution.[45] Its chronicle parallels the Free

Officers' ascent to power through the romantic drama of a forbidden and unlikely love between 'Ali (the son of a pasha's gardener) and Inji (the pasha's daughter). 'Ali owes to providence his entrance into the military.[46] First, a relational providence helped 'Ali, after he saved the life of Inji. As a reward, the pasha finances 'Ali's education. Second, historical providence assists 'Ali. Indeed, he graduates from high school in 1936, just as the military academy liberalizes its entrance system.[47] 'Ali rises to the highest circles by joining the Free Officers. The sociological reality was a different story: the Free Officers were drawn from "the middle class varying between sons of petty or high-ranking bureaucrats or some rich peasants with small properties."[48] Yet, once in power, they sported humble backgrounds. They advertised themselves as the first rulers who were true "sons of the people" in a dual national and plebeian sense. The film plays into the Free Officers' legitimizing arguments. The military rulers needed to explain their alleged rise from poverty. As a result, providence, not social networks, guides their mimesis, 'Ali.[49] Social exclusion and distinction are the *Rudd qalbi*'s overarching themes. The arrogance and egotism of the upper class contrasts with the humility, dignity, generosity, and moral superiority of the disinherited. After the revolution, the social gap that had prevented the love between 'Ali and Inji vanishes. The revolution brings together the patriotic daughter of a now demised aristocrat and the son of a now retired gardener. The film thus sanctioned a revolutionary ideology advocating a "reduction of the barriers between classes of the people."[50] In continuity with prerevolutionary ideology, it praised the proletarian rise to middle-class status through hard labor and education.

The divine does not intervene, however, in the 1959 film *Al-Bidaya wa-l-nihaya* (The Beginning and the End).[51] This film portrays the doomed aspirations of 'Ali's inverted image, Hasanayn. The antihero's father, a petit-bourgeois government employee without assets, dies suddenly, leaving his wife and children in destitution. The family then invests all its hopes, hard work, and meager resources in Hasanayn's education. The surreptitious activities of his siblings help him finance his professional military career: his brother, Hasan, is a pimp and his sister, Nafisa, a prostitute. The film reverses the moral value system. The pure are condemned to perdition in a corrupt and elitist world where social status is everything and poverty a dishonor. We have strayed very far here from the forced idealism and optimism of *Al-'Azima*. Hasanayn prostitutes his values. His immodesty and unrestrained selfish ambitions, the denial of his parentage and origins, lead to his perdition and that of his family.[52]

Dawn of a New Day

Other historical utterances favored the demotion of pre-1952 education after the 1952 Revolution. Among them were ideological ones, such as "educative Nasserism." Nasserist policies carried to their conclusion the series of measures undertaken under the khedives. These were part of a reformist "globalized" and "transnational" movement rooted in the past century.[53] However, the Free Officers pushed faster and further than the monarchy. Like the Third Republic in France, Nasser's Egypt "did not invent school; it adopted it, refashioning it to its needs and views, especially in a cultural intent."[54] Most consequential, the 1950s–60s witnessed an outstanding quantitative growth in educational infrastructures (see table 1.2) and literacy, especially in the provincial and rural areas neglected by the ancien régime.[55] "Educative Nasserism" attempted to reduce broad gaps in the spatial hierarchy, such as between north and south or urban and rural milieus.

Inequalities certainly endured, particularly the concentration of resources in Cairo and in urban–rural disparities. In 1963–64, 90 percent of urban children were schooled compared with only 65–75 percent of rural children.[56] Populations with low initial rates of literacy benefited most from these policies:[57]

> The global rate of literacy (both genders included) of those who reached the age of six in the years immediately preceding the advent of the Ra'is was 36.6%, while that of those alphabetized during the years immediately following his death passed to 65.3%.... What makes this phenomenon even more remarkable is thus that this rapid growth of the literacy rate concerns age classes whose numbers strongly rose during the period.... The numbers of the cohort of children age six reaching school age every year doubled during the Nasserian period, from half a million in 1952 to a million in 1972.[58]

Female primary schooling and literacy bloomed and the reduction of gender gaps was most remarkable. These transformations, however, were not sudden, as indicated by a 1969 Egyptian survey conducted in the two schools of a village of four thousand in the Giza governorate. The schools counted, respectively, 359 boys for 97 girls, and 210 boys for 52 girls.[59] By 1970 female education had nonetheless made undeniable progress. Most importantly to historical representations of education, mothers and grandmothers remember the lack of opportunities for women before the 1950s. Female schooling experiences thus contributed to the association between Nasserian rule and the creation of tuition-free universal education. Fictitious or factual, recol-

Table 1.2. Student enrollment (in thousands), 1952–2009

	1952–53	1965–66	1969–70	1975–76	1980–81	1990–91	1996–97	2008–9
Primary[a]	1,540	3,450	3,618	4,152	4,662	6,541[c]	7,351[c]	9,207
Never Enrolled Ages 6 to 18[b]	—	—	—	—	—	—	—	1,013
Preparatory	349[b]	574	794	1,435	—	—	—	3,964
Secondary, General[b]	182	209	293	796	2,238	4,434	4,805	797
Secondary, Vocational	25[b]	127	275	377	633	1,026	1,912	1,252[b]
University and High Institutes	52	177	161[b]	454	663	518	850	405[b]

[a] "Primary education" refers here to the sixth-year basic education (elementary and primary schools), with the exception of the period between 1991 and 1999, when the primary cycle was five years. "Secondary general" (preparatory and high school) refers to the sixth-year educational cycle based on at least five years of primary education. "Vocational" or technical schools are secondary-level schools that prepare students for a trade. "University" excludes al-Azhar, except for the year 1970. For 1952–76, figures combine data from Waterbury, *Egypt of Nasser and Sadat*, 222, as well as from the 1963 (179) and 1967 (113, 188) UNESCO *Statistical Yearbook* (UNESY). Beginning with 1975, figures include part-time students. For 1976–2009, numbers combine data from 1980, 1982, 1996, and 1999 UNESY. For vocational secondary education, 1975–96, see 1999 UNESY, II-119. For 2008–9 numbers, see Central Agency for Public Mobilization and Statistics (CAPMAS), http://www.capmas.gov.eg/pages_ar.aspx?pageid=738 and http://www.capmas.gov.eg/pdf/static/11-32.pdf (accessed 25 October 2012).

[b] Secondary vocational data for 1952–53 is based on 1950 statistics from 1963 UNESY (179). Female enrollment data is based on 1967 UNESY (113), 1982 UNESY (III-100), and 1999 UNESY (II-87). For other 1970–80 figures, see 1982 UNESY (III-175). Statistics for 1980–81 combine preparatory and high school: see UNESY 1980 and 1999. After 1950, preparatory education becomes the first cycle of the secondary level. Preparatory education becomes an independent level in 1957, but data often combine both preparatory and high school education (1980–1997), and such data is thus problematic. Statistics for primary education dropouts come from the 2006 census, and statistics for university graduates come from the 2007 census, CAPMAS, http://www.capmas.gov.eg/pdf/static/11-32.pdf and http://www.capmas.gov.eg/reports_eng/univ/frm_1_tr.aspx?parentid=1172&id=1173&free=1.

[c] Data for 1991–99 primary and preparatory education are from the United Nations Education for All (EFA) 2000 Assessment. See http://www.unesco.org/education/efa/efa_2000_assess/index.shtml (accessed 25 October 2012). Statistics for students aged 6–18 who never enrolled in basic education are based on the 2006 census. See CAPMAS, http://www.capmas.gov.eg/pdf/static/11-32.pdf (accessed 25 October 2012).

lections about the benefits of Nasserism are thus gendered and topographically defined but also socially stratified.⁶⁰ "The memory about Nasser," said a hotel manager, "totally depends on class. The poor love Nasser, and the rich hate him." Nasser did much for the poor, he thought, such as free schooling and housing. He was a great leader and a charismatic person who lived in a defunct era of charismatic leaders.⁶¹

In contrast, bitterness sharply colors feminist writer Layla Ahmad's schooling memories. Ahmad, who grew up in a privileged social milieu, bemoans the religious and national diversity of the prerevolutionary schools of her childhood. Nasser's homogenizing policies wiped out their pluralism, Ahmad wails. She discounts the depth of prejudices and exclusions that plagued prerevolutionary society and education.⁶² She also overlooks the social and cultural capital that the elite preserved during the 1950s–60s and that caused many to retain social privileges to the present day. Under the monarchy, Ahmad's brothers and sisters had pursued a British education. Thanks to her parental network and cultural background, she followed in her siblings' footsteps, despite the demotion and punitive laws that afflicted her family.⁶³ To merchants and businessmen, the laws that afflicted property owners ruined the economy and the status of the country. Whatever achievements Nasser performed—such as the High Dam—were trivial compared to the destruction he brought about through the elimination of domestic capital, wars, support to ungrateful neighbors, and suicidal economic policies.⁶⁴

Conversely, peasant women as well as urban working classes and lower middle classes acquired gains inversely proportionate to their thin social and cultural capital. Analyzing cohorts of males and females age ten to seventy-five and over, demographer Philippe Fargues has shown that,

> at the fall of the monarchy, [women] lagged 80 years behind men.... The female generation born at the end of Nasser's presidency only lagged about 20 years behind the corresponding male generation. In twenty years corresponding to the Nasserian period, women thus caught up 60 years of backwardness.... "Educative Nasserism" marks ... the first phase of a phenomenon of "catching up" of female literacy rate with its male counterpart.⁶⁵

Whereas the monarchy initiated female public education, the school system remained exclusive. The first governmental and secular secondary school for girls opened its doors in the mid-1920s. These schools numbered only seven in the mid-1930s. A handful of women entered university in the 1920s–30s.

They gradually enrolled in diverse faculties from the early 1930s and mid-1940s onward, but certain fields remained sealed until the 1950s, such as science and medicine. Accordingly, female pioneers feel pride and an acute awareness of the exceptionality of their education. They also show a strong sense of solidarity with fellow female graduates and forerunners. Nabila Husni, a retired dentist who earned her B.A. in 1953, recounts:

> N. H. We were very few [at Cairo University]; now there are a lot [of female students]. Today, for example, in dentistry, about a thousand people graduate every year. When we were there, we were overall 27 in dentistry. It was only dentistry then. There were only four women. There weren't any women entering dentistry initially ...
> M. B. Who was the first woman who entered dentistry?
> N. H. I remember her name was Karima Labib.... And she was really successful too. And Sakkina al-Ziftawi. Those were before us. Then there was one just one year before us, Bushra. See, we were four girls. Before us there were two doctors, just before us there was another one, which makes three, and then there was us four girls, four girls together. The other ones, I don't know.... I got married and lived in Port Said for fifteen years. The others lived in Cairo. One immigrated to America, Rahil. She still lives there. Another one lives here and married another dentist, and another married another doctor too, who died in '67. He did not come back.... A great number of people died in '67.[66]

Having struggled against logistical and social difficulties, and recalling their mothers' lack of instruction, women born in the 1930s–40s are keenly aware of the extent of transformations in education for successive generations. As indicated in the interview excerpt above, these women know they are pioneers and have memorized their educational lineage. The republican state accelerated the process of female integration, imposing rather than proposing reforms. Thus, Dar al-'Ulum in 1953, followed by al-Azhar in 1962, was forced to accept women.[67]

Coeducation—that is, mixed or separate classrooms within one school, theoretically limited to the primary level—does not seem to have provoked much turmoil. Selective entrance to university was more controversial.[68] For logistical and economic reasons, "some schools remain de facto mixed" at the preparatory level, especially in the countryside, either in the classroom or the schoolyard. Education remains gendered in principle. The curriculum is mostly identical except that, in preparatory schools, girls take home economics while boys study agriculture and industry.[69] Coeducation, it appears, moved along with the democratization of education in the early 1960s. According to Zaki, by "1964–1965, coeducational schools comprised 82.5 per cent of the total number of primary schools."[70] In addition, the number of female teachers almost tripled in the decade between 1953–54 and 1964–65, "[increasing] from 12,202 ... to 35,381."[71] This increase, decided on patriarchal grounds, underscores the contradictions of nationalist discourses regarding female education.[72]

The republic also consecrated the principle of female integration into the public and workspace in nearly all institutions. Female labor has remained quite low, at least officially, since many women work in the informal sector. Thus, according to a 1998 study, "no more than 11 percent of rural women and 21 percent of urban women" reportedly worked for wages.[73] Some social conservatives certainly consider such modest female integration into the labor force significant, for they view it as menacing a social order premised on male supremacy.

"The water we drink, the air we breathe"

Further accelerating female inclusion was the government's decision to open university admissions.[74] Before the 1957 law, the state assigned students to one university or another depending on their performance at the general high school exam. Universities were few, selective, and ranked:

> Students joined [university] according to their grade. The universities [themselves] were graded. Number one was Cairo University, number two was 'Ayn al-Shams University, and number three was Alexandria University. That was all. These were the three available universities.[75]

Open admission incidentally, rather than strategically, contributed to the oblivion of royalist reforms. To some, the 1961–62 laws expanding tuition-free schooling to higher education were a real political break, although here again the law sanctioned a legislative development initiated under the monarchy. These laws were one among many étatiste performances launched by the Nasser administration under the title of "Arab socialism." These notably included large-scale nationalizations.[76] Nasser dramatically announced his intention on 26 July, during the "tenth anniversary of King Faruq's abdication."[77] He correlated the dawn of the Republic with the birth of free universal education and a new socioeconomic order. State and society were now to operate symbiotically.

The state went further. It acted boldly in yet another visible political move. In 1962 it compelled the millennium-old, all-male institution of al-Azhar to integrate female students. Young women arrived in a regenerated educational environment too. As noted earlier, the government had forced al-Azhar to secularize its curriculum a year earlier and add nontheological faculties.[78] The student body subsequently increased.[79] Universal and mass education it became indeed. While primary and preparatory enrollment more than doubled between 1952–53 and 1969–70, university enrollment tripled (see table 1.2). The social composition of universities gradually changed. Anwar al-Sadat pursued Nasser's policies by developing existing structures and erecting new ones in Upper Egypt and the Delta.[80]

The reforms thus provided wider options for rural and urban populations outside and within religious establishments without distinction of gender (see table 1.2). Over the years this fostered female investment in the religious and theological realms, formerly the preserve of males.

Nasser's pledge in 1964 to offer a government job to every university graduate furnished a supplementary enticement to pursue higher studies. It was yet another avenue for female social integration too.[81] But by the 1970s universities produced more graduates than state institutions functionally needed. This consequently contributed to institutional hypertrophy and is one of the most disputed legacies of Nasserism. A massive administrative labyrinth that stands on Tahrir Square, the "place of liberation" in downtown Cairo, best embodies the criticism of the 1964 pledge. The building featured prominently in one of the most popular movies of the Mubarak years, the 1992 film *Al-Irhab wa-l-kabab* (Terrorism and Kebab), directed by Sharif 'Arafa. The film recounts the social nightmare of a father who tries unsuccessfully to obtain the transfer of his son to a school close to home.[82] The film denounces the structural ineptness of the bureaucratic state and its heavy toll on citizens' well-being.

The 1964 employment pledge ideologically benefited the government. It associated education with social opportunity and nation with state. It instituted the idea of welfare state. It also aimed to ensure the loyalty of the "children of the state." The republic sought to cement social bonds as it pushed for reforms louder, further, and faster than the monarchy did. Beyond multiplying schools and educating teachers, the government developed unprecedented public performances and outreach strategies. It organized public rallies, it established control over professional unions and associations, and it mobilized the media.[83] Many testimonies recall the riveting effect of these performances:

Z. A.   *They started by having these political rallies and demonstrations, very aggressive toward Americans. . . . [All social classes, except those directly involved in the revolution, had their goods sequestrated.] We thought of Nasser as a leader . . . Nationalism and pan-Arabism. The Arabs as a Nation. You had the Soviet bloc and the United States. The Arab world should unite and become one . . .*

M. B.   *You were very young for these thoughts.*

Z. A.   *The media. The radio. The media were important, to get some horizon. Even in '56, I was five years old. We had this feeling with Nasser and Egypt versus France, England, and Israel.*

M. B.   *Do you remember?*

Z. A.   *Yeah, very well, I remember songs, everything. You had this song "Allahu Akbar,"*[84] *it was then. . . . And there was a show for the kids on the radio called "Baba Sharu." There was this young singer, I remember his name, Amir. The song was "ya 'askari, ya abu bundu'iya" . . . "you soldier with a gun who protects the Egyptian nation." We had this really beautiful song . . . "Misr, Misr, Misr . . . [Egypt, Egypt, Egypt]." I was then at the kindergarten of the English school. Before entering in class, we would sing "Misr, Misr. . . ." I am on the verge of crying, because it is memories of nationalism, being a country with pride. Sorry . . . It was simple, but it had meaning. So it was about the motherland of Egypt. The liberation from all its enemies. Then, the United States were considered as a friend. Not as a manipulative power. The songs were very sincere. They came from protecting Egypt from the British and from the French.*[85]

This account elucidates some of the tools employed to create a new cultural and political identity after 1952. The state dispossessed some. It mobilized the masses. It indoctrinated schoolchildren in the new catechism, including in private schools. It militarized the social body. It inculcated a national pride grounded in anti-imperialism. This interview also shows the emotions that the evocation of the 1950s and 1960s sometimes raises. It illustrates the potency of Nasserist socialization policies, all the more so that the interviewee's father was dispossessed and incarcerated. Political repression affected representatives of the old order and any other force that questioned the state's political monopoly.

The New Order

The obliteration of monarchic educational achievements therefore owes to the proactive and egalitarian policies undertaken by the republic. Their corol-

Figure 1.1. Women and the making of the nation. Bronze mural, 1969. Museum of Education, Cairo. Photograph by the author.

laries were the disempowerment of the monarchical elite as well as the fostering of a new state culture, which promoted anticolonialism, social struggle, and female education. The state granted visibility and efficiently publicized educational reforms. It attacked the prominent symbols and institutions of prerevolutionary society, such as the university system and al-Azhar. It instrumentalized female secular education and participation into national industries as the reflection of the nation's modernization. A bronze mural created for the reopening of the Museum of Education in 1970 illustrates this ideologization. It shows girls and women, often alongside or behind their male companions, building the nation.

The success of historical revisionism simultaneously depended upon the recruitment of vocal advocates. Artists and intellectuals became the republic's most efficient publicists, singing, writing, and painting the revolution. The new cultural economy facilitated this mobilization. The fine arts, as with all cultural fields, passed under full state control after 1956. Governmental patronage supplanted the support of royal and private patrons. Government-sponsored exhibits replaced private galleries. By the 1940s socially conscious artists had already begun to engage in social transformation. They sought inspiration outside elite and urban circles, such as from Hammad Abdulla, Margo Veillon, and the young Inji Aflatun.

In revolutionary fashion, the Nasserist government encouraged intellectuals and artists to dedicate themselves to the state and the people. State funding of culture transformed the relationship between intelligentsia and political structure. The Egyptian government used strategies similar to those of its socialist European counterparts. It captivated minds, it enticed them, and it coerced them. The intelligentsia reacted in various ways. Some embraced the agenda of the '52 Revolution and passed over its flaws. Both personal ambitions and concern for material survival motivated individuals.

In the early years, though, the political direction of the Free Officers was embryonic and there were grounds for optimism.[86] The endurance of recollections of 1950s things past stems partly from the labor of these story and iconography makers who once co-opted the "Nasserian dream" or elements of its utopia and believed civil and national freedom to be near.[87] For instance, while the Nasserist state crushed feminist movements and leaders, women artists most visibly profited from the political project of the Free Officers. The female singer and 1940s celebrity Umm Kulthum became the unofficial ambassador of the republic.

Inji Aflatun, like some others, continued to dedicate her paintings in the 1950s to the working classes. Truthful to her feminist and social convictions, she indirectly served state populism. However, she was imprisoned (1959–63) for refusing to abandon the Communist Party. But in a tragic revelation of the inner tensions, contradictions, and operative strategies of the Free Officers, Aflatun was granted, just before her arrest, the first prize of a national painting competition. Likewise, in 1965, she received a one-year state fellowship that allowed her to present her work in international venues.[88]

In contrast, another female painter, Jadhbiyya Sirri, co-opted the Nasserian republic.[89] State populism prized her prerevolutionary inclination for figurative quotidian scenes. Throughout the 1950s her works thus continued to honor ordinary people, with a distinguishing, clumsy naivete inspired by folk and street arts. Sirri didactically painted the social struggles at play, most eloquently female ones, and addressed a popular audience.[90]

The Teacher (1954), produced a couple of years after the revolution, typifies Sirri's political commitment. The painter here becomes teacher and advocate, endorsing female education. The painting bears aesthetic resemblance to Soviet and Maoist posters. The classroom blackboard reads "love and peace" and "the people and the nation." The female teacher is receiving a white flower

/الفلقة

وكانت الفلقة من أبـرز وسـائل العقاب والتأديب في الكُتّاب

Figure 1.2. Punishment at the kuttab. Watercolor illustration, ca. 1937. Museum of Education, Cairo. Photograph by the author.

from a student. She sports a motherly, gracious, and tender pose. Knowledge is fulfillment. Her young female students attentively look up to her; like her, they are bare-headed, a few have short hair, and they wear uniforms. The scene displays the notion of a modernity defined by serenity, order, secularism, and female emancipation. This image typifies as well patriarchal, nationalist concepts of gender according to which not only females-cum-mothers are best suited to child-rearing,[91] but also for which the schoolhouse is an extension of the domestic realm (domus-home-nation), the (paternal) state providing the structure necessary to the (maternal) rearing of the child. Sirri supported the socialist idea that intellectuals and artists, as society's vanguard, carried the responsibility of educating and enlightening the masses. Accordingly, she rejected the elitist notion of art for art's sake and dedicated her talent to the social betterment of society. As it did for many others, Sirri's allegiance took a blow after the 1967 defeat.[92] Like other disillusioned artists, intellectuals, and writers, she abandoned realism and expressionism. She took refuge in the geometric abstraction and the deconstruction of color, painting houses with featureless, silenced people.[93]

The painter possibly most associated with the 1950s–60s, though, is Muhammad Hamid 'Uways. With a style similar to Sirri's and that of many others, 'Uways drew on the everyday life of simple folk, workers, and farmers. 'Uways claimed inspiration from Italian and Mexican social realism, as was common in those years among painters, writers, and filmmakers. 'Uways' work is also clearly influenced thematically and aesthetically by the Soviet school, and more broadly by the international radical artistic movement born in the interwar period.[94] In fact, even though 'Uways asserts that he developed his aesthetics and technique independently, his artistic style, social intent, and political embrace of the revolution most resembles Diego Rivera's oeuvre, particularly Rivera's early work.[95] Like the Mexican painter, 'Uways used vibrant tones, bulky structures, and a visual dynamic obtained from the decoupage of his work surface into geometric color patterns. In the early 1920s, as Mexican revolutionaries had declared that art and beauty were public property, Rivera had become, in the words of Thomas Benjamin, "the court painter to the Mexican Revolution." So, too, 'Uways became the court painter to the Egyptian Revolution. 'Uways adopted Rivera's populist and ideological themes. He romanticized the military coup "as a peasant and worker's revolution."[96] In a 1984 interview, 'Uways described his artistic conviction, in the 1940s, that "art expressing the Egyptian identity had to be attached to the existing social structures, like labor and the fellahin [peasants], but away and beyond the 'folkloric' arts."[97] Like Rivera or José Clemente Orozco, 'Uways translated this devotion to social populism into monumental figures, which he crammed onto small canvases typical of his art.[98] He painted farmers and workers and built up a nationalist imagery distinctive of the period. As evidenced by the technological artifacts of his last paintings (flowery dresses and *diacritirica*), the utopian and bucolic past continued to anachronistically haunt him unto his last days.

Like Sirri, 'Uways built the visual expression of the new discourse on educational reform. In his 1963 *Bint al-balad*, he painted his vision of the new Egyptian "countrywoman" and, by extension, of Egyptian national identity.[99] She symbolized the new times, a present anticipating the future. The painting followed by a year the extension of free tuition to higher education. The stage is an Alexandrian harbor. Invading the canvas, a young woman, seemingly a university student, walks up. Afar, a man in a bright white *galabiya* sits on the pier. In the background still, to her left, two women in traditional abaya are stopped in conversation. The depiction of these women was intended as a half-serious, half-ironic wink to Mahmud Sa'id's female representations as rendered famous by his glamorous sexualized *Girls from Bahary* (1937). Sa'id had been 'Uways' advisor at the Faculty of Arts in Alexandria. But the student wanted to depart from his former master's frivolous vision of Egypt and women.[100] His *bint al-balad* turns her back to the past.

The *bint al-balad* of 'Uways had antecedents in the past twenty years of monarchic pictorial representations of the benefits of secular female education, to which the artifacts of the 1937 museum of the Ministry of Education bear witness. Its paintings and statuettes displayed the new modern and independent Egypt through its new school girls, for example (see figure 1.3). Such representations nonetheless challenged late 1940s–50s "fashionable" visual expressions of "female social and sexual identity."[101]

The earlier "country girl" of Sa'id was popularized by cartoonist Muhammad Rakha in the 1940s–50s in the Egyptian magazine *Akhir Sa'a*. Like Sa'id's, Rakha's *bint al-balad* was sexually "aggressive, but controlled through her being firmly grounded in local meanings and customs." Rakha's *bint al-balad* differed from Sa'id's, however. While wearing the visual attributes of her "indigenous" and "often lower-class" identity, she defied European conventional definitions of modernity.[102] But the *bint al-balad* of 'Uways was not confrontational. She offered an alternative model of femininity and indigenous identity. She was a middle-class, professionally and socially active, independent, sober yet liberated, urban woman. And most of all, she was educated. Unlike the women in *abaya* and *milaya*, the body of Uways' *bint al-balad* is free of constraints, although her motion is a mimesis of the central figure of Sa'id's *Girls from Bahary*. She walks fit and strong, her hair down, displaying self-assurance. Rather than unveiling bejeweled ankles, like Sa'id's or Rakha's coquettes, the new modern woman shows tokens of her education. She holds a red book in one hand and carries a leather briefcase in the other.

Although both Sirri and 'Uways were dedicated revolutionary painters, the free spirit of Sirri contrasted with the dogmatism of 'Uways. Hence, while Sirri went into an artistic renaissance in the 1980s, 'Uways suffered irreversibly from the depressive aftermaths of the 1967 defeat, and from a change of status in the 1970s because of his earlier political loyalties. To the foreign visitor, he gave a detached picture of his earlier political involvement. He insisted on the universalism of his artistic intent. However, he could not conceal his emotion when he was invited to explain a painting hidden behind a stack of canvasses that depicted the nationalization of the Suez Canal.

Figure 1.3. Schoolgirls in uniform. Plaster statues, ca. 1937. Museum of Education, Cairo. Photograph by the author.

Even those, such as Aflatun, who were victims of Nasserian repression, succumbed to the 1956 moment: "Nasser, although he put me in prison, was a great patriot." Aflatun had celebrated Port Said's resistance with a couple of paintings, too.[103] The intelligentsia hence shared, at different costs, in the building of the Nasserian palace of memory. More exactly, they helped, in the past, advertise educative Nasserism. Some were captivated minds, others were political captives. Some accepted their roles as educators in the vanguard of the social revolution. Others witnessed the political subversion of their art. In turn, their works participate in the present and sometimes inadvertently in those historical utterances that obliterate the monarchic past.

From Kuttab to Makatib

Most artists and intellectuals and government officials alike espoused a secular project of society in the 1950s–60s. The state thus disqualified the religious educational system and its curriculum. It deprived private religious institutions of their autonomy, funding, and social function. The oblivion of prerevolutionary education hence entails the disqualification of Islamic education, para-education, and private charitable organizations and scholarships (*khayriyya*), which had once provided for the poor. The demotion of religious education predates the revolution, but the Free Officers established secular schooling as the exclusive legitimate education. This fabrication relied upon what Gregory Starrett calls the "astounding fiction" of secular government. In the 1950s–60s, the belief reigned among both European and Egyptian secular intellectuals and political leaders that "Islam [had] simply been bypassed."[104] An associated fiction consisted of defining religious forms of education as vestiges of the past, ill-suited to present needs. The exhibit of the Ministry of Education museum in Cairo displays illustrations that portray the physical violence and primitivism of *kuttab* pedagogical practices as out of place in modern Egypt (figure 1.2). School came to equate with the *maktab*, before the 1950s, excluding the religious *kuttab* as a proper form of education. This enforced a new semantic distinction. The *madrasa*, which once designated an institution of higher Islamic learning, came to designate a secular school.[105]

Pedagogical differences, infrastructural inequalities, and professional prospects also differentiated *kuttab* and *maktab*. The *kuttab* did not prepare pupils for the new professional occupations and aspirations of the mid-twentieth century. It was a private community service that pedagogically stressed memorization:

T.S.U. I entered the kuttab when I was about four and I entered school [madrasa] when I was about six . . .
M. B. Do you remember the days of the kuttab?
T.S.U. Yeah . . . I remember the days of the kuttab . . . because the kuttab

> *that was in the village, it's the husband of my paternal aunt who created it, the Shaykh Sa'd Nasr. He opened the kuttab in his house ... and we learned reading and writing. They gave us tablets called "ardoise" [slate] tablets, and we wrote on them ... the verses we had to learn, and the day after we listened to them, and after we heard them we erased them, and we wrote over again ...*

And oftentimes community members, outsiders, or family members encouraged parents to send their children to primary school (like 'Uthman's uncle). Ra'uf 'Abbas recounts:

> *Then a friend of my father, one of his colleagues, gave my father a very good advice: "This boy will not make a very good al-Azhar professor because he hates this kind of schooling, so why don't you send him to regular public school?"*[106]

Transfer to public school in those days was often reconstructed as a providential turn of fate because it was a rare occurrence. 'Uthman preferred the *madrasa* even though he did not have traumatic experiences at the *kuttab* as others did, such as Ra'uf 'Abbas:

> *There was no schooling at this time in [the] village [where my father worked]. So, I lived with my grandmother, my father's mother, in Shubra. ... There I attended Qur'anic school, because my father was preparing me to become 'alim at al-Azhar. I stayed there for two years where I recited almost half of the Qur'an. I hated this kind of schooling, because the methods of education were terrible. I was beaten every day in order to memorize carefully the wordings of the Qur'anic verses. Imagine how difficult it could be for four-year-old child, you know. ... His friends may be playing on some playground, or sent to kindergarten, if they were of a middle-class family, while I was sitting in a dark, dim room, learning the Qur'an from a half-blind, half-sighted man with a very long stick in his hand, and a child could expect to be beaten anywhere, everywhere on his tiny little body. I was not doing well in arithmetic and Arabic. ... But I had no other alternative than memorize the Qur'an.*[107]

This testimony recalls corporal punishment, a mode of disciplining associated today with religious instruction and archaic pedagogy. It also points, most significantly, to changing expectations about schooling benefits and pedagogical practices. Children knew of alternative schooling. Many stories recount physical abuse at the *kuttab*, meaningless memorization, comical and ignorant

Shaykhs (Islamic teachers)—the latter trope populates jokes and recollections. The educational and pedagogical poverty of *kuttab* teachers contributed to their demise.[108] Not long ago, though, when bridges linked secular and religious institutions, the nationalist elite of the 1920s–30s had attended the *kuttab*. However, in the 1950s, al-Azhar lost much of its social prestige due to the flourishing of new educational ideals embodied by the University of Cairo. An elitist institution in the 1930s, it became a symbol of republican egalitarianism.

This change came at a price. In 1938 Taha Husayn had written in defense of universal education and unrestricted access to university. This contradicted the position he had once held, which dissociated structural arguments (existing state structures cannot absorb everyone) from financial and social ones (universal education is too costly and leads to social destabilization).[109] Many conservative predictions came to pass, such as the unemployment of university-educated youth. But was this the result of inherently flawed, unrealistic, open-access university policies?

Egypt's first republican government had opted, like the French Third Republic, for the fall of "the pillar of ignorance." This policy accepted short-term losses for long-term benefits. Its success, however, depended on continuity. In the 1970s though, government expenditures on education underwent a sharp decline.[110] Inclusion policies were aborted, and "God preserved class distinctions," in the words of Husayn. In turn, new social divisions appeared. In any case, educational structures and infrastructures failed to accommodate social demands. The quality of education declined in proportion to demographic inflation. Classrooms were overcrowded and teachers underpaid.

Despite such shortcomings, the reforms undertaken in the 1950s accelerated the inclusion into the social fabric of disadvantaged sections of the population. These reforms also established the notions that "equal opportunity" was a fundamental human right, as Husayn had wished, and that the state was responsible for bringing about social justice. The idea that revolutionary idealism and populism are at the root of social dysfunctions and graduates' unemployment thus masks other liabilities and social realities, from deep-rooted social inequities and elitism to more than fifty years of state capitalism-cum-Infitah. Today's education policies are functionalist and utilitarian.

"In revolution one should never look back"

Egalitarianism served the obliteration of Wafdist achievements. Reciprocally, the demotion of educative Nasserism serves those utilitarian proponents of the status quo. Egalitarianism is also one of the most potent historical utterances about the 1952 Revolution. A rupture in political semantics occurred when the state embraced the concepts of equality of opportunity and of a classless society.[111] These ideas had been politically subversive under the monarchy. Even though the postrevolutionary schoolhouse preserved its domesticating function and maintained the social status quo, the republic cast off the conception of mass education as denaturation. This "new egalitarianism" was ideologically conveyed through the example of the new rulers' social trajectory, which centered on President 'Abd al-Nasser. The state built the mythos of plebeian leader or the *Ra'is* around his figure.[112] This tribute paralleled a rewriting of Colonel Ahmad 'Urabi as a Spartan, "eloquent peasant" who became a national leader.[113] This motif persists in schoolbook dialogues.[114] In the 1950s 'Urabi thus became the historical forerunner of Colonel Nasser as textbooks convey:

> Student: "Was Ahmad 'Urabi Egyptian?" The teacher said, "Ahmad 'Urabi was an Egyptian peasant from a small village near Zagazig. He received a classical religious education and entered early (at age 14) in the army, where he was quickly promoted."[115]

Nasser was unduly celebrated as the first Egyptian ruler since Pharaonic times. Both colonels were lauded as native sons (*awlad al-balad*) who helped the nation perfect its destiny. In addition, the leader was to incarnate the nation's plebeian soul. Nasser became the humble son of a mailman. Unlike Colonel 'Urabi, though, Colonel Nasser was able to drive away the invaders. As the illustrator Salah Jahin portrayed it during the Suez War, Nasser prevented another British invasion of the 1882 kind.[116]

Contesting the idea of social predestination, the Free Officers projected their proletarianized trajectories onto allegories for upward mobility. The mythology that they developed thus depicted the army as one of the few venues open to the common people in prerevolutionary times.

According to state-sanctioned narratives, the monarchy supported a hierarchical vision of society, which fostered an exclusionist education system that sustained a strict, oppressive social order ("feudalism"). The ruling class was in power by right of birth and repaid its privileges by offering its casual random benevolence. The republican utopia replaced the monarchic one. In modern republican mythology, education fosters social mobility. Educative Nasserism was thus to generate a classless society.[117] Nasserian egalitarianism is another disputable and disputed story that remains a powerful trope in historical utterances about education in the 1950s–60s.

State ideology and public policies, the expansion of free tuition, and the construction of schools all spurred enrollments. But these only contributed to the success of schooling. Educational accomplishments in Egypt ultimately depended on public attitudes toward education. Social expectations about its benefits had to change. The deepest change concerned male mentalité regarding the value, finality, and purpose of female education as well as the social status of female labor. Even in well-off milieus, many frowned on working women and especially working mothers in the 1940s, particularly outside Cairo. Female labor is still commonly stigmatized as socially downgrading in some milieus such as rural Upper Egypt. In the 1940s it was a marker of lower social status. Nabila Husni came from a Cairene educated, petit-bourgeois milieu, and her parents encouraged her studies. She became one of a few female dentistry graduates at Cairo University in the early 1950s. Her husband, a native of Port Said, thwarted her professional ambitions though. He feared public opinion about her interacting with males in the workplace. After the fortunate opening of a family care clinic and with her father's support, she obtained marital approval:

N. H.   *My husband did not want me to work. He did not want me to work. Before me, there was only one female doctor in Port Said before me, a generalist. Because Port Said was a small place, people considered this a shame. "She is working. Why is she working? Does she materially need to work?" Then, my father, may he rest in peace, was still alive, and he worked in the field of education. . . . And he was the friend of people working at the Ministry of Health and doctors. My husband said, "No, you will not work with them, because you should not be treating men." A long time ago, it was not like today. They opened a practice in the school clinic that was only for women and children. And my husband agreed. That time, my husband agreed.*

M. B.   *When was this?*

N. H.   *When this was? A long time ago, a long time ago. I first stayed home for two years before I got married. After that, I worked. The day the war started [1956], I was at work . . . and I remember this was my first day of work.*[118]

Female labor, in Husni's milieu, was thus looked down upon. It was indeed associated with material necessity, social demotion, and lower status. Husni made a number of concessions. But she pursued a successful career in dentistry and administration while rearing her children.

The alteration in general public attitudes toward education was discernible as early as the middle of the nineteenth century.[119] But the formidable expansion in school enrollment in the 1950s–60s, within the context of considerable material and financial hardships, suggests a rather drastic change. Overcoming social taboos was one hurdle; material impediments were another. The poor sent their children to school despite the lack of scholarships, the limited number of schools, expenditures (transportation and supplies), and the need for child labor, such as in labor-intensive agricultural areas. Without parental support, students struggled, especially university students, who incurred higher expenses in an unfavorable economic context with rampant unemployment. Again, historian Ra'uf 'Abbas:

> My grades at the baccalaureate allowed me to join Cairo University. But for economic reasons, because I come from a very poor family, I had to select the nearest school to the railway terminal of Cairo. That's why I joined 'Ayn al-Shams faculty, because it was in Shubra at that time. . . . I could not even afford a bus ticket at that time. I had to walk from Cairo railway station, across the bridge of Shubra, until I reached the university and the faculty, where the Faculty of Arts was located. It's still there. Now it is a faculty of engineering. . . . I used my free pass to reach home. These were really, really hard years.
>
> Through these years, I was trying to find a job to cover the expense of my education. But this was in vain. This was a problem in the fifties. I entered in university in 1957 at the peak of unemployment, from 1957 up to 1961. . . . This was one of the reasons that pushed Nasser and the regime . . . to push the Egyptian national capital to participate in the process of nationalization of the economy. . . . The country was suffering a kind of economic stagnation, so it was hard to find a job.[120]

Throughout the 1950s, low-income university students had to overcome dire material restrictions. It took time and courage to resume one's studies. While student enrollment has increased tremendously since the 1960s, similar material obstacles persist. Laissez-faire allows economically disadvantaged children to elude school. Compulsory education is insufficiently enforced.[121] Official statistics evade these realities. Since 1975 general enrollment figures include both full-time, single-shift school and part-time, double-shift school enrollment, thus distorting the picture of educational attainment.[122] Tuition-free instruction leaves a great deal of expenses to families, today as in the past. Most families do not receive any subsidies. In fact, public schools are de facto privately subsidized. Parents who cannot afford to send their children to private schools resort to in-school group private lessons for the poorer (*majmu'at*) and individual private lessons.[123] Without private tutoring, parents believe, children have no chance to pass the yearly exams because classes are too rudimentary, especially English lessons. Most importantly, today as in the past, low-income rural and urban families depend materially on child labor.[124] Therefore, the success of universal schooling demands sacrifices and involves conviction in the material and social benefits of education.[125]

Unlike the instruction of males, the education of females is most immediately and obviously beneficial. Educated girls have greater chances of social promotion than boys by way of marriage. The current investment in female schooling contravenes patriarchal notions, as in the 1950s, that educated girls were unsuited to marriage and incapable of rearing children.[126] Female intellectual emancipation brought about financial dividends to the family household. The proliferation and diversification of educational venues for females have been critical to the emergence of new attitudes. However, regional and social disparities reside. Most common in Upper Egypt, and sometimes performed outside state survey when the legal marriage age is not met, early marriage is often perceived as economically and morally beneficial. It has an obvious impact on overall literacy.[127] Yet state institutions have been promoting images of female social empowerment. They have crept today into civic education whereas they were almost absent a decade earlier.[128] The patriarchal idea of women as companions of the revolution still permeates the cultural realm, from Algeria to Egypt, in *The Battle of Algiers*, *The Open Door*, *Jamila*, or in public murals. Revolution and war remain masculine historiographical domains, as 2011 textbooks indicate.[129]

Today's educational system is consequently a hydra, discursively inclusive yet empirically exclusionist. The *maktab* replaced the *kuttab*. Technical school replaced the elementary school. As in the past, the social elite often sends its children to foreign private schools and universities at home and abroad so that the "educational system [reflects] the mixed economy and divided culture."[130] Post-Nasserian administrations are largely responsible for this situation. Sadat reorganized primary and preparatory instruction into a unique nine-year "Basic Education" that bore an uncanny resemblance to the basic elementary instruction of the khedivial age. Its program made it clear. Indeed, Basic Education was to prevent "backsliding into illiteracy," preparing pupils "for practical life within [their] own environment." To be sure, it would help pupils "forge [their] working life, whether agricultural, industrial, or commercial, by providing [them] with the necessary training."[131] Congressmen eerily professed a similar statement in 1925, agreeing that "the ideal program [was] that which [guaranteed] the eradication of illiteracy and [prepared] the pupil for working life, [improved] his moral and intellectual level at the measure of his material and social condition."[132]

The divide between inclusive populist and exclusionist educational models has only deepened today. The absence of a public education of quality has regenerated the two-tiered prerevolutionary system. The revolution maintained, rather than altered, khedivial social inequities.[133] Egyptian society thus struggles to adapt its institutions to the long-term needs of education in the face of demands of social equality, the unsettling adjustment of gender roles, and material constraints. Meanwhile, one of the legacies of the 1950s is the expectation that the state ought to embody the nation, represent its citizens, and provide for their moral and material welfare.

Several factors are thus at play in the erasure of the khedivial educational past from today's historical utterances. First, competing political forces have used the Nasserian past as a negotiating tool. Second, after the 1950s the body politic established new direct relations and means of communication with the nation through the mass media, public speeches, rallies, outreach centers held by the state-sanctioned Arab Socialist Union (ASU), and the schoolhouse. In a now vernacular language that performatively wiped out the social distance between rulers and ruled, the government reached out to every corner of Egypt. It widely publicized educational policies in the name of egalitarianism, which today's schoolbooks still echo.[134] It made visible its endeavors, building new schools in deprived areas, promoting female education and labor. It launched aggressive reforms in emblematic sites such as al-Azhar. Captive minds, the intelligentsia further helped publicize reforms and indict khedivial injustice. They thus solidified a derogatory narrative that occulted prerevolutionary reformism. It invaded all cultural fields and defined the revolution. The resulting historical misrepresentation is a double-edged sword for the Free Officers. On the one hand, Egyptians positively ascribe free universal schooling to Nasser. On the other hand, they also negatively attribute the malfunction of the educational system to the same egalitarian idealism that caused reformists to open the doors of the schoolhouse to all. In all cases, this historical fallacy has less to do with the politics of memory than with sociology.

2

The New Order

Schooling reforms in the 1950s–60s followed the path traced by the Faruq monarchy (1936–52), but the republic formulated a new political idiom. It claimed to transform the schoolhouse into the seat and backbone of the new civil order. Accordingly, in a 1961 speech, President Jamal 'Abd al-Nasser proclaimed, "The new culture we want is a reflection of the new order. . . . The culture we want is the culture of the people, hostile to imperialism, to political, economic, and social exploitation. . . . The Cultural Revolution places itself at the service of the political and social revolutions."[1]

This chapter evaluates the paradigm according to which the schoolhouse and textbooks function as a foundational and transformative tool by which the ruling order transmits its idiom, collective ethos, and historical narrative. This paradigm originates from the historiography on nineteenth-century France. It posits that the schoolhouse is central to the construction of civil institutions. For French Minister of Instruction Jules Ferry, schools were to forge a collective national culture under the control of the Third Republic.[2] Creating a nation, nationalists believed, required chanting in unison a common past. Civic education—most of all, history textbooks—became to the national community what catechetical instruction and biblical epistles were to the Church. Egyptian revolutionaries adopted the French republican model of the ubiquitous interventionist state. Accordingly, social studies were to provide pupils with a unique ontological narrative, an illustrious lineage, and a story of collective trials and self-realization. Students thus read about their "ancestors the Pharaohs," Menes, Salah al-Din; studied conflict, invasion, and colonization; and learned that the '52 Revolution reestablished Egypt's historical continuum.

The idea that the schoolhouse potently homogenizes historical representations tends to be widely accepted today. In fact, the world of nations offers many examples of persuasive historical manipulations. Some resulted in legitimizing war, from Serbia to Uganda, Palestine to Indonesia, and France to

America. We all share anecdotes of historical lies once memorized, fallacies parading as absolute truths, conflicts of memory turned into interpersonal and communal warfare. Thus, modern institutions exploit the past with the political intent of shaping the present. Yet these stories are also versatile, questionable, questioned, and fragile. One must hence prod at the Orwellian idea that "who controls the past controls the future" and "who controls the present controls the past." This chapter tests the limits of institutional hegemony by examining present pedagogical practices and the social studies and history curricula published in the fifty years between 1948 and 1998–2000.[3] It questions the reach of educational institutions.

I argue with Timothy Mitchell that the "process of producing the nation" is "more mundane and uncertain" than is often alleged.[4] The agents of production of historical utterances reside in many sites outside the schoolhouse. Diffused and plural, performative and pedagogical, formal and informal, self-aware and earnest, they participate in the unsettled making of vernacular representations of the past.

Who Controls the Present

The Egyptian school curriculum is composed of three cycles since 1957. It has had a six-year primary cycle (basic elementary education) from 1953 to 1988 and 2000 to the present, and a five-year primary cycle from 1988–89 to 1999–2000.[5] It has maintained a three-year preparatory cycle and a three-year general secondary cycle since 1957 (totaling six years of secondary education).[6] Since 1969, students learn history in primary and preparatory school within the social studies curriculum, which was "social and national education" under Nasser. This general instruction on Egypt and the world was introduced in the third year of primary school between 1953 and 1988, and then again in the last 2011 textbooks. In 1999–2000 it was part of the fourth-grade primary curriculum (see table 1.1 in the previous chapter).[7] In the past decade since 2000 the form and visual content of schoolbooks has been substantially revised—the pedagogical quality and visual quality of the books have improved, but not so much their textual historical content. Two remarkable changes, however, deserve a mention and another study. First, references to Islamic scriptures are more abundant today than a decade earlier. Second, in line with U.S. pedagogical recommendations to the Egyptian Ministry of Education, women are visually omnipresent as social actors at all levels of social studies instruction. Social studies textbooks include history, geography, civic education, and natural sciences. History becomes an independent subject in general secondary school. Only then are books drafted under the guidance of academics, and their content improves in quality and consistency.

The French Guizotian ideal of state monopoly over education inspired both Wafdist and Free Officers' reforms.[8] The Nasserian state thus nationalized and centralized educational institutions and curricula. It monopolized the production of textbooks. The schoolhouse became a tribune for doctrinal diffusion. These policies were not isolated. Rather, these were elements of large-scale policies by which the state imposed its hegemony. The Egyptian government started this process in the mid-1950s (as other newly independent states) and accelerated it after 1961–62. New political powers commonly revise history as a means of legitimation. The Free Officers and their heirs thus rewrote the past. They transfigured a military coup into a popular revolution and an oligarchy into a democracy.[9] A 1965 apologetic presidential speech summarizes this revisionism, colored with socialist ideology: "Revolution covers the whole people. Revolution means *continuous change* carried out by the people for the realization of their aspirations. A coup, on the other hand, is the work of a gang and aims at the seizure of power. What we have here is not a coup. It is a popular revolution which embraces all the forces of the working people in an alliance pledged to implement the Charter and to establish socialism and a sound democracy."[10] The Free Officers thenceforth situated their action within the continuum of the nation's struggle for self-realization. The Charter created the fictive legal framework of their demographic enterprise.

Another fiction, the reinvention of 1952 as historical rupture, further propped up this creative historiographical performance. It involved the identification of the will of the nation with the will of the state; of the state with the military-bureaucratic establishment; and, within the military, of the Free Officers with the Vanguard of the People. In so doing, the 1952 revolutionaries replaced one ideological set of beliefs and myths with another.[11] By the late 1950s textbooks displayed the redefined pan-Arab and Islamic ideological identity of the state. They substituted the phantasm of a glorious dynastic epic with the fabrication of Turkish-Ottoman oppression. Ethnonationalism, which commanded a revision of Egyptian political chronology, helped cast out the Mehmet 'Ali dynasty from national history. The institutional transition was gradual, as most schoolbooks were revised after 1958–59.[12] Between 1952 and the new textbooks, khedivial textbook narratives remained in use. Some were renamed. Others were stripped of their content.[13]

The ethnonationalization of the Egyptian past, however, preceded the Free Officers. Egyptian historiography took off with the nationalist movement after 1922.[14] Illustrious nationalist leaders, such as Mustafa Kamil and Muhammad Farid, aware that historical interpretations can shape sociopolitical actions, lent their talent to history writing. There were also anonymous, plebeian patrons of Clio, who used the schoolhouse as their *minbar* (pulpit) and history as a sword. According to 'Amm Taha, these patriots actively worked at many levels of the educational system in the 1920s–30s:

T.S.U. *Ibrahim Adham Nafadi, the director of the school, who taught us history, may God bless his soul, . . . he started class by saying: "Boys, I will tell you the true history" and he [told us]: how the English came to occupy Egypt, and what happened during the 'Urabi Revolution, and how 'Urabi was patriotic and how the khedive Tawfiq betrayed the Egyptian people, and how it's the khedive Tawfiq who allowed the English to occupy Alexandria, and the betrayal of the Egyptian feudalists and their association with the English, and how the English made fun of them. . . . And then [Nafadi] told us: "That history, beware not to write it in the lessons. . . . Beware not to write it in the exams. . . ." And he would tell us the history of the Muhammad 'Ali family and the khedive Tawfiq and the King Fu'ad and their majesty and things. . . . He would say, "That's what you have to talk about in the exams. . . ." And he told us many things about the terribly nasty conditions of the Egyptian people from the time of the Mamluks and the time of the Muhammad Ali family, . . . and I remember at the end of the year . . .*
M. B. *What year was that?*
T.S.U. *In the year '29 . . . in 1929 . . . I went to the exam and I took the exam and I was excellent and the result. . . . You know I will tell you . . . I got the 'Ali Mubarak pasha prize in Arabic [language], which was a bond from Bank Misr [Egyptian National Bank]. I received that bond during a large ceremony organized by the Society in Cairo. . . . The last day of examination, we had history. . . . My uncle used to organize a party at his house for all the students on the occasion of the end of the school year. . . . So I came in and the director of the school called me and he said to me, "Come show me the questions sheet." So I handed it to him. He said to me, "Well, how did you answer the first one?" The first question was what do you know about the Suez Canal? So I wrote what Ibrahim Adham Nafadi told us . . . "The building of the Suez Canal was the reason for Egypt's debts. . . . And this was the reason for the occupation of Egypt and this was the reason why Khedive Isma'il . . . let the English occupy [the country], because of their*

road to India. . . ." And all the people and the students stopped eating . . . and my uncle came forward to punish me. . . . [laughter] The school director held me and said to [my uncle], "Taha effendi, do not say a word." And he said to me, "By God, my son, your paper fell in the hands of a patriot and there are many of them in the educational system, that is, you are lucky. . . . If the paper had fallen into the hands of a traitor, both our fates would be in the [hands of God]." . . . When the results came out, I found out that I got 18½ out of 20, which indicated that not only my uncle and Ibrahim Adham Nafadi but the great majority of educated people were patriots opposed to the traitorous royal family . . . opposed to the English. . . . So they sympathized with 'Urabi and the 'Urabi Revolution and considered 'Urabi as a patriotic fighter. . . .[15]

This testimony reveals a long history of underground, subversive, civil patriotic resistance associating public officials, schoolmasters, and students.[16] Educators' social networks were solid enough that they could escape censorship and sanctions. They were able to exert a significant political influence on the youth. They publicized the corruption of the khedivial state, its spoliation of national wealth. They held it responsible for foreign occupation and denounced its collaboration with the British. Meanwhile, they upheld colonial, racial categories of collective identity. They believed political legitimacy to be conditional upon ethnic kinship. To nationalists, the House of 'Ali was *allochthonous*. Rejecting dynastic authority, nationalists thus Turkified it. In response, monarchist historians rejected the association between ethnicity and political legitimacy. They cited European monarchies, England more exactly and maladroitly, as examples. They strategically adopted a reading of the past according to which "independence does not consist of having rulers of one's race. Does anyone say that England was not independent after 1066? The Ayyubids and Mamluks were not Egyptian by blood, but their victories over the Crusaders [were] Egyptian triumphs."[17] Whereas apologists of the now "Albanian-born Macedonian" Ottoman dynasty also integrated the racialist paradigm of their opponents, monarchists disputed the nationalist archetype according to which the race of rulers and ruled should be coterminous. Ethnoracial concepts of identity still permeate Egyptian and foreign historiographies alike. They dominate descriptions of what it is to be, or not to be, Egyptian. In the historiography as in vernacular narratives, Nasser ended alien domination in Egypt, becoming the first "true" Egyptian head of the nation since ancient times.[18] Waterbury declares: "It is not nationalist hyperbole to state that Nasser was the first native son at the head of the state since the (pre-Ptolemaic) pharaohs. The foreign dynasts themselves were sustained to varying degrees by foreign powers, the last two being the Ottoman and British Empires."[19]

When Napoleon invaded Egypt in 1798, he acted on an analogous racial framework according to which the Mamluks, "imported from the mountains of Circassia and Georgia," were foreign rulers. French romantic artist Anne-Louis Girodet dramatically painted this racial paradigm, which justified the "liberation" of the Egyptian nation "from the hands of the oppressors."[20] The idea of Egyptian sedentary immobility and racial segmentation is a vernacular commonplace. British colonialists analyzed Egyptian society and legitimated their occupation on similar premises.[21] Disputing this essentialism, historians suggest, in fact, that identities—by nature multilayered—offer a spectrum of intersecting political, religious, ethnic, national, and parochial loyalties.[22] In contrast, nationalist narratives typically erect political antagonisms into ethnic ones. Thus, they mimic colonial narratives and adopt their analytical categories while presenting the illusion of restoring a natural, historical social order. The nationalist project, as Mitchell has noted, therefore intrinsically depends on "arbitrariness, injustice, and coercion."[23] The Nasserist state likewise used compulsion to homogenize and mobilize society.

An Anachronistic State of Being

One might reiterate that the Free Officers did not invent Egyptian nationalism. Rather, they took charge of that in the name of which past struggles had been led.[24] Nevertheless, they refashioned Egyptian nationalism with distinct political intents as dictated by their vision of national cohesion. To that effect, they carried out vigorous statist measures of homogenization and centralization.[25] In archetypal nationalist fashion—post–World War I Turkey and Iran, post-1962 Algeria, the Federal Republic of Yugoslavia—the state justified its actions on historicist grounds. To nationalists, the nation was in a phase of development: unachieved. In the 1950s–60s newly independent states often sought to achieve a unity that imperialist powers had practically and discursively denied them. A homogeneous educational program was put in place to perfect national growth.

Thus spoke Nasser:

> I sometimes consider the state of the average Egyptian family—one of thousands of families, which live in the capital of the country. The

father, for example, is a turbaned fellah—a thoroughbred country fellow. The mother is a lady of Turkish descent. The sons and daughters attend school respectively following English and French educational systems. With this, an atmosphere where the 13th-century spirit and 20th-century manifestations intermingle and interact. We live in a society not yet crystallized. It is still in a state of ferment and agitation. It is not yet stabilized in its gradual development compared with people who passed before on the same road.[26]

The family portrait embalmed in the *Philosophy of the Revolution* is a snapshot of a 1954 nationalist imagination. It resonates with a cacophony of Arabic, Turkish, French, and English voices. The "average" Cairene family described here fits the stereotypical, so-called cosmopolitan elite of the khedivial age. The manifesto equates linguistic and ethnic plurality with foreign intrusion, "ferment and agitation," and ultimately confusion. The union of the "turbaned *fellah*" and the "lady of Turkish descent" represents yet another social *imaginaire*: the marriage of material power and social status whereby a rural wealthy countryman married into the Ottoman urban elite, such as writer and feminist Layla Ahmad's parents.[27] Their progeny received a foreign instruction in European missionary schools. The parental ethnic and social divide is combined with the cultural split of the children's separate educations (French and English) caused by imperialist intrusion. Nasser construes cosmopolitanism as a degenerate by-product of colonization.[28] In proper developmentalist fashion, *The Philosophy of the Revolution* posits "tradition" as an anachronism. It further denounces the dissonance of a society wherein medieval and modern twentieth-century modes of life coexist, a paramount modernist antithesis. It also co-opts the nationalist concept that national communities are the product of natural law, and that "crystallization" and "stabilization" into nation-states is historically ineluctable. Homogenization is hence organic to history. Subsequently, the state in the 1950s was to beget concord by feeding children with the same *baladi* milk, that is, a shared collective history taught in the same tongue and in the same nurseries. Following the French nationalist model, Nasserian schoolhouses were the primary agents of "progress," "evolution," and unification.

Republican interventionist policies resulted in three important political measures: the homogenization of school curricula, the nationalization of private schools, and the rewriting of textbooks. Today, fifth-grade pupils learn about the connection between the early nationalist movement and the promotion of an indigenous Arabic education.[29] The idea of transforming the people into a nation by means of a universal instruction in the same tongue had Ottoman precedents. But in the 1890s the British demoted Arabic instruction to the effect that, by 1907, secular school curricula were either in French or in English. After the independence, Sa'd Zaghlul, then "at the head of a new 'Arabization program,' once again moved all disciplines except natural science, history and geography back into Arabic."[30] In the 1920s the Arabization process subsequently achieved broad political acceptance.[31] However, material and logistic obstacles limited its institutional use. Arabic was only used in the Faculty of Law, and even then "to a limited extent."[32] By 1948, though, the Ministry of Instruction adopted more aggressive methods. It expanded its jurisdiction to private schools and to the teaching of Arabic, civics, history, and culture. "Egyptianization" and "national" subjects made significant headway.[33] After 1952 the construction and diffusion of a new national narrative was a continuation of this project by which the state established the political taxonomy of an Egyptian past divided between foreign dominance and national sovereignty.[34]

In continuation with their predecessors, the Free Officers tightened their control over education. They enforced nationalization and curricular homogenization and, after 1954, kept foreign and private institutions under surveillance.[35] This policy received a new impulse after the 1956 Suez War, when Europeans were forced out of the country. Education became a question of national defense and sovereignty, and, consequently, its reappropriation became an act of decolonization. The new catechism of the nation extended to every pupil residing in Egypt. It was to include Islamic history, the struggle against colonialism and feudalism, Arab nationalism, and civic rituals designed to embody the ruling ideology.[36] Author and scholar Mahmud A. Faksh observes of his student days:

> This overt and general pattern of socialization might on frequent occasions take the form of celebrating Port Said Day (the evacuation of British and French troops in 1956) or Palestine Refugee Day, or any other nationalistic event.... [S]uch ceaseless efforts to bring about an identification with the regime have been somewhat successful. My classmates and I developed a strong sense of identification and pride with Arabism, anti-colonialism and nationalist leaders of Nasser's calibre.[37]

Nongovernmental schools went through measures of "repression," in the words of its critics, or "integration," in the words of its apologists, which culminated in 1958–59.[38] Private schools hampered direct state control over national instruction, since, up to the mid-1960s "6.1 per cent of primary students, 29.1 per cent of preparatory school students and 25.5 per cent of secondary students attended private schools."[39] Between 1958 and 1963, in a tense environment fraught with colonial wars and ideological struggles, the government set in motion the Egyptianization of school administrators and teachers. In 1959 the Ministry unified school curricula, issued new textbooks, demanded that teachers be politically trustworthy, and recommended the purging of libraries.[40]

The imposition of national textbooks occurred shortly after the proclamation of the 1956 National Charter. The revolution's "book of faith" was even incorporated into curricula and exams. It promulgated Islam as the state religion.[41] It thus established within the new political space of the republican nation-state the religion of the majority (Sunni-Arab-Islamic) as the culture of all. The revised National Charter of 1961, taught in schools and universities until 1970, further introduced a socialist dimension to this national catechism. In the words of Zaki 'Abd al-Mat'al,

> *It was socialism and they advocated it by [teaching] the Charter, al-mithaq. The Charter . . . speaks of equality. . . . We had to memorize chapters from the Charter and our civic studies then were chapters from the Charter. . . . We start reading the Charter starting our third preparatory year, in the ninth grade. . . . You had to remember, because in your exam they would ask you. . . . It was a socialist preparation for a capitalist society. . . .*[42]

From 1961 to 1970 the Charter stipulated that curricula were to observe the "principles of the Revolution."[43] Most suited to establishing the mythohistorical basis of national rebirth, history lessons were to act as revolutionary agent. Previously taught for reading practice, history now entered the social studies curriculum. The state thereby consciously labored to ensure the political loyalty of the citizenry.

Whether the state successfully enforced these measures involves some speculation. Individual testimonies suggest that ministerial declarations belie a more uncertain and heterogeneous process. The application of ministerial decrees varied as a function of the relationship between school administrators and public authorities. At any rate, not all foreign schools had Egyptianized their curricula by the late 1960s. Schools could include nongovernmental curricula. Additionally, there were spaces of resistance against state rules. For example, at the French Jesuit school in Cairo, Mat'al became acquainted with and was deeply impressed by French and Marxist literature. In the school's library, he discovered Marx's *Das Kapital*. He fondly recalls one of his teachers, a young Canadian, who arrived in the late 1960s. This Jesuit Marxist exerted great influence on the young man. "With him," Mat'al recalls, "the curriculum was very important.... We read André Malraux... *La peste*, and *La condition humaine*... and Saint-Exupéry's *Terre des Hommes*.... I was taken by them.... It was so revolutionary, I mean."[44] Foreign schools were not banned either. Rather, by the early 1960s, they assumed the new guise of "language schools," a denomination that survived the 1970s reprivatization of the educational system.[45]

A Castle of Clay

Egyptianization policies in the 1950s–60s resumed what the monarchy had begun, but the government innovated as well. It reconceptualized education and redefined the ideological norms of citizenship. This revolutionary socialization was ideologically heterogeneous though. As Mahmud Faksh explains, it mixed civic, religious, and political principles (Islam, nationalism, Arabism, and socialism).[46] Today's curricula inherited these ideologically composite principles. In the 1950s–60s, presidential speeches also served as an extension of the schoolhouse. Their historical didacticism resembled that of Turkish president Mustafa Kemal Atatürk's speeches. They helped diffuse the national catechism to the masses and garner popular support. Nasser's lectures explained the political situation in a revisionist populist light, such as his famous speech on the nationalization of the Suez Canal. Through radio broadcasting, Nasser reached wide audiences of adults and youth alike.[47]

Social studies textbooks were geared toward the youth but shared stylistic and structural features with public speeches and newspaper serials. As evidenced by textbooks for the nine- to fourteen-year-olds, these vulgates also clarified the present through synthetic, apologetic, affective, and didactic narratives.[48] Similar to U.S. textbooks, Egyptian manuals offered a social imaginary, a "set of shared beliefs, myths, 'meaning systems,' and historical images, forming an essentially religious structure." Likewise, they provided "symbols of political cohesion and identity" rather than "historical figures per se."[49]

How much did Egyptian textbooks, in practice, promote this ideology? A variety of sources, ranging from pedagogical studies published in the 1950s to present-day testimonies, agree that schoolbooks' dullness and teachers' performances can hardly inspire the interest of students, let alone emotions.[50] As Shams, a sixteen-year-old high school student, once deplored, "History [was] taught as a series of events without relation to each other, without any story." It gave "no sense of why and what really happened." Shams used to "love history as a kid, it was like an exploration of other worlds," but he ended up hating it.[51]

Publishing economics explain some of these issues. The absence of free competition in textbook submissions and budgetary constrictions results in low wages for writers and poor quality in the books. The task is daunting. Textual constraints are dire. Guidelines are strict, which protects students against "harmful" content, and lessons have been thickly condensed over the past thirty years.[52] As in other parts of the colonized world, foreigners wrote school textbooks during the colonial period, at least partially.[53] In Egypt, curricular Egyptianization started soon after the revolution, although as discussed earlier, major changes only took place between 1959 and 1961.[54] In 1961 the government reorganized the Ministry of Education, which resulted in substantial curricular revisions. By 1962 the government supervised all textbooks from primary to secondary levels. The state commercially monopolized textbook publishing after appropriating the printing industry in 1961–62, along with vital sectors of the Egyptian economy.[55] This was a means to "control and direct Egyptian public opinion" as well as to "form and mobilize the new elites." The state consolidated its efforts after 1960, when it introduced Arab socialism.[56] As Luwis 'Awad wrote, education and publishing "[bear] the most serious consequences on the formation of the hearts and the spirits, on the orientation of public opinion."[57] After nationalizing the prestigious Dar al-Ma'arif in 1963, the state became the largest Arab editor, controlling 25 percent of the Egyptian production. The exportation of religious publications and schoolbooks generated its largest benefits.[58] This lucrative commerce continued after the Infitah. The state still controls textbook narratives today.

But for memory-politics to triumph, a sustained commitment and a substantial material investment in the production of knowledge is necessary, which has been remarkably lacking since the 1970s. No coherent educational project has come to replace the policies and ideological apparatus set in place in the late 1950s and dismantled in the 1970s. As a result, the pedagogical production is disjointed and civic education is farcical.

Textbooks underwent major revisions at three points in the past fifty years: after the political assertion of Nasser in 1958–59, then by Sadat in 1974–75, and by Mubarak in 1990–91. Schoolbooks are discursively heterogeneous (see tables 2.1 and 2.2).[59] They bear remnants of Nasser's 1959 "Revolution," Sadat's 1971 "Revolution of Rectification," and Mubarak's "program of Enlightenment" that rhetorically marked the 1990s. Yet what do civic lessons

Table 2.1. The Nasser years in primary, preparatory, and secondary level textbooks, 1995–2000

GRADE (LEVEL)	Primary School (1st level: 5 years, ages 6–11)		Preparatory School (2nd level, 1st stage: 3 years, ages 12–14)	Secondary School (2nd level, 2nd stage: 3 years, ages 15–18)
	4th (age 10)	5th (age 11)	3rd (age 14)	2nd (age 16)
NASSER	Four pages on the Nasser years, briefly mentions Nasser in "Events and Personalities"; mention of Nasser's name, but no description.	Three pages on "Jamal 'Abd al-Nasser and the Revolution"; mention of Nasser's origins (village); identified as founder of Free Officers; death; described as "strong leader and fighter."	Four pages on the 1952 Revolution in contrast to thirty-five pages about "Egypt since the Revolution"; indirect critique of Nasser (for political/judicial oppression and censorship); Nasserian industrial and social policies described; Egyptianization; nationalization; land reform; High Dam; Pan-Arabism; nonalignment; 1956 war; anticolonialism; death of Nasser related to resistance against Israel after the 1967 setback.	Thirty-two pages discontinuous information: no text specifically addressing Nasser.

JULY REVOLUTION (event and government)	No mention of the 1952 Revolution itself, but mention of 25 January 1952 police resistance. Mention of 1956 popular resistance in Canal cities, battles of Kafr al-Shaykh and Burulus.	"Philosophy of the Revolution" program identified without mentioning specific book or author. Revolution brought an end to British occupation, feudalism, monopolies, capitalist control of power. The Revolution brought about a strong national army; social justice; sound democracy. Discussion of nationalization of Suez Canal, union with Syria, Israeli attack of 1967.	The Free Officers identified as authors of political and economic independence and economic and social development. Solidarity with Arab countries (Algeria, Syria, Palestine). Struggle against Israel in which Nasser lost his life. Discussion of 1967 as setback (*naksa*).	No text specifically addresses the Revolution, though indirect mention of the Nasser years occurs in "Egypt and Issues of the Arab World," especially the 2 pages on the Arab-Israeli conflict (1956, 1967).
FEATURES	Only 4 pages of history. Facts cited succinctly without detail. Very little text, content deployed in 2 lists; no cohesive narrative. No specified authorship.	Only 3 pages of history. Only 3 main themes; few compared to other sections of the textbook. Policies are presented as the making of the Revolution itself (as historical agent) but not as Nasser's policies. No specified authorship.	Thirty-five pages of history, but only 6 pages on the Revolution proper; 11 pages on the Arab-Israeli conflict until the 1979 peace agreement (including the 1956 and 1967 wars). First direct mention of Nasser's policies, even though text concentrates on achievements of the Free Officers. No specified authorship.	Specified authorship as regards the historical narrative: modern history section written by specialists—'Abd al-'Aziz Nawwar (historian, 'Ayn al-Shams), 'Asim al-Disuqi (historian, Helwan)—and Ministry of Education official (Radwan). Text concentrates on regional politics and diplomacy.

Note: See table 1.1 for details of textbooks used and of the history curriculum at other levels.

Table 2.2. Historical themes, primary to secondary school, 1995–2000

Themes	4th Year Primary	5th Year Primary	3rd Year Preparatory	2nd Year Secondary
Egypt eternal: unity and stability		Egypt's ancient unity and stability Menes: Founder of the Egyptian nation Unity against the Hyksos invaders: Egyptian unity founded on struggle Egypt's leadership as natural and eternal: in the Antiquity as in Islamic times Egypt characterized by its religious, social, and national unity, as exemplified by the 1919 Revolution (when Christians & Muslims were one against the British)	Egypt presented as unified and unifier	Unity granted: role of Egypt as unifier of Arabs (as embodied by the 1973 War)
Invasion and resistance	Analogy between 1973 and Pharaoh's victories—textbooks are the same as those found at the "Pentagone"	Analogy between 1973 victory and Pharaoh's victory (as against the Hyksos)	Since the Revolution Egyptian history only recounted as military history	Modern history starts with Napoleon's invasion and popular resistance against French invaders

...1973 commemorative museum, the military museum at the Citadel (Cairo), and the military museum in Port Said All but two of the events cited are not invasions (Greeks & Arabs ruled rather than invaded Egyptian land) Analogy between the invasions of Antiquity and modern colonial invasions	...Mongol invasion likened to Israel's Constant military threat and occupation indicate that Egypt must continue to fight for its independence; war threats justify the need for a strong military	...Popular resistance on the Suez Canal ('Urabi, 1919, and 1952 revolutions) Attrition War presented as a symbol of national resistance, that is, a symbol of continuous fight; Egypt was not defeated nor did it surrender. The Attrition War was an example of resistance to colonialism, imperialism, & Zionist expansion	...All modern and contemporary history organized around the Egyptian nationalist movement—from one revolution to another
Army	Pharaonic roots of Egypt's modern military power (Menes, Amosis); Egyptian army is the best on earth; Mongol invasion as means to glorify Egyptian military deeds; Ahmad 'Urabi as means to show that the army embodies the Egyptian people; textbook emphasizes the dangers of weak army (Faruq's outdated armament was the cause of the military defeat of 1948)	The trials of Egypt and the Arab world are always due to foreign intervention—threat, infiltration, or occupation	The central agent of a history is military struggle

tell us about the reconstruction of history in the 1960s? How did and does the schoolhouse fashion the historical utterances of the 1950s–60s?

Revolution, Rectification, Enlightenment

In his endeavors to wash out the traces of his predecessors, Nasser wrote Egypt's dynastic past out of school textbooks. Sadat (in the course of the "Rectification") wrote out Nasser. Nasser discredited Faruq. Sadat expurgated the *Ra'is* along with the events associated with his legacy.[60] Mubarak's administration (the "Enlightenment") perpetrated Sadat's politics of memory. As a result, school lessons barely mention 1952. Schoolbooks cite it only twice, allusively, in the fifth year of the primary level and again curtly—yet in comparatively greater detail—in the third year of preparatory school (tables 2.1 and 2.3).[61] Second-level secondary schoolbooks address the Revolution, but only within the larger framework of "Egypt and issues of the Arab world." Even then, textbooks focus on Arab nationalism and independence movements, without detailing the Nasser administration. Furthermore, schoolbooks do not venture beyond the shores of the 1952 Revolution. History ends in 1952, at which point the present begins. One has yet to see how and at what pace textbooks will be revised after the 2011 Revolution.

In contrast, under the 1959 curriculum, the '52 Revolution spread out over thirty-three pages in the fourth year of primary school. Forty years later, the same textbook does not even mention the 1952 July Revolution in its list of memorable events. Rather, it commemorates collective popular actions always led by "a great character, who did not spare his efforts to build a strong and cherished homeland."[62] It cites Sadat and Mubarak as heroes but omits Nasser. As in the 1954 *Philosophy of the Revolution* integrated in primary school curricula in 1959,[63] today's textbook further cites the achievements of the Free Officers. They brought about land reform. They ended British occupation, feudalism, monopolies, and capitalist hegemony. They established a strong army, social justice, and—finally—a sound democracy.[64] In continuation with Nasserian ideology, today's textbooks portray the state as the incarnation of a revolution translated into popular will, and the "aims of the Revolution" as realized.[65] The '52 Revolution, encompassing the present, is a historical *course* rather than a moment.

In 2000 textbooks, Nasser made his first appearance in the fifth year of primary school (table 2.4) among sixty-three personalities. The book briefly mentions his Upper Egyptian origins and that he founded the Free Officers.

Table 2.3. Events and places cited in fourth-grade 1998 history curriculum

Thirty-eight items (not counting reiterations)

Political events (20 items, 52.63%)	National heritage (6 items, 15.78%)	Urban and economic development (12 items, 31.57%)
• 1919 Revolution	• Library of Alexandria	• Foundation of Cairo
• Rosetta's victory against Fraser in 1807	• Rosetta stone	• Opening of the Damietta harbor
• 1956 battle of Burullus	• Spear of the Caliph	• Foundation of Port Said
• Resistance against the French invasion	• Pyramids of Giza	• Foundation of Ismailia
• 1906 Dinshaway event	• Pharaonic monuments (Qena)	• Memphis, first capital of Egypt
• 1919 struggle against the British	• Abu Simbel	• Town of Ahnasia
• Crusaders' defeat and capture of Louis IX		• New Valley
• Resistance against the crusades		• Textile industry
• 1956/1973 heroism of Port Said		• Qanatir
• January 25, 1952, army resistance against the British		• Sugar and aluminum industry
• October 24, 1973, Suez battle		• High Dam
• Fayyum's resistance against French invasion and British occupation		
• Beni Suef's struggle during 1919 Revolution		
• Asyut's resistance against the French		
• Arab conquest of Egypt		
• Alexander the Great visits the temple of Amun		
• Battle of Alamein		
• Liberation and reconstruction of the Sinai		
• Taba's liberation		
• 1970 battle of Shadwan		

Table 2.4. Fourth-grade 1998 history curriculum

Sixty-three listed historical characters*

Cultural & Social (22 characters)	Religious (17 characters)	Political & Military (24 characters)
• 'Abbas al-'Aqqad • 'Abd al-Halim al-Darbashi • 'Abd al-Qadir Hamza (also political) • Ahmad 'Atiyya Allah • 'Ali al-Jarim (also political) • 'Ali Ibrahim (Dr.) • Bayram al-Tunsi • Fikri Abaza • Hafiz Ibrahim • Hafni Nasif • Ibn Hawqal • Mahmud Fahmi • Manetho (historian) • Mashhur Ahmad Mashhur • Rabi' al-Jizi • Rif'at al-Tahtawi • Riyad al-Sunbati • Sayyid Darwish • Taha Husayn • Zakariyya Ahmad • 'Aysha Hasanayn (female)	• 'Abd Allah al-Sharqawi (shaykh) • 'Abd Allah al-Gharib (sidi) • 'Abd al-Rahim al-Qan'a'i (sidi) • 'Abd al-Rahman (sidi) • Abi al-'Abbas al-Mursi (sidi) • Abu al-Hasan al-Shadhili • 'Ali Yusif (shaykh) • al-Idrisi (sharif) • al-Imam al-Sha'rani • al-Sadiq 'Arjun (shaykh) • al-Sayyid al-Badawi • Dhu al-Nun al-Masri al-Akhmimi • Ibrahim al-Disuqi (sidi) • Muhammad 'Abdu (shaykh) • Mustafa 'Abd al-Raziq (shaykh) • Ibrahim (Abraham) (biblical figure) • Musa (Moses) (biblical figure) • Saint Catherine (female)	• 'Abd al-Aziz Fahmi • 'Abd al-Mun'im Riyad (martyr) • Ahmad 'Urabi • Alexander the Great • 'Ali Mubarak • Al-Mu'iz al-Din Allah al-Fatimi • Fu'ad Nasr al-Din (martyr) • Jamal 'Abd al-Nasir • Hamid al-Basil • Hasan Tubar • Khefu (pharaoh) • Mahmud Yunis ("the Engineer") • Muhammad Anwar al-Sadat • Muhammad Husni Mubarak • Muhammad M. Yusif (martyr) • Muhammad Mu'in Allah • Muhammad Salih Harb • Mustafa Kamal • Nabil Mansur ("the child")—the martyrs of 1956 • Police martyrs of 1952 • Sa'ad Zaghloul • Salah al-Din al-Ayyubi • Queen Nefertiti (female) • Shajarat al-Durr (female)

*Unless otherwise indicated in parentheses, characters are male.

His death receives as much commentary as his life. In the second year of secondary school, the textbook provides oblique information on the Nasser administration. In contrast, the third-year preparatory textbook is the first and only account in a child's education to provide in some detail (five pages in 2000, and nine pages in 2011) a history of the 23 July Revolution. The textbook concedes agency to 'Abd al-Nasser on two levels only. At the domestic level, he receives recognition for the development policies cited in the fourth year of primary school textbooks as collective actions (land reform, High Dam, Egyptianization and nationalization). At the international level, the book recalls his participation in anticolonialism.[66] Sadat is put forward in the second year of the secondary schoolbook too. His famous radio speech, on 23 July 1952, is quoted at undue length: the lesson bears the political terminology of the Infitah. The textbook indirectly but clearly denounces Nasserian corruption and repression. This repudiation is juxtaposed with Sadat's democratization. "Rectifying" Nasser's (unqualified) "errancies," Sadat "closed down detention camps, lifted press censorship, and supported the independence of the judicial system."[67] Students accordingly barely learn anything about the 1950s–60s from their schoolbooks. This historiographical absence sharply differs from the inflation of references to Nasser in vernacular discourses, in book publishing, and in periodicals.

Useful Lessons

School, some argue, is the most important source of national historical education, since only 2 percent of Egyptian students attend university.[68] One could indeed concede that such might be the case. Yet one must be cautious in presuming that school is the primordial source of production and consumption of historical knowledge and imagination. In fact, the textual fabric of textbooks, the working of the school system, and pedagogical practices all belie this idea. Political and ideological intents, such as the events that the Ministry of Education strategically selects for its textbooks, are identifiable. In contrast, it is difficult to identify a specific Egyptian national narrative. Recent textbooks about the 1950s–60s are insubstantial, typifying curricular deficiencies and suggesting the vulnerability of memory-politics. The history lesson in the fourth year of the primary level thus reads:

> "What do we learn in this lesson?" "The most important events of my governorate. The useful lessons drawn from these events. The causes and consequences of these events. The influences that led to these events."

So, what do students learn? Certainly not what really happened in the 1950s–60s or why. From primary to secondary school, in twelve years of schooling, pupils read a meager nine pages on Nasser and the '52 Revolution. Contemporary national history as a whole is elliptical. Even the more elaborate secondary level textbooks reduce modern and contemporary history to bare regional politics (see table 2.2).

Class performances further cast doubt on effective knowledge acquisition. An overwhelming number of schools today offer two-shift classes. Students memorize literally condensed history lessons for the final examinations.[69] Added to weak textual content, these practices further discourage historical intimacy. The counter history that young 'Uthman heard in the 1920s would be hardly imaginable today. The same could be said of the devoted schoolmaster who taught historian 'Asim Ahmad al-Disuqi in the late 1950s at the secondary school of Muhammad 'Ali pasha. After the revolution, the school was renamed after Mustafa Kamil. 'Abd al-Hamid Fatiha ("I never forgot his name") went far beyond his teaching obligations, and he left a lasting impression on his pupil. The teacher was a learned man, well versed in pharaonic history and in English. He encouraged students to read works in their original languages. He disregarded textbooks, taught students to love and take good care of their books, encouraged questions, and nurtured his students. Disuqi thus recalls,

> *He had a passion for history, so he made us love history. . . . So, he gave us more information than the books of the Ministry. . . . You know, when I entered university, I felt like I was seeing the program we had at school with that teacher, because we had a book, but he told us something different.*[70]

Disuqi's remarks indicate the quality of his education. Fatiha may have been an exception; there have always been exceptions. Nostalgia, confession of the birth of a passion, echo of the past, or comment on the present? We tend to remember teleologically what triggered our passions. In any case, this testimony stands in contradistinction with today's impersonal and perfunctory teaching. So, what do students really learn in their lessons? Official statistics indicate that, on average, students complete their history and civics curriculum. But statistics do not disclose what students learn qualitatively.[71] Furthermore, they do not provide the rates of drop-outs and part-timers, real-time attendance, educational attainment, school expectancy, and transition rates. In fact, many students in the Cairo, Giza, and Qalyubiyya governorates attend two-shift and even three-shift schools, and in reality receive little instruction.

I argue that rather than a national narrative, civic education conveys the "time of the nation"—that is, historicist and nationalist concepts—which predate the '52 Revolution. In the 1950s–60s they were incorporated into official and public historical representations. They have been hammered into students via curricula and public media for the past sixty years. They offer three steady motifs: national union/stability; invasion/resistance; and the military (table 2.2). The latter motif, a Nasserian pedagogical innovation, binds together the first two. Military leadership indeed guarantees stability and protects the nation against foreign invasion. It organizes and embodies popular resistance. The motifs of unity/stability and invasion/resistance potently resonate because they are rooted in prerevolutionary nationalist ideology. They echo what Yoav Di-Capua called the "national epic of 'Abd al-Rahman al-Rafi'i." "Once marginalized . . . because of his nationalist revisionism," al-Rafi'i received institutional recognition. Nasser himself quoted him in his speeches.[72] The Rafi'an model fit the revolutionary and populist orientation of the Free Officers. After 1970 Nasserian motifs were easily adapted to new state performances, for the state grounded its legitimacy in the association of military and political power. Nasser's successors established a largely fictive political continuity with the Free Officers. Finally, Sadat invented the idea that the nation had reached the final phase of its historic struggle with the 1973 "victory." Thus, preceding the revolution, and established outside the schoolhouse and state institutions, these ideological motifs penetrated public cultural fields at large.

What, then, do we learn specifically in history textbooks? Since 1952 state institutions have most steadily striven to inculcate the interdependent historical alliance of people and army. After the revolution, these forces merged into a nation defined by its resistance against foreign intrusion (see tables 2.2 and 2.3). This ideological motif appears outside the classroom most eloquently in a painting that M. H. 'Uways created after the 1967 defeat that depicts a fellah-soldier, the masculine symbol of the army-state. His body forms the canvas that physically contains and protects a nation of mostly women and children. He watches over the country's sources of prosperity (High Dam, city, and industry). The fellah-soldier iconically embodied the nation-state in public media throughout the 1950s–60s, as seen during both the 1956 and 1967 wars, in the works of Jamal Kamal and in others' illustrations. The soul of the nation, however, pictorially remained a female figure.[73]

Like 'Uways' paintings, textbooks evade altogether the evocation of domestic dissensions that would hurt the image of national unity. As has been often commented upon, unity is strategically constructed by erasing internal dissent. In the post-1973 textbooks, the victory against Israel replaces the unitary function held in earlier narratives and imagery by the 1952 Revolution. There is no national liberation without war and victory over, yet peace with, Israel. "Enlightenment" textbooks preserve the transcendental role of Egypt so crucial to nationalist ideology. Egypt freed the colonized world yesterday and brings peace today. Its function thus remains the same while its mission changes (see tables 2.1 and 2.2).

The schoolhouse has changed, but the military legacy of the Free Officers remains, invading Egyptian political culture and institutions. In the 1950s–60s young men underwent military training once a week in both public and private secondary schools. They performed the salute of the flag and presented arms under official supervision. Young females donned military attire as well for the media.[74] Today the army is physically absent from the schoolhouse. But the idea that it forms the nation's backbone still impresses the curriculum. It also informed the forgiving attitude of many people regarding military violence during the 2011 events.

Institutional history is a series of military episodes that legitimizes military rule in the faraway past as in the present. Ironically, war brings peace, and warriors become peace advocates and laureates (tables 2.2 and 2.3). The alliance between the military and the people becomes a prerequisite to national integrity. The story of Pharaoh Amosis' expulsion of the Hyksos was used under Nasser as a parable of the Arab–Israeli conflict.[75] In Sadat's eulogies of the 1973 war, it becomes a lasting image-type in reference to the Israeli defeat, an image in turn reappropriated by Islamists. Thus, the newspaper *Al-Sha'b* announced the opening of the October War Museum in Cairo in 1989 by carrying on its front page a picture of the pharaonic fresco of Amosis chasing the Hyksos under the caption "God is great."[76]

In Egypt, military museums display dramatizations of the motifs that appear in textbooks. During spring and summer, the esplanade of the Citadel's museum in Cairo swarms with school children on field trips. Like textbooks, the museum portrays governmental political and ideological strategies. In nineteenth-century Europe, "museums came to be conceived as symbols of national identity and progress, and as sites of education for the masses."[77] While it is doubtful that all museums "shape collective values and social understandings in a decisively important fashion," they do reflect the ideological messages that private and public institutions wish to communicate.[78] The Citadel museum in Cairo, the Panorama '73, and the military museum of Port Said substitute a military epic for a historical narrative. Like textbooks, museum displays link ancient pharaonic glory with the present military order. They use the same iconography as textbooks, refracting the continuum of the "time of the nation."

Yet Citadel, Panorama '73, and military museums fail to provide spaces of empathy and social mediation between ruling power and citizenry. Few citizens enter these museums of their own volition. The empty Citadel museum stands in contrast to the Citadel's outdoor esplanade, which swarms with children. Military museums are a most narcissistic form of power display. Whether at the Invalids in Paris or the Citadel in Cairo, the desertion of the modern pyramids of military power may be construed as a repudiation of the military order and as the failure of its epics to foster national membership and citizenship.

A Form without Content

The schoolhouse has become the image of the nation's political system. It embraced the form of a republic but failed to provide content or citizenship. Over the past forty years the state has deserted the schoolhouse. Pedagogical reports unanimously lambaste the dire textual condensation. They condemn rote memorization. They deplore the absence of class discussions, critical analysis, and extracurricular materials. They lament overworked teachers and the exaggerated worth of final exams. This situation points to textbooks' unsuitability to inculcate historical knowledge and influence historical imagination. Historical utterances are mostly produced outside the classroom. They result from the interplay among various political strategies, and from social, demographic, and economic factors that are often incidental.

Hence, the historical utterance according to which universal schooling is a Nasserian legacy owes to the active reconstruction of the history of the monarchy by revolutionaries and their successors. It also owes to their promotion of the republican ideal of egalitarianism and nationalist republican concepts about education. It further has to do with schooling development in formerly deprived areas. This utterance is also due, incidentally, to long-term historical changes that bloomed after the '52 Revolution—for instance, regarding the value and nature of education, particularly female instruction. Finally, the modern mass media allowed the state to reach out to wide audiences in unprecedented ways, making educational reforms known, visible, and thus likely to be remembered.

Similarly, textbooks' historical narratives in use today conform to political and ideological but also economic exigencies. Ideological palimpsests, they bear Nasserian, Sadatian, and Mubarakian imprints. In practice, the Ministry of Education opted for a bricolage of old and new narratives because the books thus produced are cheap and because some legacies are best evaded. On the one hand, the textbook industry prefers low-cost textual additions to new texts.[79] On the other hand, textbooks expose the ideological burden of the present political order. The military need the mythical Revolution, with its capital R, whereas the reality of the revolution, with a lowercase, encumbers them. Like any process of political hegemony, the pedagogical enterprise of the state is incoherent, malfunctioning, and riveted by tensions, as is the national narrative it conveys.[80]

Consequently, the Egyptian schoolhouse appears to have little agency in fabricating what the history of memory scholarship calls a "collective memory" and a "historical consciousness." Indeed, it lacks material, pedagogical, and political investment. In the 1950s–60s textbooks laid down the theoretical foundations of a new republican culture, but efforts to create a Jacobinist schoolhouse—if desirable at all—aborted in the 1970s. Schoolbooks in the late 1990s reveal present efforts at political conciliation between two sharply dissimilar legacies. They manifest the neglect and fear in which history is held. They display the uncertain politics of memory. Some aspects of Nasserian political culture and cultural politics certainly endure. On the one hand, broad historicist and nationalist concepts continue to fashion public representations of the nation's historical continuum. The commemoration of Port Said Day and Palestine Refugee Day have disappeared, yet textbooks retain thematic traces of the Rafi'i epic that the Nasserian state recuperated and that presents the army as the People's backbone.[81] Some utterances thus remain because they retain their function, such as demonstrating the inadequacy of a multiparty system and supporting the idea that only the military can shield the nation from foreign hegemony. However, the schoolhouse does not fashion a history, let alone a collective narrative of the 1950s–60s.

Where do we learn about the 1950s–60s then? People learn in other places than the schoolhouse and from other sources than its schoolbooks. In a press article, a thirty-two-year-old woman and computer engineer confided:

When I watch the movies or listen to the personal accounts of those involved in the revolution, or when I hear stories about the king and the poverty and corruption that used to prevail I realize just how much the revolution tried to do.... We take a great deal for granted these days.[82]

Knowledge about 1950s–60s things past and, more broadly, what historian Ghislaine Alleaume has aptly called "civic religion,"[83] comes from a variety of sources: one's social environment, friends' and family stories, the mass media, and—for a few—literature. Historical utterances are thus primarily generated outside official and conventional sites of cultural production.

Part II

Burn, Edmund, Burn

The Present Is Everything

In the politics of memory of the modern schoolhouse, the past is everything. Indeed, in the memory-politics of the nation-state, one's identification with a specific past that a specific community shares provides the basis for interpersonal fraternity, solidarity, and loyalty. Consequently, history becomes the site of one's inquiry into the material and immaterial but always emotional bonds that unite us with others. Yet, as the following section demonstrates, the past and its bonds are nothing without remaining relevant and meaningful to our lives. The present is everything.

This section, "Burn, Edmund, Burn," explores the performances that have for effect, yet not in intent, embodied the creation, maintenance, and solidification of communities in the present through the celebration of a shared past that is creatively, collectively, and continuously reinvented. The preceding section tackled the centralizing nation-state ideology and the instrumentalization of institutional historical narratives that functioned to perpetuate the national community, and to sustain the allegiance of the nation to the state. In contrast yet complementarily, this section studies vernacular utterances at the level of a provincial urban community. It focuses on noninstitutional and performative utterances and discusses their often conflictual relationship with central Cairene institutions. "Burn, Edmund, Burn" is the manifold story of a street performance enacted by a local community in the Suez Canal city of Port Said. Its utterances of the 1950s–60s, stories about the festival display, exhibit the instability of the "community." They thus disclose the discordance of experiences and remembrances within the local community itself, throughout the 1950s–60s and again after the 1970s. They also show the disparity between local and national spheres of historical experience.

•

> *When Lord Allenby assumed his post in Egypt, the country was a blaze of political intrigue and disaffection, but after six hard years he left it with-out a serious cloud upon the horizon. His patience, tolerance and fairness have won the admiration and even the affection of all shades of Egyptian opinion, and this was signified by the remarkable demonstrations which occurred upon his departure for England.*[1]

So wrote Raymond Savage in his panegyric to Lord Edmund Allenby, published the year of the field marshal's resignation from his office as Egypt's high commissioner (1919–25). An officer in the Palestine campaign, and subordinate of the marshal, Savage wrote a truculent archetype of imperialist literature: racist, militarist, anti-Bolshevik, and antiliberal. Slaughtering and acerbic, this biography defended the controversial cause of imperialism, painting the marshal as a valiant knight-crusader in golden armor.[2] British military and colonial literature celebrates Allenby as the hero of the Great War's Palestine campaign, the "last great British leader of mounted cavalry,"[3] and one of the towering figures of Great Britain's imperial hall of fame. But Egyptians convey a different image of the marshal. To them, he was a tyrant and a brute.

Allenby stories carry us downstream to two correlated utterances of 1950s–60s Egypt: a symbolic one of national resistance and war and a physical one, the Suez Canal and the city of Port Said. I examine this facet of Egyptian experience through the history of a street festival, the "Limby" effigy burning. The story unfolds in a to-and-fro movement. It begins with present testimonies, which lead us upstream to the critical years of the British Protectorate only to take us down again to the present. We learn the ways by which the 1950s' ideological apparatus appropriated national resistance, which was a core political motif since the late 1910s. The Limby also shows the demise of this motif in the 1970s. Limby's track leads to stories of three intertwined stories of war and peace: the Suez War, which marked the advent of national liberation; the June War, which ended the ideological phase of national resistance; and the October War, cast as the final phase of the national struggle in the 1970s.

Foretold Death

Since the end of the Great War and until recent prohibitions, participants at the Shamm al-Nasim festival in Port Said and Ismailia witnessed a particular event: the burning of al-Limby (haraq al-Limbi/Linbi). In the first instance, the effigy thus immolated embodied no less than Viscount Edmund Allenby. Beyond, the Limby ritual commemorated all wars past. Photographs of the 1956, 1967, and 1973 wars could be seen on the sidewalks of Port Said during the festival along with portraits of Nasser and Sadat. Nasserian wars were part of a local mythohistorical lore of enduring confrontation and resistance, which digs down into the history of British occupation. The story of al-Limby's foretold death is a channel by which one sees at work the capricious fashioning of vernacular historical utterances.

The effigy burning was a phenomenon unique to the Canal cities. Among them stood out the celebrations of Port Said. They consisted of cosmic rites originating from an ancient festivity (Shamm al-Nasim, Easter Monday). They included a modern commemoration (Allenby and Egypt's contemporary wars). And they mixed political and social protest in the form of masquerades and popular revelry. In the daytime, as in other places in Egypt, people strolled along the seashore. They gathered for picnics in gardens, parks, and anywhere grass grows. At night, revelers unleashed their theatrical and musical talents and their political vehemence, lighting bonfires and shouting daring rhymes.

Ahmad 'Awad recalls the celebrations of his youth, which combined sociopolitical satire, merriment, and vulgar farce. The festival retained until its latter days a socially divided and gendered space. Men performed in the street and women watched from afar:

> [During British colonialism], in our festivities in the spring, the spring means new life, in regards to the world, it means birth.... We have the spring festival, the flower festival, see, and we have celebrations.... People brought old and used clothes and they stuffed them with straw, and painted the face of a khawaga [foreigner] wearing a hat, and drew a hand like that, and they lifted that man, and after that they had a sort of procession for him.... You know, they liked to turn around [him] and sing songs....
>
> They imitated the Red Skins [Indians].... They did things that attracted the attention, like the pagliaccio [clown], who covered his face with paint and wore henna and wore a special costume and became a pagliaccio, or a pantomime or something like that.... They came out holding a drum in their hands and a stick, and things... and they played and jumped and danced.... They had walking processions.... Women were up on the balconies watching.... Shameful things, you know. Even the windows.... You see this window? It was ajar, it was a shame to open the window.... Women watched from behind the shutters.[4]

By the early twenty-first century, performances had assumed many new guises. Notwithstanding, haraq al-Limbi was an established marker of local culture and identity. But then Limby was prosecuted in 1998 and the festival condemned within a few years. It came back in the spring of 2011, after the demise of Mubarak, and one has yet to see what will become of it.

As many others, Kamal 'Id recalled not only the masquerades, crude songs, and farcical plays but also the preparations of his youth, in the 1940s. The social experience was as important as the festivities themselves. Preparations disclosed two levels of solidarity and identity, two sets of social order, both colonial and communal. First, they displayed Egyptian solidarity and resistance in the face of British adversity, a cat-and-mouse game. Neighborhoods, "alleys" or *haras*, collaborated with one another to hide preparations from the British police, while competing against one another. Second, they also revealed the social solidarity, the unity, as well as delineated the boundaries of each of the internal units of the Egyptian district within the socially and ethnically divided colonial city. Rich and poor, adults and children, men and women, all actively participated:

> *I am 74 years old and I maintain that I was born in the street, you see. I have been called Captain Ghazali since I was 11 years old, you know. A hero, and sportsman, and known all over Egypt, when I was a kid. I grew up and I found al-Limby! My father and my mother during that season told us, "Come on, everyone makes his own al-Limby!" And they bring us clothes and tell us that we have to do this and this and that.... Now, in the season, children make them, the young kids.... And streets [hara] envied each other.... So, some of the rich people brought trousers and stuff. And the poor brought galabiyas. You found someone from the neighborhood who made a galabiya, and a second made overalls, and a third made a suit ...*

Each *hara* therefore asserted and reinforced its internal cohesion. The Limby helped transcend social hierarchies.

> *Everyone collected vegetable wicker baskets to burn them.... [It was about] who burned the most and who amassed the most on the roofs of our streets.... And a month or a month and a half before, all the streets [everyone] looked who had the biggest roof in the neighborhood, and you know, the ... things they'd burn, the scraps, meaning the wood and the wicker baskets and things.... And at night, all that was [brought down] and people*

celebrated.... People made feathers and [wore] dentures and imitated the Red Indians and imitated the Africans and.... And mind you, they sang and said, say what, "Oh, Allenby," because his name was Allenby, "Oh, Allenby, oh, son of bitch, your wife is a shameless whore...." There are other words besides this, insults, that is... I am just putting it nicely for you...."Oh, al-Limby, son of a bitch... your wife is shameful and easy," or "He made himself beautiful for the usta [boss].... Who is the usta?"... That usta was also a bad guy, a traitor.... So, well, we would say al-usta... al-usta Husayn, for example.... And watch out: "He fixed himself up for the usta.... Who is the usta? Cry over him, he likes mullet.... Cry over him and make a circle around him, he loved shrimps...." And so forth and they liked to turn around the fire before the burning and that was the festivity.... But before that, they held processions and the town.... You know, before the burning also, they walked with him in a demonstration, carrying him, and on a car, and they decorated him, and things like that... [5]

Kamal 'Id's recollections illustrate the festival's carnivalesque and hybrid political and burlesque nature. It also shows the political power of vernacular oral comic and poetic rhymes and obscenity, which have inspired contemporary playwrights and poets such as Ahmad Fu'ad Nijm (1929–) and Najib Surur (1932–1978).

The competition among neighborhoods occasionally turned violent, which kept local authorities on alert, as Kamal 'Id recalls:

Alleys competed with each other... who made the biggest fire and who made the biggest al-Limby... and watch out.... Well, the alleys competed with each other.... There was my paternal uncle who was... considered the leader of the alley... and the family house, our house, its roof served as a storage for... the baskets and the things that they burned.... When I was a kid I saw them celebrate in front of me.... My uncles [started preparations] a month before.[6]

Effigy burnings took place downtown, in working-class areas, al-Manakh, but also most famously in al-'Arab, the commercial "Egyptian" and "Arab" quarter of Port Said. Al-'Arab came to embody the cohesion and identity of the nation's native community against the colonizer and the Europeanized elite. Oral accounts of the Limby present us with relics of colonial experience, social segregation, and conflict.

Port Said, Center of the Earth

Port Said plays the leading role in this story because of its intimate experience with foreign administration and its situation within the colonial transit network. In 1875 "King Edward VII, as Prince of Wales, passed by Port Said on his way to India."[7] In 1882, Port Said woke up to the presence of six hundred British troops, whose mission it was to overthrow the rebel Urabist governor.[8] In 1919 the boat transporting Sa'd Zaghlul to Malta, his place of exile, secretly sailed by Port Said. In 1925 the man who had sent the Egyptian leader to exile, Lord Allenby, forever bid farewell to Egypt from the same harbor. There is no irony here: the human and commercial traffic were intense. Also, more often than in the rest of the nation, military conflict affected Port Said. In the late nineteenth century, the small city was the theater of fierce fistfights between sailors of those countries engulfed in the Crimean War. In 1916 the port became the target of German air units because it was a critical point of passage to the Levant for the Allied troops.[9] Colonial troops from India, Indochina, Madagascar, and Algeria died in Port Said's hospitals and harbor. Australian, British, Italian, and imperial battalions lingered in the port city after World War I. In 1935 the sons of Mussolini, on their way to East Africa, were greeted by several thousand Italians accompanied by Fascisti bands.[10] During World War II Port Said was again raided by the Germans. Once more it swelled with soldiers, and with men and women of all trades.

Political and social protest thus found fertile ground in Port Said and the Suez Canal.[11] In 1947 Port Saidi demonstrators tried to prevent "supplies from reaching a [Dutch] ship" in solidarity with Indonesian nationalists.[12] By then most British troops had retreated to the Canal Zone, now the stage of a virulent anticolonial resistance movement. Nationalist riots were not new. Yet, teleologically, for nationalists, the "Battle of the Canal" was the first act of the July Revolution drama. The battle culminated on 25 January 1952 when the British retaliated, attacking Ismailia's police headquarters. Some fifty Egyptians died. The tragedy sparked the second act of the revolution, the infamous burning and looting of downtown Cairo, during which rioters targeted numbers of foreign businesses. Subsequently, the state crushed and dismantled the Canal's underground resistance.[13]

The Limby, however, summons another episode of Port Said's history that filled residents with pride and challenged their historical marginalization. After 1956 the state rewarded Port Said with the title of "Martyr City" in commemoration of citizens' resistance against alien troops. The Suez War altered Port Said's economic and political identities. Port Said was an ideal site of patriotic symbolism because it had been erected and administered by the invaders. After 1956 practically all of its European nationals departed. Another war, however, first called my attention to the city. While Port Said was the city of Egypt victorious in 1956, it paid a heavy toll for the 1967 defeat, as oral testimonies and diplomatic archives document. Several thousand lives were turned upside down. After the War of Attrition began, civilians were displaced for several years. Their evacuation is often mentioned in passing in history books, but to Canal residents the harsh time of the *hijra* (emigration) is an organizing event around which they recount their stories. In 1974 the government allowed civilians to return to their war-damaged hometowns. The Suez Canal reopened. Once more Port Said was transfigured. In the 1970s governmental change intersected with the economic boost of the Canal area. Port Said, Ismailia, and Suez became the daughters of Sadat's Open Door policy. Economic freedom (free-market) substituted for national freedom (independence) after a presidential decree established Port Said as a free trade zone in 1976 (a much older project). Once more adventurers, traffickers, merchants, and workers poured in. Nightclubs reopened their doors. Port Said regained some of the financial attraction of its early days. Yet international political pressure reversed the city's legal status in the 1990s. Denied economic and commercial privileges, bazaar merchants lost their weekly herds of visitors and their livelihood. Port Said entered yet another uncertain phase of its eventful history. The last Limby performances bore witness to Port Saidis' anger and anxiety. Meanwhile, the ban of the festival revealed political authorities' own insecurities.

Law and Order

Every year it became bigger than the preceding year, until the government suppressed it last year. God knows what this story is about. Maybe it will be forgotten, you know. Year after year, we will forget that there was an Allenby and that we were burning him and that we were, who knows what, and all these things that happen in life.[14]

By all accounts—like the preceding account of 'Abd al-Rahim Gharib al-Banna—ministerial and gubernatorial decrees, reinforced by police squadrons, produced prompt and effective results against bonfires in the Canal cities. Port Said was first hit in 1998. A gubernatorial decree accused the disorderly Limby of hurting tourism. In 2000 Ismailia's celebrations were in turn banned. A local decree pronounced that bonfires presented a safety hazard and that burning rubber tires polluted the air.[15]

> *People went and took the old wheels of cars, the tires, and things like that, and burned them and whatnot, to have fun. . . . The day of Shamm al-Nasim, the government comes, the night of Shamm al-Nasim, dozens of cars and the Central Security and they [took away] these things from the streets and in front of houses, and that's it, you know. It's been two years that the government has been doing this . . .*[16]

By 2001 inhabitants widely accepted the argument that local authorities banned the festival for safety concerns related to the gas network. On Saturday, 4 May 2002, the Interior Ministry officially forbade the Port Said celebration, threatening violators with jail sentences and fines of at least a hundred pounds.[17] On the following day, on Shamm al-Nasim, children broke the law, a witness reported, by burning small effigies made by their mothers. In the heart of town, some two hundred policemen and anti-riot trucks gathered, similar to those used against political demonstrations in Cairo. But the police in Port Said were here for the Limby. In 2000 some hundred people were reportedly "promptly arrested" for burning effigies. An official spokesman had declared that "it's something [city authorities] wanted to do for a long time because it leaves the streets of Port Said smoldering for days."[18] Sanitary reasons were likewise invoked two years later not by the Interior Minister, who refrained from commentary, but by local officials, who did not mourn "the bad habit of setting fire in the streets, squares and gardens, as it harms our health and the health of our children, spoils the beauty of our city and causes pollution." To sanitary and aesthetic reasons, authorities added safety concerns and "fears that the burning of dummies could spark a fire since a gas network was laid [in 2000]"[19]—even though gas installation had actually started a few years earlier, in 1997.[20] Anyway, Limby was also kept out of safe and fireproof areas.

Not without irony, in 2000 'Ali Abu Shadi, the head of the General Organization of Cultural Palaces, issued an obituary notice of some sort. Indeed, he approved the construction of a commemorative museum devoted to Port Said's Shamm al-Nasim celebrations while recognizing the effigy burning as Port Said's idiosyncratic figurehead. Public authorities further envisioned the financing of a documentary film on the Limby.[21] This unintentionally satirical gesture finely illustrates one process of ideological subversion by which the state controls menacing cultural practices by embalming them alive, generating innocuous fetishes of "national collective memory" in the designated palaces of the nation-state, such as the museum and the city square. To what extent these memory-politics will prove effective and whether the museum (if it ever comes to life) will attract the interest of the public remains to be seen. Like the Citadel and October War Museum, the derelict war museum on the outskirts of town reflects public disinterest for state memorialization. As in other social arenas, the state has arrogantly excluded citizens from decision-making of collective interest. It imposes its hegemony in the memorial field "as it pretends to impose itself to the whole of the social body."[22] Over recent years a museum fever has materialized this solipsistic ideology. Despite public detachment, the state has multiplied efforts to encapsulate contemporary national history using modernist tools and aesthetics and a militarist language that petrify the nation.

Equally intriguing was Port Saidis' silence in 2002 when asked about the banning of the festival. Most people curtly repeated the official transcript, the fear of fire hazards. Yet the "hidden transcript" of the ban that one reads in political and economic news was rarely mentioned. First, popular demonstrations in support of the second Palestinian Intifada raged in the spring of 2002. Like their compatriots, Port Saidis disapproved of governmental policy and inertia regarding Israel. Second, two legal decisions became effective in January 2002, which were part of the international General Agreement on Tariffs and Trade (GATT). On the 1st and 13th, Gov. Mustafa Kamil successively announced the revocation of decrees giving special status to transit storage facilities for imported goods (Customs Law 66 of 1963). He also imposed a 500 percent rise on imported goods' custom-tariffs. Five years before the date set by official decree, for "security considerations" and without prior warning, these measures rescinded Port Said's preferential status as declared twenty-six years earlier. As a result, thousands of merchants poured into the street. Protest turned into riot. Rioters destroyed government property. Finally, merchants launched a three-day strike. Security forces arrested some 140 people during the second week of January 2002. Protesters bought some time. The state first sent the army to restore order, after which President Mubarak announced the deferment of the decree in a five-year plan of gradual remission (2002–7). The city's economy was ultimately altered and the means of subsistence of many eradicated, as was the commerce that gave Port Said its urban, albeit provincial, character. Port Saidis were promised a growth in industrial activities (gas and harbor) and tourism. But for myriad traders and vendors, professional conversion was unrealistic. In addition, the ecological harm caused by industries in the area, foul beaches, and the absence of commercial and cultural attractions within the city limit tourism.[23]

Most Port Saidis, however, kept silent in 2002 about the relation between the Limby prohibition and January events and about their discontent regarding Israel. Many Port Saidis nonetheless described the festival as a metaphor for the revolt of the powerless. They also identified with the Palestinians, as Kamal 'Id's recollection suggests.[24]

> *The people of Port Said were defenseless, like . . . the Palestinian people now. . . . A state with tanks and planes and a people revolting with grenades and stones, so it was the same thing in Port Said . . . a defenseless people with nothing in their hands. . . . So they did what they could possibly do. . . . So they made the Limby effigy . . .* [25]

Utterly fragile, communal historical utterances thus compete with and at times support—in distinct contexts—official public utterances. By the late 1990s Limby stories variably recounted local opposition to the British, national resistance against imperialism, and the more inclusive, postcolonial social struggle against injustice. During the 1950s–60s the Limby had reenacted the communal and national resistance to British presence, but it had also absorbed elements of the Nasserian official rhetoric, though creatively reinvented. In the '70s the festival's meaning was reinvested. The new clothing and fabrics that built Port Said's prosperity now replaced rags in the confection of the Limby. But all the Limbies, with their historical meanings, always coexisted. Yet, while diverse, they remained cohesive because they shared "paradigmatic lines of narrative similarity": war, resistance, and rebellion, now having for canvas the Ford Foundation, the GATT, the International Monetary Fund, and "globalization."[26]

3

When Edmund Allenby Became al-Limby

> En même temps que surgissait de ces lagunes la cité maritime et toute européenne de Port-Saïd, avec ses longues jetées, ses bassins, ses monuments d'une civilisation industrieuse, on voyait s'attacher à ses flancs une ébauche de village arabe, fruste échantillon de la vie insoucieuse de l'Orient.... Fondé, d'abord par les fellahs venus à Port-Saïd pour y exercer les métiers de portefaix, de manoeuvre, de porteurs d'eaux, etc.
>
> Edouard M. Riou, *Itinéraire de l'Isthme*

Its geographical site conferred to Port Said an obvious strategic importance in traditional warfare and commercial ventures all through the twentieth century. Built on the Mediterranean shore, to the west of the Suez Canal and to the east of Lake Manzala, at the northern point where the Sinai Peninsula meets the Delta, Port Said long suffered the imperial desires of European powers, their allies, and their enemies since its establishment in 1859. Port Said was born from these desires, like Ismailia shortly afterward in 1863. It soon became the largest city on the Suez Canal.[1] In 1854 the French diplomat and entrepreneur Ferdinand de Lesseps created the Compagnie Universelle. It administered the 104-mile-long canal from Port Said to Suez. Fifteen years later it was open to transit.[2] De Lesseps' statue now stands near one of the Canal Authority warehouses. Egyptians had dethroned it, breaking one arm, after French and British troops evacuated the city in December 1956. Its bare pedestal, at the northern end of Port Said's pier, in front of the fishing harbor, reminds us both of the city's historical turnabout and of its roots.[3]

At first a simple harbor crammed with rowdy, pleasure-thirsty sailors, Port Said settled down in the 1920s. In the 1930s, maritime transit intensified. Sailors stayed for shorter periods and the city suffered fewer disturbances. A local diversified commercial life flourished.[4] The city was further tamed "under the influence of authorities concerned with order and public morality." It was now "[becoming] an honest harbor, neither better nor worse than its Mediterranean counterparts," reassuringly stated French Company agent Charles de Sérionne in the 1920s.[5] Sérionne, however, had to contend with the city's long-established, albeit little-deserved, moral discredit. A few imaginative minds had sullied Port Said. Rudyard Kipling left the most nefarious and long-lasting mark when he wrote in the 1890s that "the concentrated essence of all the inequities and all the vices in all the continents [found] itself at Port Said."[6] The periodic presence of military contingents certainly nourished this ill repute. The breakout of World War II did not help with the disciplining dear to Sérionne and other interested parties. War profiteering drew flocks of men to the Canal.[7] World War II also delayed the transfer of British troops from Port Said to the "bitter lakes," near Ismailia, as had been stipulated by the 1936 Anglo-Egyptian Treaty.[8] This enduring military presence led to the 1951 rebellion along the canal and to the insurrection of Ismailia in January 1952.

Foreign infringement upon Egyptian sovereignty was also political and economic. Until the 1956 Suez War, Port Said, Ismailia, and Port Tewfik (south of Suez) continued to be administered to different degrees by the Compagnie. *In principio*, the Canal was Egyptian territory, hence sovereign. De facto, however, it was under British control, even more so after 1914, when Egypt became a protectorate. It retained this status until 1922, wartime justifying the renewal of laws of exception.[9] Port Said certainly enjoyed greater autonomy than Ismailia, especially after the 1920s, but until 1956 foreigners, mainly the French and the British, had ascendancy over city affairs.[10] Though in name an Egyptian enterprise, the Compagnie "kept the print of its French origins. Its capital [was] in great part French and the administration council" had a French president until 1956. Only five out of thirty-two council members were Egyptian.[11]

This order of things was not anomalous in the 1920s–30s. Europeans almost exclusively owned, controlled, and managed large industries. The Compagnie's industries, however, attracted an uncommonly large permanent indigenous workforce.[12] While Port Said held about 80,000 souls in 1926 at the time Allenby departed Egypt, it counted some 178,500 inhabitants by 1956, when Eden replaced Allenby at the burning stake.[13] These numbers rose to 244,000 by 1960, 472,000 in 1996, and to 598,377 in 2009.[14] By the mid-1950s Port Said had become the principal Egyptian harbor for maritime relations with Asia Minor and the Far East.[15] Like its Mediterranean counterparts, it enticed, until the 1950s, Egyptians as well as foreigners, most of the latter migrant workers.[16]

This situation did not compare to the ancient, mythical, sophisticated, cosmopolitan Alexandria that was nostalgically praised by European travelers. Port Said could claim neither a Constantine Cafavy, nor a Stratis Tsirkas, nor an enamored visitor such as Lawrence Durrell, nor the Hellenistic ruins propitious to romantic contemplations.[17] It was a youthful, industrious, merchant, peddling, and cheeky city in the 1920s–30s. Its bards were the large working classes, who created a living musical, poetic, and lyric tradition.[18] Yet Port Said's ethnic diversity could have inspired, like Alexandria did, the eugenicist prose of Raymond Savage, for whom the "average modern Egyptian" was "in breeding an unholy mixture of Arab, Maltese, Turk, Greek, Italian, and Levantine Jew."[19] Social and religious community networks encouraged the settlement in Port Said of foreign and domestic workers.

Becoming Limby

The city's multicommunal makeup did not smooth the toll of foreign rule and wars, though. In wartime, colonial troops settled on the Canal and the British unloaded their war burden on Egyptian shoulders. However, to say that the local population hated the British would be a distortion. Army camps brought employment on the Canal, as they did in Cairo. Oral accounts testify to nuanced relationships and necessary accommodations, including with the British, for personal experiences do not obey the tropes of nationalist narratives. Conflict was not absent, but the Canal cities offered a rather harmonious coexistence and collaboration between alien and native popular classes.[20] Shipyard workers, who were in majority Egyptian, and the Egyptian personnel attending to the army eventually established courteous friendships with some of their foreign coworkers. They socialized, if not at work, then in the profuse bars of the city. Around a drink and the gambling table, all were equal in the face of misfortune.[21] Yet, by "burning Edmund," Port Saidis uncompromisingly rejected British political hegemony as well as claims that Egypt benefited from occupation.[22]

After World War II, the 1948 defeat, and nationalist agitation, the Egyptian government was no longer in a position to defend the British military presence. Armed and civil organized and unorganized resistance against the colonial order started in October 1951, when the Wafd Party unilaterally abrogated the Anglo-Egyptian 1936 Treaty. It culminated in January 1952 and continued until the spring. Dockworkers went on strike for months. The government removed Egyptian labor from the Canal Zone.[23] For months, ambushes, stabbings, fires, acid throwing, bombs, sabotage of telephone lines and mooring wires, booby traps, snipers, and gunmen were directed at the Suez Canal Company and at British soldiers, military headquarters, and boats.[24] A small photograph hanging in the living room showing a handsome young man holding a gun across his chest prompts the visitor to ask 'Abd al-Rahim Gharib al-Banna for a story to be told. In Ismailia, al-Banna had worked for the British army in the 1930s and 1940s. He recounted with pleasure his friendships with some British coworkers and their families. But al-Banna also remembered with the greatest pride smuggling to the Egyptian resistance in 1948 weapons that Muslim Indian conscripts of the British colonial army had helped steal from army supplies.[25] Later he did not hesitate to take up the arms during the underground Battle of the Canal.

Thus, a core performance of the festival in Port Said was the reenactment of national resistance. The burning of Allenby established a festival within a festival with a nationalist as well as a social dimension. First, the effigy burning elevated the particular into the universal. It asserted Egyptian national unity against the foreign occupant. Alternatively, the spatial arrangement of the festival voiced class boundaries. Centered in al-'Arab, the burning avowed the social cohesion of this working-class neighborhood against the Afranji middle- and upper-class district. Furthermore, its participants implicitly affirmed their national identity not only against the colonizer but also against estranged native elites, spatially and culturally divorced from them, whom they associated with the occupiers and profiteers.

This spatial colonial division into native working-class ('Arab) and foreign and elite (Afranji) districts remains distinctive of the old town's architectural design and economic activities. The old city districts have retained their colonial architecture, their names, and much of their geographical distribution.[26] Until today, old and new neighborhoods developed in the 1950s and 1970s assume differentiated social identities. One's spatial location indicates one's class and professional occupation as well as whether one has old or new money, and it marks the distinction between "original" residents and the successive waves of immigrants who came to Port Said in the 1970s.[27] Al-'Arab remains the heart of the city because of its historicity and its economic importance. But the borders that separated al-'Arab from al-Afranji district are now blurred, even though the latter retains some of its old families and trades, such as the now almost vanished bars and hotels owned by Greek Egyptians. Today the somewhat elusive division between "original" inhabitants and "newcomers" of the 1970s has replaced former colonial distinctions and also points to the social fragmentation of the community.

Political and social fragmentation in colonial and postcolonial times resulted both in the repression and in the emulation of the Limby festival. It refracted the city's economic and political competition of interests as well as the tension between informal and institutionalized cultural forms. It ended with the apparent victory of the latter, a fate common to many carnivals.[28] At its inception, the Limby effigy burning was much like a "political feat." Rather than politics parading as cultural event, al-Limby was a subverted cultural tradition, a performance explicitly and uncompromisingly political. There was no pretense, neither in intent nor in act. The British colonial authorities had no doubt about it. They chased revelers and tracked down their stocks of burning supplies.

As the effigy burning became ritual, as Allenby's identity became blurry, as the ritual finally transfigured the general into al-Limby, setting Edmund on fire now verily assumed the form of "masquerade politics." Masquerade politics are, in the words of Abner Cohen, "politics articulated in terms of non-political cultural forms such as religion, kinship, the arts."[29] That being said, the Limby festival and its inventive custom always kept the potential for, and the eventuality of, political feat alive. Metaphors contain this potency for materialization. In sum, burning Edmund Allenby was initially more than sheer cultural expression and contestation of the existing "economic and political power,"[30] the enactment of which "sanctioned the existing patterns of things and reinforced it."[31] Port Saidis clearly and simply expressed their wrath. To be sure, by burning Edmund, people denounced the existing order of things. Yet they simultaneously enunciated a straightforward "death wish" against the colonial order by performing an "effective metaphorical aggression"[32]—that is, a physical aggression perpetrated against the symbol of British political power rather than its actual representative. This performance gained might as people integrated the novelty into a preexisting celebration of ancient roots (Shamm al-Nasim) while preserving the latter's essential form. The potency for materialization and activation of the "metaphorical aggression" is, I believe, the primary reason why political authorities prohibited the festivities in all parts of town and all along the Canal in 1998.[33]

Inventing Innovation

In Port Said and Ismailia alike, most testimonies assert, there was no effigy burning at Shamm al-Nasim prior to Allenby's. Both the local population and outsiders commonly portray the effigy burning as a local, incidental, and spontaneous innovation. Ex nihilo, like the city. Haraq al-Limby is an "invented tradition," which historian Eric Hobsbawm has defined as "a set of practices, normally governed by overtly or tacitly accepted rules and of a ritual or symbolic nature, which seek to inculcate certain values and norms of behaviour by repetition, which automatically implies [a largely factitious] continuity with the past."[34] Human artifice is thereby reinterpreted as natural law. However, the claim in Port Said is not one of ancientness, that is, the "reference to [an] old situation" or its "quasi-obligatory repetition."[35] If such factitious continuity exists, it lies in the idea that both the symbolic meaning and ceremonial rules continued through time. It might also lie in the invention of repetition: there is no certainty that the Limby festival occurred annually since its inception. The (re)invention, however, consists in conveying the idea that the ritual was a novelty. The stress hence lies on invention, uniqueness, and genuineness, rather than on the antiquity of the present.

In fact, Port Saidis form a community that does not disclaim its recentness. Like other migrant communities, they do not claim a long established, ancient local tradition. To the contrary, they assert their innovative, unconventional, and progressive spirit. They were born or raised in an urban community of recent foundation. They formed a congregation of immigrants of varied social and national origins. In the nineteenth and early twentieth centuries, many came from the Mediterranean basin and joined in the promising European and Egyptian financial ventures. In the 1970s rural migrants flocked from the Egyptian countryside to the now all-Egyptian Canal. The following remarks by Ahmad 'Awad wonderfully illustrate the mechanisms of social integration and transformation in Port Said:

> A. A.   *And every community had a club. . . . The Italian club. . . . cultural and intellectual and social. . . . In Port Said, here, there were places for newly arrived foreigners. When these Cypriotes came, their clothes in the past were not like today. . . . Today Cypriotes, people from Cyprus, have become European. They wear a suit. But back then the Cypriote wore something called the libas [garment]; it was something like that costume that goes down, but with a long crotch [hajar] . . . between the legs. . . . Like the sailors'.*
> M. B.   *Yeah, like the Turks.*

A. A.   Like the Turks. ... And [the new immigrant] sported a red tarbush on his head, but the day after he arrived, his Greek brothers, you know what they'd do? Someone his size, for example if he had a strong body, got things from home, and another one gave him trousers, hop, and he became an effendi. And the day after, he became a khawaga [European] you could not distinguish from the other khawaga. ... That's Port Said, that's how it was here in the past. ... We saw these sorts of things. ... But today, Port Said is no more. ... The only people who come here now are from the countryside; they come to sell chicken, they sell vegetables, they sell things. ... And after that, they return on their boats. ... Or these people from the countryside who come to work in houses, they work as workers. ... And that's Port Said: the pulse of life never ceased.[36]

As this testimony shows, communal solidarity and organizations helped integrate newcomers into the local community. It also suggests that upon arrival immigrants reinvented themselves. An undifferentiated European foreign identity (*khawaga*) set apart the Cypriotes, Greeks, Maltese, and Italians from Egyptians, which was based upon erasing physical distinctions. As this testimony also implies, Port Saidis lived in a world made up of multiple streams of traditions. Today they pride themselves on their cultural singularity, including their Shamm al-Nasim customs. At the same time, they also tend to apprehend the city as a closed impervious entity. Port Saidi elders insist on an urbanity set in opposition to rurality and to the migrants of the 1970s, who redefined the town's identity. Accordingly, the effigy burning is not a rural accretion to the urban body but rather a tradition born from Port Said's urban cauldron. By contending that the ritual was an innovation, storytellers thus highlight the nationalistic and political dimension of the ontological event.[37] Simultaneously, they buttress the idea that the city possesses a quite unique character befitting a rebellious reputation legitimated by an insular geography.

In fact, we lack any sort of authoritative evidence pointing to historical practices of effigy burning that would unravel the Shamm al-Nasim mysteries. Ironically, European Orientalists furnish the matrix for present Egyptian descriptions of the festival. Edward Lane's elusive account forms the hypertext of most recent commentaries.[38] Further meager observations, written by foreign scholars, missionaries, and seekers of exoticism, reveal the extent of our ignorance of the celebration's history. Egyptian anthropology and folk studies have only lately taken an interest in such cultural practices.[39] Foreign travelers were largely unfamiliar with local society.[40] Their accounts also fail to mention either effigy burning or bonfire, maybe because these practices were not exotic to them, for burning old clothes, household items, and furniture in the spring was shared with other Mediterranean societies. One hypothesis might thus be that haraq al-Limby derived from spring bonfires, such as the religious Christian burning of the Judas, also during Easter, and the nonreligious Jewish ceremony of Lag BaOmer.[41]

Another hypothesis that might explain the Limby links Shamm al-Nasim to Nawruz's bonfire and effigy burning (the "mock king"), as does Lane. Formal and functional similarities point to shared ceremonial practices that could have fused in late nineteenth- and early twentieth-century Egypt.[42] Some foreign testimonies of this period reported the persistence of Nawruz in the Upper Egyptian countryside, even though it disappeared from Cairene records by the fifteenth century.[43] As noted earlier, the reliability and interpretation of this evidence is problematic.[44] But the point is that the burning of effigies seemed widespread in small Upper Egyptian towns, at least until the late nineteenth century.[45] One might hence surmise that Shamm al-Nasim was more diversely celebrated eighty years ago than is commonly assumed.[46] One may further infer that bonfire and effigy-burning customs lingered on in the countryside into the twentieth century in the Delta as in Upper Egypt. Rural folks could have brought the custom along with them as they emigrated to and visited the Canal.[47] Indeed, when Allenby was first condemned to death by fire between the late 1910s and the early 1920s, rural migrants flocked to the Canal. They came from the nearby countryside as well as Upper Egypt. They attended religious and profane events. Most of all, villagers, particularly women, commuted daily from their homes to the city, as they still do today, including to Cairo. As Ahmad 'Awad recalls,

> *Peasants came to Port Said to sell agricultural products. They brought cheese, they brought chicken, they brought ducks, they brought butter, they brought all that. They came from the countryside ... the villages, where from? From the governorate of Daqhiliyya. ... You know, merchants, women, who came in the launch [by] the lake. ... The launch brought them to the markets. ... The Monday market, the Thursday market, the Friday market ...*[48]

Many farmers settled in town, which offered a large array of seasonal as well as permanent professional opportunities. Until World War II, peasant workers formed the bulk of the Egyptian industrial force. Port Said offered no exception, especially during wartime inflation, when large contingents of manpower were needed. Most workers then came from Upper Egypt.[49] Oral testimonies about rural migration corroborate what scarce written records and intuition suggest. The innovation of the festival, then, was not the effigy burning itself but the transformation of its form, sociopolitical function, dimension, and meaning. Tradition was reinvented, reappropriated, and adapted to the particular context of Port Said.

Some testimonies insist in fact on the rurality of the practice. Rural folks burned effigies in surrounding villages and in the city during khamasin night, on the eve of Shamm al-Nasim. They celebrated the demise of the winter and the advent of the New Year.[50] According to anthropologist 'Aysha Shukr, rural emigrants continued to burn "khamasin dolls" after settling in the city.[51] One might imagine that on occasion the faceless effigy was dressed up in the guise of the "tyrannical king" of the day and immolated. The rural ceremony was then urbanized. The reborn khamasin doll preserved its newly given name (Limby) and its new function (social protest) in the 1920s and was thereafter dissociated from its rural origins.

Tradition thus invented did not arise ex nihilo but rather drew upon preexisting customs and rituals. However, longtime Port Saidis, such as Ahmad 'Awad, are keen on distinguishing between urban and rural traditions, setting themselves apart from rural folks.

> M. B.   *The effigy-burning custom ... that custom existed in the countryside long ago, you know.*
> A. A.   *No, the countryside did not imitate Port Said. ... We were the only ones in Port Said to have a spring burning, that's all.*
> M. B.   *I heard that this custom came from the countryside, that there were people in the countryside, that the peasants would have fires, you see.*
> A. A.   *The fires in the countryside were different from here. ... Here the burning is a festival. ... As for the burning in the countryside ... they burn the rice straw, which is normal, you know. ... As for us, we had fires with the purpose of celebrating. ... The aim was celebrating. ... Shut off [the recorder] so that we won't work forever.*[52]

This account thus rejects comparisons between urban and rural practices. It highlights the structured and political nature of Port Said's festival. Similar to nationalist views of the nation, the city here assimilates rather than integrates exogenous elements. The insistence on discontinuity asserts Port Said's uniqueness and insularity. This theme is cast onto recollections of its past as told through tales of resistance, one of which is the Limby festival.

Ceremonial Death

The effigy burned in Port Said was not merely the symbol of an abstract and cosmic power, such as the King of Nawruz and the mock king of the Coptic New Year. Rather, it embodied a tangible, political authority: Edmund Allenby and British arbitrary rule. Naturally, all allegories, including that of the mock king, may oscillate between abstract and tangible spheres of meaning. Accordingly, al-Limby was an instance of the ambiguity, versatility, and reversibility of carnivalesque performances. The effigy-burning presented "sustained public actions in which social conflicts [were] dramatized."[53] Limby performances physically played out in the streets the power struggle between British and Egyptians. The confection of the effigies was a circumvention of and a victory over the colonial order. The tyrant was tyrannized, poked fun at, insulted. Conflict was verbalized and its symbol carried out at the burning stake in full military uniform.

These dramas do not simply restate underlying social structures and divisions. They are what Victor Turner "calls society's 'subjunctive' mood." Thus, "ritual, carnival, festival, theater, and other cultural performances express 'supposition, desire, hypothesis, possibility' rather than fact."[54] The Limby burning chronotopically reveals carnivals' polysemic outcomes and their unpredictability. The festival has evolved since its first spontaneous, anarchic, improvised anonymous performances. Yet it never lost its polysemy. From the start, political authorities toiled at containing the event within the boundaries of an inoffensive parody of the social order. They sanctioned attacks against state-approved foes such as Israeli politicians and soccer referees. In 2002, after banning the festival, local powers consented instead to a preapproved performance, orchestrated by the Khudayr family, generally known for its elaborate effigies and locally reputed for its association with city authorities and for operating within authorized boundaries. The municipality was in fact concerned with the Limby's unpredictable politicization consistent with ritual performances' liminality.

Bully's Bull's Going Loose

> *You know, after you left [the café yesterday], I spoke with many people. We could not reach a conclusion . . . we could not reach a conclusion. You know, in [Ismailia], we find people burning the Allenby. Well, where did they get this from? And why? Everyone says something different. . . . This Allenby*

was in a car going where? He was ... you know, the English political center in Egypt, and whatnot. ... Nothing, it's over, the government forbade that thing ...[55]

The history of the effigy burning remains shrouded in mystery. One has yet to find authoritative records reporting the ontological event. Most oral sources safely reference the 1920s, when the nation was facing the pains of the Great War. This hypothesis, however, leaves open conjectures as to why exactly the practice started, as 'Abd al-Rahim Gharib al-Banna's earlier bemused remarks so aptly illustrate. Oral and press accounts situate the first event sometime between 1917 and 1925. This framework corresponds to General Allenby's physical presence in the Near East. Such conjectures rely on circular information, untrustworthy news articles made of stories collected on the street, and unnamed Orientalist accounts. While dating is not essential to our story, historical selections are, for they demarcate the realms of meaning and associations by which people frame the historical Allenby. Historical fictions inform us of the field marshal's reputation. They explicate colonial and postcolonial war experiences and their influence on present political perspectives.

A 2002 news piece conveniently locates the event in 1917, that is, the beginning of Allenby's mission in the Near East.[56] Yet, if the effigy burning was originally bound to Shamm al-Nasim and Allenby's political assignment, this date is unlikely. In 1917 Allenby had not yet proven himself as the "warrior-statesman," in the words of his hagiographer, "worthy to be remembered along with the greatest in the days of the Old Testament and beyond the greatest of the Crusaders in the Middle Ages."[57] Allenby, in fact, arrived in Egypt after Shamm al-Nasim. Also, contrary to popular belief, he did not linger on the Canal. First arriving in Cairo on 27 June 1917, he was a day later formally appointed commander-in-chief of the Mediterranean Expeditionary Force for the Palestine and Egypt campaign.[58] During the summer of 1917 Allenby immediately established his general headquarters in Khan Yunus, behind the front line. The field marshal spent the following months (until early 1919) in Palestine. He was promoted both to the position of high commissioner of Egypt and to the title of lordship in March 1919, in the midst of the Egyptian Revolution, whereupon he settled in Cairo. Yet Allenby's predecessor, Sir Archibald Murray (1860–1945), could plausibly have inspired the first effigy burning in June 1917 in celebration of his departure. It does, however, remain a moot proposition. Unlike Allenby, Murray failed to achieve preeminence in Egyptian history and memory, even as a villain. His deeds are not much recounted in British literature either, where he only appears as accountable for the military failures of 1916 and early 1917 against the German and Ottoman armies.[59] Allenby, however, carried on Murray's legacy and resumed some of his controversial plans. It was Murray's decision (not Allenby's) to restrict entrance to the Canal in 1916, whereby "no Egyptian or European was allowed to enter without a permit."[60] The same year, "Sir Archibald Murray's engineers [had] accomplished the remarkable feast of laying a pipe-line across the desert from the Suez Canal to El Arish,"[61] a feat entailing undesirable hardships. Fellahin had additional reasons, in early 1917, to feel disgruntled about the British army. In the name of military security and war efforts, its command pressured both the Egyptian government and civilians. In May 1917 the British, who anticipated rebellions, legally decreed that all Egyptians surrender their weapons.[62] They imposed further restrictions and demands upon the local population following Allenby's arrival.

If Limby was not born during Shamm al-Nasim or May 1917, it may have blazed in September, on Nawruz. Allenby had then just completed the "elaborate system of pipelines, railways and roads" that Murray initiated a year earlier.[63] Egyptian workers had toiled through the desert in the heat of the summer as they linked British military bases to the Palestinian front. Many lost their lives. According to colonial standards, Allenby's rule was not particularly tyrannical, but his actions during the summer of 1917, especially during the railroad construction, explain his reputation. Q. M. 'Ulawyah and M. Shuman[64] support this hypothesis in their work on popular poetry based upon local oral lore.[65]

Both the Egyptian government and the British military command in Egypt were under pressing demands from London. By all accounts, the British army was in a dangerous situation when Allenby replaced Murray at the command of the British army.[66] As a result, the British increased their requests and critically undermined the authority of the newly appointed Fu'ad I (1917–36) in the eyes of Egyptians. They thus exacerbated local hostility to British occupation. Egyptians felt that they were carrying Great Britain's burden. They were forced into dying for the occupier's personal war against the Germans and the Ottomans, which was none of their concern. The deeper the British sank into war, the greater they requisitioned local "auxiliary services."[67] At their peak, in early 1919, there were some four hundred thousand British imperial troops in Egypt.[68] In the British colonial mind-set, the recruitment of Egyptians was mutually beneficial. It was educative for natives and cost effective for the British. In a 1918 ode to Evelyn Baring (1883–1907), S. H. Leeder thus praises British coaching of Egyptian youth in the service of the army: "To-day the army service causes no wailing; the mother and the youthful wife look forward to seeing the lad again, strong and straight, a traveled man with many things to tell, and even with a little money in his pocket."[69] To imperialist clichés and arrogance Savage added a comically messianic interpretation of the Palestine campaign:

> His name, phonetically at any rate, was of deep significance to the natives, for "Alla Nebi" in Arabic means "The Prophet of God," and spelt backwards, "Ibn Allah," signifies "The Son of God." Superstition was rampant, and prophecy after prophecy was fulfilled. ... Allenby came from the West and took the Holy City, not as an arrogant conqueror, but as one respecting the place which was at once the cradle of Christianity and the third most important shrine of Islam.[70]

To my best knowledge, native prophecies did not leave any record.

The military operations in fact yielded temporary benefits to some Egyptians. The garrison town of Port Said economically profited from the war. In contrast, in the nearby countryside, mothers, "youthful wives," and "straight lads" wailed. The British ruthlessly used local labor, corvée, and provisions, "food-shortage [even] threatening some areas with famine."[71] The building of the railroad in the desert, material deprivations, and the corvée convincingly elucidate Allenby's tyrannical image. During the war, forced labor indeed supplanted paid work. British figures cite 500,000 laborers. Egyptian estimates range between 1,000,000 and 1,500,000.[72] British soldiers in the Levant were not to be envied either. By mid-1919 they were close to rebellion. Tired of broken promises of demobilization, troops organized protest actions against their commanders. Their highest commander had no more sympathy for their plight than he did for Egyptian laborers. "Some trade union microbe has got into them," Allenby reportedly declared. "I can't shoot them all for mutiny."[73]

Resistance figure, worker, grassroots activist, poet and lyricist, and a local authority in Canal folklore, Captain Ghazali supports, along with many others, the hypothesis that war deprivations and forced labor spurred the first Limby burning.

> *This Allenby is a much-hated personality. . . . He headed the British forces in the '14 War. . . . They were extending the railroad . . . the railroad in the Fertile Crescent. . . . And with the corvée, they gathered the young men. . . . They took them to build . . . to make the railroad in that whole area. . . . So, people*

called this "the torture." ... So, when they heard that he was leaving ... [in 1919], they started breaking jugs and crushing everything in front of them in celebration, because the men slipped away from work. ... So they started impersonating him. ...[74]

Even though war events and oral narratives alone do not prove beyond reasonable doubt that the effigy burning was war related, they convincingly point to the grounds for Allenby's reputation and, furthermore, to the importance of World War I in Egyptian political mobilization.

In addition, by 1919 Allenby also came to embody the repression of the nationalist and independence movement. Another version of the Limby story accordingly attributes the effigy burning to Allenby's violence against the 1919 insurrection, as poet Kamal 'Id suggests:

> *Allenby was a military leader for Great Britain ... for the region of the Canal ... or from the Sinai to ... Palestine, you know. ... Egypt was occupied by Great Britain in those times. ... In the year [1919] ... during the '19 Revolution in which Sa'd Zaghlul pasha rose ... there were demonstrations. ... So [Allenby] put down the demonstrations by force. ... So they made the Allenby effigy. ... They came up with that tyrannical Allenby ...*[75]

There is no record of the tyrannical Allenby as portrayed in this testimony. Yet oral and written accounts unanimously show that Allenby was a strong-headed man. He employed all possible means for enforcing his will. Flinching was a last resort, as Allenby's own comment about shooting his troops suggests. Even sympathizing compatriots agree on his tempestuous moods and bad temper, which they excuse as a downside of his admirable force of character.

By 1919, in fact, High Commissioner Allenby employed all possible means for restituting social order. The 1919 Revolution hypothesis is reasonable, but it does not elucidate why the event would have both taken place and been maintained specifically in Port Said, let alone on the Canal. Were disturbances and repression particularly intense in Port Said and the Canal cities? Likely so. Canal dwellers added mighty labor strikes to nationalist protest. Wartime hardships and related work grievances had led to the unrest of Compagnie workers in synchrony with their compatriots all over Egypt. Egyptian and European workers even joined forces.[76] As was customary, the French solicited British military intervention to put an end to disturbances. Curiously, the high commissioner declined, despite his disapproval of workers' solidarity and his aversion to trade unions and their association with nationalist groups.[77] The high commissioner strategically, rather than temperamentally, used violence and tyranny.

The 1919 Limby thesis dubiously befits nationalist narratives. It elevates the effigy burning to a revolutionary act, incorporating the Limby in the great 1919 Revolution.[78] In the Canal cities and in Port Said perhaps more than anywhere else, the Great War and the 1919 upheavals are strongly associated. One may easily envision, on 21 April 1919, Shamm al-Nasim revelers dressing up khamasin effigies with new clothing and shouting, in rhyme and rhythm, "Allenby, Oh, son of a bitch, your wife is a shameless whore" and "Oh, Allenby! Allenby died, Oh men! And there are lice and nits in his gonorrhea."[79] In July 1919 a Cairo police record seemingly referenced these Shamm al-Nasim Port Saidi rhymes, indicating that "in native quarters . . . streetboys, lower-class natives, seed vendors, etc., [had] been publicly singing a *new song* in the vernacular . . . [containing] uncomplimentary remarks about the G.O.C." There is little doubt that Port Saidis, like Cairenes, indulged in lewd political *zajal*.[80] This record further complicates our story and thickens its mysteries.

In the same nationalist interpretative vein, a widely spread account explains the effigy burning as a celebration of Allenby's departure on 14 June 1925. After all, the governor and his wife left Egypt from Port Said. Traveling in a "special train," the couple had been greeted by the British community with a "luncheon-party . . . prior to their embarkation."[81] Among the "great demonstrations of affection" following news of the high commissioner's departure, it seems plausible that Port Saidis organized a blazing celebration of their own. Supporting this interpretation, one story relates that upon learning about the departure, Port Saidis flocked to the train station, shouting at Allenby and British rule. This account has Allenby escape through a side exit where he is rescued by his compatriots. This day incidentally coinciding with Shamm al-Nasim, the story goes, participants baptized the effigy in the name of the marshal.[82] One might easily picture such an episode occurring behind a police cord and Allenby being escorted out. British records, however, are silent about such incident.

In another widespread patriotic account, the ontological event happened during a year when Coptic and Islamic calendars overlapped, most commonly situated in 1925, the year of Allenby's departure. Accordingly, the Coptic Eastern, the pagan Shamm al-Nasim, and the Islamic Mulid al-Nabi were simultaneously celebrated.[83] I first heard the story from Hagg Yusif, a retired merchant of Port Said. The story was later confirmed by Captain Ghazali. The hagg was my first interviewee to correctly identify Limby as the marshal. Port Saidis in their forties and younger, from earlier generations or from families of recent migration, only vaguely knew Limby's historical identity. Recollections are generational and communal historical representations ephemeral. One year—Hagg Yusif confessed that he did not know exactly when and, keen on being factual, declined to give a date, because he "was not there, it was long before [he] was born"—Mulid al-Nabi happened to coincide with Shamm al-Nasim. Crowds of people had crammed into the streets. Muslims celebrated the religious holiday, everyone enjoying the moment, when Allenby arrived in his car and proceeded to drive into the Muslim crowds. Allenby ordered his driver to move ahead, but his driver refused. So, Allenby pulled out his gun and pointed it at the head of the recalcitrant man, summoning him to either drive or die. As the driver moved ahead, people became infuriated; they stormed and burned Allenby's car. Since then, people have commemorated the event with the burning of Allenby's effigy.[84] Port Said's French consular archives record an identical event, dated 15 September 1920, which does not, however, involve Allenby but a group of sailors.[85]

The Mulid account highlights the unity of Port Saidis of all faiths, celebrating, and rising up in unison against the offender. I looked in vain in British archives for written evidence of the Allenby car incident, which many Port Saidis believe to be a complete fabrication. There are, however, factual roots to the legend. Savage, who admired Allenby, anecdotally reports that one of the general's "fads" was to have the roads cleared for the passage of his car. Savage provides convincing evidence that the marshal was renowned as a driving bully.[86] Although the details of the incident related by the hagg might have been lost or might never have existed, Savage's story lends credibility to oral accounts about the "Bull" (as was his nickname) driving into crowds.

Another version of the Coptic-Islamic-pharaonic story adds a third party: the foreign community. According to this rendering, people had gathered in al-Afranj. Revelers had partied all night, as usual. But the racket displeased foreign residents. They called in British troops, who ousted the Egyptian crowds; thus was lit the first effigy.[87] A similar yet more detailed account reported by anthropologist 'Aysha Shukr elaborates on the conflict:

> The members of a Sufi order prepared every year their outing in their processions at the occasion of the celebration of the birth of the honored Prophet. Once, the celebrations of the birth of the Prophet and

Shamm al-Nasim fell together. While the procession of the Sufi order was passing by the street Muhammad 'Ali, which separates [al-'Arab] from al-Afranj neighborhood, a group of British soldiers, who were stationed, prevented them from crossing the points of passage between the two areas, and did not allow any Egyptian citizen to cross without previous authorization. As a result of this prevention, a clash occurred between the two parties, which developed into the irruption of a bullet fired by the soldiers, in the air, to disperse the procession. The situation transformed into a patriotic demonstration, in which the people expressed their anger by lighting fires and shouting out against the occupation.[88]

Here, the religious ("Islamic"), national (the Egyptian "al-'Arab"), and nationalist ("patriotic demonstration") characters of the actors' performance are set against foreign and military occupiers. The power struggle between foreign and Egyptian protagonists takes metaphorical expression through spatial divisions and border crossing. First, the coalescence of Islamic and secular celebrations is ecumenical. Nonetheless, this is an Islamic religious (mystical) order that leads the rebellion and the community against the colonial order. Second, the street that separates Egyptians from non-Egyptians was named after Muhammad 'Ali, who, to some, opened the way to European penetration and, to others, was the first modern Egyptian ruler. Muhammad 'Ali Street was most of all the spatially dividing line between "Arab" (to the west) and "European" (to the east) sides of town. The attempt to cross Muhammad 'Ali Street materializes the protest against colonial sociopolitical exclusion and segregation, revealing the British alliance with, and protection of, the foreign and economic elites who were enclosed in one impenetrable space. In Ismailia, Muhammad 'Ali Street similarly divided the city and offered a spatialized interchange and segregation:

M. B. *And was the division real? You know, for example, the westerners would not go on the side of. . . . At first there was . . .*

A. B. *No, no, no . . . There was interaction, you know, in the cafés and in the workshops and whatnot, and in the streets, and during festivals. There was no such thing [then] as a* khawaga *and an Arab, no, no. . . . But you know. But the French thought they lived in their homeland and came all alone on their own . . .*

M. B. *On their own?*

A. B. *Yes, on their own . . . [whereas] when you had no Egyptian friend,* you did not come [in Egyptian quarters]. . . . Initially, that Muhammad 'Ali Street . . . the streets were divided. [And] if you were inside [the city] going [outside] to the countryside . . . the English kept you in custody. You know what the soldiers would say? . . .

M. B.   Really?!

A. B.   Yeah, "It is forbidden to enter here."[89]

Thus, parade participants, the story goes, had legitimate claims and peaceful intents. Police brutality betrayed British fragility and substantiated Egyptian moral superiority. Furthermore, the British used violence because colonial boundaries were threatened. The procession disputed colonial politics as reflected in the mapping of the city. The use of force dispersed the crowds. But there was a sweet taste of victory in the political defiance embodied in traversing Muhammad 'Ali Street and entering al-Afranj, in the crossing of physical and symbolic colonial boundaries, and in burning Allenby and British power.

This story conjures up social segregation and prejudice. It is instructive of the Egyptian colonial experience in which colonial and native institutions coalesced as the Egyptian police watched over foreign privileges:

M. B.   And the burning took place in al-'Arab or in other places as well?

A. A.   No, in al-'Arab and al-Manakh, but not in al-Afranj, because in al-Afranj there were customs and traditions that we were against. . . . They knew we were against them. . . . Against colonization . . .

M. B.   But in the quarters . . . a quarter . . .

A. A.   The popular ones, only the popular ones . . .

M. B.   And al-Manakh as well?

A. A.   Al-Manakh is popular . . .

M. B.   But in the quarter of al-Afranj there were also Egyptians, right?

A. A.   Yes. . . . For example, the merchants of the neighborhood, . . . they lived in al-Afranj, people with property, and tradesmen, and sea merchants, and engineers, and the people who were, say, "riches."

M. B.   And in al-Manakh?

A. A.   Workers and bourgeois and peasants and small merchants and carpenters and blacksmiths, these were the . . . people . . .

M. B.   Yeah . . . and wasn't there any foreigner among them?

A. A.   None at all, none at all, they didn't live with them, no. That is, these had their quarter and those had their quarter. There were some in al-'Arab . . . but not inside of al-'Arab, no. . . . On Sa'd Zaghlul Street, there were shopkeepers who sold things for the, what, groceries. . . .

M. B.   But [foreigners] would not live inside?
A. A.   Inside there was property.... His house ... was on Abu Hasan Street or Thirtieth Street (Thalathin).... Close to al-Afranj.... Close to Muhammad 'Ali.... There were foreigners.... And there were foreigners in al-Manakh, but they were not merchants ... alcohol and things like that.... There was something called the protégés.... It was forbidden to pass through them.... A phone call at once.... The police protected them.... They took care of them.... Yeah, really.... The protégés.... There were the English ethnic groups.... The French ethnic groups.... Every country had an ethnic group here.... The ethnic group was responsible.... All of Port Said was ethnic groups.... Nobody could pass in front of a foreigner ... because the government itself.... Like that. The English removed them and brought a new government the day after.... This is the meaning of colonialism.... Meaning what? That "I own you, and don't move until I tell you ..."[90]

As James Scott wrote, "Who wins the duel is symbolically irrelevant; it is the challenge that restores honor."[91] Here the bravado of the procession symbolically restored people's honor in the face of colonial exclusion, social subordination, and political repression. The reiteration of the story in the present, however, functions as a site of remembrance of the loci of such honor (faith and community) in the face of universal oppression. It is hence a site of empowerment. The hyperbolic version of the story, in which the incident took place both on Shamm al-Nasim and on Allenby's departure, on June 14th, operates as a nationalist predicate. In 1925, alas, Coptic Easter was celebrated on April 19th, thus invalidating this thesis.

Communitarian Cohesion

In November 1921 a caricature appeared in the satirical magazine *Kashkul*. It portrayed Egypt as a countrywoman lamenting the loss of her livelihood, her earthenware jug lying broken on the ground. Allenby faces her, brandishing a stick bearing the trace of his crime, and declares irritatingly: "It's really strange that after all that, you don't love me!" By 1919 Allenby had broken too many jugs already. The correspondence of the revolutionary upheavals and labor strikes with Shamm al-Nasim in the spring of 1919 supports the first al-Limby appearance on 21 April of that year. This does not preclude out-of-season and prior offenses separately from Shamm al-Nasim. The occurrence of the Limby effigy burning might exist independently from its ritualization.

In all occurrences, these chronicles all point to one collective signification, whether the burning first occurred in 1917, 1919, 1925, or some other year. None of these glorifies the acts of one single individual. Rather, they underscore the communal making of the event, national (Allenby's departure and revolution) and local (Mulid and World War I). Occasionally, they also highlight the antagonism between Egyptians and foreigners. But all of these stories, like the festival itself, symbolize national and local communal cohesion.

Thus, two planes of interpretation and social belonging, and two social spheres of historical utterances, coexist: the local (the Canal region and the city of Port Said) and the national (Egyptian) community. At times the loyalties and interests they cover coincide and nourish each other. At other times, though, they come into conflict as revealed by performances that defied municipal authorities. The affirmation of one's local, special, unique identity feeds itself in contradistinction from, but also alternatively by appropriation of, the national. The public utterances that result from individual, communal, and national dynamics are hardly predictable.

Limby is but one of many casualties caused by this conflict between the state, positing as nation, and local communal interests at times set against and at times coterminous with the nation. Thus, whereas Limby bravely survived colonial hunts, he succumbed to the iron fist of national politics. Institutions best subdue dissidence by appropriating or subverting its form. The state used force and claimed the tradition by arranging its burial with a commemorative museum.

Festival stories betray the pervasiveness of the rich capital of emotions and political drives inherited from World War I and passed onto the nationalist movement of the 1920s–40s. They also bring back other emotionally rich events, such as the Suez drama. One may imagine the masquerades organized for the evacuation of the British army. After 1956 and until the city was hit again by another misfortune, the festival became entangled in a new political chapter of Egyptian history that washed out the historical identity of al-Limby.

4

Port Said, Martyr City

M. B.   *When you were young, how was the festival? What did people do, and has the festival changed here compared to a long time ago, you know?*

A. B.   *Not at all, the same processions, exactly the same. ... There were small processions; now there are big processions.*

'Abd al-Rahim Gharib al-Banna interview, Ismailia, 1 November 2002

Between the end of the World War I and the Free Officers' Revolution, our story of haraq al-Limby relies on elders' recollections. They reckon that celebrations remained much the same until recent years, only varying in size. When people assert, as 'Abd al-Rahim Gharib al-Banna does, that the festival did not change, most speak of its corpus delicti. What have remained are its essence (resistance) and basic forms (bonfires, processions, etc.) rather than the detailed manifestations of the effigy burning (confection materials, actors, etc.). Whereas most agree that no significant changes occurred until the 1950s, testimonies converge to emphasize that there was a specific historical moment after which the festival became a sizeable *zahira* (phenomenon, event). For some, the *zahira* dates from the 1952 Revolution and the Suez War. For others, it dates from the June War and the post-1967 evacuation.

Proponents of the revolutionary landmark support nationalist interpretations of the festival. In fact, some of the evidence supports this date, which coalesces the overthrow of the monarchy and the end of British military presence, political independence and sovereignty, 1952 and 1956. In my early inquiries, reports binding the festival to the 1956 events were so dominant that they obscured the connection between Limby and Allenby. This raised the question as to whether the historical character and the earlier meaning of the ritual had been buried with the Suez War. This association also nourished my suspicions as to whether nationalist interpretations overstated the impact of 1956 on the festival. The street-to-street random search for the historical

Allenby yielded an overwhelming number of fantasies. But they also corroborated the narrative according to which the Suez War significantly affected Shamm al-Nasim celebrations. While burning Edmund did not lose its anterior social functions, for about a decade the reinvigorated festival embodied the fulfillment of national emancipation from foreign economic, political, and military hegemony.[1] Limby stories flesh out the historiographical commonplace that the '56 moment—the nationalization and the Egyptian political victory—was the keystone of Nasser's popularity. Communitarian accounts of 1956 thus help understand both public myths about and experiences of the 1950s–60s.

Burning Eden

One might ascribe the preeminence of 1956 memories in festival accounts to the crystallization during the Suez War of long-muffled anticolonial and nationalist sentiments. Such sentiments found an outlet in the effigy burning. Al-Limby was truly born when the historical Allenby died, when British troops landed on Egyptian soil for the last time. Earlier festivals had demonstrated the strength of communitarian unity against the colonial order. After '56, the festival channeled local celebrations of the victory of a long struggle. The Limby might have appeared during the 18 June 1956 national "Evacuation Day" celebrations. Since World War II more than eighty thousand troops had been stationed in British bases that occupied two-thirds of the Canal. Following the October 1954 Agreement, the "British quietly [gave up the] Suez base to Egypt." In 1954 Brig. John H. S. Lacey gained the title of "last British soldier" to leave the Canal. In 1956 he lost this honor.[2]

The 1956 Suez War was the perfect occasion for appropriating the Limby. The state created a body of representations about the war, for which tropes persist today, erecting memory stones and monumental paper palaces to the city's heroism. It exploited Port Said's symbolic resources, anointing it as the "Martyr City" and the Egyptian Stalingrad through speeches, press, cinema, and exhibits. Public authorities renamed streets after the heroes of the resistance. This enthronement was somewhat denied to another center of enduring patriotic resistance, which actually hosted the administrative center of the Compagnie: Ismailia. Was it because Ismailia also sheltered the Muslim Brotherhood, a competing nationalist movement that the Free Officers sought to eliminate? Certainly, the resistance was nationalist and Nasserian or it was not.

In 1956 the national appropriated the local and apposed its official seal on the resistance of the Canal. At the same time, national politics furnished conditions propitious to the local independent revitalization of the Limby celebrations. Oral evidence suggests that the urban practice of effigy burning before the 1950s was contingent on confrontation with the colonial order. This implies that the effigy burning only became ritualized after the 1956 War, in the sense of becoming an annual event, set in time and place, defined by a series of steady elements, and serving a specific function. The occasion was the invasion of national territory by Israeli, British, and French troops. As one witness recalls: "You know, it started in '56 . . . as something strong that is . . . a big festival."³ Kamal 'Id's memory of an effigy burning has more violent overtones.

> *That started in '56. . . . Even when we were . . . occupied. . . . The English and the French entered in Port Said and stayed about two months. . . . Two months, you know, minus ten days. . . . You know, I wished it were two months. . . . You know, not me, you know . . . the youth, the . . . countrymen. . . . I remember a burned motorcycle that the children had brought in the middle of the place. They gathered around it and stood it up and what did they put on it? Eden, that is al-Limby, and they wrote on it "Eden" and insults and things like that. . . . All day long, with the [British] patrols. . . . I remember that I, that I was watching al-Limby from afar . . . when two people came, like that, and they came down in front of me, and there was my brother with me and my sister's husband . . . and the English came down. . . . The English from the . . . chiefs, with the lion on their shoulders. . . . He took a grenade like that; I swear he ran behind us. . . . I [suddenly] found myself running ahead of my brother. . . . We ran . . . and he was behind us with the [hand grenades] . . . Why? Because we were standing watching al-Limby.*⁴

As this testimony makes evident, effigy making was a politically powerful and seditious act. The foreign invaders fueled national feelings. The youth were actively involved. The effigy spontaneously appeared on the streets during the winter of '56, poking fun at the enemy. The effigy was so powerful that it angered the higher British military ranks. Also, this testimony dissociates the Limby from Shamm al-Nasim. The multifunctional effigy burning expressed merriment. But it alternated rebellion and alliance between revelers and authorities.⁵

"Port Said Is Your Graveyard"

The widespread anachronistic quid pro quo between Allenby and a second lieutenant captured during the Suez War hints further at the simultaneous independence from, and vulnerability of, Port Saidi communitarian recollections to political manipulation. It indicates a new phase in the history of the effigy. Official scripts and public utterances reveal complex, uncertain dynamics. I heard the story of the lieutenant many times in the streets of Port Said during random encounters, as on Shamm al-Nasim 2001 from Muhammad, a street vendor in his thirties, who sold counterfeit Adidas clothing in al-'Arab. Muhammad rehearsed, as did many others, the story of fire hazards such as gas pipes and streets filled with fabric and clothing made of flammable acrylic materials. He explained this was the reason for banning the festival. He certainly regretted the ban, but he understood. Along with others, he agreed that even though nothing had ever caught fire, gas pipes sometimes ran dangerously close to the surface of the street. Celebrations used to take place all over the city, in each street. Nearby, on Nabil al-Mansur Street, there was a man, Khudayr, a calligrapher, who went to a lot of trouble every year to set up a performance, a play, complete with effigies and all. "Nabil Mansur" Street had been named after a young boy, "not taller than that" (Muhammad pointed to a passing girl, eight or ten years old), who had thrown three hand grenades at the British. The soldiers had been taken by surprise; they did not expect a blow from such a young boy, Muhammad explained. Many streets were like "souvenirs," he said. People learned effigy making because it ran in the family, as with the Khudayrs. Now that man, Khudayr, had stopped. The government had forbidden the celebrations downtown, "So, they say, if you want to celebrate, you can do it on the beach." There had been celebrations as long as Muhammad could remember. He said it started in '56. People sang songs like "Oh, Canal! Oh, Our Sea!" In 1956, he continued, people captured and encircled al-Limby. After he disappeared, the British police searched but could not find him. People had burned him, said Muhammad.

Muhammad's account typifies the imaginative recollections of those of his generation who did not live through the events, particularly those whose families came after 1974. It points to the role of toponymy as repository sites for the past, but only when it is sustained by active communitarian lore. The account mentions as well what used to be a front-page story during the Suez War but that history books now barely mention.

The names "Manhouse" and "Mulhouse" came out several times in the course of other conversations about the war. He was a British officer captured in '56, people recalled without elaboration. Hagg Yusif knew better when questioned about "Manhouse": this was another event altogether. Like Allenby, "Moorhouse" was a British officer. He was the "son-in-law" of the Queen of England. During the invasion of Port Said, the resistance (*fida'iyyin*) had captured him not far from British quarters." They hid Moorhouse in a trunk. The underground did not want to kill the officer. Rather, they wanted to use him as a means to bargain with the British government because he was the queen's son-in-law. Yet British searches in the neighborhood prevented the *fida'iyyin* from returning to their prisoner. So he died. This was not the fault of the underground but a consequence of the British house-by-house search. Moorhouse stayed in his trunk for three days. When his corpse started to smell, Hagg Yusif said, people put some dead kittens near the dumpster in which he had been ditched so that the British would not be alerted by the stench.[6]

Even though Hagg Yusif adorned the Moorhouse story with royal panache, fatal debasement, and tragicomic detail, the basic facts are accurate. Alessandro Portelli has written of the virtues of factual inaccuracies, anachronism, and asynchrony. Here, the anachronistic interlacing of Allenby and Moorhouse in part exposes the physical trauma endured by Port Saidis in contrast with their compatriots who lived far from the warfront.[7] Yet there is more to this equation. The general and the lieutenant are symbolically bound. They both embody the whims and arbitrariness of British power. Moorhouse's fatal end stands as an allegory for that of Great Britain's. Moorhouse was the realization of a death wish earlier pronounced against Allenby alias British imperialism. Furthermore, burning Allenby and capturing Moorhouse, as historical acts and mythicohistorical stories, both call attention to the allegorical triumph of the powerless over the powerful. The recurrent analogical motif between the Limby protest burning and Palestinian uprisings, and between Port Saidi and Palestinian resistance, needs to be understood in that light.

Egyptian stories about the '56 War thus recall the arbitrary violence of the British and Egyptian payback ending in moral victory. The French were curiously absent from the recollections I gathered. They do, however, appear in contemporaneous caricatures as inoffensive feminized characters, as appears in a Zaki cartoon, in which Egyptian troops recognize a French plane by the feminine leg and hand sticking out of it.[8] Certainly, British troops outnumbered the French ("6,500 at top strength").[9] In some instances, interviewees were respectful of my national feelings, too. But many considered, without fear of paradox, that France's actions had been justifiable. Whereas the British unduly sought the restoration of their empire and the overthrow of Nasser, the French defended their financial and political interests. They reacted to the loss of their assets caused by the Canal's nationalization and to Nasser's assistance of the Algerian independence movement. The 1956 War was emotionally charged for the French army. However, interviews suggest a lack of empathy for Maghrebi colonial experiences. They indicate that French "Arab politics" in the 1960s mended Egyptian injuries, engendering lasting sympathies toward France, Général Charles de Gaulle, and his political heirs.[10]

In contrast, nothing has alleviated the memory of British misdemeanors. Traces of Moorhouse's infamy linger in the local military museum in Port Said, in which hangs a painting of his kidnapping. Portrayed nearby is the assassination of Major Williams, who "like Moorhouse, was a bad guy," as Hagg Yusif recalls.[11]

> *One day, William [sic] was riding his motorcycle, that William was one of the [bad officers], he always hit people, he was on al-Nahda Street, coming from Ramses, where there were the military checkpoints, they were here in that corner, just in front them, there was a boy, from the popular resistance. . . . William liked to run over people with his bike, in the streets. So that one day, a man called out his name as he was riding by: "William!" William turned, and the man threw a hand grenade at him. In the incident, he lost his eye, and his legs were injured.*[12]

Hagg Yusif was present when the incident happened; he saw it with his own eyes. Then the British arrested a civilian called Muhammad Mahran, the hagg recalled, and they plucked out his eyes to give them to "William." After the war, Nasser established Mahran as a hero, decorating him, even though Mahran was a common man. And Mahran married his nurse, the Hagg concluded. A Maj. James Williams, intelligence officer and long-time British colonial agent, was indeed wounded on 13 December but suffered only "a compound fracture of one leg and lesser injuries to the other."[13]

These testimonies thus mix personal experience, historical facts, urban legends, and state propaganda (Mahran's plucked-out eyes). Historical utterances are synthetic; they embody a process by which events drawn from our direct experiences are integrated within a larger narrative that borrows eclectic aspects of public scripts. The characters recalled by Hagg Yusif might mean very little to most Egyptians and historians today, but they are part of

Port Said's heritage, however fragile. The nineteen-year-old soldier Mahran, who lost his eyes in battle and who recounts the story of his abduction and torture to this day, is a local celebrity and a living Nasserian edifice.[14]

The Queen's Son-in-Law

In addition to reporting the daily violence of the occupation, British official records and newspapers covered the unfolding of the Moorhouse episode with a great wealth of details. At the time, the kidnapping created such agitation among the British military and general public that its absence from European historiography is puzzling.[15] The "Queen's son-in-law," twenty-one-year-old second lieutenant Anthony Gerard Moorhouse, had no relation to the royal family.[16] But such affiliation in local lore endows him with a special status that elevates his kidnapping to an act of heroism and makes him worthy of contempt.

British official records do confirm some of the Egyptian oral accounts. On 11 December, shortly after operating as platoon commander in a raid conducted against "terrorist" headquarters, Moorhouse ventured out alone in his jeep and was kidnapped. One source indicates that he was caught tearing down posters of Nasser. Most describe his kidnapping as retaliation against his arrest of seven Egyptian commando suspects when searching a dentist's apartment. He was captured with his own pistol while questioning a man in the street.[17] British archives recount that he later "was tied to a bed, his captors intending to exchange him for some Egyptian 'resistance' prisoners. When British troops began combing the area [on 15 December] he was locked in a small metal cupboard. His captors returned once to feed him but, as the search intensified, they felt it unsafe to return and he was left for two days." On the night following his kidnapping, "British armored cars [had started rumbling] in and out of the slum quarter . . . reinforced sentries [hovering] around tiny bonfires." But British searches did not start in earnest until four days later. Moorhouse died of suffocation and "was buried in the house where he was held."[18]

The British did not spare their efforts to find Anthony Moorhouse. Leaving the lieutenant behind threatened Eden's prime ministership.[19] Contradictory news of Moorhouse's fortune held the British public in suspense until 31 December. For a while international newspapers had reported, allegedly based upon Egyptian official informants, that the "fanatic Muslim Brotherhood in Port Said" was responsible because the "secret terror organization . . . was attempting to embarrass President Nasser."[20] The confusion reached its peak just before the evacuation when once more, for a short time, new information rekindled British hopes. On 23 December, as the search had become pressing and desperate and with Port Said now back in "Egyptian hands," Major Wicks, a UNEF officer, witnessed seeing Moorhouse "alive and well," after the underground had "taken him blindfolded to a house." He added that Egyptian authorities had "issued an order for his release but as he [was] in other hands it [was] uncertain when this [would] be."[21] Two days later, however, Egyptians disclaimed Wicks' report. Nasser might have long known about the lieutenant's demise. He told Moorhouse's "family [that they] should prepare for the worst."[22] Only after the complete departure of British troops on 31 December did Egyptian military authorities officially declare the death of Moorhouse.[23]

In light of archival records, the legendary tale of the second lieutenant seems tragic and his capture rather pathetic. Yet Port Saidis recall the landing of large enemy forces sent by three enemy nations equipped with planes, tanks, and war ships and far outmatching Egyptian defense capacity. They remember the shelling, wreckage, casualties, and war atrocities. Thus, for Port Saidis and other Egyptians who supported the resistance, the kidnapping, which occurred in the midst of a neighborhood occupied by the enemy, remains a message of empowerment that bespeaks the resolution of the Egyptian people.

The Moorhouse incident further satisfied the Nasserian government's sardonicism and revenge. To British dismay, in 1959 *Al-Ahram* announced the opening of a "Moorhouse museum" in the house where the young lieutenant had died. The museum was to open for the third anniversary of the Franco-British evacuation and contain "drawings showing how he was kidnapped, the box in which he was kept, the rope with which he was tied, and pictures of the heroes who captured him."[24] Some of these artifacts are on exhibit today at the war museum on the outskirts of town. The Suez section of the museum encapsulates heroic scenes and actors of the Battle of Port Said, which in turn betrays 1950s politics of memory. Imitating an American B-movie snapshot or a pulp fiction cover, a large painting dramatically reenacts the Moorhouse kidnapping, showing six sleekly dressed kidnappers pushing the lieutenant into a Chevy. A legend recalls their names for posterity. Another painting by the same artist commemorates young Sayyid 'Aslan's earlier attack on Major Williams. Photographs show state officials' visits to the mutilated Muhammad Mahran. On the opposite gallery wall hangs a portrait of Sami Khudayr, who eluded description in the 1950s because of his fame, but whose heroism people rarely remember today. Another part of the gallery hosts an icon of public political memory: Nasser standing at al-Azhar's *minbar* (pulpit), reconstructed as a handcrafted miniature in a mosque's interior with little figurines. Other stories, such as Nabil Mansur's, as well as other faded relics, fill this derelict exhibition. Judging from the state of these objects, the Suez episode seems condemned to dust. In contrast to the fifty-year-old hall, commemorative pieces dedicated to the October War shine nearby, such as fresh war paintings graciously created in the 1990s by the same Korean artists who contributed to Cairo's military museum and to "Panorama 1973."

The museum accordingly appears as a palimpsest, whereby late 1950s memorabilia linger. Unlike the fighter Khudayr, the "child Nabil Mansur" highlights instances where memory politics built alcoves, at least provisionally and locally, in the immense and fragile palace of memory. Nabil Mansur is the only "fighter" Muhammad the street-vendor cited. He also stands out as the only civilian, among the otherwise anonymous "martyrs of '56," still mentioned fifty years later in fourth-grade history textbooks alongside great national figures. Yet, despite this citation, Mansur is not really known outside local confines. For the nation, the resistance was national and collective. For Port Saidis, it was local and communitarian.[25]

The Moorhouse exhibit is also a window to contemporaneous propaganda as found in the press, in songs, or in films, such as the 1957 *Bur Sa'id* (Port Said).[26] Although a commercial failure, this film illustrates pointedly Nasserian ideological aesthetics. Three other features that also describe the Canal resistance were released a year after the war. While Niazi Mustafa's unmemorable 1956 film *Sijin Abu Za'bal* (Prisoner of Abu Za'bal) and *Bur Sa'id* both anathematized the "tripartite aggression," Kamal al-Shaykh's 1957 *Ard al-salam* (Land of Peace)[27] honored the "struggle of Egyptian *fida'iyyin* on the canal against the Zionist enemy for the liberation of the 'land of peace,' Palestine."[28] Both *Sijin Abu Za'bal* and *Ard al-salam* are now little known. In contrast, *Bur Sa'id* became the television feature commemorating the 1956 nationalization of the Canal. Ironically, it was not deemed "nationalistic enough" in its own time.[29]

Bur Sa'id begins formulaically, like a British spy thriller spiced with sexual intrigue, romance, and battle scenes. It also ends conventionally, in patriotic sacrifice. Both Lieutenant Moorhouse and Major Williams are its villains. Liable for war crimes, they meet their rightful deaths at the hands of brave civilian fighters. Most importantly for ideological purposes, the film portrays the struggle of ordinary people, the working classes of al-'Arab. It uses documentary footage to add real-life feeling to the fantasy. Tulba, a simple, brave man played by actor Farid Shawqi, leads the physical and patriotic resistance. In turn, his fiancée, the blind, virtuous, and pure Wafiyya, embodies spiritual resistance.[30] As Walter Armbrust pointed out, Wafiyya personifies the vulnerable nation, while Tulba defends Wafiyya and the honor of the nation.[31]

But the defense of the nation is collective, rather than individual. Men, children, and women—by order of appearance in *Bur Sa'id*'s scene of weapon distribution—unanimously volunteer to defend the nation. They endure loss, torture, and all sorts of humiliations. Only when hope declines, when guerilla barricades are breached, does the underground regular army arrive on stage. Dressed in civilian clothes, it transcends social distinctions: the resistance was primarily a grassroots movement. The people's enduring and spontaneous resistance, not international law and covert operations, thus brings about the cease-fire and victory.

How influential are films such as *Bur Sa'id* in the context of Egyptian historical utterances? How many of these characters ('Aslan, Hamdan, Moorhouse, and Williams) do people remember today outside the Canal? How many have slipped into oblivion? This is difficult to evaluate. I argue that *Bur Sa'id* portrays both the debility and the power of propaganda machines in creating enduring historical myths. The film's characters have had a different imprint on the Canal's lore than on national mythology because, in order to take hold, official utterances need not only reiteration but also a cohesive social framework that sustains their relevance. Port Saidis have a stake in their community's history. Some directly witnessed the events. Others knew their participants. Mythologized figures, such as Moorhouse and Williams, then provide anecdotal material that fleshes out and colors local stories. These figures help establish the dramatic Manichean structure of Canal lore as well as plant key story-telling characters. Take, for example, Hagg Yusif's narrative, from our 15 April 2001 interview:

> When Mina Hawas was kidnapped and hidden, . . . [Williams], the leader of the British Secret Services, . . . had been in Egypt . . . for twenty years. . . . [Williams] went out with the English and came back with the invasion. . . . And he knew Arabic and he knew Egypt and the whole map of the Canal. . . . So when he came and Mina Hawas was kidnapped, Port Said waited and if Mina Hawas did not appear, Port Said would destroy. . . . So, of course, this Sayyid 'Aslan [the fida'iyyin] gave him a grenade and he looked for [Williams] until he found him and he entered in the office

of grievances. He went also in front of [everyone] and the people there at the police. . . . So, he, Sayyid 'Aslan, . . . he stuck the grenade against his leg and carried it on him and he asked for a paper, like that . . . under the pretext that he was going to present a complaint, to whom? . . . To the one they thought was the leader of the secret services, [he conned Williams into getting into the car and] that Sayyid 'Aslan, he was also my friend at work . . . at the Suez Canal. . . . This is the true story . . . that he told me himself.

In his story, Yusif subjectifies Port Said but then shifts to the collective form, thus reinforcing the sense of a communal action as well as pointing to local membership and solidarity.

While these stories nourish Canal lore and a discrete sense of communitarian belonging, public media do not much debate the 1956 events and their historical significance. National history curricula are evasive too. Indeed, these events evoke Nasserian glory and as such are discomforting to Nasser's successors. Furthermore, the "1956 moment" is too precious ideologically to be publicly contested. Indeed, the nationalization and the war are together a metaphor for liberation. Because of these historical elisions, to the larger nation, the Battle of Port Said may evoke no more than the fictitious heroes and scoundrels of a black-and-white movie. Anecdotes are but ornamental when detached from a larger social framework and from creative acts of commemoration. I argue that *Bur Sa'id* contributed significantly to Moorhouse's impersonation of Allenby, to the confusion between the events they connect to, and to the frequent mention of "William" and "Moorhouse/Manhouse," even among people without a clear idea of the conflict.

In contrast, local lore in Port Said kept Moorhouse alive. Personal accounts circulated within the community, even in exile. In addition, commemorative performances reinforced the recollection of the events, including among Port Saidis of recent stock. Allenby-Moorhouse-Eden burned during the festival of Shamm al-Nasim in the 1950s. People also created rhymed prose and songs. Surviving beyond the long Canal War (1967–73), lyrics such as "Moorhouse"—which accurately describes the incident, including its memorialization—passed from one generation to another. The famous Port Saidi *simsimiyya* musicians, the Tanbura, an attractive local alternative to commercial music, have included such pieces in their repertoire:

Moorhouse
Moorhouse, but why did you come from London and here behave brutally, and act as an oppressor,

Well, leaving nothing intact?
And here you found your death when you entered that house
Moorhouse but why did you come ...
Empowered by the Atlantic Alliance?
You thought you were still in Gandhi's time
[But] Egyptians are Arabs and free
Who told you to come down to my country?
Moorhouse, but why did you come, etc.
You thought we were your supporters
But the problem is we are free men who fight night and day
We are not afraid of colonialism
Moorhouse, but why did you come?
On our land, the resistance saw you, they pledged not to let go of you,
   and in a black taxi they kidnapped you
The news reached your mother and father
Moorhouse, but why did you come?
In the neighborhood over there, they kidnapped you, and in a trunk
   they locked you
You have a museum and people come see you
And if only, oh soldier, they did not bring you, etc.
Moorhouse, but why did you come?[32]

In the winter of '56, some people experienced their "first exile" (*hijra*). Most people returned home within a couple of months of their evacuation. Songs old and new circulated once more among the exiles after the long *hijra* following the Six-Day War. People "found solace" by visiting one another. During the successive *hijras*, resistance became a powerful motif of local identity, which was reinforced by repeated conflict, evacuation, and destruction. The Tanbura musicians, devoted to keeping alive the Suez War songs, have sustained the eulogy of Port Said the Resistant. Thus, they help maintain utterances of anticolonial struggle where the past stands as a protest against the present social and political order of things.

Black, Gray, and Other Creative Dialectics

While British historiography provides paradoxical accounts of the war, especially with respect to military damage and human losses, British archives give a sense of the physical intensity of the military attack, the chaotic atmosphere that prevailed, and the force of propaganda on both sides of the conflict. Most importantly, they point to the violence into which civilians were drawn. The British public had been moved by civilian casualties, as captured for *Life* magazine by Larry Burrows. Burrows photographed two women in black searching for relatives, barefoot, and covering their faces with the edges of their veils to try to keep out the stench emanating from the corpses lying strewn on the ground around them. Photographer David "Chim" Seymour (killed by an Egyptian bullet while covering the war) captured the city's desolation after its bombing, British tanks sullenly penetrating narrow streets.[33] Naval bombardment pounded the city. A U.S. journalist reported seeing a "yellow Coca-Cola truck [roaming] the rubble-filled streets picking up bodies of Egyptians," walls torn away, potholes, "water [running] from burst mains."[34] A few thousand people lost their homes.

Photographs and news reports became weapons in the diplomatic battle that accompanied the invasion. As official records noted with some reserve, there "certainly [were some] very unpleasant stories and pictures being circulated."[35] French, British, and Egyptian war propaganda have been researched.[36] The scholarship indicates that both the Egyptians and the Alliance engaged passionately in a contest over international sympathy and support. Both sides extensively used black, gray, and white propaganda—that is, different degrees of public deception—in pursuit of their goals. Among such propaganda, civilian casualties were the most provocative and controversial.

Official documents reveal military templates in that domain too. Conventionally, armies of occupation do not publicize civilian casualties unless they wish to strategically instigate fear and confusion. Military strategists understate human harm. They blur boundaries between civilians and fighters, and they restrict public broadcasting to reporting military losses. The most prominent British estimate on Port Said casualties, prepared for the British parliament by Sir Edwin Herbert, president of the Law Society, suggested a "confidential estimate of Egyptian casualties military and civilian combined [according to which] 650–700 [people were] killed, 850–900 seriously wounded (hospital cases), 1,200 lightly wounded (walking cases)."[37] His (confidential) estimate regarding civilian casualties reached an average of 25 percent.[38] Both Mr. Middleton's anodyne telegram statement and Herbert's report suggest that the latter adopted the relatively reliable figures for military casualties and then simply deducted civilian numbers based on an arbitrary percentage (25 percent). British official records leave no doubt as to the undervaluation of civilian casualties. A British counterpropaganda document thus warns:

I think we may get some collective denial of the worst Egyptian atrocities stories.... Please send by emergency telegram details of the worst stories affecting the conduct of British troops and the honour of the Allies forces.... [Stories] should refer to massacres and atrocities and not (repeat not) civilian casualties incurred during the operations. Press may well state that they do not believe our figures of casualties, but we must get these two issues separated.[39]

Accordingly, British authorities insisted that they had attempted to "limit damage and loss of the lives and property of Egyptians and other nationals" and the "dangers to which they exposed themselves to this end." Damages were superficial. The attacks had been precise. Egyptian forces aggravated civilian casualties, the British claimed, by using civilian homes and public places for "storing ammunitions and weapons" and by inciting civilian rebellion and "dissent."[40] Herbert likewise pointed out that military and civilian boundaries were fuzzy. His report thus concluded "that three quarters of the casualties were incurred by military or armed civilians."[41] British authorities broadly discredited "assurances . . . that it was against the Egyptian government policy to encourage armed opposition to the Allies." General Stockwell indicated that "recent events in Port Said [directly contradicted] those statements, and [proved] conclusively that a coordinated and sustained campaign of violence [was] being directed against the forces under [his] command, and that this campaign [was] increasing in intensity." Herbert concurred with stories of civilian insurrection. But he also noted that Nasser's recruiting campaign appeared inefficient.[42] Although the incident casting Limby-alias-Eden on a motorcycle does not figure in British records, those records report the countless ambushes, machine-gun fire, snipers, rocket launchers, and grenade attacks that awaited the invaders on a daily basis in December 1956. "Eleven separate grenade throwing incidents in 24 hours" were reported on 14 and 15 December.

Both sides, however, understood that the most crucial combat was to be led on the public relations battlefront with creative dialectics.[43] Throughout the occupation, small local clandestine and national publications were distributed to the population. The Egyptian press praised the courageous underground while the occupiers criticized clandestine publications for inciting violence.[44] On 9 December the British uncovered a local "subversive printing press" that had been "actively engaged in [the] printing of subversive posters, bills, and newspapers" that added to the numerous "subversive and offensive slogans marked up on the walls," as seen in *The Battle*. British patrols and Egyptian rebels relentlessly tore down one another's posters, some at the expense of their lives. Pamphlets were sneaked in from outside the occupied city. Indicating a perverse sense of political legitimacy, a British report recounted that the "Red Cross/Red Crescent status [had been] abused by attempting to deliver on train to Port Said a highly subversive and provocative issue of an Egyptian newspaper, overprinted and put into the train by the Egyptian Liaison Officer to UNEF at Kantara."[45]

The political and cultural magazine *Ruz al-Yusuf* published articles throughout the conflict that focused on the ordinariness of exceptional acts of resistance: the common folk were courageous by nature. *Ruz* used simple and edifying stories. It lauded with novelistic prose the spontaneity and unanimity of a popular resistance that transcended age, gender, origin, and class.[46] Scripts were accompanied by Soviet-style illustrations of workers and peasants united in defense of the homeland, as in an illustration by cartoonist Zahdi that shows the united nations of the world backing the Egyptian national struggle and that reads, "We are not alone."[47] Nasserian schoolbooks recycled this theme, which lingered into the Mubarak years.

Expectedly, British records depict the *fida'iyyin* in less than complimentary terms. The British held the Egyptian government "responsible for the restlessness in Port Said."[48] They condemned the "indiscriminate issue of arms by Egyptian authorities to the local civilian population, including women and boys aged 12 and upwards."[49] These arms transformed every civilian into a potential threat and rendered British military operations extremely delicate. On the Egyptian side, Nasser argued that the military superiority of the invader required civilian mobilization.[50] On the eve of allied landing, in the night between 5 and 6 November, Egyptian government vehicles cruised through the streets with loudspeakers announcing the distribution of weapons and ammunitions. Arms supply to civilians offered a convenient counter-propaganda tool. It helped the British explain civilian casualties and harsh military measures: every *galabiya* could hide an armed soldier and "every little boy could become a sniper and many did."[51]

Whereas Egyptian statements manufactured for international consumption during the conflict were ambivalent with respect to underground activities, later publications are unequivocal. The youth were politically mobilized for national and international campaigns. In 1958 the Egyptian academy of Rome exhibited "drawings by school children of Port Said on the Fight for the Defence of the City." In the academy's brochure the minister of education saluted children as "living symbols of love for the Fatherland."[52] A 1964 commemorative governmental pamphlet used as proof of valorous popular mobilization a foreign source that (disapprovingly) cited children's enlistment, the distribution of weapons, clandestine presses, and the military use of civilians. Preventing foreign troops from penetrating further into national territory overran Egyptian concerns about civilian safety.[53]

By the 1960s the 23 December Suez commemoration, or "Victory Day," was well established. It became one of the top national celebrations. Nasser inaugurated the tradition of delivering national addresses on the site that was the symbol of the victory, Port Said. Given its role as an exaltation of Nasserian glories past, this tradition died with Nasser. Still, in 1965 a French official communiqué reported on the occasion of a presidential commemorative speech in Port Said: "It is in this town (shall we recall?) that the Chief of State has pronounced a great part of his most famous orations. Addressing the inhabitants of the 'martyr city,' he usually drifts off into his most popular verve."[54] Reporting in 1966 on a presidential speech given for the tenth anniversary of the evacuation, Roux compared the enthusiastic celebrations of the "Heroic City" with Cairo's dullness. This highlights once more the contrasting historical experiences between the capital and its province and among the varied parts of Egypt:

> Through the press, radio, and with the support of the [Arab Socialist Union], the government tried to give a *high relief* to the celebration of the "Battle of Port-Said." In reality, this anniversary did not seem to much rouse the population, at least in Cairo; the atmosphere was very different in the "Heroic City" to which had converged youth groups, coordinated by the Socialist Union, which had come from diverse parts of the country in a victory rally.[55]

According to a contemporary foreign correspondent, throughout the Nasser years, 'Id al-Nasr (Victory Day) stood second in importance after only the July Revolution. The commemorative Suez War museum had been built under the municipal square. Its "Tomb of the Martyrs of 1956" became a conventional stop for foreign dignitaries. In 1963 Premier Zhou Enlai "placed a wreath at the foot of the 150-foot-high marble monument" and visited the museum. A year later Soviet premier Nikita Khrushchev and Iraqi president 'Abd al-Salam 'Arif followed in his footsteps. Khrushchev purportedly declared: "There are holy places on the globe where man feels the greatness of heroism and sacrifice. . . . The city of Port Said is foremost among these places."⁵⁶ Nasser's successors relocated the museum's memorabilia and militaria to a new place devoted to all Egyptian military exploits. After the 1973 War, 6 October replaced Victory Day and 'Id al-Nasr fell into oblivion.

"When They Hit Them, They Hit Them!"

> With the English and French occupation of Port Said, the resistance had become very active. Every day it broadened, as more and more women and men joined. Under organized leadership the units scattered, concealing themselves in homes and clinics, in shops, in every corner of Port Said.
>
> Latifa al-Zayyat, *The Open Door*

Outside the literary world and less theatrically than Zayyat,⁵⁷ many Port Saidis responded to governmental injunctions and joined in the resistance against the invaders even though this was not the full mobilization officially announced. Some acted out of civic duty and patriotism, exacerbated by what they saw as a forceful display of imperialist power, running against historical time, now that the world was wholly engaged in shaking the "yoke of imperialism." Hagg Yusif recalled Port Said's battles with thrill and pride:

> *The first thing we saw is the British hitting us with planes, and the French, and they said there is an attack, an attack, a big attack, and people were coming from left and right. The government had given us weapons. We take the weapons and run, and we fired on the troops that came to occupy. We sit down and after some hours we became many, many, many [people]. The rest, of course, on the side of the defense of the state that came to occupy [us], directly before the occupation, they took the decision to encircle the town and a popular resistance rose from the people inside Port Said. They never let them breathe, not a day. [The Allies] shoot them without any respite. They were scared all the time and could not stay in place, the English. The French are in Port Fouad, the English in Port Said. They were afraid and they couldn't stay. They taught them a lesson, you know, they gave them a hit on the head. When they hit them, they hit them!⁵⁸*

In turn, with his characteristic sobriety, Kamal 'Id explained that accepting the arms distributed to civilians was a matter of self-defense. Using weapons was a necessity. He was not a fighter and received limited training. But this was his duty as the eldest son. Neither he nor his brother ended up using their hand grenades; they both returned their weapons to Egyptian authorities:

K. I.   [Britain] left in June 18 or 6.... They occupied us for seventy years... and after three months they came back...
M. B.   Do you remember the tripartite attack?
K. I.   But that's [what I am talking about] the tripartite aggression...
M. B.   How old were you?
K. I.   I was around twenty years old.... It's taken hold of men.... We were sleeping, from five... at five at night we were sleeping.... There was no light, like that. Like it was planned in Israel, like that. You know, from five o'clock until seven in the morning.... If you walked at night after five, you were shot down. Me, of course, I lived all these things until they left.... And I had a grenade.... I was not a resistant.... And I never held a weapon in my life.... But there were cars, and he said to the people, "Everyone take a grenade and you'll get trained...." So, I took a grenade and the soldiers and the fida'iyyin of Port Said taught me how to load it and how to throw it, and things like that.... And I kept it... to protect my family.... Because I am not a hero, I am not a combatant resistant.... But I wished I did to protect my family, that's all. If they had attacked me... and my house, since I was the oldest in the family, I had to defend it....[59]

Like 'Id, many remember when Edmund Allenby metamorphosed into Anthony Eden and Guy Mollet in that winter of 1956. They recall the "malicious joy" of defying the enemy with effigies and the "rage," too, of seeing the colonizer come back "after three months," the pride of expelling him. Battle accounts convey a strong sense of civic duty. Port Saidis remember the solidarity among civilians, but also the association with government authorities. The occupier severely punished sedition such as burning Limbies and holding, distributing, and hiding weapons. As 'Id recalls

> We lived in al-'Arab... in the neighborhood of al-'Arab.... And of course the English entered and they said, those who have weapons have to surrender them.... Those hiding weapons in their homes will be shot.... My paternal uncle took my grenade and unscrewed the top.... The top was made of wood.... It was all made of wood; it was good, that is. He unscrewed the top from underneath and pressed the grenade and nailed it back together... until the English left Port Said.... I gave it back.... Someone from the revolutionary leadership came, his name was ['Abd al-] Latif al-Baghdadi, he was a colleague of 'Abd al-Nasser.... He came for the hand-over from the people. Every day there was a hand-over of weapons.... I went to return my grenade and my brother as well [came] along with me.[60]

Participation in unlawful activities solidified mobilization, whether or not people engaged in combat. Prominent public personalities signed up to boost public morale. For instance, the attendance of a prominent Free Officers Committee and Revolutionary Command Council member like Wing Commander 'Abd al-Latif al-Baghdadi during the restitution of weapons, mentioned in the previous anecdote, did not go unnoticed. General Fawzi visited the ailing Muhammad Mahran. Encounters with famous officials reinforced the value of civilian association with the politico-military authorities. Nonmilitary celebrities volunteered their patriotic diatribes on radiophone news and in songs. Singers Umm Kulthum and 'Abd al-Halim Hafiz, composer Riyad al-Sunbati, and poets Bayram al-Tunsi and Salah Jahin eulogized the army, its leader, and national sacrifice.[61] In 1956 Umm Kulthum sang "It's Really Been a Long Time, Oh, My Weapon" and "The Liberator, the Unifier, and the Guide of Arab Nations":

> You liberated the Nile from intruders
> Now wrecked and clueless
> Today in Egypt you ignited the lighthouse
> Which radiance the others revived
> Unifying the Arab Nation.

Umm Kulthum sang about taking up arms, courage, and sacrifice during the attack of a city assailed but never conquered, as in "The Voice of Peace":

> Three nations in arms, but none ever held foot in Port Said
> The voice of peace, victorious, prevailed,
> And our blood, spilled on the ground, shall
> Never be wiped off from our land.[62]

The fanfare of propaganda does not invalidate altogether the solidarity between civilians and politico-military authorities: there was a sense of righteous fight against invaders' illegitimate use of violence.[63] Simultaneously, civil-military unison does not dominate personal recollections and should not be overstated either. One must distinguish this mobilization from official statements, such as those of *Sawt al-'Arab*, that appropriated civilian insurgency.[64] One must thus differentiate between spontaneous popular resistance and regular army and be wary of presuming that state propaganda persuaded civilians to fight, although the war stirred up patriotism. Certainly, though, the media built up a general tension and "suffocation" in the words of Najib Mahfuz.[65] They reiterated the indispensability of the military. They underscored the historical necessity of civilian action in cases of national defense. In a special feature, "Know Your Weapons," *Ruz al-Yusuf* recast Egyptian popular resistance within a broad historical continuum. One article, "How Can You Become a Resistance Fighter?" mixed medieval and contemporary analogies. It denounced the oppressor, once victimized, now tyrannizing. The article compared the first anti-imperialist Egyptian patriot—who allegedly fought in Salah al-Din's army against the Crusaders—to British World War II resistance fighters against the Germans, American Revolutionaries against Great Britain, and Koreans against the Americans.[66]

In revolutionary mode, the press also commended the universality of the resistance: citizens found roles suited to their age and sex. In the intrinsically male culture of nationalist revolutions, roles are gendered. As Armbrust observed, while nationalists discursively include females, they "construct men as socially dominant."[67]

Correspondingly, men treated female participants protectively and paternalistically in 1956. Such gendering is also a cliché of the war film in the 1950s–60s, in Hollywood as in Cairo. Patriarchal politics thus tainted Egyptian war movies, such as Yusif Shahin's 1958 *Jamila Bu Hirad* (Djamila the Algerian) and 'Izz al-Din Dhulfiqar's 1957 *Bur Sa'id* (Port Said). They also marred war literature, whether written by women such as Latifa al-Zayyat or by men such as Yusif Idris. In Egypt, Morocco, or Algeria, men cast women in supportive roles. Women conducted light operations and sabotage missions.[68] They carried ammunition, hid or encouraged male combatants, and mended men's wounds. Civilian underground resistance and "secret defense" organizations (that is, al-muqawma al-sirriyya, or the secret resistance movement), monitored by army regulars, formed the military front of fida'iyyin, among whom older and younger men were engaged in dangerous missions, suggests *Ruz al-Yusuf*, while women's love uplifted their hearts.[69] Historically, female participation to resistance movements has been instrumental, but few of these women—such as Zaynab al-Qafrawi and Fathiyya al-Ikhlas—have been officially honored. Ideologically, though, women's involvement in 1956 legitimized nationalists' claims that they represented the whole nation.

Interestingly, post-Nasserian reimaginations of the war attribute greater agency to women on the battlefield than in 1956 representations. Over the past twenty years, commemorative illustrations in Port Said have reconstructed women as armed combatants mimicking Palestinian female fighters. Such reinvestment of a profitable past—like the painting of a Port Said school and the newer paintings of the museum of war—reflects female political empowerment (see figure 4.1). The present anachronism of 1956 muhaja-bat mujahidat—female resistant fighters in full Islamic garb—but also their masculinity, contrasts with the romanticized, stereotypical, and overtly feminized women of 1964 paintings.[70] Present reconstructions in effect desexual-

Figure 4.1. Munaqiba combatant as portrayed in this detail from a Port Said school painting, 2007. Photograph by the author.

ize women and reappropriate their bodies as symbols of a national struggle reinvented as egalitarian and religious.

In contrast, the Suez War had provided in the 1950s a discursive space for a radical, revolutionary, and secular utopia of patriotic love delimited by conservative gender boundaries. Such utopia allowed existential (no fear of death) and class transcendence ("a worker can lead a phalange of engineers or doctors and men of science!").[71] Revolutionary ideologues identified the army with the national body and the nation with the fellah as appears in a multitude of illustrations. The romanticization of popular resistance, what Mahfuz called "the tales from Port Said,"[72] came with literary-like anecdotes, such as the fictive fiancée smuggling bullets hidden in flower bouquets.[73] However, the influence of propaganda on popular perceptions of resistance, social behavior, and political attitudes remains difficult to quantify.

While not a historical reality, the unified resistance between Canal citizens and the national army became a literary fact. Many writers paid tribute to the Battle of the Canal and the Suez War and joined institutional scripts. They described the 1951 and 1956 battles as unified episodes of a saga embodying the universal drive for national and individual liberation.[74] This motif structures the 1960 novel *Al-Bab al-maftuh* (The Open Door). This work by Latifa al-Zayyat was published as the "earlier optimism [of the preceding decade] was wearing off, after a period in which 'Abd al-Nasser's regime had imprisoned many of its opponents and had strictly curtailed freedom of expression and the right to organize."[75] The core of Zayyat's work, her powerful statement regarding female emancipation, has not faded. Yet what interests us here is its utopian nationalism. Its "revolutionary optimism"[76] illustrates the synchrony between much of the contemporaneous literature, on the one hand, and the public transcripts that appeared in the mass media during the war, on the other hand. That said, while often characteristic, this optimism was not unanimously emulated either. However, Zayyat's literary style found a welcoming terrain in the 1950s–60s. The novel and its cinematic rendition typify nationalistic symbolism. The blast of de Lesseps' statue thus seals the novel as a firework would visually end a movie: "It was a symbol of the ages of slavery and colonialism that they had inherited, a symbol that pulled them back into the loathsome past, that put a barrier between them and a finer future. That symbol must be shattered."[77] Another firework awaits, as the heroine (Layla) breaks away from an unwanted engagement. She reaches out to her true love (Husayn) and achieves her own liberation. Like Nasser in the story when he nationalized the Canal, Layla expects her decision to bring about foreign retaliations, while her companion in battle sighs, "Finally . . . we're there." Freedom comes at a price at both the personal and the collective level. The couple softly discusses ends and beginnings. They pronounce the connectedness of individual and national destinies and self-realization and construct liberation as a historical stage of evolution.

Zayyat pays tribute to Port Saidi *fida'iyyin* and the ideological canons of the moment through grandiloquent patriotic dialogues as well as gruesome battle scenes. In contrast to public media, she emphasizes female participation in armed combat, where courage is—and can only be—ferocious and merciless. Zayyat's female fighters recall French public depictions of 1870 Communardes: they are plebeian, wild, and brutal. In contrast with the French Revolutionaries, though, female violence in *Al-Bab al-maftuh* is not a deprecating indication of gender denaturation. Rather, it points to women's natural, instinctive, defensive reaction when the nation, as family, is in danger.[78] Zayyat thus obeys, overall, nationalist gender conventions. Accordingly, Layla and Husayn conform to those roles according to which the "male representative of the nation . . . is more active and articulate than his female counterpart [in consonance] with most local practice, which assigned more active public roles to men than to women."[79]

This holds true for the main characters of another contemporary work, *Qissat hubb* (Love Story) (1956), in which, as in *Al-Bab al-maftuh*, the male protagonist arouses the woman's national consciousness and leads her to action.[80] This first novel by Yusif Idris chooses the 1951–52 Canal Resistance as a backdrop to recount national liberation with an idealistic and populist verve similar to Zayyat's. Idris equally develops the Aflaqian Baathist notion that self-achievement results from the abnegation of one's personal interests through dedication to the nationalist cause. Correspondingly, national liberation parallels self-emancipation. As in *Al-Bab al-maftuh*, a man and a woman are united in their shared love for the nation. They overcome the ethical dilemmas inherent to their social class (the same as the Free Officers') when they have to choose between national (i.e., moral) duty and personal (i.e., selfish petit bourgeois or middle-class) comfort. This book inspired Salah Abu Sayf's 1963 film, *La waqt li-l-hubb* (No Time for Love). The same year appeared *Al-Nasir Salah al-Din* (Salah al-Din the Victorious), one of two nationalist movies by Yusif Shahin. Both *Salah al-Din* and *La waqt* celebrated the auspicious ghost of 1956. Like *Al-Bab al-maftuh*, these films were produced in the wake of the failure of the United Arab Republic and the 1961 radical reforms and in the midst of an acute domestic and regional crisis.

In such context, Abu Sayf and Shahin, like many others, made ethical concessions. They resorted to patriotic images of resistance and unity, and exalted secularism and interconfessional unity. In *Salah al-Din*—as in *Al-Bab al-maftuh* and *Bur Sa'id*—Muslims and Copts fight side by side while Muslim clerics often pose as the people's spirit or consciousness (in *Jamila* as in *Bur Sa'id*). Traitors are foreigners parading as Egyptians (*Bur Sa'id*). Oftentimes neither Copts nor Muslims, these are interchangeably Jewish, atheist, or amoral men.[81] As commonly argued, Salah al-Din's battle against the invading Crusaders was the obvious mimesis of Nasser's war against the 1956 enemies. Shahin's other pan-Arab film, *Jamila*, about a heroine of the Algerian War of Independence, also capitalized and was built on the 1956 momentum.[82] Movies such as *Jamila* or *Salah al-Din* served a similar purpose as Frank Capra's "Why We Fight" series, produced during World War II in the United States, which extolled the morality of the Allies' combat. Like *Bur Sa'id*, *Jamila* resorts to documentary footage to convey the historicity of the fiction. This film also situates the resistance in an indigenous working-class milieu and likewise uses social clichés. Thus, al-'Arab in Port Said and the casbah in Algiers are interchangeable studio arrangements.[83] As with the propagandistic *Bur Sa'id* and *Ruz al-Yusuf*'s articles, the core of the resistance in *Jamila* resides within the common folk: national interests ultimately unify all social classes.[84] First, the underlying Suez War motif in *Jamila* underscores the shared suffering of the Algerian and Egyptian nations. Both were martyrs of colonial aggression. Second, drawing a parallel between the Battle of Port Said and the Battle of Algiers fuses both conflicts as liberation struggles. Hence, the Suez events provided the Egyptian administration with the war of independence that the '52 revolutionaries had been missing. Accordingly, they mobilized mythmakers, such as the film industry, into merging '52 and '56 into one long liberation struggle. A military coup smoothly brought the Free Officers to power. But as revolutionary leader Bin M'Hidi avows in Gillo Pontecorvo's *The Battle of Algiers* (1965), the hardest part of a revolution is after it is won.[85] In 1952 the Free Officers had been short of the plebeian endorsement necessary to validate their self-proclaimed popular movement. The '56 moment gave them such sanction.

In fact, *Jamila* is less about the 1957 Battle of Algiers than it is a eulogy of Nasser and the 1956 Battle of Port Said. This is evidenced by the contrast between Pontecorvo's *Battle of Algiers*, on the one hand, and *Jamila* and *Bur Sa'id*, on the other hand. In *Jamila*, Egypt prompts Algerian liberation. Played by the Egyptian star who sponsored the film, Jamila herself is Egyptianized.

The actress does not even disguise her accent. The film ends with credits to Egypt for supporting the Algerian Front of National Liberation and for alerting the international community to French war crimes.[86]

In contradistinction, shot on site, coproduced by and written after the memoirs of Algerian revolutionary fighter Sa'di Yasif—who plays himself and served as technical advisor—Pontecorvo resorted to oral interviews and used an Algerian cast mainly of amateurs. This Italian-Algerian coproduction humanly and dispassionately analyzes the complexities of guerrilla war, the mechanisms of civil violence, the notion of legitimate violence, and the coercive ways by which revolutionaries enforce national cohesion. Analogies to the Battle of Algiers in Nasserian state propaganda encapsulate an important motif of historical utterances of the 1950s–60s: Nasser's aid to independence movements. This idea remains, some have argued, the real cause for the Suez War in "most Egyptian primary and secondary sources."[87] This motif lingers in both written and oral evidence. It points to the idea that France attacked Egypt because Nasser supported the Algerian resistance. Consider, for example, Kamal 'Id's explanation:

> Here in '56, why was Port Said attacked even more? Because we ... were helping Algeria ... the liberation of Algeria. ... Egypt supported ... Algeria with weapons ... so the attack [on Port Said] was violent. ... It was the position of Egypt with Algeria. ... So, it was like that, you know.[88]

The historical scholarship supports the suggestion that the French viewed "Nasser's downfall [as] the key to Algeria continuing as a French possession."[89] Nasser thus used the 1956 moment as a metaphor for the Egyptian and international struggle for national sovereignty. First and foremost, national liberation was the resistance to all forms of imperialism. Independence required autonomous political and economic structures—hence, nationalization. Indeed, shared aspirations for sovereignty brought together to the same site *fida'iyyin* of diverse political persuasions in 1951–52 and again in 1956.

Historical utterances accompanying the '56 moment form a cluster that includes the revolution, the nonalignment movement, and the universal aspiration for national liberation. This transcendent understanding of '56 elucidates why, in '58, in the wake of the Suez War, Ahmad 'Awad christened his barbershop the "Bandung Salon." 'Awad was, he explained, "blinded by that history." He avoided discussing his former political beliefs, although he spoke with some sarcasm behind his apparent detachment.

> *Bandung was a city in India where 'Abd al-Nasser traveled and made the first conference that [discussed] world peace. . . . So, I was blinded by that history and I wrote on the salon "Salon Bandung." . . . But it became clear that there is no peace there and there is nothing except for colonialist thought, and colonialism has its own ways. . . . It does not necessarily need to be with weapons, that is the military, not at all. Colonialism reestablished itself through sex films, that's the way they call them, and that we call the blue films, all the blue films are films . . . that have sexual content, that's all. . . . And soccer, and the debilitating songs and the drugs and these new cuts for the hair . . . the bang and the kaburia, and the clothes, like the shirts that come here from the West. We got nothing from that Infitah [open door policy], that's it.*[90]

I heard about "Bandung" inadvertently. I had asked about 'Awad's address, showing his picture around. Some men I encountered knew him only by "Uncle Bandung." In the early 1970s 'Awad had replaced "Bandung" on the façade of his barbershop with "Misr" (Egypt). The partial discoloration of the salon frontage bore traces of this erasure, even though the barber-poet kept his nickname. In fact, to some extent, the Suez victory cursed Egyptian political life. As Layla Ahmad wrote, "In Egypt henceforth there would be no bar to Nasser's doing whatever he wanted—anyone even mildly critical of him was purged or somehow silenced or got rid of."[91]

The reception enjoyed by the film *Nasser 56* showed no sign of Ahmad 'Awad's and Layla Ahmad's criticism. Released on the fortieth anniversary of the 1956 events, this blockbuster no doubt evidenced a demographic shift, for the majority of the audience did not live through the 1950s–60s and did not share elders' mixed experiences. The historical distancing of present audiences and the ideological disinterest of Egyptian youth explain the attraction of some to Nasserian things past. They are fed its photos, cinema, music, and stars, and nourish a "prosthetic memory" that can be inspirational. Nasserian memory has become a commodity. As such, it is stripped of its contentious elements, as testified by a 2011 exhibit sponsored by Nasser's daughter that took place in a Cairene private art gallery.[92] The organizers of "Abd El Nasser, the Dream" thus arrogated the January 2011 Revolution as a legacy of Nasserism.

A Nasserian iconography developed independently from and in spite of history and politics. Nasser has become a retro, countercynical, young forever, charming, and charismatic icon. Like John F. Kennedy, Nasser was a brave man struggling against dark forces, prematurely gone, and tragically lost. The appeal of the 1956 moment and the social consensus that might arise from its utterances derive from this generational estrangement from the past as well as from the commodification and subversion of history. On the one hand, this distancing has masked the darkness of the 1950s–60s. Nasser offered the idyllic promise of bright tomorrows but also the somber reality of thirteen years of a state of war (the Suez, Yemen, June, and Attrition wars) as well as dispossession, expulsion, repression, imprisonment, and torture. On the other hand, distancing generates utopia, and the Nasserian utopia provides a balm for troubled times in contradistinction with the promises of the past, such as economic independence, social welfare, and employment.

Memory-politics is also liable for the reinvested presence of this period. Politicians and intellectuals, whom Sadat had silenced, reemerged in the early Mubarak years. Some contributed to the neo-Nasserist revival. The ailing Egyptian economy, free trade regulations' effects on the domestic market, widening social inequality, unemployment even for the overeducated—yet badly educated—youth, corruption, the absence of political vision: all these ailments belie postcolonial promises of social and individual liberation. The July Revolution established the political and economic foundations of this condition. It brought about a new class of pashas, a new set of usurped legitimacies, and new waves of corruption. But Nasser is commonly absolved. He is represented as a Prometheus whose creation ran amok. He was a tyrant yet a well-intentioned, patriotic one.

Evidently positions vis-à-vis Nasser depend on personal experience, class, political and ideological leanings, and notions of justice and of the role of government. A handful mourns constitutional monarchy. Many view Nasser as a strongman who lacked political know-how, who dispossessed the middle class and thus destabilized society, and who founded the present military, authoritarian state. Others grieve socialist pan-Arabism and Egyptian economic independence. They consider economic failures as the root of all political illnesses. Others condemn Nasser for leading the nation astray from its Islamic national identity and for trying to shape it into a secularist socialist nation. They dream of a just society that would be spiritually guided and true to itself. Some simply, like Zaki 'Abd al-Mat'al, bemoan their youth, whenever it was.

> *We thought of Nasser as a leader. . . . Nationalism and pan-Arabism. The Arab as a Nation. You had the Soviet bloc and the United States. The Arab*

world should unite and become one.... You had this song "Allahu akbar" [the opening song in the film Port Said]. And there was a show for the kids on the radio called Baba Sharu. There was this young singer, I remember his name, Amir. The song was "Ya 'askari, ya abu bundu'iyya." ... "You soldier with a gun who protects the Egyptian nation." We had this really beautiful song... "Misr, Misr, Misr" [Egypt]. I was then in kindergarten at the English school. Before entering in class, we sang "Misr, Misr." [sobbing] I am on the verge of crying, because [these are] memories of nationalism, [of] a country with pride. Sorry.... It was simple, but it had meaning. So it was about the motherland of Egypt. The liberation from all its enemies.[93]

While discussing his early childhood, Mat'al expressed genuine nostalgic emotions despite the fact that his father was a cabinet minister under the monarchy who was periodically imprisoned in the 1950s–60s even though he had abandoned politics.

Another testimony by a witness of another generation, Raf'at 'Adli, also accounts, more clearly than official scripts, for the vitality of the 1956 experience today:

Raf. A. *I had a room, in which I had been for a long time, and I would have my studio, an atelier room in which I would work. That's where we would meet.... You know, these days were wonderful days.*
M. B. *When was that?*
Raf. A. *That was at the time of school ... that is in the '50s. We grew up through the '50s and we were mature by '56. This was a very beautiful thing. In the time of the attack on Port Said, we came down ... in our street, there were soldiers. Everywhere in Heliopolis, and around the airport, in that area, there were soldiers. We had a tank standing in the street.*
M. B. *A tank?*
Raf. A. *A tank with soldiers, and we would sit with them, and we'd bring them tea and food. Like friends, you know. We would see the planes shooting at it and the machine guns, and things like that. Of course, we were not very affected in Cairo. There was much more going on in Port Said.*
M. B. *What do you remember exactly of '56?*
Raf. A. *Well, recollections made of beautiful patriotic feelings. Of course, we were too young to join ... the volunteers. We were still in high school. During high school, we did not have a military presence as in college, but there was simply some kind of preparation. But there were patriotic feelings.... The beautiful songs of this period ... and ... the youngsters would sit*

with the soldiers when they were shooting with machine guns at the planes that flew over the military airport. The military airport was next to us. Of course, even the soldiers that were there, we sat with them, and of course, there was no school. Everything closed down. We sat with the soldiers all day long, and stopped studying, and even after the war stopped, and they had gone, of course, we kept corresponding, and things like that, because this created strong friendships. In the whole country.[94]

Institutional utterances helped create the 1956 moment, that "second Nasserian Revolution." This being said, political manipulations and wistfulness do not satisfactorily explain widespread recollections of national unity and fraternity. To a large extent, 1950s nostalgia reveals a yearning for a time of innocence in an age of individualization and globalization, for a precapitalistic, preindividualistic, small communal world. Neighbors knew one another; workers were not alienated from the fruits of their labor; and "there was no such thing as Muslim or Christian." A world where, in the words of Ahmad 'Awad, "everybody loved each other."

You know, there are, in Cairo, places that are fine. . . . Calm, you can't hear a cry; you can't hear a noise. . . . But here in Port Said, its distinctive mark was that every day, at sunrise, the vendors of jasmine walked and arranged it in the form of a chaplet or the form of a palm-leaf stalk. There is a stick and he wraps around it the jasmine buds and sells them. . . . You found the smell of the streets replete with the jasmine seller. . . . The beautiful spices and their beautiful smell. . . . And there is no more jasmine, it's over, and there are no more vendors. . . . Port Said was famous. . . . There were a lot of families whose work was to sell jasmine at sunrise. . . . And the milkman in Port Said walked with his cow, calling. . . . He comes with his cow and you want some milk and he milked her for you . . . and he gave you milk from the cow itself. . . . Port Said was a family and this is something that distinguished it from the other [cities]. . . . We all knew each other and our streets and our houses were one same beehive. . . . It was not partitioned like today. . . . Today they're strangers.[95]

This poetically recounted utopian moment was shaped by, and predates, the Infitah, at which point intercommunal strife became commonplace. Currency inflation affected basic commodities. Demographic inflation ran amok. Pollution darkened the waters of the Nile, and so forth. These are features of industrial capitalism. For instance, the Tanbura musicians do not simply carry the past into the present. They rather endeavor to recall and recreate a defunct pre-Infitah society. They wish to resuscitate its communal atmosphere. They enact the culture of artisans, fishermen, workers, and an egalitarian social order. They gather a faithful audience of fans of all ages who strive for congenial folk music and a social culture otherwise lost in commercial entertainment and consumerist Egypt.[96]

One Same Beehive

The Tanbura sang and Limby rejoiced when British presence came to an end in 1956. The festival shifted away from death wish to merry celebration of the funerals of all Limbies, past, present, and to come. After the 1950s, the Limby should not have been a threat to political institutions, but the ritual was sporadically banned under Nasser. Rulers dread unruliness, and the Limby could take so many forms: Moorhouse, Eden, the referee of a Zamalik–Ahali soccer game, Israeli and Egyptian politicians. Port Saidis' creative spirit goes beyond the festival. Local singers and poets may be the Canal cities' brightest jewels. Their compositions are Port Said's communal heritage, as anthropologist Mas'ud Shuman explains:

> *The region of the Canal was in confrontation with the enemy, generally speaking. So this is a region with strong roots in its heritage. . . . It has the* dimma *song, the* simsimiyya, *resistance songs. . . . And of course, troupes grew out of this region. . . . Acts of resistance were expressed through song. There was the troupe of Captain Ghazali, who was in Suez. . . . And he produced several collections of songs that the troupe of "Sons of the Land" used to sing. . . . And the title "Sons of the Land" is not accidental. . . . The "Sons of the Land" never stopped being devoted to the Land and its defense. . . . The troupe of "The Resistance fighters" in Ismailia . . . meaning steadfastness against the enemy . . . the steadfastness of the resistance. . . . The troupe of the "Youth of Victory" . . . who called for victory against the enemy, or victory against negative things, and victory against all these things. . . . Then the "Youth of the Renaissance" . . . because they were outside . . . in Ra's al-Barr. . . . And they had their poems, and they had their songs written by poets, and then these personal songs transformed into popular songs.*[97]

The war thus fueled Canal patriotism and inspired nationalist organizations as well as songwriters and poets who created a distinct "Canal" cultural identity. Limby celebrations were also reinvigorated when city authorities proclaimed the city an emblem of national sacrifice after '56. Port Saidis accepted the honors and cultivated this image locally. State institutions, intellectuals, and artists in turn sustained it in national public utterances, songs, literature, cinema, and the press.

Oral evidence suggests that the historical Allenby was lost in the blasts of the Suez War. Thus was Limby born, wrapped in Moorhouse's shroud. Limby was not alone to undergo alterations after the war. As in other Egyptian cities after 1956, Port Said's political, social, and economic mapping was transformed as "foreigners" left.

Another great change was yet to come after the June War, from which Port Said and the Limby reemerged radically altered. Anticolonial resistance became obsolete, and the festival, like Egypt itself, entered its post-Nasserian stage. For all that, anti-imperialist motifs have not disappeared. Individual utterances of the 1950s–60s carry into our present the notion that new forms of imperialism have replaced old ones and that liberation is yet to come.

5

The End of History

And the sage recited:
Your boon companions lied to you;
These years are full of war and tribulation.
. . . .
You have wisdom and vision and justice,
But you let corruption gnaw at the land.
See how your orders are held in contempt!
Will you order till there comes one who will tell you the truth?

Najib Mahfuz, *Adrift on the Nile*

Depictions of the Limby festival leap from the mid-50s to the mid-70s, when "it became big." There is simply not much to tell (*hiyya*), some Port Saidis said, of a festival that remained unaltered in the decade following the nationalization of the Canal. There is even less to recount, as 'Abd al-Rahim Gharib al-Banna suggests, of a festival with neither revelers nor a place to celebrate in the five to seven years after the June War.

> See . . . what happened is that we did not come back to Ismailia. . . . We emigrated, we were forced to emigrate, transfer to Upper Egypt. . . . We did not come back until the year '73 . . . that is, we came back in the year '74–'75 when we got the Sinai back and there were no Jews [anymore] and people, you know . . . went back to their homes.[1]

Although its army did not pull back from the Sinai in 1975, Israel withdrew half of its frontline troops from the vicinity of the Canal. Narratives about 1960s Limby celebrations are elliptical. They omit or brush off the reason for their discontinuation: the 1967 War and the evacuation of the Canal Zone in its aftermath. Limby undoubtedly made some occasional appearances—in the guise of Moshe Dayan, as Kamal 'Id recalls.

Came '67. We disagreed with Israel, for example. We brought Moshe Dayan who was their leader.[2]

But he essentially vanished from 1967–69 until about 1974, when he returned in new clothes.

Transition was more arduous after the 1973 War than it had been after the brief Suez War. Material damages had then been limited. Also, the passage from a European-controlled to an Egyptian-ruled economy and Canal had been smooth after 1956. Government and private companies replaced foreign businesses. The disappearance of the British did not traumatize the local economy either, as Ahmad 'Awad relates:

A. A.   *Colonialism had here in Port Said something called the "camp" for the drivers of the cars.... There was another camp called the "Sauveteur," and so forth.... You know, there were camps everywhere, ... all the power was in the hands of the British.... But when came the revolution, the power became Egyptian ...*
M. B.   *Well, the British troops ... the soldiers, when they walked, the military men, did they walk like that in the streets?*
A. A.   *They walked.... Here in Port Said, the English went to the cinema, that is, the soldiers. And they bought things from people, you know, normal.*
M. B.   *Were there a lot of them?*
A. A.   *A lot.... When ... a new theater play came to town ... [as is] normal. And we interacted and worked with them ...*
M. B.   *And then, when they left, Port Said changed ...*
A. A.   *Port Said, after that, the Minister of Labor came and said, "The group of people who works with the English! Come and we will give you work. We will give work to the workers of the English." Someone who had worked for the English was paid 10 sagh a day to leave.... So they took [the money], and they served the country: some worked in the health sector, some worked as servants, some worked as guardians of a business, and some worked as bridge keepers, you know. They took them, and they gave work to whoever had skills. You know, that's the way that the transition problem was resolved ...*
M. B.   *Well, did the city become calmer after the troops left?*
A. A.   *No. It's not a matter of better or worse.... People want to eat. Like today. Today, the Free Zone has been revoked, or it is on its way of, what,*

> *disappearing. They say that they will make new projects. . . . Something takes the place of something else or some things change into other things. You know, things turn into other things, you know. What we have now in Port Said is natural gas. But nobody in Port Said wants to buy, who knows why.*[3]

Indeed, in a long-term historical perspective such as for the elders who remember sailboats and steamboats, workers carrying coal to the docks, and armadas of *bambuti*—the famous rowboat peddlers—things "simply turn into other things." In the short term, the transition from a decade of stability to post-1967 difficulties was rough and the history of Port Said and Limby turbulent. The War of Attrition and the October War were turning points.

Archival records and some oral recollections partially fill in the gaps in the Limby story. They uncover one of the final pieces of the Nasserian experience: the short time between 1967 and 1970. The sudden death of Nasser on 28 September 1970 concluded a series of commotions in which the '67 *naksa* (the "setback," a Nasserian euphemism for "defeat"), the War of Attrition, and "Black September" '70 had followed one another. Teleologically, Nasser had it coming. He had sustained a military state on the rhetorical grounds that the revolution was ongoing and perpetual. War against colonialism, imperialism, and reactionary forces in general was ineluctable because these forces constantly adopted new forms. Yet no state, no nation, can sustain for long such acute ideological and military conflict. So Nasser's successor shrewdly played the card of "peace and prosperity." This assured Sadat both a popular domestic base and U.S. support. Ultimately, it was not the peace, per se, but the terms of the peace with Israel that alienated Sadat's former supporters. Egyptians were saturated with the Nasserian state of war. Its end was a relief. Canal residents therefore embraced the festival's exuberance in the '70s. After '74, Port Said, once a symbol of armed resistance, now embodied the motto of the 1970s: peace, prosperity, and capitalism. Port Said celebrated the official transfer of power to civilian hands on 5 June 1975.[4]

"There Is War All Around Us"

The 1967 fiasco and the War of Attrition damaged the capital of sympathy Nasser had gained in 1956. Consequently, the ideological war of resistance to which Limby and Port Said had been drafted were demoted. It had become ludicrous, such as when the governor of Port Said, in '67, during the mounting crisis between Egypt and Israel, turned a display of civilian order and resistance into a satirical "Borgesian tale," in the words of its narrator. Hoping to win political credit in Cairo, the governor had summoned male civilians to perform paramilitary drills on the public place. Men were forced into an improvised exercise of fire rescue, which aborted dramatically. The drills ended in anarchy, disaster, and death. They turned into a mockery of political ambition and arrogance.[5]

Oral testimonies reveal the ambivalence of utterances regarding the period after the defeat. This ambivalence is bound to war experiences, such as Nabila Husni's. Her house was located "right in front of the harbor" of Port Said. It was one of the areas most damaged during the Suez War. The city was shelled, houses were ransacked, and civilians were taken by surprise.

N. H. *The war had started in '67. June 5th '67. It lasted from '67 to '69. When the Jews entered in the Sinai, they entered during these two years, as far as I can remember. There was war during all that time in Ismailia and Suez. . . . There were fewer raids on Port Said. We stayed [in Port Said] until 1969 and then we came here [to Cairo].*

M. B. *Do you remember that time?*

N. H. *I remember very well, I remember very well. 'Abd al-Nasser had nationalized the Canal. And they threatened us. We heard them say on the radio: "We will attack Egypt, because we reclaim the Canal. . . ." Because he wanted to build the High Dam, and they did not accept to help, something like that . . . I can't recall exactly, you know. When we first heard that they had attacked, we did not believe it; we were in Port Said. I was in Port Said. My mom and my dad were here in Cairo, and my siblings were here in Cairo. The day after, I went to work as usual, and I received a phone call saying, "there is war all around us," because we were living right in front of the harbor. . . . I had a young son, the oldest was about a year, maybe even younger than a year. . . . We came back. . . . We went to the house of my mother-in-law. . . . The children, I said to their nanny: "Take the children and go to the house of grandma." I could not get in [my own house] because the war was hitting really hard. So we stayed a little while. France, England, and Israel came. They landed on the country with parachutes, and they occupied all the places on the sea, and they closed them up with barbed wire. They occupied [these places] so that they could be directly on the harbor, all alone. My house, the house I lived in, was occupied by the same French command. If I remember the man was called Stockwell, their chief, Stockwell.[6]*

> We stayed there a little bit, then came the ultimatum of the Russians, [who] forced them, by order, to stop the war. And they stopped the war, and the days of killing stopped. We came back after they left, in my house, three days after, exactly. We pretended to be journalists.
>
> M. B.   *They fled?*
>
> N. H.   No, they did not flee. They left with all their stuff, and they stole every valuable that was in my house, like they stole from all the houses in which they had been. I remember very well the first time I came back to my house . . .
>
> M. B.   *How long were you gone?*
>
> N. H.   I think . . . I don't remember exactly . . . but I believe it was two months, until there was October '69, the war. We went to Cairo, we stayed two months I guess, and after the Russian intervention we came back. . . . They went back to their boats stationed in front of the house, on the harbor . . . and left. . . . We came back home. They came back in 1967. We were evacuated again.[7]

This vivid and informative narration deserves ample consideration both for its human details and its narrative structure because, as she set out to recount the June War, Husni remembered the tripartite attack, even though she knew the chronology of the '67 events. She was conscious of recounting the 1956 war ("They came back in 1967. We were evacuated again"), but she nonetheless interchanged narratives. Interrupted and asked to date the events, she then became confused and mixed up days and years, the war of 5 June 1967 and 1954—the year she got married and settled in Port Said—while being aware that she was not describing the June War.

> M. B.   *Do you remember when these events happened?*
>
> N. H.   *The first time, it was five days on June 5, '55.* This was at the time of the birthday of my son. The men . . . attacked us again on the 5th of June '54 . . . I can't tell, I can't recall exactly. He was one year old. I can't remember exactly, the war was, the nationalization was in '69, '67, or it was in '54. I recall in '54, we came back to live there, in Port Said, from '55 until '67. There was another war in '67.

Husni apologized, taken aback by her confusion, even though she had accurately dated these events both earlier and later in the interview. This mix-up is not an isolated incident. Another interviewee, Fa'iq Rida, married in 1967 and lived in Cairo throughout the 1950s–60s. Rida showed a similar tendency to blend war narratives when I asked him about the date of his wedding.

F. R.   *I got married the year of the aggression, the tripartite aggression, you know?*
M. B.   *No, I don't know, I don't understand . . .*
F. R.   *In 1967, Egypt was attacked by Israel and France and England. That's called . . .*
M. B.   *That's 1956 . . .*
F. R.   *Yes, that's 1956, 1956, I was wrong. But in 1967 also, but then it was only Israel, Egypt and England. But during this attack I was also here. That's true.*[8]

Yet another time, when I asked about Suez, al-Banna recounted a minor incident that took place during the June War. He was in Suez in 1956 and in Ismailia in 1967.

M. B.   *And '56?*
A. B.   *'56, the Tripartite Aggression . . .*
M. B.   *Were you here in Ismailia?*
A. B.   *Yeah, I was here in Ismailia . . . I was here in Ismailia, yeah . . .*
M. B.   *Tell me.*
A. B.   *I was an employee at the time, in electricity. I had moved. I got a transfer in Ismailia, because that's my home, see. . . . We were going to work and we were standing at the door of the town's council, that's on Rida Street, in the passage. . . . As we were standing, what do we hear? The Israeli attack. . . . Planes and tanks . . .*
M. B.   *Could you tell me what happened in '67 in Ismailia?*
A. B.   *In '67 what happened? But I told you that we were standing in front of the door of the theater [City Council] . . .*
M. B.   *I thought this was during '56, I did not think . . . you were speaking of '56 . . .*
A. B.   *Yeah . . . I am sorry.*[9]

These mnemonic overlaps divulge a similarity in people's experiences of the 1956 and 1967 wars. They signal the mental association between two webs of antithetical experiences, ideas, and emotions. Politically, people perceived both wars as imperialist ventures.[10] At a personal level, both wars brought devastation. Even though, in contrast to '56, foreign forces did not occupy Port Said in '67, Israeli bombing wrecked the city. Husni sourly remembers material losses in '56, the mayhem in her house, the gratuitous violence:

We entered and we were shocked. The whole building. . . . They had taken down . . . for example, all the furniture of the dining rooms, and the tapes, the gramophones, all these things were on one floor, and they had established their kitchen there.... When I entered my apartment, I was dumbfounded.... I found the apartment totally miserable, the chairs, of what used to be the salon, had been slashed [by a] bayonet ... Everything had been stolen, they took everything. The carpets were gone.... They had destroyed the apartment, you see, they had destroyed the flat.[11]

In '67, Husni found her house intact.

N. H.   *When we came back after 1967, nothing had been broken, no nothing. We came back in '69. On the Canal, Suez, and Ismailia, the war was very hard. In Port Said it was not. There was a raid, then they left, attacked, then left. It kept on going [like that]. Because on the harbor, there were deep-water bombs meant for the boats. We'd be sleeping and the house was shaking, like that. At night I was very scared, but [my husband would] say: "Don't be afraid, don't be afraid, that's the deep-water bombs attacking." But of course I was scared. And I had the two boys, in '69 I went down with the boys, but during the first war I only had the first one.*
M. B.   *How did you learn about the war?*
N. H.   *I remember that day, in that year '67, I was at work, and I was told that there was an attack. And we went out, we went out running.*
M. B.   *Were you scared?*
N. H.   *Of course, there was an attack and we went to the garage of the building. We went down the six floors of the building, down to the garage, and when the attack ceased, we went back up. But nobody ever wanted to leave the country. In '69, it's the government that evacuated people. Even the first one was about the nationalization of the Canal, the Tripartite Aggression was about the nationalization of the Canal. As for the second war, I can't recall, I can't recall what Israel wanted, you know.... 'Abd al-Nasser gave the order to attack so that we would take back the Sinai. But we were not prepared, militarily we were not prepared. So they came back walking, I remember very well. My brother was still alive, and he was an officer doctor. He was a doctor, but a military doctor. He came back walking from the Sinai.*[12]

There was a sense of vain suffering in '67, as there had earlier been in '56. This time around, the Egyptian command was responsible for the pain of troops and civilians. The deadly march of conscripts from the confines of the Sinai to the Canal is one of the leading utterances about the war. Contemporaneous news and witness accounts alike recount the long walk that illustrates the absurdity and cruelty of the war. It comes second only to the lies about Egyptian victories diffused by the radio during the week of 5 June. Every Egyptian family had relatives on the front. A number died. Some came back to tell their trial. Others remained on duty. They endured the War of Attrition, and some were even dragged into the October War.

At times, the June War brings people back to the moment at which the defeat most betrayed the ideals of the revolution. Conversely, recalling the '56 victory stimulates recollections of the event that overshadowed it, so these wars are two faces of the same coin.

In the realm of public utterances, in his novel *Buyut wara' al-ashjar* (Houses behind the Trees)—published in 1993 in the early Mubarak years and set against the backdrop of the evacuation of Port Said after the June War—Muhammad al-Bisati personifies this duality as monstrous, morally and physically hideous twin brothers who endlessly bicker about the revolution. One brother carps that "the government gives lying information to the papers and they publish it. Then sons of bitches like you read it and believe it." His twin later observes that "the Canal's a curse; it's the cause of all our misfortunes. It's a whore of a Canal. . . . It's not the Canal. . . . They came to strike at the revolution. Everyone says that. If only you'd listen to me and we hadn't left the house."[13]

The identical twins of the novel are a metaphor for the divided memory of the Egyptian nation over the Nasserian legacy and its most contentious aspect, the June War. They mirror the nation's split opinion regarding the Free Officers' achievements and the respective responsibilities of the president and his government in the conduct of public affairs. One voice portrays the revolution as a reified higher power, stifled by reactionary, warmongering, counterrevolutionary forces. The other voice accuses revolutionaries of deluding credulous people and manipulating national media and institutions. In this bivocal, deaf dialogue, the Canal physically embodies the mental and emotional fragmentation of the national self.

As in his other writings, Bisati rarely provides in *Buyut* any context for his story. He confounds, teases, and keeps his readers on alert. He parsimoniously dispenses historical allusions. Rather than using individual dramas to flesh out history, he uses historical resonances to tell eternal human dramas. *Buyut*'s stage, the village, is a timeless place, whereas the nearby city of Port Said is cast in time. Urban space, unlike rural space, is therefore a site of history. History seeps through the village when war refugees arrive: "Thousands of people, millions, [leaving] their homes and [wandering] about like stray dogs."[14] As differing notions of time divide rural and urban life, historical consciousness itself is divided, and thus memories are spatially distinct.

Overall, the presence/absence of the war in the novel refracts its presence by absence from historical utterances at large. Personal recollections about the '67 war are elusive. Public utterances are elliptical. Over the past thirty years, institutional, official, and media sources have focused on military resistance on the Canal and, after the October War, on victory. In fact, the fate of civilians as well as human casualties between '67 and '75 have been buried even deeper than the *naksa*. In the Canal cities, in contrast with the larger nation, war recollections are unavoidable because the conflict intimately shaped individual and communitarian lives.

Politically, the '56 and '67 wars present other analogies, such as the manner in which they were conducted.[15] In 1967 Nasser adopted the strategy that had led him to victory a decade earlier. As French ambassador Jacques Roux noted in June 1967, Egyptians themselves had very much in mind the Suez War during the May–June crisis. This caused a flare of enthusiasm, Roux noted, among people who believed that they were reliving the fall of 1956:

> While the army was trying to face up and dissimulate its first setbacks by victory announcements, leaders seem to have rapidly gained an understanding of the seriousness of the situation. . . . Obsessed by the memory of Suez, President Nasser and the whole population probably judged that a demonstration of strength was ineluctable or a soviet ultimatum which would turn upside down the issue of the battle as well as the dimensions of the conflict.[16]

The memory of '56 facilitated governmental manipulations of the public. Egyptian authorities repeated domestic propaganda but also strategies previously tried out in '56. They claimed that Egypt was within its rights and expected the same outcome as a decade earlier. Speeches, newspapers, and radio announced an incoming victory for which there was no likelihood. Just as in the past, the government recruited celebrities and set up "spontaneous" policed gatherings, as Zaki 'Abd al-Mat'al remembers:

> [Everyone] was mobilized psychologically toward a war. I remember President Nasser in May ['67] in a famous press conference, in Heliopolis, . . . we thought that we were going to win the war, like this. The Arab Socialist Union [held] gatherings. I remember going as a young man to a gathering near the Arab League, in which there was this famous actress, . . . the

> brother of Nasser, Halim Shawqi 'Abd al-Nasser, and the ASU secretary for Cairo, Mr. 'Abd al-Majid Karim.... They [talked] about mobilizing the people to go to war against Israel. We [shouted] slogans, like ..." [America] take back your money, 'Abd al-Nasser is going to crush you tomorrow" or "'Abd al-Nasser, your next step will be in Tel Aviv." We went to many demonstrations on the road toward the American embassy, but unfortunately, although we [supported] the government, the police gave us hell.... We did not know then that our forces were not available to go to Sinai. We had to call the [military reserve] to fight in the war. I saw pictures after the war in Life magazine, showing some of the reserves who did not even have uniforms. They [wore] galabiyas. The media machine [pumped], and we [followed].[17]

Fabrications regarding the situation in May and June are an outstanding feature of war recollections. Archival records and personal testimonies vividly recall the lies circulated by the media between 5 and 9 June 1967. After six days of victorious slogans, Nasser's revelations on the extent of the defeat came as a violent, physical blow. In the words of Ambassador Roux, news of the ceasefire "took Cairo by stupor."[18] Zaki 'Abd al-Mat'al recalls how early elation gave way to shock and rage.

> On June 5th, 1967, we were sitting, taking our mathematics exam when we heard the sirens. We were told that the war had started. All the driving in Cairo stopped, so that we had to go back to school by foot [the exam was taking place in another place]. No bus was functioning. Everything stopped. The radios declared that the anti-aircraft artillery had shot down five planes, six planes, 20, 100, 200, so we were very euphoric. The start of the call had been at nine o'clock in the morning; we had this math exam and we were so happy to stop it.... We returned back home and at once I joined the civil defense. It was created for students and it was very primitive and naive. We were organized in patrols of three people, one carrying a bucket of sand, one a fire extinguisher, and one being the captain of the team. We could stop fire by any means. We were posted near our houses in the street for eight hours. It was voluntary.... Sawt al-'Arab, the "Voice of the Arabs" [radio] station, was pumping news telling that Israeli planes had been shot down and that our troops were on their way to Israel. This famous speaker, Mr. Ahmad Muhammad Farid, was on the radio shouting, "Where are you, Golda Meier? Where are you, Dayan? Come, we are ready to finish." In the night we had a total blackout. Our civil defense guide had told us that at the

sound of the sirens, we should go from building to building [and] see if there were any source of light to turn off. The second day, more planes [dropped]. On the third day, since my father listened to the BBC on the radio, he heard different news. But we were not so convinced. We started rationalizing things. [We had] a neighbor [whose] father [was] working with the Egyptian secret services. . . . And I told him that the BBC had announced our troops were retreating. He told me that this was a tactical retreat. This was meant to let the Israelis [into] the Sinai, so as to surround them and crush them. . . . In the morning, I took my sister and we went to my mother's place. I remember on the evening of this day, Nasser came on TV. My stepfather was there, and so was my mother, in the apartment, and we were watching TV. Nasser came and stated that he had to take the blame for this. It was not a defeat, but what they called a setback [naksa]. . . . "We were waiting at the east, they came from the west, and the United States were to blame, because there was this famous ship, Liberty, jamming transmissions." I was shocked. . . . Simultaneously, there were demonstrations in the streets . . . and a sort of fictitious air raid, with all the anti-aircraft guns banging in the sky. I became very furious then. I started insulting Nasser, at the TV screen.[19]

Here split recollections, elated and enraged, coexist. 'Abd al-Mat'al's sense of betrayal and ironical farce dominates his account.

In the realm of public utterances, many have recounted such feelings, emblematized by Nasser's admission of defeat and by his resignation. One of the earliest films to portray the event is Yusif Shahin's 1972 *Al-'Asfur* (The Sparrow).[20] Set shortly before the June War in an Upper Egyptian village, *The Sparrow* was the first movie to evoke the war and political corruption. At the same time, this Egyptian-Algerian coproduction avoids iconoclastic denunciations and political libels, in contrast with the staple of Sadatian revisionism, 'Ali Badrakhan's 1975 *Al-Karnak*.[21] *Al-'Asfur* first appears to embrace the idea that a few corrupted (capitalist) elements, such as Shahin's unscrupulous businessman, caused the *naksa*.[22] But the film also narrates the collusion of high public officials and entrepreneurial circles. It recounts the baffled emotions—disbelief, anger, sadness—brought about by news of the defeat. In a memorable ending, the main protagonist, Bahiyya, rushes out into the street accompanied by swelling crowds that shout their refusal of the defeat. In the background plays a patriotic song by banned dissident singer Shaykh Imam 'Isa and poet *engagé* Ahmad Fu'ad Nijm.[23]

Disappointment was proportional to previous endorsement. Mat'al was among those disillusioned supporters. His testimony conveys the ideological conditioning of Nasserian youth. Mat'al had enthusiastically volunteered on a civil defense patrol when Nasser's secret police arrested his father, an "old regime" outcast. His testimony also highlights that the English and French educated middle and upper class had access to sources of information outside domestic ones, inaccessible to other strata of society, such as foreign-language news media.

The national media had been creative, but 1967 fictions had, contrary to common opinion, a precedent. On the eve of the '56 tripartite attack, government vehicles had roamed the streets with loudspeakers. They announced the imminence of World War III, the bombing of Paris and London, and the coming of Soviet reinforcements. Local songs recall Egyptian black propaganda, reinvented as the invaders' fabrication:

At night, we saw a car, going telling the Russians were coming.
It turned out that this was a deception plotted by the Brits,
And the French, with the Jewish gang.
Oh dear, oh dear, oh dear,
Oh dear lord... [24]

Egyptian government agencies had recycled Soviet propaganda. They compared the Battle of Port Said with the Battle of Stalingrad. These calls were meant to foster a civilian army. Regardless of their own propagandistic exaggerations, British accounts convincingly point to the irresponsibility of the Egyptian command in recruiting and delivering weapons to inadequately trained civilians.[25] Past events often seem to furnish clues to present states of affairs. But Egyptian 1956 propaganda was not taken advantage of in the years to follow. However, it puts into perspective the mechanisms of the *naksa* and reveals the workings of the state that produced it. In other words, the nationalistic propaganda that embroidered the 1956 shrine was the epitaph of the 1967 War. Little remains of the 1956 deceit because the war appeared to be virtuous and incidentally ended in victory. Aggressors left and the nationalization was successful. The newspapers, radio, cinema, songs, and literature further occulted the contestable aspects of the war. Furthermore, international struggles gave imminence to national ones. The Korean, Vietnam, and Algerian wars along with the U.S. civil rights movement invaded daily news and marked many lives. They shielded the Suez War from criticism because the war had become larger than itself.

In 1956 the reified revolution hence found its uppercase, its legitimation, fusing "memory, myth, and history."[26] The construction of the '52 Revolution bears many similarities to the Mexican Revolution, such as the pragmatic, eclectic, antisectarian, populist, reformist program adopted by 1920s Mexican leaders. Under President Álvaro Obregón, as under Nasser, "la Revolución became the government and the government was la Revolución." Similar to Mexican revolutionary scribes and emulating historian 'Abd al-Rahman al-Rafi'i, the Free Officers created an omnipresent revolution that "inhabited the past, present, and future."[27] The reification of the Mexican Revolution into myth took time. In contrast, the Egyptian revolutionary leadership hastily reified and institutionalized the *thawra* (revolution) into Thawra (Revolution) and monumentalized the present into History. Also different from the Mexican Revolution, the Free Officers dispelled political and ideological competition, political disagreements, and alternative accounts of the '52 events. Egyptian authorities imposed their monopoly over the mass media and historiographical production. Moreover, the '56 historical moment, which facilitated the historiographical transformation of a military coup into the glorious '52 Revolution, relied on the idealization of Nasser. As a result, disputing the colonel's probity risks desecrating a moment that still carries much emotional charge.

Nonetheless, historical utterances about the '67 events always bring about the question as to whether the President was responsible, liable, or ignorant of the activities of his subalterns. Those who hold the man of 26 July as champion of national pride tend to dissociate him from the man of 9 June, that is, the master of deception. The most indulgent not only separate the president from the state (army, party, government) but also from Field Marshal 'Amir and ASU Chairman 'Ali Sabri. To borrow Bisati's image, a schizophrenic memory disconnects the president from the power structure. Right after the defeat, Nasserists themselves publicly acknowledged institutional corruption in order to rescue the revolution and avoid large-scale political indictments. In fact, Nasser was responsible for rewarding allegiance to the state rather than honoring individual competence. Egyptians often discuss the political legacy of this cronyism, as it is here by 'Abd al-Rahim Gharib al-Banna:

> See, [in '67] we knew [in Ismailia] that they had hit the planes and the airports, and of course, this was a mistake. . . . Why? Because the authorities had a problem with people of knowledge. . . . These [people] were kept out [of power], and the people who are the friends of the revolution were those who, you know, took their place. And they miscalculated things, you know.

> There were people from the army who said that we should hit Israel first. 'Abd al-Nasser said: "Absolutely not, we will receive the first blow." . . . If I take this stick and hit him on the head, what can he do? Yeah? That's what Israel did, and with the position of 'Abd al-Nasser, God bless his soul . . .²⁸

The Suez War might indeed have been a curse, for it postponed the judgment of the Nasserian chain of command and presidential responsibilities for building a clientelist, authoritarian, and military state fraught by corruption.

The Hijra

The curse was a site of comfort for the people of the Canal in the late 1960s. Recollections of the Battle of Port Said were kept alive in exile. To most, the evacuation is known today as the second *hijra*, although elders who experienced World War II evacuations call it the third *hijra*. The *hijra* thus most commonly describes the exodus of civilians from the Canal Zone gradually from 1967–1970 and from 1974–1975. For a couple of years after the June War, the residents of Port Said, Ismailia, and Suez sustained episodic Israeli aerial attacks and military skirmishes. Israeli troops on the east side of the Canal occupied advanced observatory posts spread out every kilometer. These stations were so close, Nabila Husni remembers, that Port Saidis could hear Israeli loudspeakers taunting them.²⁹ 'Abd al-Rahim Gharib al-Banna recalls similar goading:

> We would go on the canal and find the Jews sitting defending the other bank. . . . "Hey, Egyptians!" And they insulted us. And if [they wanted] to pull out a grenade and attack one of us, that was possible, you know. It was very common, you know. So, we were ridiculed in '67, not in a small way, you know.³⁰

Archival records corroborate oral testimonies. In late June 1967, for example, Israeli troops set up "a loudspeaker that, almost every night, broadcast for [the Company's employees and workers], a quarter of an hour to twenty minutes of news and commentaries in Arabic."³¹ In addition to such provocations, Canal residents suffered from economic destabilization. Fishermen lost their jobs. They risked the same fate as fida'iyyin if they dared venture too close to the shore. After the breakout of the June War, some Port Saidis briefly left the city. Most stayed in town as long as they could, probably less by virtue of their indomitable character—as patriotic explanations would have it—than, as Ahmad 'Awad explains, to preserve their "interests," jobs, and property:

> *People left depending on their interests here and shops. . . . Their families and children went away because of school . . . so that young children could go to school in another place. But the father would stay here. . . . He'd tell you: "What am I going to do there, for example, with the peasants? There are mosquitoes there. . . . There is an atmosphere there that's different from. . . . And I won't be able to make any profit, I am a man, a Master Ironer. . . . What will I do there? It's better if I stay here and I work here. . . ." And they worked here and lived. . . . You know, it was a horrible period, but it was . . . in my opinion, it was all a scenario . . .*[32]

Women and children went to the nearby Delta, in the midst of peasants and mosquitoes, while men stayed behind. But after the War of Attrition began (March 1969–August 1970), following several months of permanent alert, public authorities ordered a general evacuation, as Husni describes:

> M. B. *Did you leave after the attack?*
> N. H. *After they attacked us? No, we stayed in the apartment for two years, from '67 to '69, in Port Said, because Port Said was not hit as much as Ismailia or Suez. We could sustain this. You went down [in the basement of the house], went back up. . . . In 1969, it's the government . . . that asked [people] to leave in order to evacuate the town. . . . How [else] could we make war at our ease and get our land back?*
> M. B. *Did people accept to leave?*
> N. H. *Nobody wanted to leave at all. Especially since we were doctors, all our men were doctors. So that the first time we left, only women and children left. I was a doctor. . . . But because my child was young, I left. I can't recall exactly, what precise events happened, before what . . . these are old things, you see.*[33]

A few thousand civilians remained between 1969 and 1975, catering to troops. There were between twenty-five thousand and fifty thousand civilians in the Canal area in 1973.[34] 'Awad reluctantly, yet humorously, spoke of the atypical solidarity born out of people's dreadful existence in this period:

> M. B. *In the period between '67 and '74, did you stay [in Port Said]?*
> A. A. *Staying, staying, yeah . . . I stayed . . .*
> M. B. *How was the atmosphere?*

A. A.   *It was an atmosphere of silence . . . [with irony]. There was a mutual affection between dog and cat. . . . You know, both were hungry [laughing]. . . . You know, when someone threw something, the two ate it, there was no counting. . . . There was the sense that there was no use for hostility and that we had to eat together. . . . Animals were affectionate with one another. . . . The army controlled [Port Said].*[35]

During the second *hijra*, discounting the brief '56 evacuation, civilians went to the many corners of the nation. Family members were often separated for economic reasons. As the novel *Buyut* shows, and as its cinematic adaptation melodramatically illustrates, employment was often hard to come by in exile. The state provided subsidies, al-Banna recalls:

A. B.   *The hijra took place via the government. . . . For example, they brought 20 trucks in Ismailia, for example. They brought people. . . . The government knew that such and such people will go to Kafr al-Saqr, others will go to Upper Egypt. . . . Those ones will go to Mansura, those will go who-knows-where. . . . So . . . they made shelters for people . . . schools . . . government facilities that were closed, and whatnot. Those who had relatives went to them, for example; they did not go at the expense of the government. And then, all these people who emigrated, the government gave them money to live . . .*
M. B.   *They helped people?*
A. B.   *Yes, sure . . .*
M. B.   *Could they find work to help themselves, find work?*
A. B.   *Whether you worked or did not work, every family got ten piasters* [sigh] *per person per day . . .*
M. B.   *Was this enough to live?*
A. B.   *Ten piasters, for example, a family, you know, for example, let's say six people, 60 piasters, 18 pounds . . . a family could live on it. And people even came back with money . . .*[36]

Some people stayed with relatives. Others were hosted by government offices. Subsidies were insufficient for many families, though.[37] People overall managed on their own. The government had trouble accommodating the sudden mass of refugees. At the end, relocation was contingent upon personal networks, as al-Banna explains:

Yeah . . . Ismailia emigrated three times. . . . [We] emigrated in '40 or '41 because of the German raids. . . . You know, in many streets here in Ismailia, many people died from the raids of the Germans. . . . The second emigration was in the year '56, the tripartite attack of Israel. . . . The third emigration happened in the year '67. In these emigrations . . . many people . . . did not know the land of the Delta and the north of the Delta and these sorts of things. They did not know this region. . . . When we emigrated, we, for example, we were from Dekernes and went to our family. . . . If you were from Port Said, you stayed in Port Said in your family and if you were from Alexandria, from Mansura, from who-knows-where. . . . We, when we emigrated in '67, Cairo did not advertise anything and if you did not know where the shelters were, you did not know anything, no nothing-in-the-world.[38]

Temporary shelters often evolved into lasting accommodations. In *Buyut*, Muhammad al-Bisati aptly describes the exodus of Port Saidis to the countryside and the emergency shelters:

They had moved in small groups in hired lorries. . . . They would then split up, to meet again after some days in some new village. . . . They went through . . . the open hall of a hospital, the courtyard of a mosque, schools. These all resembled one another. . . . They were sited beyond the village houses . . . . The school pupils as though expecting them, ran to the houses as soon as they saw them coming to gather up loaves of bread, clothes, and blankets. . . . "All of you ask for schools . . . . There is no longer a single place in them . . . . Many are coming. We form the second line. The hospital is crammed full, even the corridors, with families."[39]

Limby was the lesser war victim, but what happened to him in exile is unclear. Some say that people individually made and burned the dolls. For all that, by most accounts, refugees did not re-create communal celebrations.

Cairenes had an easier experience of the war and could hardly relate to the refugees' ordeal. Soon after the defeat, diplomatic reports recall, Cairo swiftly returned to prewar conditions. In early July "new foxholes," "sandbag enclosures, and machine gun emplacements" were no more to be seen. The government publicized that it was organizing a front of "popular resistance." It coordinated the "physical and military training of youth to join the 'shock troops.'" On 13 July the press declared that "400 girls from the higher institute of physical training" had completed their instruction.[40] By early August these youth groups created before the war now refrained from ostentatious performances. However, according to U.S. sources, youth "'recruitment' [continued to be] systematically carried out by door-to-door neighborhood canvass and woe to the youth who fails to appear for scheduled sessions of training which includes instruction in judo and karate."[41] Barely two months after the war, Donald Bergus, permanent head of the Interest Section at the American embassy, reported:

> Cairo continues to convey an atmosphere of detachment and listlessness. Bridge guards remain but appear less warlike as the days pass. Observed military vehicular traffic has been almost nil and the once daily regular overflight of Migs has become sporadic. The Hilton washed out most of its blackout blue early in the week and most car owners have done the same to their headlights. Moveable barbwire road blocks remain in ready position along edges of airport road. Such outward reminders of the war grow daily fewer.[42]

Many news items depict the rapid normalization in Cairo after the war contrasting with the fever of May and June. This period was one of "stagnation" in "which 'the home front was spellbound as though struck by tempest.'"[43]

Cairene indifference to the Canal's misfortune and to the consequences of the June War in Palestine thus became a fact of life in the early '70s. Some, especially members of the leftist intelligentsia, such as filmmaker Sa'id Marzuq, deplored this disinterest. His 1973 film *Al-Khawf* (The Fear), released shortly before the October War, declaimed atrophy in the face of national tragedy. This posttraumatic movie tells of the impossible romance of a young couple in Cairo (a cinematic cliché) in the wake of 1967. He (Nur al-Sharif) is a Cairo photographer who shoots pictures of Suez in ruins after the Israeli bombing. War has indeed destroyed about 80 percent of the city.[44] He is a voyeur. She (Su'ad Husni) is a war survivor whose family has perished in the blast of Suez. He loves fun and girls. Mourning consumes her. Prisoner of her memories, she feels alienated by Cairo's ubiquitous frivolity, superficiality, and consumerism. He is intrigued by her melancholy. Lingering sexual tension parallels social and political tension (the Palestinian drama and the War of Attrition) and composes the film's narrative thread.

An otherwise political statement of poor aesthetic quality, albeit well intentioned, *Al-Khawf*—like Abu Sayf's *Hammam al-Malatili*, also released in 1973—condemns moral and political hypocrisy.[45] It also dictates the patriotic duty to remember. Marzuq suggests that while the past provides guidance, one must act upon the present in order to assume one's collective and individual responsibilities. The nation should remember constructively: indulging in either mourning (she) or hedonism (he) is destructive, paralyzing, and infertile, like the couple's aborted sexual craving. *Al-Khawf*'s intellectualist language of mortification and its complacency in the bizarre, however, embody the schizophrenia that it condemns. This appears to be a typical paradox in post-1967 productions.[46]

To a certain extent, public expressions of normalization in Cairo came and went in waves from 1967 until Nasser's death in 1970. To Cairenes and provincials alike, war had become a fixture, "[occupying] a prominent place in the Egyptian media," even though its saga of flamboyant victories and fallen heroes, according to American reports, left "little visible impression on UAR public." By contrast, the physical remains of the '67 and '73 wars, such as bomb shelters and districts in ruin, persisted in Port Said until at least the late 1970s.[47] In Ismailia and Suez, though, civilians had been hit harder and fled earlier. Al-Banna witnessed the destruction of his neighborhood in Ismailia. Like Husni, he felt that war damages had been gratuitous, for "Jews . . . have no pity." Today "Jews" and "Israelis" are used interchangeably.

> *After the War of Attrition, around '68 . . . you know, for example, I went out of our house, that short time I am telling you about, where there was a twenty-four hours raid . . . not an air raid, an artillery raid. . . . I look around and I see that all the houses that are around me have been demolished, gone, except for our house, that's it, that was not destroyed. . . . You know, the Jews, they have no pity . . .*[48]

The long 1967–73 state of war depopulated the area. Cities and villages became ghost towns and military outposts. A bare five to eight years separated the Six-Day War from civilians' return, but they dramatically altered the lives of exiles from Port Said, Ismailia, Suez, and surrounding towns and villages. Whether in Port Said or Ismailia, the second *hijra* therefore frames individual accounts of the 1960s–70s. Anyone born before or during the exile vividly remembers disturbances, flight, and resettlement. The war begot a distinct exodus narrative. After a period of uncertainty, tarrying, and dispersion, exiles came back estranged. Not everyone returned. Strangers moved in. Communities were fractured.[49]

People thus offer countless stories of loss. The demographics of the post-1974 period contributed to this alienation. Among old-stock residents prevailed the sentiment that their cities had been spoiled by the influx of outsiders in the '70s. Before this mainly rural migration, "there was no mud, there was no dirt." Al-Banna describes how newcomers "ruralized" the city:

M. B.   *After people came back [1974], . . . did everyone come back or did some people stay in . . . ?*
A.B.   *Yeah . . . You just said a very important point. There are people who stayed [in exile] and did not come back. And there are people who came back bringing with them other new people, you know. I have a son who married for example a girl from Mansura, so he brought her when he came. There is in Mansura a railroad line with Ismailia. And that happened a lot, you know, like that. To the point that we felt in Ismailia that we, this is not our town, those who came outnumbered us. . . . [When they came], there was no mud, there was no dirt. Someone came and sent for his brother and sent for the son of his paternal uncle and sent for who-knows-whom.*[50]

These bitter commentaries corroborate stories of Limby's transformation. Hence, for Canal residents, 1960s–70s recollections are emotionally charged. They compound remembrances of the *hijra*, war, cultural dissolution, and economic and demographic inflation. These discrete communal utterances set the isthmus apart. Also, they illustrate one facet of 1950s–60s nostalgia that is not a bereavement of Nasserian things past but rather the mourning of a cohesive, altruist, organic, pre-mass-industrial society.

Many changes associated with the post-*hijra* period were initiated in the 1950s–60s, though, such as demographic growth. Stimulated by trade and industrialization, the population in the Suez governorate grew between 1947 and 1960 by 90 percent, with 57,100 migrants. Compared to the national average of 37 percent, this made for the highest growth rate. Internal migrants accounted for 28 percent of the Suez governorate population in 1960.[51] In the 1960s Nasser sought to increase foreign investments and initiated measures of economic liberalization, including the project of duty-free zones along the Canal. Despite this private capitalistic overture, Nasser insisted on the continuity of his political vision. In contrast, his successors emphasized the rupture with the past and ideologically advertised it in the 1970s by promoting the Canal's duty-free zones and chanting the *'ubur* (crossing).

"Prosperity, Peace, and Love"

Whereas *al-'ubur* literally designates the military crossing of the Canal during the 1973 War, it authorized and figuratively ratified the transcendence of Nasserian things past. The vaunted military prowess of the October War helped Egyptians come to terms with the Six-Day War. Accordingly, recollections about the '67 defeat and the '73 victory are as intertwined as narratives about 1956 and 1967. On a live television broadcast transmitted on the 10th of Ramadan 2002, film director 'Ali 'Abd al-Khaliq was invited to speak about his recollections of the 1973 victory as an introduction to his latest work, which dealt with the October War. Khaliq acquiesced, "Yes, very well," and proceeded to recount a long story that started with, "I was on the way, driving to Ismailia, and I saw the bombing," and ended with, "This was the first day." "The first day?" "Yes, June 5th." Khaliq had, indeed, recounted the beginning of the Six-Day War. His account was soon followed by the embarrassment of both the artist and the program anchor.[52] Almost twenty years before, in 1971, 'Abd al-Khaliq had authored *Ughniyya 'ala-l-mammar* (A Song on the Passage), which perhaps clarifies the situation. Set during the June War, *Ughniyya* was a patriotic ode to national unity. It relates the hopeless resistance of a few isolated conscripts of various ages and social classes. The sole survivors of their battalion, they sacrifice their lives to defend their military outpost and national honor. The film also criticizes the corruption of the '52 Revolution, albeit with the usual leniency of the 1967–70 period. Despite its mildness, like the 1968 theater performance by 'Ali Salim on which it was based, the film incurred state censorship because of its implicit message. It received popular acclaim for the same reason. On the one hand, this drama successfully dealt with "the problems of society in both a comic and serious vein."[53] On the other hand, the languishing pace of the characters, moving toward their certain death, conveyed a sense of deep despair and absurdity that outweighed its political concessions. In 1971 spectators saw *Ughniyya* not only as a condemnation of the *naksa* and the War of Attrition, like the theater play, but also as a call for the military repossession of the territories that Israel had captured. Diplomatic treaties, though, not war, brought about this recovery.

While the October War did not expunge the defeat, it brought about redemption. For a few years, Egyptians had derided Sadat's postponing of war operations. Officially for strategic purposes, he had repeatedly declared the imminence of war and soon thereafter retracted. This became the topic of many popular jokes.

Sadat finally declared and sustained war on 6 October 1973. While critics might remain cynical about its outcome, they salute the technical expertise displayed during the crossing of the Canal. This prowess sharply contrasted with the 5 June fiasco. Above all, the nation "reclaimed the Sinai" and, as Husni and many others recall, Sadat thus established his political authority and reestablished the national honor that Nasser had destroyed:

After that [1967] [the Israelis] came back, and we received them well, and God gave us victory. In 1973, we attacked them, and we reclaimed the Sinai.[54]

Fa'iq Rida echoes Husni's memories and sentiments:

Yes, all Egyptians loved Sadat after the victory against Israel in 1973. He was victorious. What did Nasser do, glorifying the army? 1967, he brought defeat. Sadat brought victory.... Peace is the best thing that happened to Egypt.[55]

During the 1950s–60s, continuing conflict had become a collective feature of life, an anathema. Al-Banna relates:

M. B.   *Did you get scared [during the 1967 War]?*
A. B.   *Not at all, we did not get scared.... How many years did we spend in wars, you know?*[56]

Military involvement in Algeria, military participation in Yemen's war of independence throughout the 1960s, the chronic state of alert and fear, domestic conflicts, and the militaristic culture of the state had strained civilians. Consequently, most Egyptians then welcomed peace with Israel and applauded Sadat. They saluted another *'ubur*: the passage from regional to domestic priorities. Ironically, Nasser had isolated Egypt from the rest of the world while neglecting national welfare in the name of internationalism. In contrast, Sadat adopted *Misr al-awwal* (Egypt first) as his mantra but reopened Egypt to the outside world. The primacy of domestic interests was the foundation of Sadat's distinct political identity, in opposition to his predecessor's call for transnational solidarity.

Port Said: Hong Kong of the West

By 1974 the Egyptian government had cleared the Canal of the mines left by the '67 and '73 wars. Repopulation soon followed, envisioned as the face of New Capitalist Egypt. Port Said, officials announced and foreign newspapers repeated, was to become the "Hong Kong of the West."[57] Sadat chose 5 June 1975 to inaugurate with great pomp, wearing a Pahlevi-like white admiral uniform, the reopening of the canal to maritime circulation three months after its announcement. Israeli troops conciliatorily became invisible. Subsequently, the commemoration of the Canal's recovery strategically replaced the anniversary of the '67 defeat,[58] even though the celebrations did not survive Sadat or erase the memory of the defeat.

Limby made his comeback as well. Most significant to the becoming of the festival, Sadat established free-trade zones in the Canal cities. Port Said was the avant-garde of his master plan. Earlier duty-free legislations, in 1902 and 1920, had established limited trade uses, confined to the harbor area. In late 1965 Nasser planned on establishing a 1.1 million-square-meter free-trade zone within the next two years. The government wished to attract new industries and trades, such as oil refinery and petrochemical industries, and foreign consumer goods. The state needed hard currency. The war in Yemen was pulling the country into a financial abyss. Port Said's harbor, hurt by airline tourism and the transit trade competition from Aden and Djibouti, would hopefully be revitalized.[59] The June War cut short this project.

The "Leader of the Crossing" reawakened the free-trade idea with the reopening of the Canal. In May 1975 he declared all of Port Said a duty-free area. The goals had not changed. Import tax exemptions were to boost the Canal's redevelopment, fill in the vacuum created by the withdrawal of foreign capital in the 1950s, and heal the scarred cities and industries of the Canal. Foreign products indeed poured into the country. The "free cities" (*madina hurra*, pl. *mudun*) were transformed into commercial centers swarming with small retailers and avid buyers. A "kind of pilot project for the rest of the zone," Port Said turned into a construction field, the largest marketplace of the Canal, a consumerist pilgrimage, and a contrabandist paradise.[60] This reputation outlasted tax exemptions.

Throughout the 1990s customers flocked in, attracted by lower prices and foreign merchandise. Cheap products, especially clothing and electronics, as well as high duties at the customs fostered smuggling. Some made a living out of it. According to a 1978 news article, more than 40 percent of the goods shipped through Port Said evaded custom duties, smuggled in fishing boats through the marshes, hidden under vehicles' backseats and tires, and so on. Government officials themselves were involved in small and large trafficking, including drugs.[61] Port Said came to embody the opportunistic *mentalité* of the Infitah itself. It became notorious for its lawless adventurers, its easy money, and its rampant corruption. This reputation invaded the media, as in the film *Ahl al-qimma* (The People at the Top), directed by 'Ali Badrakhan and released in 1981. In the film, the boundaries between moneymakers and crooks, businessmen (Muhammad, the owner of an import-export company) and criminals (Za'tar, an ex-con hired by Muhammad to help with his grimy business) are hazy. *Ahl al-qimma* metaphorically brings to mind the trajectory of a capitalist entrepreneur born to a humble Ismailia family, 'Uthman Ahmad 'Uthman (1917–99), probably the richest man in Egypt in the 1980s. His company headed the reconstruction of Port Said and the canal's deepening. Sadat chose 'Uthman as minister of reconstruction (1973) and minister of housing (1974–76). The president's intimate friend thus became "at the same time a minister who could issue tenders for contracts and a contractor who could bid on them." 'Uthman's company assets and profits skyrocketed between 1972 and 1981.[62]

Al-Banna's testimony about Ismailia resonates with *Ahl al-qimma*'s story:

M. B.   *And the economy of the city? Did it change after the war?*
A. B.   *After '74, you mean?*
M. B.   *Yeah. . . . Because after Sadat, for example, made Port Said . . .*
A. B.   *A free city . . .*
M. B.   *Yeah, a free city and all that, you know . . .*
A. B.   *People said that those who did not make any money in the days of Sadat will never again make money in their life. . . . He made a huge opening. . . . Sadat. That was not a small thing, you know. . . . He was . . . . You know, this is a rare phenomenon in history, seriously. . . . He did not get his due . . .*
M. B.   *What kinds of people profited the most in the seventies?*
A. B.   *Who profited? Thieves . . .*
M. B.   *Thieves?!*
A. B.   *God yeah! . . . You know, look at the people who got all the good high positions in the country . . . the thieves. . . . And the honest man, even if he is going to starve, he will not hold out his hand, that's it, he is honest, you know. . . . The upright man shows contentment. . . . The man who's half-half walks and follows the crowd, and that's it, you know . . .*[63]

The experiences of Canal cities in the 1970s illuminate national developments. As al-Banna stated, the breakdown of the state-controlled economy opened up a wealth of opportunities for new capitalist ventures, especially in the circles of the new apparatchik elite, as did the collapse of the East European block.

The "resulting new prosperity" brought about by the Infitah owed less to genuine expansion "than to the increase of imported consumer goods that [flowed] into the interior of Egypt, legally or illicitly."[64] The results were quite opposite to the goals professed by policymakers, that is, "[increasing] Egyptian-made exports" and decreasing national dependency on imports.[65] First the Suez War, now newcomers, consumerism, and capitalism radically altered the Canal cities' identity in the 1970s and changed the face of the Limby.

A Gift to the World

Peace and capitalism drove Limby to his deathbed. After '74 in Port Said as in Ismailia, Limby festivities turned into a celebration of wealthier times to come. To those born in the 1920s–30s, the 1970s opened a third and last episode in the history of the festival. After the 1970s the festival became an exuberant display of the new fortunes, expanding under the rush of financial capital. Residents born in the 1960s and after tend to view the festival in the light of its post-1974 history, where new fabric and clothing replaced rags and used clothes in the making of effigies. In our interview, Captain Ghazali recalled the post-1970 festival's capitalistic buzz:

> *The event grew with the Free City, people's machines, and the clothes of the cotton bale and things. People have money, and it became in a certain way a form of advertisement! You know, those sons of Khudayr. . . . And the sons of Zakariyya, and all these children. They gather money from the shops and from the capitalists to make the festival. They were doing it at [great] expense, see, performing and bringing artists, and then came in painters! And the artists deviate from the festival process, that is, its spontaneous form, where there is no neighborhood without a Limby hanged and suspended in the streets for a month [before the burning]. These are customs that recede, especially every time the government is, you know, in alert, so it counts every gathering as an opposition. . . . The government doesn't want this. . . . Now they want a settling down. . . . And artists come from Cairo who perform a couple of good-for-nothing nights here and . . . get it over with.*[66]

For the nouveaux riches of the Infitah, the effigy burning was the occasion for displaying newly gained wealth and social status while reinforcing networks through the collection of Limby funds. In Ismailia it is said that the biggest effigies were set up by a well-known affluent figure: a butcher. In Port Said the well-connected Khudayr family became celebrity. Some people in Port Said, as in the earlier testimony, believed that this take-over of the "capitalists" showed the victory of Infitah "fat cats" who usurped the festivities.[67] As Captain Ghazali pertinently points out, these individualized and delocalized events undermined the spontaneity, originality, and collectivity of the festival. In the pre-1970s period, the confection of effigies took place at different scales, but it was always a collective action that delineated the spatial and social confines of the neighborhood:

> C. G. *In the streets, it was spontaneous. In every street, the children collected money from one other and revived that ritual. That's like what we have during Ramadan, the month of Ramadan. People meet each other in cities and make banners and lanterns, and this and this and that. ... So what happens [now], see, is that different people collect from the shops to make something big. That's an opportunity. Opportunists don't miss a chance.*[68]

In the pre-Infitah period, each trade, artisan, and *hara* had its own cart. This was indeed, as Captain Ghazali noted, very much in the manner of a religious procession. With the advent of the Infitah, however, this practice waned. The structure of the festival dominated by individuals from the economic elite reflected the new socioeconomic realities, such as the disappearance of guilds and the fracture of tightly knit *haras* and families. Formerly anarchic, communal cultural creations thus became trivial, hierarchical, individualistic, and produced for mass consumption. Yet evocatively, the national press defined the Khudayr performances as communitarian.

Beginnings and Ends

By the mid-1970s celebrations in Port Said and Ismailia pointed toward a displacement from anticolonial and armed to social and ethical resistance. The demotion of 1950s notions of national resistance preceded the Infitah: Egyptians were disabused by the hollow semantics of pan-Arab nationalism, its manipulative slogans, and its militaristic ordeal. The June War and Nasser's death in 1970 unveiled this order of things. Whereas the 1950s was an age of utopian ideals, the 1970s begat the age of cynicism. Sun'allah Ibrahim's 1992 *Dhat* (Zaat) typifies this turn. *Dhat* ruthlessly tells of the obscenities of consumerism, conformism, capitalism, and modernization.

Limby performances refracted the climate of the time, and Limby stories convey perceptions of such times. Hence, recollections of the effigy burning in the 1940s–50 period expose colonial segregation and recount the existence of intimate urban communities. They also summon armed conflicts suffered and peace welcomed. They remind us that nostalgia for an ante-high-modernist, preconsumerist, and preindividualistic society is generational.

Starting in the late 1970s the effigy burning manifested people's adaptation to, and relish for, consumerist and capitalist pleasures. The new festivities borrowed old motifs (Allenby) but also forged other ones that conveyed contemporaneous mundane, political, and economic preoccupations. Limby burnings always operated as free, open social commentaries, all at once spontaneous, wild, and structured, organized, subversive, and officially endorsed. Limby performances henceforth reckoned Port Saidis' materialistic indulgence; their favorite soccer team; their derision of the Lewinski scandal; their solidarity with the Palestinian struggle; and their resistance to controversial economic policies that made little case of their personal fates. Yet Limby will remain or die the Limby: these revelries eventually turned into protest against public authorities. Economic expansion fell short of 1970s figures and the promised Hong Kong of the West.[69] In fact, past and present Limbies reveal the analogy revelers drew between old and new forms of exclusion and oppression experienced throughout the nation. The following section returns to Cairo and questions one particular form of exclusion and oppression as well as another distinct realm of communal experience as it turns to religious and spiritual utterances and the Coptic Church.

III

St. Mary, Mother of Egypt

The Past Is Everything

The previous section, "Burn, Edmund, Burn," argued that the presence of the past lies in the continuous reinvention and renewal of the communal covenant that makes the past relevant, rather than in the stale rehearsing of old stories, as the schoolhouse does. But whose covenant, and what community? Could local social and cultural distinctiveness survive the alteration of Port Said and Ismailia? Different populations indeed inhabited the Isthmus in 1956, in 1967, and in 1974. The members of the large foreign communities either left or were expelled in the 1950s. And internal migrants changed the Canal cities in the 1970s. One might surmise that the social fabric and structures, spaces of social intimacy and familiarity, nurtured a sense of local distinctness rather than created consistency. This sense of endurance is also based upon the historical exclusion of those elements that contradict the idea of communitarian cultural integrity. Post-1956 historical utterances, such as Limby stories, thus assimilate all foreign nationals and protégés to colonial society. Ironically, Greeks, Italians, Maltese, French, Croatians, Englishmen, Jews, Christians, Muslims, and others—most of all the working classes among them—contributed to fashioning the cultural distinctness of Isthmus urban societies.

Communalism in the Canal cities was built as well in contradistinction and opposition to political authorities, to the state, and to Cairo. As seen, Canal cities have a long history of trade unionism and political activism, which sets the region apart to this day. The political and financial interests of Canal city workers have often been at odds with those of the central government. The ban of the Limby festival at the turn of the past century and the particular violence that the state exerted against the protest movements of the Canal in 2011 are testimonies of these social tensions and political antagonism.

•

In the present section, "St. Mary, Mother of Egypt," I explore further the relation of community and nation, and community and nation-state. After the national and the local, I study a third level of historical utterance and community. I investigate the religious community and one last facet of 1950s–60s utterances: national unity and interfaith harmony. The question that revolutionaries faced in 1952 remains relevant after the 2011 Revolution. What community do new state representatives seek to represent? What commonwealth? The covenant drafted by the newly elected political appointees following the 2011 elections will define the *civitas* and delimit fraternity.

I also question more broadly what becomes of cosmological arguments when religious movements after the 1960s have in fact flourished in an age dominated by scientist and rationalist concepts of modernity. What becomes of religious distinction? I suggest reevaluating religious and spiritual movements as well as the question of national unity in the post-Nasserian era under the prism of the structuring and homogenizing corporatist, textual, competitive, global, and capitalistic aspects of the modernizing process.

One such aspect is theological and religious competition. The Coptic Church responded to it, and to its loss of hegemony and fear thereof, by affirming its theological and structural continuity and its apostolicism. The endorsement of miracles, such as the apparition of the Virgin Mary to the north of Cairo in 1968, was a means of affirmation of this apostolicism. The Coptic Church was the repository of Christian tradition. Here, the past is everything.

I start with and articulate this section around the same historical hinge as the last one: the June War. The conventional political tale about post-1967 things past is that the defeat marked the downfall of Arab nationalism and secular politics. The vacuum thus created propelled the politicization of religion, and sectarian conflict followed. The veil, the beard, and faith-based social networks of all kinds are thus commonly interpreted as the ideological defeat of a European secularist model of modernization or as countermodernist phenomena. Correlatively, Coptic political activism is often narrated as a response to Islamic violence and persecution.

In the 1950s–60s modernization brought about social dislocation in some arenas and greater social control in others. On the one hand, some processes disrupted the social fabric and value systems, such as rural migration, social mobility, changes in gender roles, urban atomization, and theological competition. On the other hand, other mechanisms reinforced social cohesion and hegemonic processes instigated a few decades earlier. These facilitated institutional and public, but also sectarian and private, control of the social body.

The state imposed its political and ideological hegemony by dissolving the multiparty parliamentary system. The one-party system thus reformulated educational institutions and curricula. It regulated public services and civil organizations. Starting in 1955 and culminating in the 1961 Reform Law, the state asserted an outstanding control over, and redefined the civic mission of, al-Azhar.

Noninstitutional religious and secular actors congruently reinvested religion by recodifying practices and theology. They disputed institutional hegemony. Groups such as organizational networks, youth groups, grassroots religious education, and charitable organizations multiplied. Most remarkable was the simultaneous and unprecedented centralization and reinforcement of state power along with the diversification of such civil agencies that worked both with and against governmental institutions.

Within the Coptic community, secular and clerical organizations had roots in the late nineteenth and early twentieth centuries, although Coptic "Renewal" came about in the 1940s. This renewal consisted in communitarian Coptic spaces, built around the Church, that fulfilled social and political, educative and cultural, religious and civic functions and that were socially inclusive.[1] By the 1960s the Church's civic and polyvalent role was solidified. Some historians have attributed this crystallization of sectarian life to Copts' minority status and alienation. Accordingly, Copts reacted to Muslim oppression and to the Islamicization of public life in the 1950s–60s.[2]

Yet this interpretation is only partially satisfying. The affluence and integration of Copts before the '52 Revolution can hardly be generalized. While Copts' civil rights struggle and throes are real, interpreting their history against Muslim hostility is reductive. Among other things, it disregards and fails to explain transformations and issues within the rest of society that are similar to Coptic ones. The tensions between religious clergy and state, the discordance within, and the heterogeneity of the religious community itself are common to Christian and Muslim communities.[3] I argue that clerical centralization and social polyvalence are organic to the modernization processes.

The Coptic Church has faced the instability inherent to a postindustrial world that gives easy access to a large array of theological, spiritual, and ritual commodities. The Church adapted and redefined its functions, doctrines, and practices in response to perceived threats, many originating from other Churches.

Maintaining the façade of its doctrinal immutability is part of those strategies. Thus, the past is everything. It has for purpose to symbolically preserve the Church's structures and demarcate it from other Christian rites. As Victor and Edith Turner pertinently wrote, "While one religion prevails, social and cultural structures seem immutable. However, structures, and the symbols which manifest them, do break up and crumble. What often persists is *communitas*, no longer normative or ideological, but waiting to be given new form by a new religion."[4] The Church is apprehensive about the conversion of the *communitas* to more universalist and theologically reformist cults. It is aware of its vulnerability.

In 1968, when the Virgin appeared in Zaytun, the nation was undergoing times of anxiety. The Zaytun utterances thus display responses to the insecurities following the 1967 defeat. The war shaped the meaning of the apparition, and conversely the apparition shaped interpretations of the war. Zaytun became to ecclesiastical and political orders, similarly to Fatima in 1940s Portugal, "a fact of contemporary history with a projection throughout the world. Not only [was] this a confirmation of the supernatural and of faith, but it [was] also a guarantee and a testimony of the spiritual unity of the nation."[5] Its utterances, though, since the past forty years, have exposed the spiritual fractures of national and religious communities, and political strain. They have revealed "dissent and schism" both inside and outside the Church. Hence, the flare of Marian worship that followed the Zaytun event has been a "source of inspiration and strength against heresy and subversion" mainly, in Egypt, against Protestantism, Evangelism, and other competing sects.[6]

6

The Science of Miracles

[Governor-general Ortai] reported that on the last day of the tenth lunar month of the previous year—the emperor's fiftieth birthday—glorious five-colored clouds were seen circling the sun for many hours above one of Yunnan's most sacred shrines. The amazing sight, repeated the following day, could be seen by countless people across a great range of countryside. Clearly, Ortai wrote, this was a "completely unprecedented omen of good fortune."

Jonathan Spence, *Treason by the Book*

On 5 May 1968 the Egyptian media offered rather unusual news. Kyrillus VI (Cyril VI), the 116th pope of the See of Alexandria (1959–71), head of the Coptic Orthodox Church, had announced that St. Mary; Theotokos, the God-bearer; al-'Adhra', the Eternal Virgin; Sittina, Our Lady; al-Mustafiyya, the Chosen One[1] had appeared on Easter, 2 April 1968, at a church located in Zaytun, to the north of Cairo.[2] National newspapers printed photographs of the phenomenon. The following day the news had reached the rest of the world. A Copt recalled in the late 1970s, "All the newspapers, even the Muslim newspapers, spoke about the Mariophany or apparition of the Holy Virgin. They even spoke about it on television."[3] The front page of *Al-Ahram* showed a nocturnal, human-shaped halo of light surmounting one of the domes of the church. A few days later, 10 May, the weekly magazine *Al-Musawwar* published the images of a ghostly luminous form rising between two domes, crowds of believers standing around the church, public officials attending the events, and photographic evidence of supernatural cures.[4] Mainstream media reported miraculous sights at the Zaytun shrine for a year after the first apparition. Some say that people continued flocking to St. Mary's church for two or three years.[5]

News of the apparition came about during a volatile international political situation. As seen through *Al-Ahram*'s headlines, these were days of righteous struggles. On 7 May, *Al-Ahram* reported Martin Luther King Jr.'s critique of the World Bank. In the United States, the civil rights movement was at its height while anti–Vietnam War demonstrations raged. Czechoslovakia had just started a promising democratization program. And the Palestinian resistance began a new phase of its twenty-year history. On the domestic front, the "visitation" of the Mother of Light had occurred three days after Jamal 'Abd al-Nasser's 30 March Program Speech.[6]

The event's commemoration did not wait long. In 1969 Pope Kyrillus instituted a liturgical annual feast in honor of Our Lady of Zaytun. Some forty years after the apparition, pilgrims still regularly visit the Zaytun church during the Marian month of August in hope of seeing the Virgin.[7]

Doves and Clouds

The international press conference during which the pope had announced the apparition gathered some "150 Egyptian and foreign journalists."[8] Athanasius, the bishop of Beni Suef, read the papal statement aloud. At his side stood an illustrious delegation composed of archbishops Ibram, Samuel, Gregorius, and other officials:

> The pope Kyrillus VI announced in a statement issued yesterday at the papal residence the veracity of the manifestation of the Virgin at the church of Zaytun. . . . She has continued to appear incessantly until now and some nights She appears for a period up to two continuous hours. The pope said in his communiqué that the apparition of the Virgin manifests itself by snow-white clouds, or in the form of a light preceded by the emission of spiritual figures like the dove.[9]

On May 4 the Ministry of Tourism circulated a document that confirmed the apparition.[10] Newspapers, magazines, radio, and television echoed the story. It made *Al-Ahram*'s front page for three days, until 7 May. It then vanished from the daily's cover until the dramatic events of 20 May, when crowds heard the false rumor of another apparition. Some ten thousand people rushed to St. Michael's church in Shubra, a northern suburb, and now, like Zaytun, an overpopulated Cairo neighborhood. Fifteen people were trampled to death and many wounded.[11]

Even prior to the patriarch's authentication in April '68, news of the Mariophany had spread beyond Cairo's precinct through the Coptic press. People captured the Mother of Light on camera; one such photograph is sold today at the church as an anonymous picture of the Virgin (figure 6.1). As Church records suggest, periodicals and word of mouth prompted many to go see for themselves. One Coptic Orthodox publication, *Al-Watani*, reached the formidable circulation of 220,000.[12] "When I read about the appearance of the Virgin," testified Riyad Najib 'Azir, "I asked [permission from work] to travel to Cairo, so on the evening of this past April 21, my mother accompanied me and stood by me in the crowd on the street of the church at Zaytun." In a description that matched *Al-Ahram*'s 5 May photograph, Riyad recounted: "And suddenly, my sight was caught by the dome where I saw a clearly defined illuminated body, wearing nun garments, suspended in the air above the dome of the church."[13] A graduate of the Faculty of Commerce in Alexandria, Riyad became one of the key "witnesses" that the Church Committee of Investigation selected. His was a serious case of miraculous sight worthy of certification, historical recording, and recollection. Like others, after reading *Al-Watani*, the lawyer Zaki Shanuda, another "certified witness," went to the church on Easter Sunday, 27 April.

Figure 6.1. Marian apparition at the Church of Zaytun in 1968. Devotional photograph; photographer unknown. Collection of the author.

Nearly twenty years later, in 1986, *Al-Watani* would publish daily reports during what became the first "return" of the Virgin. As in 1968, *Al-Watani* claimed exclusivity on the news.[14] Many collective visions of the Virgin were to follow, always at Coptic churches, the last one, at the time of this writing, in 2009–10. Now, after its 2008 anniversary, images and testimonies about the ontological Mariophany have spread on Coptic and other Christian Web sites. Only the meaning of the 1968 event has changed.

In 1968 the papal communiqué transmitted the finely detailed visions of clerical and lay witnesses. The story was a hit. By 5 May thousands had gathered in the vicinity of St. Mary. This modest church had been built in 1924 under the auspices of Tawfiq Khalil bey, son of Khalil Ibrahim pasha. Much in concordance with premodern religious revelations, legend has it that the Virgin appeared to Khalil in 1918.[15] She asked him to dedicate a new shrine in her name on the exact site where the Holy Family had rested during its flight to Egypt. "Presira," the one whose mediation is most authoritative, promised in return that she would appear fifty years later.[16] Upon his father's death, the wealthy lawyer from Asyut thus erected a mausoleum and a family church on the said site. A year later, the beloved bishop of Beni Suef, Athanasius, consecrated it.

St. Mary's Church is now integrated into Coptic Mariological piety. Its pilgrimage memorializes the 1968 visitation and historicizes the Holy Flight. Shanuda III, who succeeded Kyrillus VI in 1971, built a massive cathedral near the church. The cathedral bolsters Marian devotion at the same time as it hallows the 1968 event.

On 4 May the Virgin had shared the public tribune, though. The media had loudly announced the results of the March 30 program referendum. For the previous month, discussions of Nasser's 30 March speech and political promises had monopolized the media. Protest rallies had occurred throughout Egypt earlier in February. Nasser had responded by calling for a national referendum to sanction his agenda. A public vote effectively took place on 3 May 1968. The preliminary result forecasted "a clear Yes. Yes. . . . Clear and strong." One day after, the minister of interior announced the outcome without generating much surprise. *Al-Ahram* titled: "99,989% [sic] said: Yes." The officious press organ had long advertised the program with praiseful articles illustrated with photographs of workers and fellahin sweating for the country's industrial and agricultural reconstruction. On 4 May, picturing long queues of men in *galabiya* heading to the voting polls, *Al-Ahram* averred that "the *naksa* [had] more than one reason; images of required changes [are present] everywhere; with the energy of the referendum ... a reminder of the passage to the path of victory."[17] These political performances were simulacra of democratic inclusion. The same political refrain, however, vaunting national renaissance, resistance, and the renewal of the democratic covenant continued throughout the War of Attrition.

News of the apparition cast a sensational halo around the new governmental program. But burlesque state performances, outward determination, and optimism only highlighted the political gloom subsequent to the defeat. The reputedly professional *Al-Ahram* columns framed the Mariophany as a common historical occurrence:

> Many saints, prophets, and pure people answered to the prayer of believers, and their spirits appeared to them, supporting and encouraging them in times of difficulty and hardship. ... The souls and spirit of saints are a spiritual manifestation sent by the Creator to believers ... : "They called me in times of hardship, and I answered."[18]

God had sent His most ecumenical messenger, revered by both Christians and Muslims. Moreover, she appeared during the Coptic week of the Passion.[19] The press praised the transcendence of religion, class, and nationality. It boasted about the massive participation of "several thousand citizens, from different religions and confessions," who "witnessed this appearance, [as well as] foreigners, and groups of men of religion, of science, and trades of different levels who established with absolute conviction what they saw."[20] Crowds arrived by all means of transportation, causing great turbulence. This was the occasion for clerics, military men, and statesmen to display their cooperation and solidarity.

The Church committee had received 120 letters from witnesses who testified they had seen the Virgin. As a result, clerical authorities set special mailboxes to accommodate this epistolary overflow in the building of Abba Louis, the papal seat, and at the church of Zaytun.[21] The press provides a sense of the event's extraordinary dimension. Thousands indeed reached Zaytun aboard "92 trains, departing every 10 minutes and carrying about 900 people each, and 50 buses, 8 lines all passing by Zaytun."[22] People occupied every inch of the area: houses, streets, walls, trees, and even streetlight posts. As on Tahrir Square in 2011, vendors and commercial activities of all kinds proliferated. There were no little profits. Chairs went "for three piasters the hour! And there were only 8 chairs left, which means that the owner of the chairs' vehicle made 576 piasters in coin of the realm!!"[23] Picturesque characters got a large share of the stories, which underscored people's union, but also the resourcefulness of simple folks:

> On the other side, in the direction of the church, "Umm Sabir," a woman over forty years old, gathered about 50 chicken cages. She put several mats on top of them and divided the remaining cages among her nine children ... she fixed the seating price at one piaster the hour. At 10:30, the whole place around the church and in the surrounding streets was transformed into a beehive flowing with individuals of all ranks ... and all religions.[24]

As the night went by, people bought drinks, food, and pious images. A Mr. Harib sold tea for two piasters a glass. The café tender made up to two pounds a night, "of which he would not have dreamt of all his life." People rented a seat for "a bottle of coca-cola or a tea at one single price: five piasters!" Water sellers made good money too. According to *Al-Ahram*, the crowds bought 150,000 bottles of sparkling water every night. People sat on the walls of the surrounding houses and the Transport Organization, where now stands the cathedral. The Muslim church guardian rented out the church wall. Most neighbors leased their roofs. The practice was so widespread that the press honored those who contravened to it, such as "the family of Sonia Labib, from the Faculty of [Literature]," which was the "only family that [allowed] people to see the spirit of the Virgin on top of their house without remuneration."[25]

Whereas Church officials kept busy with religious matters, government authorities backed up the event and sent dignitaries at the service of the population. A public committee arrived on 6 May at 2 p.m. The governor of Cairo, Sa'd Zayyid, headed it. He was accompanied by Cairo's chief of security, Gen. Mahmud al-Siba'i, and governorate officials and engineers. Zaytun soon offered a show of efficiency, unity, and cooperation among the state, the Church, and the people:

> A special commission investigated the area of the church of the Virgin hours after the diffusion of the patriarchate's statement ... and it suggested: the execution of a big road in the direction of the church; the preparation of the organization of traffic in the area; removing all the trees blocking the view.[26]

Al-Ahram printed a picture of the dome where it all happened, of the church pastor welcoming state officials, and a map of the neighborhood. *Al-Akhbar* published a photograph of the glowing church. The special committee took upon it "to prepare the planning and organizing" required by "the thousands of people that arrived there together in hope of seeing the Virgin Mary."²⁷ *Al-Ahram*'s news article with its staged photographs obeys the dramatic features of a television show. Thus, government authorities arrive accompanied by men in black (political figures), men in white (police *apparati*), and men in blue (construction workers). A hundred workers had been dispatched to the scene before the arrival of the public committee. They fixed a post "dislocated" by the crowds. They sanded part of Tuman Bey Street and cleaned up vehicles' oil spills. They paved roads and sidewalks. They trimmed and cut trees in the church garden. The performance did not lack solemnity, acted out as it was by government officials, the governor, the police chief, and their crew of "experts." The highest political authorities thus assumed direct responsibility and action. They listened to constituents, aided by a civilian and military work force. The military put themselves at the service of the nation: the news article stylistically evoked a photographic close-up on the general listening to and answering the pastor's requests. But the general also took steps forward. Entrepreneurial, looking to the future, he helped develop potential tourism opportunities. He requisitioned an adjoining mansion to that effect. He also recommended using public transportation for panoramic tours. One might imagine the pastor accompanying his guests and explaining that the abundant trees surrounding the church hindered the view of the dome, the journalist's pen drawing circles around the neighborhood, all the while followed by a bunch of intrepid kids.

Our Lady of the Palestine Liberation Organization

If the practical management of the Marian affair was in the hands of political authorities, the social and religious interpretation of the Mariophany ("manifestation," "visitation," "apparition") was imparted to the head of the *oratoribus*: namely, the Coptic Orthodox patriarch. First, in accordance with doctrinal tradition, the pope interpreted the apparition as a call to "return to faith" and piety. Second, he pointed to the visitation's universal meaning, that of a theophany, a manifestation of God's presence to humankind.²⁸ Furthermore, he invited Egyptians to consider the miracle as multilayered. He summoned them to pay greater heed to God's presence as manifested in the lesser miracles of everyday life. Thus, the divine miracle was not restricted to the Mother of Light's apparition. It also included its adjunct, scientifically inexplicable cures. The Marian event consequently offered means of redemption for those believers who "went astray from [God]." It gave an opportunity for "a multitude to repent and change" their conduct.²⁹ The pope thus explained these "two injunctions":

> First, the reinvigoration of the spirit of faith in God, in the Hereafter, and in the saints, and secondly, the occurrence of one of the splendid wonders of the healing miracles for many whose healing had been scientifically established as impossible. In his communiqué, the pope called for this apparition to be a symbol of peace between the peoples of the world and *baraka* for the beloved homeland, and a blessing for the Egyptian People, of whom the divine Revelation said that they were "the blessed People of Egypt."³⁰

This theological position was in many ways similar to Islamic ones regarding the '67 defeat, whether it was the opinion of conservative independent Muslim scholars such as Yusuf al-Qaradawi or that of state-approved authorities such as the *'ulama* of al-Azhar.³¹ In 1968 Hasan Ma'mun, State Mufti (1955–60), and Shaykh al-Azhar (1964–69)³² said of '67 that it was a religious trial, so "that [believers] may go back to Him."³³ Religious authorities, Copts and Muslims alike, "right after the defeat of 1967, at the moment where the Nasserian regime came out weakened by the trial of the *naksa*" indeed "[used] the theme of military failure in order to call consciences to come back to the memory of their religion."³⁴ The Mariophany was a cosmological sequel of the war; 1967 and 1968 were thus two sides of the same heuristic coin. Now with rather than in spite of Nasser's assent, God entered the public space.

Israeli religious milieus exploited as well the political and theological opportunities that the '67 defeat—that is, the victory of Israel—offered. As historian Michel Abitbol observed, Jewish religious trends, while they were "themselves divided into a multitude of 'chapels,'" gradually gained authority in Israeli historiography after 1967. They consequently "brought God into the Israeli public space where secular Zionists once thought to have kicked him out . . . some decades earlier."³⁵ Similarly, then, Egyptian religious scholars together with politicians brought God into the public space where, a decade earlier, secular nationalists had thought to have kicked Him out. This political turn, with regard to the exploitation of religious symbolism and institutions in the late '60s, opened the path to Sadat's politics of piety.

Atypically, though, whereas the patriarch's first injunction was social and religious, the second was political, expressing solidarity with the *pugnatoribus*, the political-military order. In tune with the ecclesiastic pronouncement, official press reports associated the miraculous apparition with the defeat. It turned a religious event into a heavenly political statement of support not only for national recovery but also for the Arab struggle against Israel, as Abba Gregorius confided to *Al-Ahram*:

> [*Al-Ahram*]: Why after the setback? Is there an explanation for the occurrence of the event of the apparition in this precise moment after the setback?
> [Father Gregorius]: Maybe because this is a good messenger and a heavenly sign that God is with us and He will not abandon us.... We hear since this past June that God has forsaken us, and if this was the cause of the setback, this appearance however—which took place in front of thousands of us—means that God is with us, and that He will support us, so that everyone realizes that this is only a mild crisis, and that Heaven always stood by us ...[36]

Simultaneously, the Church announced through Father Gregorius that the Virgin was condemning "Jewish" acts perpetrated in the Holy Land, which God had placed under her protection. Father Gregorius pursued his reading, saying that she had "[come] to announce her anger to humans and her sadness, calling for liberation." The Virgin's spokesperson ascribed her a new and unexpected role: she was politically committed and called for the repossession of the land lost to Israel. This interpretation of God's favorite mediator ideologically echoes contemporaneous liberation theologians in South America. In 1968, at a conference in Columbia, South American bishops pronounced that "'God [had] sent his Son so that in the flesh he may come to liberate all men from slavery which holds them subject, from sin, ignorance, hunger, misery, oppression.'... theologians and activists produced a consistent reading of Christian social understanding as radical as it was orthodox."[37] Brazilian liberation theologian and priest Leonardo Boff extended Christ's prophetic mission to the messiah's mother, advocating "an image of Mary as the strong, determined woman, the woman committed to the messianic liberation of the poor from the historical social injustices under which they suffer."[38] A decade after the naksa, Khomeinist revolutionaries in Iran would likewise iconographically and ideologically imitate leftist Christian liberation theology.[39] Yet, Boff alerted, "in a law-and-order society whose masculinizing powers have received such wholehearted ideological support from Christianity, will it ever be possible for people to assimilate the ethical indignation of a Mary who prays for God to . . . topple the mighty from their thrones . . . ?"[40] In a similar sense, the mighty and corrupted Nasserian state publicizing liberation and ethical indignation through the Virgin in 1968 was a grandiose irony and a bold deflection of responsibility.

The marriage of radicalism and orthodoxy as well as the manipulation of symbols of social liberation and oppression are key here: a political rhetoric positing itself as radical, framed within a religious terminology positing itself as orthodox dogma, both serving the purpose of maintaining a "law-and-order society." The miracle abruptly, albeit briefly, diverted people from these other political matters that had made the front page for months. Just as Israel had trumpeted that its military conquest in '67 was due to divine intervention, so the Almighty now uttered a counterstatement through the Mother of Light less than a year after the war.

The timing of the apparition propped the dramatic plot of the rather predictable soap opera of reform announcements. The patriarch had waited for the end of the ballots' result before handing out his verdict on the miraculous phenomenon, which had started about a month earlier. Was this delay strategically planned and instrumental? On the one hand, the seeming connivance between Church and state points to this interpretation. On the other hand, this postponement might suggest the patriarch's reluctance to collaborate, violate ethical boundaries, and breach his cherished quietism.[41]

Whatever the agreement between Church and government, timing supported moralist interpretations of the defeat. The endorsement of the miracle opposed the scientific and rationalist principles that structured Arab nationalist thought and therefore contradicted the state's elementary ideological principles. The state certainly disagreed with Islamist and other theocentric commentaries: no, God was not punishing Egyptians in their greatest time of need. Egyptians had lost a battle, but not the war. Nonetheless, state agencies endorsed theological rhetoric and episteme: God Almighty makes history.

In contrast with the 1858 Lourdes apparition in France, political and scientific circles in Egypt spared the 1968 Zaytun event from attacks.[42] Cynics and skeptics were in fact ostracized outside of national borders too. Most famously, Syrian Kantian and Marxist philosopher Sadiq Jalal al-'Azm (b. 1934) spoke out at great cost in 1969. Although banned throughout the Middle East, his analysis of the '68 miracle was widely circulated. Al-'Azm denounced Egyptian governmental statements as "nonsense" and "more pathetic and dangerous than myths." He blamed the Arab Socialist Union (ASU) for the "religious hysteria that swept the great majority of [Egyptian] citizens."

He reprimanded intellectuals for their collaboration. He denounced above all the devastation of modern, rational thought and of long-standing efforts at separating creed from scientific epistemology. The Egyptian state made a mockery of popular beliefs, he argued, and diverted people from real issues:[43]

> Everything we heard in the wake of the ['67] defeat about modern science, technology, [the use of] scientific methodologies in thinking, planning and preparing ourselves, and about measuring our words, declarations and attitude, disappeared into smoke and fine dust in one instant, because of this flaring religious hysteria. . . . To be sure, the entertainment of the Arab masses with the occult, the preternatural, miracles, and such stories, in the second half of the twentieth century but most particularly at this critical moment, will never help the peasant resolve our urgent temporal issues; this will not help us realize our vital national rights whether the Virgin got angry or not at the loss of Jerusalem.[44]

Thus, unwillingly or not, St. Mary gained the protection of Arab governments. She disclosed herself iconographically and discursively as at once anticolonial activist, modest, feminine, politically radical, and socially conservative.[45] Together, religious messianicism and scientific seal of approval complicated this portrait. It made indeed a mockery of people, religion, and science.

Soon a criminal law professor, Dr. Ra'uf 'Abid, put his legal expertise at the service of politics, religion, and science. Authoring the first "Scientific Study on the Truth of the Apparition of the Virgin at Her Church of Zaytun," the 'Ayn al-Shams University professor solemnly declared that the "miracle [would] continue until the Arab city of Jerusalem [would] be liberated from Zionist terrorism."[46] St. Mary thus named her foe. The Church was certainly not oblivious to the resonance of such an act, for miracles "have a precise function which concerns the whole of Christianity; they bring crowds to conversion . . . above all *conversion of the great enemy of the saint* and the God."[47]

In '68 the saint's greatest foe was occupying the Holy Land and Egyptian land. When the Virgin reappeared in Shubra in the 1980s, the miracle retained this exorcistic function. But the adversary had changed, as had the relationships between Church and government, Copts and Muslims, and clergy and parishioners. The retrospective meanings of the '68 miracle and its historical utterances have evolved congruently with these unstable relationships. Nonetheless, Marian apparitions are still publicly framed in the terms of that ontological appearance, national unity, and salvation, whereas a disjunction has sprung between public and intimate, national and communal accounts of miracles.

Anitra B. Kolenkow writes that "the Hebrew world used and changed ancient myths," so that biblical stories, hagiographies, and miraculous events could be reappropriated and reinterpreted to talk about the present.[48] The Church thus speaks through biblical stories and saints, and has spoken through the 1968 Mariophany since the 1980s.[49] Because God's will and his intent are in essence mysteries, the interpretation of religious utterances is malleable. For God reveals his will and intent in times he deems appropriate and in ways that neither positivist nor theological explanation can ever fully grasp. Like the heart, God has his reasons that human reason cannot possibly and, in fact, should not try to comprehend. In 1968 the Coptic Church addressed an audience familiar with the heuristic, Abrahamic method of communication and its subtexts. Its connivance with the state granted it a margin of immunity it profitably used in years to follow. The Church continued addressing its parishioners through the Virgin after the 1960s, but in subtext it now spoke of the conflict with the political order and of its fear of losing its grip on its *communitas*.

The Poetics of Miracles

The patriarch might have temporized for other reasons than spiritual and political dilemmas:

> Coptic spirituality needs marvels. Signs of God, miracles, apparitions, [and] relics are part of everyday life. These manifestations of the supernatural . . . are common in our days. Paralyzed people healed by the pope [Kyrillus] VI . . . are countless, as well as the miracles of the monk Youstous of Saint Anthony, who died in 1976. And what should be said of the apparitions of the Virgin in two popular neighborhoods of Cairo, in [Zaytun] in 1968 and in Shubra in 1986, which the Church officially proclaimed as blessed?[50]

Miracles are thus both serious and trifling matters. To inquirers who "asked why it had taken him a month to come and visit," the pope accordingly gave a savory yet humorless answer, "[downplaying] the rarity of the occurrence, saying that the Virgin had been appearing to him regularly for years."[51] For Coptic clergymen, seeing and talking to saints serves in fact as "poetics," that is, "that performance of an individual designed to evoke archetypal categories which would identify an actor with 'ideological propositions and historical antecedents.'"[52] Miracles are thus poetic performances constitutive of Coptic communality.

Familiarity with the saints is a hagiographic archetype.[53] It emanates from the "communion of saints," a doctrine espoused as well by other churches and which "posits a spiritual solidarity" between the dead and the living "in the organic unity of the same mystical body under Christ."[54] Through their personal testimonies in which they relate seeing or talking to saints, monks confirm their spiritual and ecclesiastical status. Familiarity with the saints proves spiritual purity. Theologically, this intimacy certifies the seer's capacity to witness and intercede for miracles. Monks hence validate their doctrinal status as "angels on earth." They mediate between Heaven and Earth and sanction the Church's spiritual hierarchy. In turn, by aspiring to be familiar with the saints, by emulating monks, and by acknowledging miracles, laypeople spiritually become one with the Church, the living, and the dead. The past is everything, for it provides the spiritual and material substance of the present.

The particular communal poetics of familiarity with the saints thus operates as historical utterance. That is, it is a shared narrative repertoire that establishes spiritual and historical bonds between the community of believers and its representatives and that links the earthly and the heavenly. In this creative process, believers do not simply imitate past narratives. Rather, they reenact, in the present, the experience of those early fathers and mothers of the Church whom "absolutely nothing could amaze"[55] and who lived in times of great marvels. The poetics of talking to saints and the reenactment of the tradition's utterances performatively generate a sense of communal historical continuity.[56] Thus, present miracles are a reinvestment of the scriptural tradition. And adherence to such tradition reinforces the cohesion of communal narratives.

Kyrillus VI enjoyed immense veneration because believers first and foremost measure sainthood according to the number of miracles performed during the life and especially after the death of an individual.[57] Glass sarcophagi preserve the incorruptible bodies of saints, and devotional miraculous images remind believers of such miracles.[58] The cult of saints is widespread among Muslims, too, even though Islamic theologians have been divided on the subject. Mahmud Shaltut, rector of al-Azhar from 1959 to 1963, condemned it.[59] Nonetheless, despite the popularization of purist dogma since the 1970s, the worship of saints and the belief in their miraculous powers after death persist.

It usually takes decades before ecclesiastical authorities officially recognize sainthood. Coptic Canon Law requires fifty years after the death of an individual before canonization. Kyrillus VI, however, was widely regarded as a saint during his lifetime by the Church and worshippers alike.[60] This might point to a doctrinal turn. Perhaps it was also a political strategy devised by traditionalists who counted Kyrillus in their ranks. Throughout the 1960s political and doctrinal tensions agitated the clergy, which mainly opposed "modernists" and "traditionalists." Among the modernists was the future pope Shanuda III, who wished to restructure clerical hierarchy and stimulate Coptic advocacy. Institutionalizing Kyrillus' sainthood solidified the position of traditionalists against their rivals. Kyrillus reputedly "'talked' with [the Virgin and Mari Mina (St. Menas)] and sometimes appeared to believers accompanied by one of them."[61] He is thus commonly represented on devotional pictures with his patron Mari Mina, an aura of angels atop his head (figure 6.2). Kyrillus' hagiology circulated in periodicals prior to his death. Unlike

Figure 6.2. Devotional image of Pope Kyrillus VI and St. Menas. Collection of the author.

the life story of his successor renowned for his worldliness and political outspokenness, Kyrillus' hagiology emphasized his mystical powers.[62] Miracles were indeed the late pope's distinctive mark.

Papal miracles speak of a rather ordinary conception of human welfare. The pope bequeathed fertility, good health, and fortune. God and His saints succeed where positivism fails to cure, resolve problems, and explain misfortune. Hence, Kyrillus' hagiography recounts here the distress of a longtime sterile couple; there the torment of a person afflicted by an incurable disease; and then the misfortune of a man who lost important belongings. The couple gave birth, the sick were healed, and others recovered material losses.[63] The countless pictures, stickers, and palm-size miraculous illustrations, which Copts post at work and place in their wallets, testify to the veneration that the late Kyrillus VI still enjoys today. Kyrillus' votive pictures may even be found in Haifa and Jerusalem Christian Orthodox grocery stores, even though shopkeepers might not know the saint's name. Today hagiographies, thaumatologies, and pamphlets as well as "hagio-tapes," "thaumato-videos," and Web sites, all compose a prolific and ever-expanding ecclesiastical catechism and market designed for both adults and youth.[64]

Like the lives of saints, the 1968 apparition was also commodified. The commercialization of Lourdes and its pilgrimage prompted debates in nineteenth-century France about the articulation between faith and commerce and the nature of modern religiosity.[65] In Egypt, all kinds of petty trades developed around St. Mary's church and the Zaytun pilgrimage as well. In 1969 al-'Azm harshly criticized ecclesiastical opportunism and the equally "inappropriate" greed of Minister of Tourism 'Adil Tahir. Sacred sites are universally coveted sources of revenues, which often induce tensions between parish and municipal authorities.[66] Church and state have continued to compete for the control of revenues that Zaytun generates. A 1981 *Al-Watani* article by respected journalist Mus'ad Sadiq points to these financial frictions. Sadiq criticized a development project that the minister of tourism projected in the area. Back in 1968 the Church's spokesman had positively greeted governmental plans. In 1981, though, *Al-Watani* reminded its readers of the late Nasserian Socialist Union's financial abuses as a cautionary tale. According to Sadiq, the ASU had imposed a ten-piaster entrance fee on visitors who wanted to access the area.[67]

In 1968 the Coptic Church generated its own sources of income, too. The Mariophany was commemorated contemporaneously with the manufacture of a medal. It showed the Virgin above the dome of the church accompanied by doves. There were also devotional images, which were later adapted to the St. Damiana 1986 apparition, thus associating the two Mariophanies. Miracle stories have since the 1960s been objects of mass advertising and commercialization. They have engendered a wealth of religious publications and by-products through Church publishers with accredited writers.

Some publications were produced outside ecclesiastical monitoring, through the populist press, pamphlets, and Web sites. These miscellaneous products, which have their Islamic equivalent, stir people's curiosity. They play into religious practices and beliefs shared by devout Muslims and Christians alike. Testimonies to the ecumenical appeal of this literature are sidewalk booklets. One such booklet, which addresses a Muslim audience in its foreword, is a collage of eclectic documents with minimal presentations and minimalist analysis. It emulates the Coptic hagiographies printed since the 1960s.[68]

As Coptic commentaries retrospectively note, one cannot ascertain whether the 1968 Mariophany was the "ultimate recognition of Kyrillus' capacity as a holy man" and a sign that the Mother of Light honored the living saint.[69] One might, however, safely argue that "the greatest miracle of the century" and later Mariophanies functioned as a means of asserting the apostolicism of the Orthodox Church. A complex set of interests motivated the Church to defend the truth of the event and other truths.

Truth and Other Truths

As noted earlier, the patriarchate took its time to investigate the Zaytun case before issuing a statement. Certainly, the patriarch's accountability was at stake, and its opinion had theological implications. In any case, the Church managed the affair with great care. It was important for the spiritual accreditation of the apparition that ordinary people saw the Virgin. Indeed, in contrast to the literati, their hearts are unadulterated by skepticism and other ills brought about by education. But the Church also recognized that their faith might concurrently be considered naive, credulous, and superstitious. Clerical authorities thus needed science to support faith, and the literati to approve commoners' testimonies. This contradiction reveals one of the haunting tensions of modern faith. It embraces epistemics yet deflects its intrinsic positivism.[70]

The Church gathered its theological experts in miraculous matters and, when relevant, joined forces with secular authorities. In their quest for the "truth of the event," the Church and its advisors indicated their rational, logical, and scientific approach to the supernatural phenomenon and its satellites, such as the nocturnal doves and wondrous cures.

The media mentioned the education and social rank of witnesses in several instances, including the faculty student, Riyab Najib; the lawyer, Zaki Shanuda; and the benevolent professor, Sonia Labib. Believers counted among them many men and, less so, women of knowledge. Among these were physicians, lawyers, students, and the like. Muslims provided an additional guarantee of objectivity inasmuch for their faith as for the national unity that their support demonstrated.

Bishop Gregorius headed the investigation committee with the assistance of Fawzi Mansur, the pope's hagiographer, who "[gathered] documents and information on the appearance of the Holy Virgin" and for the "verification of the miracles." In 1967 His Grace Kyrillus VI had judiciously nominated Gregorius as Bishop of Higher Coptic Studies. The bishop, known for his theological work, was a man of both religion and science. He had helped create the Coptic Institute of Higher Studies in 1954 and publish a "final and exhaustive text of the Holy Book." He purportedly founded as well a "huge scientific organization for the establishment of a Coptic encyclopedia" and ambitiously attempted "to restore" the oral tradition of "Coptic chants."[71]

> Father Gregorius, President of the Committee, said that the committee had asked all those who saw the Virgin's spirit to write down *clear* reports recounting what they witnessed with *precision*, to make of these reports testimonies on the *veracity* of the event of the manifestation of the Holy Virgin. . . . Then, [the witness] will have to write down his name, his address and age, so that each witness will bear—as Father Gregorius says—the responsibility of this *historical* testimony, that the orthodox church will present to future generations.[72]

Scientific advisers reviewed these testimonies and only "the cases confirmed by the doctors' reports" were retained. Ecclesiastical releases included the "reports of the men of religion responsible for the verification of the event" and then the approved accounts of witnesses.[73] Father Gregorius ensured that the Church's scientific method of inquiry was sound, as two triads of physicians and psychologists examined "clear" and "precise" evidence through systematic observation, analysis, and interpretation. As in other churches, witnesses' miraculous experiences had to conform to the norms set by iconography, liturgy, hagiographies, scriptures, and tradition integrated into historical time. These norms defined the truth and rightfulness of miraculous experiences, and the typology of extraordinary phenomena.[74]

Rejections are equally part of the process by which the clergy shows its phenomenological standards. After a woman named Marcelle reported seeing the Virgin at her home, ecclesiastical authorities were able to prove their methodological rigor. They discarded Marcelle's account. This case illustrated that conformity to tradition was a precondition for scientific and historical knowledge. *Al-Ahram* reported:

> We read the story told by the citizen Marcelle about the visit of the Virgin in her home, after which "foam" appeared on her son's mouth, and [when she wiped] the foam from his mouth with a handkerchief, it left the print of a palm, with a cross in the middle. . . . The following day, the pope issued an unequivocal denial of this story, while confirming other remaining stories . . .
>
> There is no definite time for miracles, they exist, they can happen any day, at any moment. . . . What is unacceptable is to profit from faith. . . . And this is what happened in the case of the story recounted by the citizen Marcelle. . . . The investigation revealed that there was an order of evacuation and demolition pending on the place in which this lady resided, because it was [about to] collapse.[75]

As in Catholicism, the Church's "central concern, however, [was] whether an apparition [was] of divine or diabolical origin."[76] The committee's inquiry disclosed the discrepancies between Marcelle's story and how holy things "normally" happen.[77] According to scriptural tradition, the Virgin's apparition "does not necessitate the window to open," the committee professed. Marcelle should have known better than to describe her window as yielding to "a destructive violent wind." As a rule, the Virgin appeared as a "delicate breeze," the committee said. This divergence established the speciousness of Marcelle's vision. The committee's judgment was further positively, empirically, and scientifically confirmed. Analyses showed that the "blood on the handkerchief was not real and [the pope] warned the faithful not to believe everything they hear."[78]

Possibly more than the fake blood and the evacuation order, Marcelle's heterodoxy proved fatal to the authentication of her account. In the typology of visions, Marcelle's testimony fit the oh-so-human type: it combined good and evil. Examiners could have simply denounced Marcelle as a charlatan. But they issued a harsher punishment by concluding that her vision had "dubious," devilish origins. Marcelle had abused sacred and ecclesiastical domains.

She had faked an ability that even saintly monks reluctantly report, lest they be thought immodest.[79] Eventually, Marcelle's story proved that the Church could distinguish between fraudulent and genuine mirabilia. It demarcated faith from credulity while combining religious and secular, theological and positivist methods of inquiry.

Blue-Eyed Virgins and Palestinian Maidens

Ultimately, scientific inquiry stopped where the sacred and inviolable started. Some questioned then, as decades later, the conformity of witnesses' descriptions of Marian features to the ecclesiastical iconographical tradition. In fact, there was no such Coptic tradition per se. The cult of Mary was itself a recent development.[80] By the 1960s, however, blonde, blue-eyed pale Virgins originating from European devotional imagery had invaded Coptic Marian pictures. Egyptian iconography and the Zaytun Mariophany thus inscribed the Coptic Church within a global market dominated not only by European Christian aesthetics but also by Western doctrinal trends.

In many places outside Egypt, European representations of Mary gradually replaced earlier symbolism and images of the Theotokos (child-bearing mother). Thus, she now became "an autonomous figure who takes initiatives on behalf of mankind, often intervening in the midst of the economic and political crises characteristic of industrialized mass society."[81] Ecclesiastical and populist interpretations of the '68 apparition as a universal message of peace signaled a similar adaptation of the Virgin in Egypt to mass-market, industrial capitalist society. The Coptic Church integrated global religious trends concomitant with a sense of spiritual identification with the larger Christian community. Concurrently, Zaytun utterances echo the tensions and contradictions regarding the nature and mission of the Apostolic Church and how it is to exist and survive in the competitive doctrinal market.

The iconographic paraphernalia point to shifts in popular piety, too. In 1968 the Virgin appeared alone, arms outstretched and palms open, on Zaytun commemorative medals and devotional pictures and in the Coptic press. This image originates from the vision of a nineteenth-century French Catholic nun, which generated "an image type that became known as the Immaculata of the Miraculous Medallion."[82] This archetype now figures in countless Coptic pamphlets and booklets (see figure 6.3). It signals one of the transformative effects of cultural imperialism and missionary work on Egyptian religious imagination.[83] It also attests to the empowerment of female figures in religious practices, which in turn refract women's enfranchisement.[84] As signaled by Turner and Turner, Marian revivalism and its polyvalent symbolism point to women's changing social roles. Similarly, in Egypt, by the 1960s the Virgin came to embody resilience and struggle, signaling female self-empowerment and social agency. Fertility and motherhood remained important signifiers of femaleness, but they ceased to exclusively define women's function.

Another Catholic iconography, the Mater Dolorosa, which is "very popular in central and southern Europe," also pervades today's Coptic Mariological piety.[85] In 2000 the popular magazine *Akhir Sa'a* reported on the apparition of the Virgin in Asyut and printed side-by-side Coptic and Mater Dolorosa illustrations. Such representations reflect here as well the global market with which indigenous productions compete and which they co-opted. The Islamic paraphernalia similarly offer products aesthetically influenced by global religious fashion and market trends. For instance, high-collar Saudi-style *galabiyas*, Gulf-style *abaya*, or the *hijab* worn along with a miniskirt over opaque stockings redefine Islamic modesty and piety.[86]

While general publications turned to an exogenous iconography in 1968,

Figure 6.3. Devotional image of the 1986 apparition of the Virgin at St. Damiana Church, Papadouplo. Collection of the author.

the Church insisted on the apparition's conformity to ontological biblical representations. The past is everything. In a 1968 inquiry, the outcome of which was predetermined, the press tactfully unveiled iconographic controversies. As the product of human imagination, religious pictures cast doubt on the divinity of an apparition that mimicked them. The question of iconographic and visions' conformity to historical reality was brought back again during the 2009–10 Mariophany. The problem, *Ruz al-Yusuf* recalled, arose back in '68. Displaying the Immaculata of the Miraculous Medallion, the magazine asked: "Does the Virgin appear with European features, as Renaissance artists painted Her, or does She bear the features of a Palestinian maiden from Nazareth?"[87]

In 1968 Father Gregorius reminded skeptics that the sanctioned iconography in fact had a sacred genealogy. Artists were

> without exception, either inspired by the real features of the Virgin, or added them to their pictures, as they appear on the painting executed by St. Luke the Evangelical . . . [who] personally drew the picture of the Holy Virgin, which can still be found today in Jerusalem. . . . The pictures of the Virgin that we presently have are authentic; her features are a copy of the original painting executed more than 1,900 years ago.[88]

Gregorius used arguments rooted in Christian mythology but phrased historically. He emphasized continuity with apostolic testimonies. Such statements not only deny the theological dynamism of the Coptic Church, and any church for that matter, but also rebuff alien Mariological influences. They deny history. The historiography on Coptic liturgical pictographic art points to its heterogeneity in the premodern period. Modern and contemporary liturgical pictography syncretized Byzantine, West European, and indigenous art forms. Today's "tradition" would have its roots in the legacy of late seventeenth- to early eighteenth-century iconographers such as Ibrahim al-Nasikh and Yuhanna al-Armani. The tradition would have received another impulse in the late 1960s to early 1970s under the artistic direction of Isaac Fanus, who prescribed new standards.[89]

The notion of unaltered and authentic culture is largely mythical, anthropologists remind us. But such a notion is a tenet of religion. Gregorius thus defended a mystified religious identity that refuted the "transnational flows of populations, ideas, images, and commodities" that in fact characterize our societies. Indeed, identifications "are hybridized constructions which are crafted out of the materials that are neither entirely local nor entirely global."[90] Marian depictions of the 1960s point to the hybridization of Roman Catholic and Eastern Orthodox models of paraphernalia and imagery that are globally distributed and that flood the Egyptian devotional market. This hybridization suggests that the Coptic doctrine has concurrently been sustaining great theological and social pressures.[91]

Divine Sapience

At the end, however, by declaring the apparition "beyond any need for statement or confirmation," Gregorius' final statement remained one of faith. It set the limits of positivist inquiry where the sacred realm started, precisely when history enters mythical time. By such reasoning, divine sapience informs culture and society. Witnesses thus gave "unanimous" descriptions. This position is in opposition to the idea that culture shapes the forms of the divine, or rather that men shape God in their image. Ecclesiastical authorities formulaically obeyed scientific reasoning while, once more, subordinating science to the divine.

Most importantly, ecclesiastical reasoning posited sacrosanct religious norms ("orthodoxy") as the basis upon which any phenomenon ought to be evaluated as natural, supernatural, human, divine, satanic, true, or false. Science instrumentally verifies religious tradition (Sunna). Modern science's "discovery" of a concordance between scriptures and empirical reality proves the marvelous nature and *hikmah* (wisdom) of sacred texts. When validated, the supernatural phenomenon alternatively might be of divine or "dubious" origin. Here also, malefic phenomena are gauged according to orthodox scriptural standards. The citizen Marcelle was not condemned with a piece of devilry, but her descriptions matched malevolent phenomena. Evidence meant conformity to orthodox iconographic, liturgical, and scriptural representations of the saint. The press laid out this orthodoxy by producing reports of identical events, visions, and scenes. Their uniformity argumentatively confirmed the veracity of the Marian miracle:

> This apparition, [that took place] during many different nights, ended in different forms. Sometimes the complete body [appeared]; sometimes the upper part, surrounded by a halo of glittering light, [which came out] from the dome's apertures, on the roof of the church, and at other times [She appeared] outside the dome, moving and walking above it, bowing in front of the upper cross, as She shed a dazzling light, facing the witnesses and blessing them with Her own hand, and

nodding Her holy head. She sometimes appeared as well with a body that looked like an immaculate white body, or in the form of a light following the emission of ghostly figures, like a very rapid dove. The apparition lasted for a long time. . . . A great number of people agreed on a single description of the scene regarding its shape, location, and the time [of the apparition], while unanimous testimonies described the apparition of the Holy Virgin, Mother of Light.[92]

The press cited a plethora of witness accounts. It gave lively descriptions of gathering crowds in colorful and at times touching modes. It transcribed colloquial and plebeian warmth. Faruq 'Atawa, a bus driver, thus reportedly declared:

> On the night of April 2, I was standing in front of the book of attendance in the garage facing the church. I heard some women in the street shouting obscure words and I came out. . . . I saw our Lady, and She was wearing white clothes standing above the western dome as if, by Herself, She was about to come down onto the street, and I shouted: "Be careful. . . . Wait!" But She did not move from Her place, and one of the people standing exulted that this was the Virgin. I looked more carefully and saw without a doubt that She looked like a nun. . . . And suddenly, a white dove flew over Her. All this lasted a few minutes, after which everything disappeared.

Archpriest Constantine Musa (Moses), pastor of St. Mary's, casually recounted the dramatic setting of the event:

> That's true. This was about two and a half hours after sunset, and I was at home, a few steps away from the church. . . . When 'Ali Ibrahim entered terrified, he said in a shaking voice: "In truth, our Lady . . . the Virgin appeared on top of the dome." So I sent my son Nabil . . . , who came back in no time confirming the news. . . . So I went . . . and I saw Her with my own eyes: a semi-illuminated picture of the Holy Virgin. . . . By then a number of workers [had] tried to overpower the illuminated image with a searchlight, but [they failed]. . . . On the night of April 9, I had no doubt anymore, after I saw Her in full . . . as She appears in Her well-known image, holding the Christ. On April 10, I saw Her a third time, She was also of normal size, but this time, She extended Her hand . . . holding an olive branch, some white doves flying over Her.[93]

This account corroborates the bus driver's testimony. It also shows once more the circumspection of ecclesiastical authorities. The Archpriest had first sent his son in reconnaissance. This act was trivial, but its recording was not. The Zaytun narrative was crafted with an awareness of, and a concern for, its consumers. Public accounts thus maintained in 1968 a discursive equilibrium between skepticism and religious faith. This testimonial has become one of the foundational texts upon which utterances of the 1968 apparition and later Mariophanies continue to be formulated today.

Commodification of the Sacred

As indicated by Archpriest Moses' serial visions of the Virgin in "her well-known" appearance, and as discussed earlier, the Church assimilated an iconography, practices, and beliefs that are part of a transnational Christian consumer culture. The politics of Kyrillus VI, who initiated the ecumenical movement, facilitated this hybridization. But consumer capitalism and culture did too. The boutiques of Coptic churches display global market strategies and trends. Worshippers can purchase videotapes and DVDs about the apparition.[94] The reconstruction of the official Zaytun Web site for the apparition's 2008 anniversary confirms the Church's astute adaptation to new forms of advertisement, technologies, and marketing strategies.

Much has been written on the commodification and commercialization of the sacred.[95] There has also been great speculation as to why, in 1968, the Zaytun miracle was "produced and consumed, what it was used for, what demand it satisfied."[96] People believed in miraculous phenomena as manifestations of divine action. But Zaytun was the first publicly recorded theater of apparition of the Virgin in Egyptian secular history. Here, as in many other places, canonized miracles did not simply replace pagan marvels, and science did not wash away religion. Rather, different spheres of interpretations fulfilled diverse purposes. They complemented one another, hence guaranteeing, in part, their epistemological coexistence. Likewise, the Mariophany's historical utterances dialectically engage and "unfold on more simultaneous levels than a Bach Fugue."[97]

There was and is nonetheless a modern hierarchy of interpretative *bienséance*. The naturally irrational and chaotic world submitted to the absolute judgment of science, if only by contrived reverence. This insistence on scientific methods of inquiry tacitly acknowledges the supremacy of positivist reasoning over cosmological interpretations. The Zaytun "marvel" was codified by political and religious structures, themselves obeying the ritualistic performances commanded by this interpretive hierarchy, including the integration of the Mariophany into historical order. As Le Goff suggested, visions are situated in mythical timelessness. Religious authorities integrated the apparition to metaphysical history (biblical time), state authorities to political history (ideological time),[98] and both religious and state authorities to the moral order.

Whether the miracle took place or not has no relevance here. Reports of the apparition possess historical value. As historian Boaz Shoshan pointed out, hagiographies "tell us what people believed in, and, in their turn, they probably reinforced popular belief." The moralizing and ideological recuperation of the vision certainly leaves no doubt. It had antecedents, too: St. Mary thus historically intervened against Muslim invaders; she converted Jews in late medieval Spain; she also converted the Nahua and others in colonial Mexico.[99]

The 1968 Mariophany shows that the Church conceded science's supervision over spiritual phenomena. It appropriated positivist inquiry. At the same time, it asserted that miracles were natural phenomena that, at the end, escaped scientific explanation. The Church thus reconciled empiricism and metaphysics into the fold of faith. The 1968 and later Mariophanies inform us of believers' spiritual expectations, of their relationship to religious and political institutions, to the global Christian community, and to the Muslim community. As seen in the following chapter, she mediated between Christians and Muslims and reminded the world and the Coptic community that God chose the Coptic Church above all other churches.

7

Globalizing the Virgin, Nationalizing Religion

Supernatural visitation, psychological manipulation, technical artifice, collective hallucination. The aporia that the Zaytun Mariophany has generated since 1968 carries enduring cultural, religious, and ideological implications. Zaytun utterances are as malleable as conceptions of the national community, interfaith relations, spiritual practices, and religious doctrine.

In 1968 some "saw," hundreds of thousands "came to see," others "wanted to see," and some did not bother. Among those who stood together at the same time and place, some did not see, some pretended to see, and others maintained that they truly did see.[1] March and April 1968 unfolded in the shadow of the defeat, widespread protest, and the Nasserian rehabilitation campaign, which insisted on Egypt's eternal renaissance. As dramatically illustrated by artist Jamal Kamal in *Ruz al-Yusuf*, Egypt was to rise again from its ruins.[2] Some people then and now considered the Zaytun phenomenon as a shameless political mise-en-scène that fed on the credulity and vulnerability of Egyptian masses. Conveniently, Zaytun was a lower middle-class and religiously mixed neighborhood.

More than forty years have passed since 1968. Despite lingering 1960s utterances, Mariophany accounts have been largely monopolized by the Church. They have also shifted paradigm as the last 2009–10 Mariophany made very clear. The Virgin now serves new functions. She has been both globalized and nationalized.

The antiquarian varnish and former symbolism of the event still shield, to some extent, those who wish to subvert the meaning of Zaytun. Within three years of the apparition, two national icons died, Nasser (1970) and Kyrillus VI (1971). Two other icons replaced them, Sadat and Shanuda III, who redefined the decade to come in regards to the relationship between state and religion. Within four years of the apparition, intercommunal strife of a new kind appeared in Egypt. This chapter explores the experiences, values, ideas, and feelings that Mariophany utterances and their paradigm shift have been conveying since the Virgin came to Zaytun. It analyzes the discursive motifs of 1968 and subsequent apparitions. Recollections of the 1968 "visitation," I argue, have come to compose the propaedeutics of ecclesiastical self-narratives, particularly in relation to other churches, to Coptic theological and religious identity, to the broader national community, and to positivist modernism. As seen in Coptic celebrations of the fortieth anniversary of the apparition in 2008, these narratives are responses to some aspects of the global modernization process. They also reflect the ethnicization of both Coptic and Islamic religious identities. Thus, the Nasserian past retrospectively becomes a historical moment associated with interconfessional respect and harmony.

Discursive Strategies

The Virgin has visited Egyptian churches and homes a few times now since 1968, although alternating geographical location. Whether they relate collective or individual visions, spiritual or physical healings, stories of the visitations are of two types. The Port Said or Lourdes archetype conveys individual spiritual experiences: a Port Said woman saw the Virgin in 1990, after which she recovered from an incurable disease. Abundant, these stories sometimes reach mainstream and non-exclusively Coptic publications. In mainstream sources, they are confined to the column of wondrous curiosities. Yet most figure only in Coptic periodicals (such as *Al-Watani* or *Al-Kiraza*), pamphlets, and Web sites, with the purpose of edifying readers. The Port Said archetype serves a spiritual purpose. It extols prayer, faith, and everyday divine intervention. In 1990 the patriarch corroborated the Port Said miraculous healing, but he did not authenticate the apparition itself.[3]

The Zaytun archetype in turn relates to collective sightings at Coptic churches with a national reach. This archetype presents a spectrum of issues reaching beyond questions of religion. Coptic publications have reported (conservatively) such occurrences in 1980, 1982, 1983, 1986, 1997, 2000, 2009, and 2011.[4] A few reach mainstream media and garner public attention. The two most widely publicized events were in 1986 and in 2000. The St. Damiana 1986 apparition at a church in Shubra was the first Marian return since Zaytun. In 2000 her apparition at the Church of St. Marc, in Asyut, coincided with the Christian Jubilee (figure 7.1).

People recall other events, too. Rami, a young man in his early thirties, learned in the summer of 1997 that the Virgin had appeared at Shantana al-Hajar, in the Munufiyya region between Quwaysna and Tanta. The appari-

Figure 7.1. Mahmud Salah, "Is this... the picture of the Virgin Mary?" *Akhir Sa'a*, 20 December 2000, 7. By permission of *Akhir Sa'a*.

tion took place on the sixteenth of the Marian month of August. Four times Rami left Cairo with a group of friends, in what seemed a jolly good trip. But neither he nor his friends saw anything. Just a huge light, "a light that could not be man-made." His mother saw, though. "She always does," Rami smiled. Some people saw the Virgin and went: "Look, look!" But Rami still did not see anything, he remembered laughing. The pope did not recognize the apparition anyway, not really. Shanuda remained vague. In 2000 Rami was at a meeting in Toronto. He heard the pope speak. The only apparition the pope recognized was Zaytun. This was a real apparition. She appeared full-bodied. People saw her, not just lights. Rami's mother saw. There was even a huge dove. And all those who attended saw. And it was in all the papers. It was in *Al-Ahram*.[5]

Rami's attitude mixed skepticism and faith. He stood between rationalism and irony, and showed a readiness—even possibly a yearning—to accept spiritual phenomena. Yet there was no irony in the case of Zaytun. Both attitudes were mediated by the story of someone else's spiritual experience. The miracle of Zaytun was "real," yet other phenomena were suspicious ("But did you hear of the Virgin in Asyut?"). Ultimately, Rami trusted the position of the pope, for whom he expressed unmitigated sympathy. Rami interpreted the pope's answers as politically conditioned, but he disagreed with my suggestion that papal pronouncements were cryptic.

1968–1986: An Incurable Darkness

New Mariophanies always bring back the Zaytun story. Many people may have forgotten its location, yet they remember that it happened around the *hazima* (the '67 defeat). Zaytun is the ontological event that foretold a series of "visitations" and is now divorced from its initial ideological context. Preambles to Mariophany stories have maintained almost verbatim both the ontological public discourse on national unity and depictions of accompanying miracles. Post-1968 visitation narratives have also preserved the Church's social and theological capacity as both public depository and interpreter of Marian matters. Neither state nor media dispute today such monopoly. In fact, the semantics of historical utterances depend upon the sphere of discourse in which they are recounted. Thus, public, national, public inter-Christian, intimate, or (Coptic) communal spheres alter acts of speech. Intimate and communal utterances often invert the meaning of the ontological motifs of the Mariophany. "Unity" conveys division, "continuity" signifies discontinuity, and "peace" indicates strife. *Al-Watani*'s January 2012 Christmas issue shows that discursive inversions and indirect allusions are a primary mode of public communication of the distress experienced by the Coptic community.

The "Red" revolutionary Virgin lost a battle she never led. The historical public/national meaning of the story has disappeared. Gone is the Arab-Palestinian revolutionary nationalist Virgin who supported Nasserian reforms and called for the repossession of Arab territories lost to Israel. Today's periodicals and pamphlets never recall this panoplied Virgin. She has become the Virgin of Peace, like her Catholic counterpart. Allusions to the June War are succinct. They serve at best as a historical canvas. More often than not, they reinforce theological interpretations of history that blame the defeat on people's "loss of faith." Like the war itself, Zaytun forecast the return of the nation to spiritual consciousness, prefiguring Egypt's religious renaissance.

Present Mariophany utterances have nonetheless preserved the nucleus of the ontological public/national discourse—interfaith spiritual union—but it has been somewhat modified.[6] Gone are stories of shared devotional practices. Much alive are stories of ideological disagreement, fear, and defamation. Voices yesterday rallying against foreign enemy forces now rise against an internal sedition, which splinters the body of the nation. In the 1970s national intersectarian, intrasectarian, theological, and spiritual divisions refashioned the meaning of the ontological Mariophany. Post-1970s conflicts thus define present interpretations of the 1960s Zaytun events and by extension have redefined vernacular memories of the Nasser years.

As in twentieth-century Roman Catholicism, while a "source of inspiration and strength against heresy and subversion, the cult of the Virgin also underlies dissent and schism."[7] Hence, the intra-Christian discourse mirrors some of the ecclesiastical and theological debates that animate the Christian community and the Coptic Church, for "secessionists" continue to challenge the authority of the Mother Church of Alexandria. Mariophany literature abundantly depicts the return of apostates, who had abandoned religion or the Church and joined "foreign confessions" and "non-Orthodox" Coptic churches and, most threateningly, reformist denominations.

The 1968 scientific "committee of inquiry" offered a defense against the latter case. It sanctioned the authority of the Apostolic Coptic Church, shelter of God's elected people within the communion of saints. It interpreted Marian intercession as a plea against dissension and desertion.[8] The edifying stories of Mariophany accounts thus tell of lost sheep and prodigal sons and caution against "deviances." The emigration of Copts since the 1950s, rising with religious violence in the 1980s–90s, has endangered the social fabric, the religious integrity, and the tenets of the community both domestically and within the diaspora. Shanuda devoted himself to building Coptic churches abroad. The Church thus intends to preserve its extraterritorial spiritual dominion. It has had to adapt its language to the culture and conditions of the diaspora. For example, a pamphlet relates the story of an expatriate who "entertained foolish thoughts" of conversion but came back to his senses after seeing the Virgin in Zaytun: "I went back and looked for a wife from my Church ... far from the foreigners [whom I had dated]."[9]

This story also underscores the ideological centrality of women as keepers of the faith. This patriarchal precept has only been growing since the 1960s, as testified by the political weight of and insistence on endogamy in both Muslim and Christian communities.

Similar to Roman Catholic strategies, through the renewed promotion of the Marian cult and mirabilia, the Coptic Church polemically casts doubts on other denominations. Moreover, mirabilia stories challenge reformist, modernist epistemology.[10] At stake are the conservancy of the Church's doctrinal authority and integrity but also metaphysical notions of the laws of nature on which the Church and other denominations depend.

Equally defying modernist systems of thought are intracommunal narratives, verbalized in chosen circles and encrypted in Mariophany tales that contradict statements of national unity. Combining theological, religious, and political meaning, this category of discourse denounces the injustice, discrimination, and violence directed against the Coptic community. Allusions, incongruous appositions, and the crying presence of events and characters often reveal the line between the lines. I asked Yusif, a Coptic custodian in his thirties, why the Virgin had appeared throughout the 1980s and 1990s: "Why 1981? I understand 1968, but 1981, why?" "Because there were things going on," Yusif answered allusively, not esoterically. In public speeches, the Church uses Coptic communal utterances, such as historiographical tradition, as allusion. Thus spoke the Patriarch of holy apparitions: "History abounds with many examples of holy apparitions.... Saint Ignatius of Antioch ... appeared after his martyrdom to his colleagues who were with him in prison and he empowered them and gave them strength. Thus appeared the Virgin, and Saint George, and many other saints ... dispensing miracles and acts of mercy."[11]

When examples abound, why choose a paradigm of martyrdom, of fidelity to clergy and doctrinal orthodoxy? Why St. Ignatius' address to his captive companions? "Thus appeared the Virgin": in similar fashion or under similar circumstances? The clergy thus talks through saints, scriptures, and tradition, especially about religious persecution.

Miracles and other stories are a supplication for faith and unity that play both into the theological praise of redemption through suffering and into the religious historiography of Coptic martyrdom. They are a rallying call against persecution, heterodoxy, and apostasy. They underscore the uniqueness of Coptic history, too. They further assess the superiority of the Church over other denominations: all apparitions occurred at Coptic sites. They strengthen Coptic communal identity while revitalizing tradition. The pathos of martyrdom, persecution, and alienation reinforces here the political, rather than the spiritual, cohesion of the group. Here again, the past is everything.

The Age of Miracles Is Over

Collective visions stopped under the presidency of Anwar al-Sadat (1971–81), although the Virgin was much in need. This period was wracked by religious intolerance, governmental confrontations with the patriarchate, exponential economic inflation, economic hardships, and growing social disparities.[12] Sadat expressed his personal sympathy for Copts, but he co-opted Islamists. Political and scripturalist Islam gained open access to mainstream media, and its proponents strengthened their ideological influence. This context stimulated the patriarchate's political activism, which Sadat treated as religious chauvinism. To Sadat, the patriarchate's political positions amounted to a war declaration. This conflict broke open in September 1981, a month before the president's assassination. Sadat incarcerated numerous intellectuals and political figures and confined the pope to house arrest in the monastery of St. Bishoi.[13] After 1968 the Egyptian government did not sponsor any more Mariophanies or any other miracle. Mariophanies had become a divisive topic rather than an ecumenical symbol.

The political use of the Virgin as national icon in 1968 was hazardous in the first place. Despite her veneration in Islam, the saint remains a core figure of Christianity. Moreover, Marian veneration is controversial within Christianity itself, as Sadiq al-'Azm noted, let alone the "substantial" theological differences between Islam and Christianity. Her most common Christian attribute, "Mother of God," is anathema to Muslims. The absence of son or mother of God in Zaytun utterances demonstrates the uncomfortable truth of religious divergences between the two faiths.[14] Muslim scripturalist militants, who loathe the cult of saints and religious syncretism in general, gained ideological ascendancy in the 1980s. They used miracles as proof of the religious incompatibility between "rational" Muslims and "superstitious" Copts, invalidating the Church's central tenet. Marian stories were from then on left to the discretion of polarized mass media.

The fortieth anniversary of Zaytun in 2008 went almost unnoticed in the mainstream media. In December 2009, when rumors spread of a new apparition in Giza, south of Cairo, which lasted into January 2010, mainstream newspapers focused on religious controversies. Wasn't the age of miracles over? Doesn't Satan customarily appear in the shape of saints? Was it appropriate for Muslims to visit the Giza church?[15] Should Christmas be banned in Islamic countries?[16] These debates have remained alive and well at the time of this writing. One year after the Giza Mariophany, on New Year's Eve 2010, a bomb exploded in Alexandria at the Church of St. Marc. It claimed twenty-five lives and wounded many more. Theopolitical discussions about banning Christmas again populated the mainstream media during Christmas 2012.

In 1968 as in 2011, politicians and nationalists, such as Muhammad Hasanayn Haykal, are prone to blame extremist and foreign elements. All avoid troublesome discussions about civil inequities. Despite—and because of—this climate, Mariophanies continue to provide "encouragement in dark times" to the mystically inclined, as do apocryphal stories and revelations "put in ancient mouths."[17]

In the 1980s, when Mariophanies resurfaced in rather dark times, the Virgin had remained God's preferred mediator. In a tense atmosphere, a 1985 pamphlet by Rev. Father Boutros Gayed, then rector of the Zaytun church, recalled the Virgin's customary role. It cited the Zaytun apparition to illustrate Egyptians' historical communion. Conventionally using edifying and heuristic stories, the publication cited, in one instance, a Muslim woman who had sought Presira's intercession for her husband's return and her child's healing. God heard her prayers. In another instance, a Muslim man broke into an irrational rage against Copts and entered a church. But the Virgin appeared to him. She first scolded him and then calmed him down. Repentant, the man apologized to the priest. The pamphlet additionally cites miracles set during the 1973 War that honor the patriotism of Coptic combatants of both the infantry and the high command. Miracle stories thus counter Islamist accusations of disloyalty and conspiracy that thrived during the 1970s and 1980s and that seemingly predate this period.[18] Marian narratives thus play the role of social mediation and intercession on earth. They are also a means of political empowerment for a diminished and dispersed community.[19]

In 1986 mainstream media spectacularly advertised for the first time since 1968 the first Marian return. It took place at the Church of St. Damiana and Her Forty Virgins in the Papadouplo district of Shubra. This neighborhood was sociologically similar to Zaytun.[20] The national publicity hints at a rapprochement between church and state.²¹ But within the realm of intimate and communal utterances, St. Damiana also helped Coptic interests. By the 1980s the collective repository of the Zaytun recollections had indeed tapered.

Coptic publications sustain that visitations had started a few years earlier before and after Sadat's assassination (such as Nabruh in 1980 and Edfu in 1982). These utterances link the Mariophanies to the patriarch's political confinement. The nationally publicized Shubra event followed the release of Shanuda, the pope returning to the head of his congregation in January 1985. In the 1960s both state and Church nationalized the Virgin. In the 1980s the Church reappropriated her for itself. Within a decade, the Holy Mother of Egypt went through a dual process of indigenization.

St. Michael Wore a *Galabiya*

The indigenization and nationalization of saints is a widespread socioreligious phenomenon. In Latin America the indigenization of St. Mary—most notoriously the Virgin of Guadalupe—helped spread Catholicism. Across Christian sects mausoleums as well as pictorial representations of saints are means of territorializing faith. The belief espoused by Copts and Catholics alike that saints inhabit their icons strengthens this appropriation. Thus, in 1995 and 1996 an indigenized Archangel Michael wearing a *galabiya* appeared in the region of Sharqiyya.²²

Church and state nationalized the Virgin in the 1960s by anchoring her topographically and historically to national space. The Church later indigenized the Virgin by rooting her to Coptic sacred space (Zaytun, Shubra, Asyut, Warraq al-Hadar) and history (contemporary tradition and martyrology). This monopolization took place on different fronts: theological reinvention, ecclesiastic reforms, Mariophany publicity and marketing, and so on. The Coptic Church thus claims the land of Egypt as its own. Simultaneous national and communal appropriations are theoretically compatible. God indeed chose Egypt above all nations; Christianity is Coptic and Egyptian; and catholic historical precedence does not exclude tolerance toward Muslims. This monopolization was nonetheless manifest during the fortieth anniversary of Zaytun.²³

Apocryphal writings and apostolic dreams and visions, such as the "Flight of the Holy Family" narrative, fortify this monopolization.²⁴ Each new visit of the Virgin since '68 occurred in a new location later identified by the Church as a halting place of the Holy Family during its escape to Egypt. Shortly mentioned in the Gospel of St. Matthew (Matt 2: 13–15), the route became an object of commemoration in the Coptic Church between the fourth and the seventh centuries CE. Today's mythical topography would be based on a medieval script. In the late nineteenth century, as their economic prosperity swelled, Copts added to the route a number of halting places, especially in Cairo and the Delta. Later, in the early twentieth century, religious patrons also erected new shrines and restored old ones, which they grafted to the route based on their ancientness.[25] As a result, they redrafted the topography of the sacred in time and fashion similar to the remapping of the Holy Land. In the process the Coptic community and the Church extended biblical territory and nationalized Christianity itself. When did the flight become a central doctrine? When did it become part of a broader Coptic imagination? How new is the theological link between twentieth-century Marian visitations and the flight? Opinions are divided on the question.[26] Whatever the case is, the route hallows Egypt, but it also functions as a testament to Coptic historicity, asserting Coptic precedence over the Muslim community. Thus, Zaytun and later Mariophanies authenticated not only the route but also historical and spiritual seniority.

One finds evidence of the secularization of the flight story in Nasserian primary school textbooks as early as 1955 (the Holy Family "passed by") and with greater emphasis in 1963 (the Holy Family "stayed one or two years").[27] In 1968 the secular media firmly established through Zaytun the correspondence between contemporary visitations and the route. The religious belief was widespread by the late 1970s.[28] Historicized, it composes today a central motif of ecclesiastical and Coptic communal utterances. The Ministry of Tourism, the Coptic Church, and foreign-language papers capitalize on the story. They advertise the route to tourists. They promote Mariophany sites as historical heritage. Religious tourism's revenues are an incentive for maintaining healthy relations between religious and state institutions.[29] While some Coptic sites might receive more attention these days from foreign than Egyptian tourists, as a novel by Baha' Tahir bemoans,[30] Zaytun remains a twice sacred domestic site of pilgrimage.

In some respects the Virgin's indigenization dissociates the Coptic community from the larger national community. It also helps the Coptic Church vie with other denominations. Simultaneously, it indicates the fragility of the Egyptian social fabric because it belies the conventional narrative of unity and harmony that structures Mariophany stories and any official discussion of interfaith relations.

Table 7.1. Mariophanies in the national press, 1968–2000

Date	April 1968	March 1986	February 1990	1997	August 2000
Site of the Mariophany	St. Mary Church, Zaytun (Cairo)	St. Damiana Church, Shubra (Cairo)	St. Bishoi Church, Port Said	St. Mary's Church, Shantana al-Hajar (Munufiyya)	St. Marc Church, Asyut
Press references (not exclusive)	*Al-Ahram* *Al-Musawwar* *Al-Watani*	*Al-Watani*	*Ruz al-Yusuf* *Al-Watani*	*Al-Ahram Weekly*	*Akhir Sa'a* *Sabab al-Khayr* *Cairo Times*
Type of event and message	Collective vision; national revival and unity; condemnation of Israel Divine support to Egypt in times of hardship	Collective vision	Only a couple of witnesses; apparition followed by miraculous healing of one seer and weeping icon Site of the apparition is on the road of the Holy Family's visit The people of Egypt are blessed	Collective vision	Collective vision; national unity; Pope's position vis-à-vis Asyut diocese and "miracle" Condemnation of terrorism Affirmation of orthodoxy
Historical or political context	1967 defeat; demonstrations against the Nasserian government; Nasser's March 30 speech and political plebiscite	Confessional tensions and violence between Muslims and Copts; political tension between Coptic church and government; Pope released from house arrest the previous year (January 1985)	Specific context unknown	Riots between Muslim village residents and Christian visitors	Celebrations of the Holy Family's visit in Egypt New millennium

Narration and Validation

As noted earlier, 1968 utterances have set the elementary structure and motifs of later Mariophany narratives for the 1986–2009 period, between the first nationally mediatized recurrence in Shubra and the last one in Giza.[31] Pope Shanuda III himself declared his "[contentment] with the account [*dhikr*] recorded for us by the Church synaxarion on her first visit to her Church of Zaytun, as a living example for the rest of her visitations to churches."[32] However, Mariophany and Limby utterances alike are polysemic. Mariophany stories' semantics and structure hence display ecclesiastical precepts, Islamic and Coptic doctrinal positions, and religious politics. They share the following motifs and structure:

- Have a Muslim "announcer" (bus driver in 1968, witness in 1997, church guardian in 2000; church custodian and coffee shop employee in 2009)
- Different site each time, later identified as halt of the Holy Family in Egypt
- Collective vision—crowds first authenticate miracle
- Ecumenical transcendental experience (faith, class, nationality)
- Identical physical features since 1968 (blue and white gown, Immaculata)
- Silent
- Nocturnal
- Identical accompanying miracles since 1968 (the appearance of doves and light, the occurrence of miraculous cures, such as restored sight, restored speech, healed of diseases)
- Papal designation of special Committee of Inquiry; local parish refers to pope
- No papal visit
- Delayed papal judgment
- Church-approved evidence evaluated by Pope (testimonies in 1968; same plus videos and photographs in 2000 and 2009)
- Recognition of apparition by committee (diverse levels of endorsement, but always "familiarity")
- Papal approval of committee's statement after careful evaluation
- Logistics and security managed by political authorities
- Clergy not surprised—miracles are part of everyday life, but people do not pay attention

The first motif is critical, for these Muslim announcers mediate between Muslims and Christians. The "man who broke the story"[33] in 1968 and "who was the first one to announce the apparition of a white light moving very slowly above the domes of the church of Zaytun" was "the driver Faruq Muhammad from the Public Transports."[34] Faruq purportedly mistook the ghostly apparition on the roof for a distressed woman.[35] Often mentioned in recollections of the event and in media and religious pamphlets, Faruq is the initial messenger and conveyer of the miracle. Later witnesses confirm his vision.

Naturally, being Muslim outsiders, Faruq and the announcers of 1997, 2000, and 2009 bore greater authority as witnesses: "at the beginning, it was a simple bus driver who noticed her; and he was himself a Muslim: so there was no reason why he would make things up."[36] In 2000 both the announcer and the church guardian were Muslims. This narratively serves as communion but also as a reminder of Islam's customary protection of non-Muslims. Faruq's modest social background reinforced the sense of authenticity of his account. Here again, colloquial, verbatim, humble speech functions narratively as authentic and sincere (rather than true) testimony. Humble speech also facilitates the reader's identification with the narrator. In addition to using these mainstream media strategies, the Coptic press also builds validation on (more or less authoritative) foreign-language sources. *Al-Watani*, more than any other source, thus cites non-Arabic Egyptian publications and second-rate foreign newspapers, in the fashion of populist religious pamphlets.

Seers' collective urban experience (1968, 1986, 2000, 2009) further distinguishes the Egyptian apparitions from their international, mainly rural counterparts.[37] It facilitates the social ("simple souls and influential people"), confessional, and national ecumene of the event. As in the 1968 scripts, Mina Thabat, *Akhir Sa'a*'s reporter of the 2000 Asyut apparition, recounted that the viewers were from "a variety of denominations, classes, cultures, nationalities, religions, and denominations . . . press agencies' foreign correspondents and Upper Egyptians in *galabiya* . . . university youth . . . pupils . . . visitors from both rural areas and cities . . . doctors and generals, government employees from all trades . . . simple souls and influential people . . . the epitome of the whole of Egypt!"[38] Thabat's descriptive contrasts have the effect of formulaically praising the religious and social heterogeneity of the nation. Simultaneously, it reproduces and sanctions a stereotypical social order (rural and urban; army, literati, bureaucracy, and peasantry).

The uniformity of testimonies regarding the appearance and message of the Virgin validates the spiritual experience of seers themselves. Seers unanimously described a Virgin who sometimes moves but never talks. Fortunately, the Church speaks in her stead. Silently, she reaches out to the crowds and establishes personal contacts with worshippers, responding to individual prayers, as the Virgin does. Descriptive uniformity also reflects the standardization of ecclesiastical and vernacular imaginations of the Virgin, even though seers sometimes convey atypical visions.[39] In the 2000 visitation, when asked about Marian "features," an elderly witness who might have remembered St. Mary's 1968 Arab nationalist garb hence replied: "Always ... she wore a white gown and a blue cloak ... and she appeared with the features of a young Oriental woman ... from Palestine."[40] The Virgin thus appeared to him in her sanctioned Immaculata garb, yet as a Canaanite.

Figure 7.2. Immaculata of Zaytun keychain. Collection of the author.

Most testimonies do not Orientalize the Virgin but rather concur on the form and nature of the Mariophany. This indicates again both the theological standardization of Coptic Mariology and Roman Catholic influence. Religious paraphernalia in today's Coptic market demonstrate the pictorial standardization generated by global Christian commercialization (see figure 7.2). The elderly witness thus recalls that "One of the elders of the Christian men of religion—from the Catholic denomination—told [him] that the apparitions of the Holy Virgin Mary were always connected with a message, and this message was always: peace, love, and penitence."[41]

Peace, Love, and Penitence

Ultimate validation for the *communitas* emanates from the pope. In 1968 Kyrillus authenticated the miracle after about a month. In 1986 it took about a year for the Commission of Inquiry to draft its report and for the pope to ratify it. In August 2000 St. Mary visited Asyut when the pope was abroad. He described the apparition as "a message of comfort from heaven and one of confirmation of the faith of Copts that heaven is aware of their struggle and is pleased by their perseverance."[42] The patriarch approved the conclusions of the Committee of Inquiry on 10 December 2000 and shared its reservations as well.[43]

In 2000 and 2009 authentication was built on new forms of proof. Eyewitness accounts and healing miracles did not suffice as they did earlier. Modern technology and visual evidence now had to validate "signs."[44] Thus, Pope Shanuda recognized divine intercession but expressed reservations as to whether the 2000 phenomenon was a Marian apparition. Immediately after the events he declared:

> Based upon what I saw in a video recording...: it consisted of a very dazzling light, stronger than any normal light, and disappearing.... That is, it wasn't a light that lasted a very long, long, long time, no. Once on the steeple, once on the dome, and once on the façade, etc. Of course, the appearance of a light of this kind is, without doubt, something divine, a spiritual phenomenon, especially when this light totally illuminated the cross. So, this is matter for rejoicing.... This matter points to a divine apparition. But a Virgin, no. I can't say that a light on the steeple, on the façade, and on the cross is the Virgin.... My opinion remains based upon what happened at the date of this video.[45]

In view of video recording and with circumspection, the pope restricted himself to declaring his "familiarity" with the phenomena in 2000 as in 2009. Clouds of light and doves indeed commonly accompany Mariophanies. Bishop Picenti declared his "familiarity" with the picture of the Virgin published in *Al-Ahali* but expressed caution too. In December 2009, the pope said the Giza phenomenon was a "blessing." But he reserved further qualifications prior to analyzing the full evidence.[46] Ultimately, and beyond religious politics, Mariophany utterances thus indicate the Church's assimilation of exogenous theological tenets and positivist concepts of truth while it formally insists on its fundamentalist biblical position.

The Monosemy of Modern Identities

Other Marian utterances disclose the Church's embrace of another modern axiom that is both archaic and potent today but was absent from 1968 utterances: sectarianism. This axiom appears in the speeches accompanying the 2008 Zaytun commemoration, which took place between 31 March and 3 April 2008. None of the newspapers that had publicized the apparition of 1968 now announced the forthcoming anniversary of 2008, except for *Al-Watani*.[47] Even the magazines that generously covered the 1986 and 2000 apparitions (*Akhir Sa'a* and *Hilal*) remained silent.[48] A few papers, the local mainstream *Al-Qahira News*, as well as both the English and the French weekly editions of *Al-Ahram*, ran articles *after* the commemoration. The independent paper *Al-Masri al-Yawm* announced the coming anniversary, but it also questioned the veracity of both the apparition and Coptic theology. *Al-Masri* thus quoted a Protestant "expert" opinion according to which the "system" used the phenomenon as "lure" and "anesthetics" following the defeat.[49] A 1968 *Ruz al-Yusuf* illustration by Salah al-Laythi, "Miracles at the Church of Our Lady the Virgin in Zaytun," displayed the ambivalence of the event, depicting a character brandishing a banner that read "Problems of the Middle East."[50]

People attended the 2008 celebrations in vast numbers, though. It took three hours for the pope to part the crowds and reach the cathedral.[51] *Qahira* only printed a couple of lines on the festivities but offered a thorough narrative of the '68 event. It seemingly mixed past and present news and testimonies.[52] *Al-Watani* ran a speech delivered by the late Father Gregorius sometime after the event (it is not dated): "To the church of Zaytun rushed tens of thousands of people of all colors, gender, religion, and language. . . . *Prec-*

edents to the apparition: In and of itself, the apparition of the Virgin Mary is not a new event, especially in our country to which the sky has bestowed ample blessings in the past. God favored it more than any other country in the world."[53]

Not new, yet unique, banal, yet serious, it was a Coptic history familiar with the miraculous especially in times of adversity, conversions, and newborn believers. One recognizes '68 elementary motifs. Nevertheless, the citation contained new inflections. God "favored Egypt more than any country in the world," and the Coptic Church above all. Most of all, Gregorius' speech wittily betrays the diplomatic tension with the Roman Catholic Church: "When journalists and reporters from news agencies contacted us asking whether the Vatican had authenticated the apparition of the Virgin in Zaytun, I was smiling; I was amazed by such inquiry. And I said: 'When we saw the Virgin with our own eyes, what need is there for the Vatican to authenticate the vision while [the Vatican] is thousands of miles away!?'"[54]

Gregorius thus derides Catholic supremacy and spiritual authority. The passage reproduced by *Al-Watani* in 2008 is noticeably more ecumenically "Christian" than forty years earlier. "And those who doubted went," *Al-Watani* reported, "saw, and came back believing not only in the apparition, but in God, in the world, in the spirit, in the hereafter, in judgment day, in reward, in punishment, and in all the Christian values." In the description of crowds, "color" and "gender"—markedly North American cultural speech categories—occupy the narrative place that faith once held. In 1968 *Al-Ahram* had mentioned "several thousand citizens, from different religions and confessions [had] witnessed this appearance." In 2008 the *Weekly* referred to "thousands of Copts," in contrast with the masses of "Christians and Muslims alike" of 1968.[55] As a result, one reads with circumspection the narrative hierarchy of Gregorius' proclamation that "all knew for certain that they were in front of a significant event [in 1968], which certainly forecast momentous matters [threatening] the future of our Church, the country, and the whole humanity." Thus, "a herald and a warning of events soon to befall [Egypt] and the Middle East, and in the far future the whole of humankind," the Zaytun apparition forecast the future rather than the present.[56] The message selected by *Al-Watani* in 2008 and the Zaytun celebrations have become distinctly sectarian.

While the media did not make much of the 2008 commemoration, mainstream newspapers mentioned Zaytun in May and June 2008, when it became a site of violence. In place of Mariophanies past, the media evoked the ghost of 1970s sectarian strife.[57] More than a year later, the announcement of a new apparition in Giza engendered virulent press debates and "[drew] the ire of skeptics. The media especially appeared either disbelieving or wishing to disbelieve."[58] The reception of the Warraq apparition thus signals the loss of Zaytun's ecumenical potency.[59] Sectarian strife now haunts Egyptian society. Mariophany utterances not only do not conjure up national concord but, to the contrary, miracle stories in the media underscore sectarian divergences.

Communitarian unity comes with shared practices, all stories tell. In the 1950s–60s people shared in syncretic religious performances or in stories thereof, particularly in places with mixed communities, such as Zaytun or Shubra. Even though this intimacy is not without ambivalence, stories and experiences of religious and spiritual familiarity enable solidarity. However, stories and rites of social intimacy have largely disappeared. Crystallizing national ecumene and the loss thereof are 1956 utterances. Here, in Raf'at 'Adli's remarks, the Virgin meets the Limby:

> *And this was also one of these great moments. Everybody loved each other. This is a thing that we totally lack today. Everybody . . . neighbors opened their door to one another. There was no such thing as Muslim or Christian, not at all. It did not exist.*[60]

Egyptian communitarian belonging surpasses, in 'Adli's account, religious loyalties. It reproduces the 1950s and 1960s as a period of interconfessional unity.

M. B.   *There were no groups? Muslims or Christians?*
Raf. A.   *No, nobody. . . . All my friends were Muslims. All my friends. In this period, from school to . . . I did not think over it, a friend is a friend, and that's all. Even in college, I was in love with a Muslim girl.*[61]

This memory of unity contrasts with the sectarian individuation of today. People now apprehend mingling with shrines and symbols of the other faith:

M. B.   *Do you know whether in Shubra Muslims went to church?*
Raf. A.   *A lot, there were a lot. There were . . .*
M. B.   *On what occasions?*
Raf. A.   *There are until now, there are until now. But of course, they act with fear. They fear other people.*
M. B.   *Today?*
Raf. A.   *Of course. Today a Muslim, even if he feels, for example, if he loves the Virgin, and venerates her, and wants to light a [votive] candle*

for her . . . he'd also fear that somebody saw him. Today, there is no trust between one another. And there are feelings that "no, this is this and that is that." This is not right. . . . When you become. . . . That's the shame of our times, of course.

M. B.   *People, some time ago, in the 50s and 60s, Muslims of that time would they go to any church? Was there any particular church they would go to?*

Raf. A.   *Any churches. Even Coptic churches like St. George, and the churches of the Virgin, they went there all the time . . . [St. Theresa], the church of the Virgin Mary, and they went to the Icon of the Virgin, to light a votive candle. This was very normal.*

M. B.   *This was normal?*

Raf. A.   *Totally normal.*[62]

Historically, the polysemy of devotional practices—polytheist, Christian, and Islamic—organized around religious sites, shrines, and rites has existed in many places outside Egypt.[63] Indubitably, polysemy entails ritual and theological and spiritual boundaries. Copts did not ordinarily visit mosques, for, as 'Adli explains,

to some extent there was nothing, like, nothing in a mosque, nothing to make vows, except for Sayyida Zaynab. There was nothing to light up a candle, the tradition of lighting a candle, in mosques, there is no such thing, what would a Christian do if he came in?[64]

However, Christians frequented and made vows at Muslim saints' mausoleums, such as Sayyida Zaynab. They attended mulids (birthdays of holy figures). Muslims sometimes accompanied Copts in their fast during the Marian month. At other times they joined in Christmas celebrations, as recounted by novelist Baha' Tahir in his story of an Upper Egyptian Orthodox monastery:[65] "In my boyhood . . . my father used to take me along with him on Palm Sunday and on the 7th of January (the Coptic Christmas) to offer holiday greetings to the monks. Among the boxes packed with cookies that my mother used to charge me with delivering on the occasion of our Lesser Feast was 'the monastery's box.'"[66]

At mausoleums, in churches, at religious festivals, people acted out rituals that, like the Limby, were without masters. People were spiritually united by their shared recourse to talismans and religious figures, which catered to their secular concerns. Raf'at 'Adli observes:

When I was in Shubra, we went to the neighbor who lived upstairs, the Hagg Mustafa and ... his daughters, and we spent the entire evening there. His daughter believed so much in St. George, that when she got sick, a miracle happened to her from St. George, and we went upstairs to see this miracle, and how she was healed and all her clothes had been anointed with crosses of blood. ... I saw her! She was a Muslim called Fatima. This was not at all something reserved, not at all [for Christians].[67]

Those shared spiritual practices and beliefs, which formed a social ground on which communities met in the 1950s–60s, have today largely become unorthodox, shameful, potentially socially harmful, and ideologized. In addition to the erosion of syncretic devotional spaces, religious scripturalism has deepened confessional alienation.

Literal religious interpretations—according to which, in the astute words of 'Adli, "this is this, and that is that," which proscribe vernacular religious practices—have gained Muslim and Christian sympathizers alike. Viola Shafik situates a religious paradigm shift within the Coptic Church in the 1970s. In her 1998 documentary *Umm al-Nur wa-banatiha* [The Mother of Light and Her Daughters], she traces the roots of Coptic revivalism in the 1950s monastic movement. It produced a new, highly educated clergy that was more prone to scriptural interpretations.[68] Religious revivalism and scripturalism were the expression of structural socioeconomic mutations, which produced an "urban bourgeois educated religiosity." Its emphasis on text and its denigration of vernacular rituals gained momentum in the 1970s. Belief in the "truth" of scriptures (Torah, gospels, Qur'an, tradition) easily leads to rejecting competitive interpretations. It encourages theological uniformity and monosemy.

Religious literate scripturalism is a modernist ideology, for it posits the power of religious and secular science and methodology to reveal God's will. It embraces the modernist distinction between religion and superstition. Scripturalist religiosity further demands individuation because objective, material boundaries and categories are the foundation of modern epistemology. What follows is that the idea of a homogeneous religious ideology and practice is "modern and largely mythical."[69]

The 1950s–60s provided a fertile soil for cultural myths of theological uniformity, according to which (theological) identity = (religious) reality, "as if, in the end, everything must necessarily and absolutely be one and the same." The Nasser state embraced modernization theories, positivist science, urbanization, industrialization, and the homology between cultural uniformity and national realization. The Free Officers reacted in part to what they perceived as the denaturalization and fragmentation of colonial society. They aspired to restore national authenticity through Arab-Islamic nationalism and the monitoring of educative, social, and religious organizations under the umbrella of the military, the ASU, and its satellites. But the Nasserian republic failed to create binding civil rituals. The state borrowed republican forms but left out their content. Its coercive strategies profoundly influenced later and present articulations of communitarian identities.

"The Love That Was There"

Sectarian politics were not a novel concept in 1970s Egypt. Yet the domestic and international conjuncture helped their ascent. Some trace back the sectarian divide in the 1930s–40s to the rise of the Muslim Brotherhood. Others argue that 1950s–60s Arab-Islamic nationalism and the attack against Christian elites caused a confessional alienation that surfaced after the '67 breakdown.[70] All concur that, starting in the nineteenth century, non-Muslim communities enjoyed social and economic opportunities and favors that resulted, in the twentieth century, in their disproportionate representation in national institutions.[71] King Faruq's government counted a majority of Copts. Christian fortunes indeed benefited from their association with European interests and the privileges (tax exemptions, foreign passports) that derived from it.[72] But did the majority of Christians enjoy these benefits? Did the primary loyalty of the Christian elite lie with their coreligionists or with their social class?

In the 1950s–60s the July revolutionaries effectively demoted the Christian elite by purging the state of the individuals associated with the monarchy, by establishing a one-party system, and by sequestrating and nationalizing private lands and property.[73] Wafd reforms further damaged a community dependent on the social and economic capital of the wealthy and on ecclesiastical services.[74] Some have convincingly argued that this demotion caused a transfer of Coptic social identification from secular to ecclesiastical authorities coinciding with the ascension of a reformed, more political clergy.[75] The Nasserian state thus ideologically supported civil equality but institutionally eroded the civil and social emancipation of Christian commoners in majority rural folks.

Secular nationalism in the 1950s presumably protected Christian citizens, though. Nasser treated with equal deference the rector of al-Azhar and the pope. Muslim and non-Muslim properties and elites were equally hurt by Nasserian policies. Educational reorganizations affected the entire educational system. Curricular homogenization and restrictions aimed to bridge cultural and social divides. In a 2011 article a Nasserist, Nasser's son-in-law, thus echoed the old idea that (generic) colonial institutions favored (generic) Christians, that they offered minorities a sound education while intently maintaining the Muslim majority in a state of ignorance, and that Christians collaborated with colonial powers.[76] Non-Muslim elites were thus deprived of their property on the basis of their financial and political affiliation with European imperialism, the monarchy, and capitalism—not religion. To Nasserian apologists, political and financial abuses were thus deserved, accidental, and sporadic, and wrongdoing must be understood within a context of imperialist attacks, national threat, and state building. In the 1970s as in 2011, mainstream media and prominent political figures have continued to reject the responsibility of sectarian strife on foreign powers and Christian acquiescence.[77]

To Islamists, non-Muslims have historically proven their disloyalty and secessionist tendencies. They point to Copts' identification with the ancient Pharaonic past and the Christian era. They unduly generalize Coptic ethnonationalism and collaboration with outsiders. Some Coptic militants in turn disparage Muslims as Arabs and foreigners and claim Egyptian racial authenticity (*al-Umma al-Qibtiyya*).[78] To ethnoreligious nationalists, politics is conterminous with religion. Religion is the matrix of national identity. And Identity = Reality. Islamists view secular projects of society and universal citizenship as foreign imperialist imports, Western cultural hegemony, and intellectual and spiritual denaturalization.

Republican ideology opposed sectarian politics, yet it paved their ground. Sadat sanctioned them by introducing Islamic jurisprudence as early as 1971, prompting Copts to confront the state and defend civil rights threatened by religious distinctions.[79] In the 1970s political strife helped the racialization of religion. It turned religious membership into ethnonational belonging. Elsewhere, sectarianism was the result of the particular conjunction of European racism, imperialist intervention, Ottoman discriminatory reform, and parochial rivalry.[80] In Egypt, legal civic reforms took place in the context of European colonial pressures and triumphant ethnonationalist ideology. Ideas of sectarian homogeneity permeated Egyptian territorial nationalism in the 1920s. They equally influenced supranationalism (Young Egypt) and the Muslim Brotherhood in the 1930s. Republican reforms institutionalized the Ottoman constitutional paradox between civic emancipation, on the one hand, and the subordination of non-Muslim communities, on the other.

The Mehmet 'Ali dynasty could not afford ethnoreligious ideas of political legitimacy though, whereas the Free Officers could. The monarchy's political and economic subsistence depended on a multicommunal and multiethnic notion of the nation ancillary to its social hierarchy. In Egypt as in Lebanon, then, "differentiation" and "discrimination" discourses were "subordinate to and enmeshed in a range of competing discourses of obedience, allegiance, and loyalty inherent in local society [and these formed] no significant barrier to a social order founded on the shared values and interests of a nonsectarian political elite."[81]

Nationalists, however, introduced new notions of citizenship and nationality in the 1940s that "reinforced communitarianism as much as [they] promoted nationalism" and that thrived in the 1950s–60s.[82] The state mobilized educational institutions and the media to enforce the new project of society, a homogeneous nation. It adopted both European racial semantics and Arab nationalist mythologies. State policies led to the departure and eviction of most *mutamasirun*.[83] Hence, the tensions inherent to Ottoman dynastic reforms, which were never addressed by successive states, crystallized around the only substantial non-Muslim group that remained after the 1960s. The "Coptic question" is thus about the meaning of democracy, civil equality, identity, citizenship, race, religious loyalty, and so on. The Nasserian state paved the way for present sectarian identities and the racialization of religious ethnicity when it constitutionally nationalized Islam as state religion. It continued the process of national essentialization that had started in the 1930s–40s. It is not uncommon to hear people say that there is a "Christian" and a "Muslim" physiognomy, and "Christian" and "Muslim" values. Sectarian distrust, the normalization of social discrimination, and religious intolerance are rather universal phenomena, but what interests us here are their historical origins in Egypt. Raf'at 'Adli remarks:

> *My daughter grew up these days and she does not sense the difference.... She sees the present situation, she goes by it, and that's all. But those who were very affected are those who saw life a long time ago, and saw people and the love that was there, and see the estrangement that exists now. It's a sad thing, sad thing.... All my friends are Muslims, until now.... That's because we belong to a particular intellectual class of people, they don't have these feel-*

ings. As for simple people, in [daily] interactions, when I go to the [police] station or to the DMV [I also experience alienation. The treatment received there] denies respect to families, [it's an obstacle when] getting papers, you know. . . . I will be kept in a corner. And in the banks, they don't serve me right away and keep me waiting. These are very simple things, but you feel something. [pause] Horrible. That's what happens.[84]

Since the beginning of the Nasser years, civil and political institutions avoided public debates about the meaning of citizenship and the nationalization of religion. Moreover, the religious Christian/Muslim paradigm instrumentally occults discussions about the roots of social and economic inequities.

In effect, the Nasserian state discredited republican social ideals when it excluded citizens from civil participation in the concerns of the state and the nation, when it precluded controversial discussions, when it assimilated state and nation. Moreover, Nasser institutionalized violence, further blemishing civil institutions. Most worrisome has been the banality of police and military brutality, as seen in the aftermaths of the Maspero or Tahrir events of the fall 2011, whose victims, many ordinary citizens say these days, had it coming. Egypt has thus entered yet another uncertain phase of its republican history. Will the newly elected representatives bring about social justice, as they promise? And if so, to whom? Will the army continue to parody republican rites or let democracy take its unpredictable course? So far, Nasser's heirs have retained their hegemony on information and political processes. They have used, as did the Free Officers, violence, coercion, imprisonment, and misinformation. This unbearable presence of the past.

Conclusion

"What Revolution?!"

Cairo, years ago.

I asked the grandmother of a friend of mine, who lived all her long life right behind King Faruq's 'Abdin palace: "Tell me about the revolution . . ." "The revolution? What revolution?!" She answered earnestly. There were tanks, and he left, and that was it. As for the revolution, she did not see it coming. Nothing new really happened after either. And that was almost all she had to say.

Port Said, some years ago.

Ahmad 'Awad had just put an end to our interview about Port Said, the Limby, the 1950s . . . I had once more bored him to death with my questions. Poet-barber, witty and beautiful mind . . . no ordinary man, he was. All in elegant prose and rhyme. *God have mercy on him.* He never spoke politics to me. Yet once, just after our interview, as we were walking by a crate (or was it a casket?) manufacturer, he said: "Nasser had a police called the 'police of the dawn.' Many of the people they arrested were never to be seen again. Only their coffins."

The Nasser years were a countercynical age that yielded much cynicism. Indeed, the times themselves generated hope among many people throughout the world, outside the likes of my friend Karim's sharp and caustic grandmother. But Ernesto "Che" Guevara now appears on T-shirts, car stickers, and in Hollywood movies. Fatima Ibrahim "Umm Kulthum" al-Biltagi inspires kitsch coffee shops and home décor. Nasser appears in the graffiti of the 25 January Revolution (figure C.1). Mao Tse-Tung is best known for his cherubim-like, acidulated silkscreen portrait as illustrated by Warhol. Che, Umm Kulthum, Nasser, and Mao are mass-market commodities, for these figures as well as the times they mimic are dead and buried. They have entered pop culture and prosthetic memory. Nasserian things past are largely

Figure C.1. Graffiti of Nasser on the side of a public building in Qena, 2012. The Arabic translates as "The people are the leader and the teacher." Photograph by the author.

mythical. Their function is often cynical. Their reality is intangible. Most Egyptians today have not experienced the mid-twentieth century.

"Bread, freedom, and social justice"

The 2011 events rekindled domestic discussions about the legacy of the Free Officers. Some people have been busy reviving the memory of the '52 Revolution and its utopia. Others have been keen on reminding the nostalgically inclined of the unbearable burdens of the Nasserian past. Nasserists argue that the spirit of Nasser was behind the spring of 2011. Social justice ... revolution ... freedom ... these were ideological dicta in the 1950s. Political scientist Huda 'Abd al-Nasir thus recalls that during the January 2011 events, she mulled over writing a book titled "Jamal 'Abd al-Nasser, a presence-absence." She reflected upon the "profound revolutionary heritage" binding the July and January revolutions. On 25 January, as on 23 July, she wrote, the youth instigated the revolution—the difference being that in '52, it was "the officers' youth [that] was the revolutionary avant-garde."[1]

Colonel Nasser's daughter thus reproduced in January 2012 a Nasserist cliché, that is, the idea that the army represented but also acted for the benefit of the people, a people that then followed in the army's footsteps. Accordingly, 1952 was like 2011 a *popular* revolution. As discussed in this book, the army ideologically enforced the revolutionary Jacobinic principle of fusion among government, state, army, and people. In contrast, state institutions were separate from government under British and Khedivian rule, during the thirty years or so of constitutional monarchy that preceded Nasser's coup.

Jacobinic principles could explain the feeble indignation of many citizens in Egypt after the deaths of Maspero and Muhammad Mahmud Street in the fall of 2011. People did not react much except for incidents relating to female dignity. They stood behind the army because the army was the state. The collapse of the army would result in the collapse of the state. At best, its political demotion would endanger the sacrosanct stability of the country since civilian institutions have not yet been built. People thus legitimized army and police use of lethal force.

Many people did not question the veracity of main media accounts, which cast aspersions on civilians and *baltaga* (thugs), and which claimed, as in 1956 and 1967, that external elements were intermingling in order to splinter the nation. Some thus argued that at Maspero the military acted in self-defense. Others professed that protesters prevented the police and army from doing their duty on Tahrir Square, thus causing deadly skirmishes.

Alternative mass media hardly made their way to the masses. Here, as in other domains and in other countries, class defines access and consumption of information. Media censorship, discussed in this book, intervenes at diverse stages of the publishing process. The army-state, which controls printing presses and applies emergency law as it pleases, can prevent the diffusion of independent news until the very final stage of its production.[2]

Popular leniency regarding police and army violence are certainly understandable in a postrevolutionary context of turmoil, incertitude, and anxiety. Necessity—more exactly, the need for institutional stability—often overrides concerns with human and civil rights, as Sadiq Reza points out: "Necessity is of course the mother of exceptional measures. . . . In 1954, Nasser cited the need 'to secure the Revolution first' to justify the exceptional People's Courts. . . . In 2000, . . . the minister of interior insisted emergency rule was 'an indispensable deterrent . . . [to] guard . . . against the criminal forces who are still intent on seizing all possible opportunities to incite unrest and hit national interests.'"[3] The Supreme Council of the Armed Forces (SCAF) eerily used the same terminology to justify the brutal repression of Square demonstrations in 2011.

The cardinal assumption behind popular indulgence toward state savagery is that state violence was the only recourse against civilian violence. Such concept of legitimate institutional violence is a Nasserian legacy. As many have pointed out, Egyptians have lived under an almost uninterrupted emergency rule since the British occupation in the late nineteenth century. Institutional violence thus precedes 1952. Colonial violence is premised on similar principles as those just described. Yet today's state of emergency is largely modeled after the republican judicial and constitutional framework established under the Free Officers. The "comprehensive emergency law" of 1958 and the Free Officers' military courts—the Court of Treason, the Revolution's Court, People's Courts, and so on—are its foundation.[4]

By accepting the military rulers' justifications, by opting for stability by any means necessary, people thus co-opt the banality of evil, for the Free Officers created the form of a republic without civil content. The Nasserian state indeed made a mockery of republican institutions and revolutionary ideals. For without popular participation in the making of the nation and the state, without independent civil authorities that monitor governmental actions, citizenship is meaningless.

The Free Officers like the SCAF justified laws of exception in the name of stability because of external and internal threats. Both Free Officers and SCAF cynically legitimized the use of violence because of the threat of violence. Such justifications, which play on fear, can be perpetually renewed in all kinds of constitutional contexts, including democratic ones. The monitoring of political and religious freedoms, however, continues to inspire ingenious and inexhaustible ways and means of social and political contravention. This social resistance is proportional to the hurdles people face. Thus, both the form and content of the republic need to be reinvented and are now in the process of being reinvented.

Ideals and Their Subversion

Some Egyptians as a result rejected these republican institutions that theoretically advanced democratic ideals yet in practice denied democratic representation to citizens. Nasser subverted social justice, but the idea itself triumphed, so much so that it was the main motto of the January 2011 protestors, including Nasser's main rivals, the Muslim Brothers. The media famously encapsulated this political unison, some remember, by publishing the photo of a Christian woman pouring water onto an ostentatiously "Salafi" man for his ablutions. As months passed, the unison of January 2011 broke into discordant voices—as is the case with any democratic project of political reconstruction that ineluctably brings about a variety of opinions. But most still agree on the overall aims of the revolution, which echo Nasserist promises—"social justice," the "leveling of social differences," and "political partnership."[5] However, the failed promises of republican institutions have invited political reassessment and innovation. God's law inspired some of those who believe that ideals can meet social reality and offset human fallibility. However, man always mediates divine wisdom. Thus, a constellation of religiously inspired parties lays claims to political guidance. Dominating this Islamist cluster are the Muslim Brotherhood's Hizb al-Huriyya wa-al-'Adalah (Freedom and Justice Party) and the Hizb al-Nur (hardliner The Light, or Al-Nour Party), which together won 71.5 percent of parliamentary seats in the recent 2011–12 elections. Unlike Islamist groups, most of the various liberal parties are new to the political scene (Egyptian Bloc, Reform and Development Party, The Revolution Continues, Al-Wasat). They are also commonly associated with the middle class; the well-off, educated strata; intellectuals; secularism; and with a political idealism out of touch with basic popular needs. "Bread" takes precedence over freedom and social justice. In contrast, religious political activists have long operated as grassroots movements and organizations. The social, spiritual, and economic support that they have offered for decades has facilitated their electoral victory. Most also share the concerns, language, and culture of the working class. In that sense, then, the popularity of Islamist movements is a grassroots expression of the demand for social justice and welfare that secular republican institutions promised but failed to provide.

    The Nasserian legacy is thus contradictory. On the one hand, the Free Officers established a political culture of violence, which they inscribed within the national republican judicial and constitutional system. On the other hand, the social ideals they subverted historically prevailed, most forcefully social justice and egalitarianism. Ironically, these ideals led citizens to call into question the politically cynical system that had produced them.

The Nasserian Pledge and Its Present

As "Retelling Salah al-Din" pointed out, republican education did not fulfill its egalitarian pledge. By the 1970s the state ceased to invest in public education. Schools did not or could not accommodate the surge in new cohorts of students. Following in the monarchy's steps, the republic thus yielded educational structures that reproduced socioeconomic inequalities. Many political commentators consider the failure of educational institutions the main reason behind massive youth, educated, middle-class involvement in the 2011 Revolution. Yet the republican ideological apparatus also planted the seeds of republican and democratic ideals with regard to the duties and responsibilities of state institutions. Even though these ideals have their roots in prerevolutionary liberalism, the 1950s–60s both witnessed and helped engineer a large-scale conceptual shift. The republic promised that educational state institutions would bring about welfare and prosperity. Indeed, throughout the 1950s–60s, the government promoted mass education, women's inclusion into the work force, and the leveling of class distinctions. Educational policies were announced in the grandiloquent and didactic fashion typical of radical times.[6] Neither the ideas themselves nor the methods were new. Yet Nasserian rhetoric contrasted with the elitist political culture of the khedivial era. Egalitarianism became the chief axiom of state ideology after 1952. Universal and free education was its chief performance. This act of speech enacted social change, no matter the intent and the effectiveness of state policies.

"Burn, Edmund, Burn" likewise shows the contradiction between republican ideals of social equity and the oligarchic nature of Nasserian power. Against the republican ideals of liberty, the state used violence and repression. Against ideals of fraternity, it appropriated national resources. The struggle against colonialism and imperialism cultivated a sense of national dignity, political purpose, and ideological unity for a few decades. Intimate forms of sociability, communal solidarity, and interdependency—which functioned independently from politics—further solidified national cohesion. But the revolution, as historical moment, betrayed the promise of a social justice that the republic, as proclaimed set of ideals, was supposed to generate—quite the opposite, because new classes of profiteers and new forms of inequity emerged after the 1950s.

"Burn, Edmund, Burn" also illustrates the tensions between civil and governmental political agencies and interests. The effigy burning was a means of resistance against all forms of subjugation and tyranny. Port Saidis' local identity was grounded in their political activism. Their experience of the 1950s–1960s was in disjunction with national experiences. Yet the state usurped, altered, and reified Port Saidi experiences. Institutions strive to subvert particularism when it threatens the myths and the social order their power relies on. The "Martyr City" became the emblem of universal anti-imperialist resistance, resilience, and freedom, which discursively bound together the national community. Political propaganda incidentally made its way into vernacular Canal tales. In the 1970s the Canal was once more appropriated to fit the new ideological blueprint. The Limby festival reached its "political coming of age."[7] After the evacuation of the Canal, festival revelers, in the image of the nation, fashioned a new social and economic landscape that glorified the free-market economy. Limby abandoned its rags. This feast lasted as long as did the fragile prosperity generated by tax exemptions. In the late 1990s, new developments and financial planning shattered merchants' and workers' prospects. Limby became all but mundane, and in 2000, against the background of the Second Intifada, the government aggressively banned the festival. For decades, festival actors creatively demanded social justice and defied politico-military repression. Limby accounts extol justice, equity, and agency in contrast with present political and social exclusions.

In similar fashion, "St. Mary, Mother of Egypt" discloses the tension between inclusive and exclusive political principles. Mariophany utterances speak of an egalitarian republican concept of citizenship embraced by the revolution-as-utopia that the revolution-as-historical-agent betrayed. Zaytun utterances further point to processes of ethnoreligious homogenization within and across sectarian lines. New modes of social distinction came about in the 1950s. A clergy educated in reformed seminaries along with literate parishioners promoted scripturalist orthodoxy. Kyrillus was a monk, Shanuda a history graduate. Literacy bolstered scripturalist religious doctrines, which came to prevail over polysemic theological interpretations and syncretic spiritual practices. The space of sacred performances (*mulid*, worship of saints, etc.) common to both Muslims and Copts shrank. The international and domestic market of religious commodities and ideas further fostered the distinction between religious denominations. Competition also stimulated the homogenization of spiritual and religious practices within each community. The Free Officers had publicly embraced a secular national identity in which love for the homeland transcended religious distinctions. At the same time, they promoted a unity premised on cultural and ethnic homogeneity. Arab nationalism's predicament after 1967 forced a reassessment of secular political morality. Some thereafter condemned the secular republic and associated notions of citizenship. Ideological tensions among religion, politics, and national identity are now debated through the "Coptic question."

Longing and Belonging

Now, all this being said, all these political betrayals being told at an intimate level of historical experience among those who lived the Nasserian present, a sort of longing often prevails among those who were not directly afflicted by dispossession and repression. This longing is not political, though. It is rather a longing for belonging to a world of social intimacy.

In fact, a similar longing permeates oral testimonies of Egyptians who lived through the 1950s–60s and much of the world literature, such as Orhan Pamuk's youthful tales of Istanbul. The longing for a quiet and simple life that derives meaning from human social intimacy is a familiar emotion in postindustrial societies. One of the costs or virtues, depending on one's perspective, of twentieth-century modernization has been the depersonalization of social relationships. Congruently, technology intruded into private lives and personal occupations. So, like others, Raf'at 'Adli, who spent his childhood in Shubra in the 1940s–50s, mainly associates post-Nasserian things past with the dissolution of social intimacy.

> ... the rhythm was simple and life was very quiet, and everybody in the afternoon enjoyed their time as much as they could. Families went to the cinema, men on their own sat at the café with friends, chatting and drinking coffee. Of course, there was no television. That was life. Radio programs were the most important things, around which people gathered, be it series, cultural programs, stories. And that was, I believe, for me, what I liked the most about the people in this period, and about the period itself. When you listened to a play on the [radio] you'd start imagining the events for real ... that developed people's imagination much more than today. You see the series and their décor on TV, that's it, you've seen it. You can't imagine the scene anymore. This was one of these essential things, I think, that destroyed the imagination of people. No more imagination. Everything became ... Why would I imagine things?[8]

The 1950s–60s were not only the years of 'Adli's early adulthood. These were also, in his view, "simple times." The years that followed brought about interconfessional alienation, the disintegration of personal bonds, and the dawn of free thinking and creativity. 'Adli's meditations are distinct from political nostalgia. But like schooling, Limby, and Mariophany stories, 'Adli's recollections recount the demise of a utopia. This demise started after post-1967 confessions of public corruption, followed by attacks on the Nasserian ideological and social edifice. Yet despite the downfall of the Nasserian utopia, the idea of egalitarianism itself triumphed far and wide in the decades following the '52 Revolution. The idea that the state ought to bring about a just and equal society informed the 2010 widespread social protests in and outside Egypt and the 25 January 2011 events. The meaning of egalitarianism, however, how the state ought to establish it, and what sort of state it should be, continues to be debated in Egyptian society. One has yet to see how and for whom the victorious Islamist coalition intends to establish social justice. It would be most remarkable of the military state if it were to bow to political ideals and relinquish without a fight the valuable political and financial capital as well as the social privileges its representatives have accumulated for several decades. All the more as the Free Officers and their political descendants shared with the monarchy a patronizing distrust for those plebeian classes that are demanding their share of power. However, Egyptians are not afraid anymore to oppose the authorities that be. And their demands are forceful, because they go beyond a regional "Arab" phenomenon. Rather, they are a protest against the "misère du monde," our global contemporary social and economic inequities, which need to be addressed globally as well as locally.

Abbreviations and Acronyms

ARE   Arab Republic of Egypt
ASU   Arab Socialist Union, Egypt
CADN   Centre d'Archives Diplomatiques, Nantes
CEDEJ   Centre d'Études et de Documentation Économique Juridique et Sociale
DEPSTATE   United States Department of State
FO   Foreign Office, British Public Record Office
JE   Egypt, British Public Records Subseries
MAE   Ministère des Affaires Étrangères, France
MOE   Ministry of Education
NARA   United States National Archives and Records Administration
PRO   Public Records Office, Great Britain
RG   Record Group
SECSTATE   United States Secretary of State
SITREP   Situation Report
UAR   United Arab Republic
UKDEL   United Kingdom Permanent Delegation
UKSU   United Kingdom Salvage Unit, PR records
USINT   United States Intelligence Agency
WO   War Office (British records)

Key to Interviews

A. A.   Ahmad 'Awad
A. B.   'Abd al-Rahim Gharib al-Banna
A. D.   'Asim Ahmad al-Disuqi
C. G.   Captain Ghazali
F. R.   Fa'iq Rida
H. Y.   Hagg Yusif
K. I.   Kamal 'Id

M. A.	Mona 'Awad
M.H.U.	Muhammad Hamid 'Uways
M. S.	Mas'ud Shuman
N. H.	Nabila Husni
O. F.	'Umar al-Faruq
R. A.	Ra'uf 'Abbas
Raf. A.	Raf'at 'Adli
T.S.U.	Taha Sa'ad 'Uthman, aka 'Amm Taha
Z. A.	Zaki 'Abd al-Mat'al

Notes

Introduction: This Incurable Otherness

1. Taha Sa'ad 'Uthman (T.S.U.) (b. 1916–d. 2004), interview by author, Cairo, 10 December 2003. In Arabic. Unless otherwise noted, all interviews were conducted in Arabic by the author (indicated in the text as M. B.). Formal interview excerpts appear in the text in italics; these I translated from tape recordings and transcripts. Informal conversations, set in roman type and embedded in the text, are reconstituted from handwritten notes taken in the field during and immediately after the conversations.

2. Nora, "Entre mémoire et histoire," in *Les lieux de mémoire*, xxxiv.

3. Emphasis added. Rousso, *Le syndrôme de Vichy*, 140.

4. Halbwachs, *Les cadres sociaux de la mémoire* and *La mémoire collective*; Bakhtin, *Speech Genres*; and Portelli, *Battle of Valle Giulia*.

5. Bahloul, *Architecture of Memory*, 6.

6. Halbwachs, *Les cadres sociaux de la mémoire*, x–xi.

7. Two exceptions are Saad's dissertation, "Peasants' Perceptions of Recent Egyptian History," and his article, "Two Pasts of Nasser's Peasants," 11–23. Pioneer histories exist, such as Beinin and Lockman, *Workers on the Nile*, and Cole, *Colonialism and Revolution in the Middle East*.

8. Baghdadi, *Dhubbat yunyu* (June Officers); Fawzi, *Harb al-thalath sanawat* (Three-Year War); Haykal, *1967: Al-Infijar* (1967: The Explosion); Ramadan, *Tahtim al-aliha* (Destruction of the Idols); Kerr, *Arab Cold War*; Gordon, *Nasser's Blessed Movement*; and Beattie, *Egypt during the Nasser Years*.

9. Among others, see Clancy-Smith, *Rebel and Saint*; and Khater, *Inventing Home*.

10. Bahloul, *Architecture of Memory*, 6.

11. As opposed to the distinction established by Nora, "Between Memory and History," 8.

12. See Lury, *Prosthetic Culture*; and Landsberg, *Prosthetic Memory*, 143.

13. Bloch, *Apologie pour l'histoire*, 48.

14. See Spence, *Memory Palace of Matteo Ricci*.

15. Portelli, *Death of Luigi*, ix.

16. Halbwachs, *Les cadres sociaux de la mémoire*, 51–52; and Frisch, *Shared Authority*, 13.

17. Portelli, *Battle of Valle Giulia*, 58.

18. Ibid., 93.

19. Handler, "Is 'Identity' a Useful Cross-Cultural Concept?" 29, 30.

20. The history of representations covers ideologies, *mentalités*, imaginaries, symbolism, historiography, and memory. See Le Goff, *Histoire et mémoire*, 23, 109.

21. Henri Bergson (*Matière et mémoire*) and Emile Durkheim influenced Halbwachs, who introduced the notion. One example of equation between social and collective memory is Roudometof, *Collective Memory, National Identity, and Ethnic Conflict*, 7.

22. Halbwachs, Marcel Mauss, and Henri Lefebvre were concerned with multidimensional (individual, collective, psychological, and social) dynamics. For Mauss and Halbwachs, the social dominated the psychological. See Mauss, *Sociologie et anthropologie*; and Lefebvre, *La production de l'espace*.

23. Halbwachs' *Les cadres sociaux de la mémoire* argues that discrete groups generate discrete apprehensions to the past, as well as modes of social behavior.

24. Halbwachs' answer to the plurality of memories, as seen in *La mémoire collective chez les musiciens* (originally published in *Revue Philosophique* [March–April 1939]: 139–65), recalls Bakhtin's concept of pluriglossia. Gérard Namier describes the epistemological break between *Les cadres sociaux de la mémoire* and *La mémoire* in his postscript to *La mémoire collective*, 243.

25. Halbwachs, *La mémoire collective*, 29.

26. Thus, Halbwachs likens memory to ways of perceiving and living life—which departs from *Les cadres sociaux de la mémoire*.

27. Halbwachs, *La mémoire collective*, 58. On oblivion and narration as generating coherence to the past, see Lowenthal, "For the Motion," in *Key Debates*, 211.

28. Dakhlia, *L'oubli de la cité*, 6.

29. After the translation of Nora's *Les lieux de mémoire* and Halbwachs' *Les cadres sociaux de la mémoire* into English in the 1990s, the "history of memory" became rapidly popular across the Atlantic. It thus came to a crisis at the height of its popularity, as discussed in Lavabre, "Usages du passé," 481. Among others, Dakhlia cautions that the model of a "convergent and assimilationist history" is inappropriate to North African societies (*L'oubli*, 14).

30. On resistance to assimilation, see Joutard, *La légende des camisards*.

31. Hobsbawm and Ranger, *Invention of Tradition*.

32. It is not the case that Nora claimed that religion and spirituality were dead, as has been argued by Winter and Sullivan: "When Nora argues that society has banished ritual, or claims that it has no further use for the sacred, and that literature is dead, he displays the weakest links in his position. Anybody observing the difficulties attendant on the assimilation of Muslims into French society would scoff at such claims." Different issues (political, social, religious, and cultural) are conflated here regarding Islam. Nora cautions that one must distinguish between religion and the sacred. And that positivism changed the sacred as we knew it. See Winter and Sullivan, *War and Remembrance*, 2.

33. Lavabre, "Usages du passé," 481. Nora uses history against memory and modernity against tradition.

34. Favret-Saada, *Les mots, la mort, les sorts*.
35. The problem of reception remains critical, as noted by Winter and Sullivan, *War and Remembrance*, 18.
36. Bakhtin, *Speech Genres*, 91.
37. Ibid., 89.
38. Rousso, *Le syndrôme*.
39. Zemon Davis and Starn, "Introduction," in *Representations* 26, 2.
40. Bakhtin, *Speech Genres*, xiv. In contrast, Halbwachs assumes the coherence of collective memory and the national group, leaving a narrow space to dissonance and incoherence.
41. Dening, *Death of William Gooch*, 14, 16.
42. Anthropologists tend to study memory as orality/tradition in opposition to literacy/modernization. This dichotomy is similar to the secular/religious conceptual dichotomy disputed by Starrett in *Putting Islam to Work*, 15.
43. Valensi, *Fables de la mémoire*; Rousso, *Le syndrôme de Vichy*; Gillis, *Commemorations*; Ory, *Une nation pour mémoire*; Fussel, *Great War and Modern Memory*; and Winter and Sullivan, *War and Remembrance*.
44. See Zemon Davis and Starn, "Introduction," in *Representations* 26, 2. On historical hegemony, historicity, and textual authority, see Rappaport, *Politics of Memory*; Swedenburg, *Memories of Revolt*; Shryock, *Nationalism and the Genealogical Imagination*; and Messick, *Calligraphic State*, 123, 53.
45. Portelli, *Battle of Valle Giulia*, 8.
46. Only four chapters deal with the cultural history of the Nasser years in Podeh and Winckler, *Rethinking Nasserism*. See also Gordon, *Revolutionary Melodrama*; Armbrust, *Mass Culture and Modernism in Egypt*; and Danielson, "Performance, Political Identity, and Memory," 109–22.
47. Bakhtin, *Speech Genres*, 2.
48. Burguière, "L'historiographie des origines de la France," 41–62.
49. I will henceforth use "Mariophany" to indicate Marian apparitions and "Mariology" to designate both theological and scientific studies of the Virgin Mary.
50. Loraux, "Pour quel consensus?"

Part I. Retelling Salah al-Din

1. The parallel with eighteenth-century "absolutist" reformers in Prussia and Austria is striking. See Melton, *Absolutism*, 114–15.
2. 'Ajati, quoted in Farag in "La construction sociale," 74. See Starrett, *Putting Islam to Work*, 30: Cromer's 1905 position on *fellahin*'s education echoes 'Ajati almost word for word.
3. On British and Egyptian elites' shared interests, see Bakkar, "Qualitative Aspects," 5.
4. On student political movements, see Abdalla, *Student Movement*; and Waterbury, *The Egypt of Nasser and Sadat*, 219–20.

5. Elementary schools were established in the early twentieth century but legally redefined in 1919 under nationalist pressures. See Starrett, *Putting Islam to Work*, 67.

6. On school fees, see Farag, "La construction sociale," 43, 44, and Farag, "Isma'il al-Qabbani," 57.

7. There are additional disagreements about the chronology of institutional changes between the 1940s and the 1980s.

8. Farag, "Isma'il al-Qabbani," 57.

9. See Ezzat, "Revolution Revisited," 6.

10. See Waterbury, *Egypt of Nasser and Sadat*, 235; Cochran, *Education in Egypt*, 42; Zaki, "Guidelines for Improving the Preparation and Selection of Textbooks," 17, 28, 43–44; Bakkar, "Qualitative Aspects," 7. See also El-Din, "Egypt National Report"; Abdalla, *Student Movement*, 27, 104, 105, 109; and Szyliowicz, *Education and Modernization in the Middle East*, 264; or see Sika, *Educational Reform*, 38.

11. On census categories, see Fargues, "Note sur la diffusion," 116; and Baz, "Méthodes d'assimilation," 230.

12. Farag, "Analyse de presse," 284.

13. Ibid., 284–85. In 1993 a neo-Wafd author advocated limiting free education to "basic" literacy schools that "teach and educate."

14. On oblivion, see Ozouf, *L'école de la France*, 92–93.

15. In 1932 5 percent of teaching time was allotted to social studies. After 1963 it rose to 7 percent—roughly equivalent to 1932 science and physical education allotments. It dropped to 4 percent in 1981, equivalent to music. See Starrett, *Putting Islam to Work*, 83.

16. Michel Edmé-Petit, quoted in Ozouf, *L'école de la France*, 99.

Chapter 1. Farouk Is Gone, Long Live the Revolution

1. See Awad, *Literature of Ideas*, 134.

2. Luwis 'Awad (1915–90) might have identified with Husayn. A socialist liberal, he was imprisoned in 1959, but he continued to speak out after his release. Husayn's fate spoke of the general castration of the Egyptian intelligentsia. See Aclimandos, "Louis 'Awad (1915–90), un philosophe iconoclaste," 165–66.

3. See Awad, *Literature of Ideas*, 134–35.

4. See MOE, Egypt, Husayn et al., *Fusul Mukhtara* (Selected Texts), first-year secondary (1955), with an introduction by Husayn. See also Buhayri, *Ta'rikh Misr*, 173. Unless otherwise noted, all the textbook materials cited in this book for the 1948–86 period are from the documentary collection "Muqararat al-Tarikh" (History Regulations), in the archival series "al-Jughrafiyya wa-al-Tarikh" (History and Geography) located at the Mathaf Wizarat al-Ta'lim wa-al-Tarbiyya (Education Museum and Documents Library), Cairo.

5. French minister Jules Ferry (1832–93) is mostly renowned in France for secularizing the school system.

6. MOE, *Al-Dirasat al-ijtima'iyya* (Social Studies), fourth-year primary (1998–99), 37.

7. See Husayn, *Mustaqbal al-thaqafa fi Misr*. The "unabbreviated" Glazer English trans-

lation (*The Future of Culture in Egypt*) provides an idea of the content of the work, but many of its sections have been considerably abbreviated and altered. Some of the book's ideas were not new, but Husayn was a most eloquent advocate, as discussed by Farag, "Enjeux éducatifs et réforme sociale," 199. See also Galt, *Effects of Centralization on Education in Modern Egypt*, 14–15.

8. See also Szyliowicz, *Education and Modernization in the Middle East*, 260.

9. See MOE, *Tarikh al-watan al-'arabi* (History of the Arab Homeland), third-year preparatory (1959), 186.

10. See MOE, *Tarikh Misr* (History of Egypt), fourth-year preparatory (1954), 252. This is the first post-Faruq history book for this educational level.

11. Directed by Kamal Salim, Egypt, 1939.

12. Armbrust, "Egyptian Cinema On Stage and Off," 79–80.

13. See Shafik, *Arab Cinema*, 130.

14. Reid, *Cairo University*, 109. Official reports and studies based on such reports, such as Lloyd et al., "Impact of Educational Quality," endorse the idea that the 1923 constitution brought about free universal public schooling.

15. Secondary school cost LE20 a year including books in 1926. See 'Awad, "Bonnes feuilles," 168.

16. T.S.U. interview, Cairo, 10 December 2003. 'Uthman was an amateur historian of the labor movement, a retired factory worker, a Communist Party member, a unionist, and a poet.

17. After 1971 the textual quality of textbooks abruptly declined. See MOE, *Tabaqan li-al-manahij al-mawhida* (Application of the Unified Curricula), third-year primary (1971), 26. Despite steady improvements since 1993, curricula still rely on memorization rather than interactive learning; see Sika, *Educational Reform*, 236–37.

18. See Cochran, *Education in Egypt*, 23: "elementary" schools "taught no foreign languages and were conducted for a half day" in a six-year cycle as opposed to the four-year "primary" level.

19. Husayn, *Mustaqbal*, 104. Few scholars consider the temporal gap between legal and social reform. Also, the literature concentrates on governmental education, especially universities, and foreign schools. Lower-income, female and/or non-Islamic elementary instruction has been neglected. There were Coptic and Jewish *kuttabs* (religious schools) too, and charitable organizations funding vocational education, such as the Tawfik Coptic Society. But there were no higher Coptic and Jewish institutions in the 1930s. On Copts, see Heyworth-Dunne, *Introduction to the History of Education*, 87; and Nasim, *Ta'rikh al-tarbiyya al-qibtiyya* (History of Coptic Education). On artisans' education, see Chalcraft, *The Striking Cabbies of Cairo*, 162–63.

20. Stoler, *Carnal Knowledge and Imperial Power*, 131.

21. In 1933 90 percent of elementary instruction was religious education, writing (Arabic), and counting (arithmetic). Starrett, *Putting Islam to Work*, 68–69.

22. In 1949 the textbook used in the third year of primary (ibtida'i) school was also used in the fifth year of basic elementary (awwali) school, covering the modern period

up to King Faruq. See MOE, Egypt, 'Abd al-Rahim and Ibrahim Namir Sayf al-Din, *Qisas wa muhadithat sahla* (Simple Stories and Events), third-year primary and fifth-year elementary (1949), 54.

23. On basic education, see Farag, "La construction sociale," 43–44. On free tuition in 1944 and 1951, see Faksh, "Consequences of the Introduction," 46. On nineteenth-century schooling, see Boktor, *School and Society*, 115, and Starrett, *Putting Islam to Work*, 27.

24. In contrast, the children of the elite evaded conscription. Husayn, *Mustaqbal*, 107.

25. Ibid., 105, 108.

26. Ibid., 93.

27. Similarly, Muhammad Farid spoke of the emancipating and disciplinary virtues of literacy in 1913. He praised the "condition of [Egyptians'] brethren in Europe." He culturally positioned himself among Western intellectuals. Farag, "Enjeux éducatifs et réforme sociale," 200.

28. Husayn, *Mustaqbal*, 103, 104.

29. Ibid., 104.

30. Ibid., 104, 105. Husayn advocated open access to university for the middle and upper classes.

31. Ibid., 104.

32. Ibid., 106.

33. T.S.U. interview, Cairo, 14 December 2002.

34. Thoraval, *Regards sur le cinéma Égyptien, 1895–1975*, 31.

35. Armbrust, "Egyptian Cinema On Stage and Off," 82.

36. There were 368,710 televisions in Egypt in 1966, 259,055 of which were in Greater Cairo. Wahba, *Cultural Policy in Egypt*, 14.

37. See Ghosh, *In an Antique Land*, 292–93.

38. Consider, for example, Muhammad Sha'ban's film *Al-Sharaf* (The Honor) (Cairo, 1998). The historical background of the film (1967) allows the filmmaker some sartorial license, the main actress (Jiran Fadil) appearing in revealing short dresses. See also Belli, "Le 'moment 1967,'" 41–55.

39. See Lury, *Prosthetic Culture*, 1, 2.

40. Two famous examples of cinematic sociopolitical allegory from the 1930s and 40s are *Lashin* (Lachine), directed by Fritz Kramp (Egypt, 1938), and the acerbic film *Al-Suq al-sawda'* (Black Market), directed by Kamal al-Tilmisani (Egypt, 1945). The 1948 censorship law was a result of the latter film.

41. Except for Tilmisani's *Al-Suq al-sawda'*.

42. Armbrust, "Egyptian Cinema On Stage and Off," 77.

43. Dramas set in prerevolutionary times could always become subversive. Consider the 1969 film *Shay' min al-khawf* (A Bit of Fear), directed by Husayn Kamal, and director Henri Barakat's 1965 *Al-Haram* (The Sin).

44. Directed by 'Izz al-Din Dhulfiqar.

45. Armbrust, "Manly Men on a National Stage," 263.

46. Dialogues highlight elitism and patronage: "The military academy is not for us or our children," and "The most important thing is connection."

47. See Gordon, *Nasser's Blessed Movement*, 41.

48. Waterbury, *Egypt of Nasser and Sadat*, 275.

49. Meanwhile Sulayman Zaki, a student of modest means, wins over the selection committee after an impertinent nationalist and egalitarian speech. All Nasserian schools (al-Azhar included) offered military training. See Platt and Hefny, *Egypt*, 124.

50. See the Ministry of Education pamphlet by Harby and Afifi, *Education in Modern Egypt*, 26.

51. Directed by Salah Abu Sayf, *Al-Bidaya wa-al-nihaya* is based on the 1949 novel of the same name by Najib Mahfuz.

52. The novel is more subtle in its portrayal of characters than this movie, as is Mexican director Arturo Ripstein's 1993 emotionally complex adaptation of Mahfuz's novel, *Principio y Fin*.

53. See Stoler, *Carnal Knowledge*, 120, 264n21.

54. Crubellier, *L'école républicaine, 1870–1940*, 5.

55. See Waterbury, *Egypt of Nasser and Sadat*, 218, 220.

56. Szyliowicz, *Education and Modernization in the Middle East*, 264.

57. Regional disparities were important: in the Delta, rural female literacy increased considerably (7 percent to 47 percent for 1944–69) while in Upper Egypt this rate was low (3 percent to 27 percent). Compare also male and female literacy in urban and rural settings, north and south, from 1919 to 1969. See Ireton, "La lettre et le chiffre," 169, 173.

58. Ibid., 164.

59. "Cultural Development in the Countryside," unpublished 1969 cultural field survey by the United Arab Republic Ministry of Culture, cited in Wahba, *Cultural Policy*, 12.

60. See Saad, "Les deux passés des paysans de Nasser."

61. M. (thirty-year-old hotel manager), informal conversation with author, Cairo, 29 November 2002.

62. Ahmed, *Border Passage*.

63. The return, in recent years, of the prerevolutionary aristocracy and bourgeoisie stems in part from that cultural and social capital, in addition to the underestimated preservation of some of their financial assets.

64. Salah S. (owner of a furniture business in his thirties), informal conversation with author, Cairo, 22 December 2011. In Arabic.

65. Fargues, "Note sur la diffusion," 120. See also Ireton, "La lettre et le chiffre," 166.

66. Nabila Husni (N. H.), interview by author, Cairo, 23 March 2000. Born in 1930, in Cairo. According to Raye Platt and Mohammed Hefny, there were about 10 percent of women in universities in 1958, 15 percent in secondary schools, and 35 percent in primary schools. In 1954–55, there were 6,766 women in universities out of a total of 55,051 students. See Platt and Hefny, *Egypt*, 125.

67. According to Reid (*Cairo University*, 105), six women entered the Faculty of Medicine at the University of Cairo in 1928. Yet engineering, agriculture, and veterinary science,

"far removed from upper middle class female roles in Egypt," only enrolled women after World War II.

68. See nineteenth-century French coeducation debates in Furet and Ozouf, *Lire et écrire*.

69. Coeducational schools have either mixed or separate classrooms. See Lloyd et al., "Impact of Educational Quality," 444, 450. Also see Crabbs, *Writing of History*, 97.

70. Zaki, "Guidelines for Improving," 52.

71. Ibid., 52: "Most educators agree that female teachers are preferable to male teachers at the primary level."

72. Khater, *Inventing Home*, 130.

73. Amin and Lloyd, "Women's Lives and Rapid Fertility Decline."

74. Reid, *Cairo University*, 174. Waterbury also mentions the conflict between educational planners and the elite and the pressures to which both Nasser and Sadat relented in *The Egypt of Nasser and Sadat*, 235.

75. Ra'uf 'Abbas (R. A.), interview by author, Cairo, 3 and 9 July 1997. In English. 'Abbas (b. 1939–d. 2008) was Chair of the History Department at Cairo University at the time of this interview.

76. According to Abdalla, university fees were reduced twice in 1956 and 1961 before being abolished in 1962. Abdalla, *Student Movement*, 105. According to Waterbury, selective entry to university was abolished in 1963. Waterbury, *Egypt of Nasser and Sadat*, 236.

77. Reid, *Cairo University*, 174. Reid further points out that "by 1955, 71 percent of university students were already attending free, because of financial need or because of scoring at least 75 percent on their examinations. Nasser finished what the Wafd had started"(ibid., 110). See also Abdalla, *Student Movement*, 105.

78. Consider the late nineteenth- to early twentieth-century reforms of Dar al-'Ulum. See Aroian, "Nationalization of Arabic and Islamic Education," 41–42.

79. Abdalla, *Student Movement*, 105. See also Zeghal, "Nasser et les Oulémas d'al-Azhar," 106–7.

80. Reid, *Cairo University*, 175.

81. See Waterbury, *Egypt of Nasser and Sadat*, 236.

82. *Al-Irhab wa-al-kabab* (Terrorism and Kebab), directed by Sharif 'Arafa (Egypt, 1993). See Armbrust, "Terrorism and Kabab," 283–99. Students who achieve 90 percent and above on the primary school exam choose their school, although they rarely know their scores, and not all districts offer such choice. See Lloyd et al., "Impact of Educational Quality," 459.

83. Egyptian TV was inaugurated in 1960. By 1962 three channels diffused some twenty hours of programs per day. There were about twenty-nine thousand televisions in 1960, and five hundred thousand by 1969. See Pignol, "50 ans d'histoire de la radio et de la télévision en Egypte," 26–27.

84. "Allahu akbar fawqa kayd al-mu'tadi" (God is above the plots of aggressors), as Walter Armbrust explains, is a "stirring march composed to commemorate the victory of the tripartite aggression" (Armbrust, "Manly Men on a National Stage," 263).

It is also the opening of the 1957 film *Bur Sa'id* (Port Said), directed by 'Izz al-Din Dhulfiqar.

85. Zaki 'Abd al-Mat'al (Z. A.), interview by author, Cairo, 27 April 2000 and 4 May 2000. In English. Born in 1951, Zaki 'Abd al-Mat'al is a lawyer.

86. Karnouk, *Contemporary Egyptian Art*, 7.

87. On state propaganda in magazines, see Armbrust, "Manly Men on a National Stage," 247–75.

88. See LaDuke, "Egyptian Painter Inji Efflatoun," 477, 483, 481.

89. Jadhbiyya Sirri (b. 1925) graduated from Cairo's High Institute of Fine Arts for Girls in 1948. She taught art at Helwan University from 1955 to 1981. See Saad el-Din, ed., *Gazbia Sirry, Lust for Color*.

90. Among her pre-1952 reformist works are *Motherhood* (1951), *In the Classroom* (1951), and *In the Kitchen* (1951). Among her postrevolution works, consider *Umm Ratiba* (1952), *Swinging* (1956), and *Popular Marionnette* (1957). Others, like *Song of the Revolution* (1952), *The Two Wives* (1953), and *The Teacher* (1954), are more didactic.

91. Cooper and Stoler, eds., *Tensions of Empire*, 90, 91.

92. Consider *Grief* (1967), *Disintegrated Houses* (1967), *Fall of the Hero* (1969), and *Frightened Houses* (1968–69). See also Saad el-Din, *Gazbia Sirry, Lust for Color*, plates 41, 42, 49, 52.

93. See her "People-Houses" series of paintings, realized in the wake of 1967.

94. Muhammad Hamid 'Uways (M.H.U.), interview by author, Alexandria, 16 May 2002. 'Uways (b. 1919–d. 2011) was not only committed to the 1952 revolution; he also held an influential position at the University of Alexandria. He was reputed for his autocratic teaching methods.

95. Compare to Diego Rivera's *Festival of Flowers* (1925).

96. See Benjamin, *La Revolución*, 74–75.

97. 'Uways, quoted in Karnouk, *Contemporary Egyptian Art*, 18. Zaynab 'Abd al-Hamid, Jadhbiyya Sirri, M. Hamid 'Uways, 'Izz al-Din Hamuda, William Ishaq, Salah Yusri, and sculptor Jamal al-Sighini were the core of the Modern Arts Group who "found their momentum in the early 1950s" (qtd. in Karnouk, *Contemporary Egyptian Art*, 15).

98. Sometimes for material reasons. M.H.U. interview, Alexandria, 16 May 2002.

99. On the concept of *ibn* (son) and *bint* (daughter) *al-balad* (literally "of the land"), see Messiri, *Ibn al-Balad*, 1. Also see Armbrust, "Manly Men on a National Stage," 248–49; and Ryzova, "I Am a Whore but I Will Be a Good Mother," 13–15.

100. M.H.U. interview, Alexandria, 16 May 2002.

101. Ryzova, "I Am a Whore but I Will Be a Good Mother," 14.

102. Ibid., 13.

103. LaDuke, "Egyptian Painter Inji Efflatoun," 483, 480.

104. Starrett, *Putting Islam to Work*, 16.

105. The madrasa was an Islamic school providing an elementary instruction, like the *kuttab*, and a more advanced education, like al-Azhar. See Platt and Hefny, *Egypt*, 120.

106. R. A. interview, Cairo, 3 July 1997.

107. Ibid.

108. *Kuttab* instructors often had a liminal education and lived on the fringe of poverty. See Husayn's description of his teacher, who smoked in class and asked students to run errands for him (Husayn, *Al-Ayyam*, 30–31); see also 'Uways, *Ta'rikh alladhi ahmiluhu 'ala dahri*.

109. Husayn, *Mustaqbal al-thaqafa*, 39.

110. This assessment is partially based upon my examination of some fifteen schoolbooks available for the 1948–86 period at the archival center of the Ministry of Education, "Geography and History" archival series. This sparse archival collection is most substantial for the fifth-year primary (ten textbooks for the 1953–86 period). Mubarak slowly redressed the percentage of state expenditure even though he manipulated compulsory education (see table 1.1). In 1970 the total expenditure on education as a percentage of total government expenditure had reached 15.8 percent. In 1981 it had dropped to 9.4 percent, but by 1995 it had climbed back up to 14.9 percent. Current ordinary expenditure on education as a percentage of current government expenditure was 23.8 percent in 1970, 10.1 percent in 1981, and up to 16.7 percent in 1995. See UNESCO, *1999 Statistical Yearbook*, "Total and Current Public Expenditure on Education," table II-18, p. II-492; and Sika, *Educational Reform*, 41.

111. Harby and Afifi, *Education*, 13; and Bakkar, "Qualitative Aspects," 8. Also see UAR, "Address by President Jamal Abdel Nasser at the Great Popular Rally at Gumhuriya Square," 15.

112. Nasser only earned the title of "Ra'is," just as Guevara earned the title of "Che."

113. Blunt elevated Ahmad 'Urabi to the stature of a heroic fellah-soldier and Egypt's first nationalist leader in *Secret History of the Occupation of Egypt*. He also equated the notion of fellah to racial authenticity. On Urabist historiography, see Mayer, *Changing Past*, 27.

114. See MOE, Al-*Dirasat al-ijtima'iyya* (Social Studies), fifth-year primary (1996–97), 68.

115. Ibid., 67.

116. The illustration shows Nasser defiantly facing the British fleet. Salah Jahin, "Jamal ('Abd al-Nasir): 'That kind of thing belongs to 1882. It does not work in 1956!!'" *Ruz al-Yusuf*, 5 November 1956, cover page.

117. See Williamson, *Education and Social Change in Egypt and Turkey*, 108, 109. Williamson argues that 1920s–40s politicians carried "a suspicion that the Egyptian people were not yet properly educated to a responsible role in politics." Some promoted primary education as a precaution against rural revolts.

118. N. H. interview, Cairo, 23 March 2000. Husni's father was a teacher and her mother a homemaker. She was raised in Cairo, married a pharmacist, and moved to Port Said. She moved back to Cairo in the late 1960s.

119. Foreign schools, immigrants, and emigrants influenced public attitudes in Lebanon somewhat earlier than in Egypt; see Khater, *Inventing Home*.

120. R. A. interview, Cairo, 3 and 9 July 1997.

121. In spite of penalty principles against parents, results are unsatisfactory. Article

139 of 1981 extended compulsory "basic" education to children age six to fifteen (instead of six to twelve), thus including preparatory school. See Cochran, *Education in Egypt*, 79.

122. See UNESCO, *1999 Statistical Yearbook*, "Gross Enrollment Ratios by Level of Education," table II-8, p. II-271.

123. Primary and preparatory school certificates determine whether a child enters a technical or general track. Only a third of pupils enter the latter. See Herrera, "Scenes of Schooling," 47–48.

124. According to a recent statistical study, male dropout rates vary as a function of the family's socioeconomic situation. On the financial aspects of female education, see Lloyd et al., "Impact of Educational Quality," 463, 465.

125. See Bourdieu and Passeron, *La reproduction*.

126. Barbara S. Mensch, Barbara L. Ibrahim, Susan M. Lee, and Omaima El-Gibaly, "Gender-Role Attitudes Among Egyptian Adolescents," cited in Lloyd et al., "Impact of Educational Quality," 463. See also Taher, *Aunt Safiyya*, 77.

127. According to a 1980s study conducted in Upper Egypt, 44 percent of women were married before the legal age of sixteen. See UNICEF, "Early Marriage."

128. Newer textbooks show improvements in display and in the textual and visual integration of females. See the section on women's emancipation and social role—including Suzanne Mubarak—in MOE, *Al-Dirasat al-ijtima'iyya* (Social Studies), third-year preparatory (2009–10), 119, 122–24; see also MOE, *Al-Dirasat al-ijtima'iyya* (Social Studies), second-year preparatory (2009–10), 37, 47.

129. See the section on the '52 Revolution in MOE, *Tarikh al-watan al-'arabi* (History of the Arab Homeland), third-year preparatory (1959), 75–86.

130. Cochran, *Education in Egypt*, 54.

131. Ibid., 79.

132. Cited by Farag, "La construction sociale," 72.

133. National data reports 97 percent primary education enrollment in 1993 and 100 percent in 1996. See UNESCO, *1999 Statistical Yearbook*, "Primary and Secondary Education: Enrollment Ratios by Age Groups," table II.9, p. II-369.

134. UAR, *Al-Dirasat al-ijtima'iyya* (Social Studies), third-year preparatory (2009–10), 76, 81.

Chapter 2. The New Order

1. 'Abd al-Nasser, "Science Day Speech," 18 December 1961, quoted in Abdalla, *Student Movement*, 116.

2. Crubellier, *L'école républicaine, 1870–1940*.

3. I explored schoolbooks published between 1948 and 1999, focusing on textbooks published at the time of the first Mubarak curricular reform yet before the passage of Law No. 23 of 1999, which reestablished the sixth-year primary level suppressed in 1988–89. On state reassessment of compulsory education, see El-Din, "Egypt National Report." On curricular revisions since 1997, see Tadros, "Hitting the Books," 16.

4. Mitchell, *Rule of Experts*, 183.

5. Under Nasser, compulsory "basic" education was limited to primary school (age 6–12). It was extended to preparatory school in 1981 by education Law No. 139 and reinforced by Law No. 23 of 1999. See El-Din, "Egypt National Report."

6. Between 1925 and 1949 schooling was divided into an up to eight-year basic education cycle and a five-year secondary education cycle. Preparatory school legislation dates from 1949. See Harby and Afifi, *Education in Modern Egypt*, 21. Unfortunately, statistics often lump together preparatory and secondary schooling under the "second level" category.

7. A similar change took place in the United States in the same period. See Zaki, "Guidelines for Improving," 49.

8. A French statesman, François Guizot (1787–1874) established (male) public primary education in the early 1830s. It was extended to girls in 1850.

9. See Buhayri, *Ta'rikh Misr*, 170.

10. Emphasis added. UAR, "Address by President Jamal Abdel Nasser at... Gumhuria Square," 70.

11. Reid, *Whose Pharaohs?* 205.

12. Revisions were directed by Sa'id al-'Uryan. See Buhayri, *Ta'rikh Misr* (History of Egypt) and Maxime Rodinson, "Préface," in Carré, *Enseignement islamique*, ix, 8.

13. Coudougnan, *Enseignement de l'histoire pré-Islamique*, 25.

14. Crabbs, *Writing of History*, 205.

15. T.S.U. interview, Cairo, 10 December 2003.

16. On Islamist nationalism, see Wickham, *Mobilizing Islam*, 154.

17. *Al-Mujmal*, quoted in Reid, *Cairo University*, 205. This textbook, *Al-Mujmal fi-al-ta'rikh al-misri* (The Survey of Egyptian History), was written in 1942 by scholars, in contrast with the 1960s revised textbooks. The Ministry of Education worked again with scholars (such as Dr. 'Asim al-Disuqi) for its 1999–2000 primary and secondary level curricular revisions.

18. Cochran (*Education in Egypt*, 41), however, reclaims the first Egyptian presidency for Muhammad Najib. On nationalist rewriting of Ottoman rulers as aliens, see Fahmy, *All the Pasha's Men*, 23–24.

19. Waterbury, *Egypt of Nasser and Sadat*, 233.

20. Moreh, *Napoleon in Egypt*, 24, 25.

21. See Cromer, *Modern Egypt*, xvii–xviii.

22. See Bhabha, *Nation and Narration*; Makdisi, *Culture of Sectarianism*; Garcia-Arenal and Wiegers, *Man of Three Worlds*; and Clancy-Smith, *Mediterraneans*.

23. Mitchell, *Rule of Experts*, 179.

24. Farag, "La construction sociale," 17.

25. On centralization, see Bakkar, "Qualitative Aspects," 7.

26. Nasser, *Egypt's Liberation*, 41.

27. Rural notables and their "Turkish" wives moved to the capital to seek an education for their children unavailable in rural areas, as was also common among army officers. Tewfik Aclimandos, private conversation with the author, Cairo, 10 October 2001. As discussed in this chapter, the Turkification of the Ottoman Egyptian elite is largely a

product of Egyptian nationalism; in the scholarship on Ottoman Egypt as in ordinary speech, this term is more often than not an anachronism.

28. President Habib Bourguiba of Tunisia expressed similar ideas. See Obdeijn, "Enseignement de l'histoire dans la Tunisie moderne," 49.

29. Under the leadership of Sa'd Zaghlul. See UAR, *Al-Dirasat al-ijtima'iyya* (Social Studies), fifth-year primary (1996–97), 72.

30. Crabbs, *Writing of History*, 206.

31. Abécassis, "Une certaine idée de la nation," 7, 8. Kamil and Zaghlul (who held the title of minister of education) had pressed for Arabization.

32. Crabbs, *Writing of History*, 207.

33. Hassan, "Choix culturels et orientations éducatives," 19. Law 40 of 1936 stipulated the imposition of Arabic and government supervision. On the other hand, as Cochran explains (*Education in Egypt*, 29), "Foreign schools could include other curricula" and the language of instruction was not specified.

34. On national taxonomy, see Abécassis, ""Une certaine idée de la nation," 8. On the 1955 Nasserian reforms of personal status and confessional tribunals, see Abécassis, "L'enseignement étranger," 709.

35. Abécassis, "L'enseignement étranger," 733.

36. See Williamson, *Education and Social Change in Egypt and Turkey*, 121.

37. Faksh, qtd. in Ibid., 121.

38. On requisitions and biblioclasm, see Abécassis, "Enseignement étranger," 14, 732. I use the term "private" to designate nongovernmental schools that were nationalized to different degrees. The status of nongovernmental institutions is in fact a more complex issue than presented here.

39. Abdalla, *Student Movement*, 104.

40. Abécassis, "L'enseignement étranger," 731, 734, 740. On Law 583 (1955), also see Cochran, *Education in Egypt*, 29.

41. Abécassis, "L'enseignement étranger," 715.

42. Z. A. interview, Cairo, 4 May 2000.

43. Withdrawn from university curricula in 1970. Abdalla, *Student Movement*, 116.

44. Z. A. interview, Cairo, 4 May 2000.

45. Abécassis, "Une certaine idée de la nation," 20.

46. See Faksh, "Consequences of the Introduction," 51–52.

47. According to an unpublished 1969 report on a Giza governorate village, 38 percent of households possessed a radio (mostly transistors) in addition to the radios owned by shopkeepers and the two village cafés. In 1968–69, Voice of the Arabs, the local and overseas radio service conceived for Arab audiences, provided twenty-six hours of broadcasting a day (inclusive of all programs, home and abroad) while the main general program broadcast for twenty hours a day. See Wahba, *Cultural Policy in Egypt*, 12, 67–68.

48. See Buhayri, *Ta'rikh Misr*.

49. Frisch, *Shared Authority*, 31, 46.

50. Al-Sayyid Abdalla, "Improving the Teaching of Social Studies in Egyptian Sec-

ondary Schools," 84–85. The first examination of primary schoolbooks was conducted in 1954. See Zaki, "Guidelines for Improving," 120. Shams (age sixteen) and Mu'taz (age nineteen), informal interviews by author, Cairo, 1 September 2001.

51. Shams (age sixteen), informal interview by author, Cairo, 1 September 2001.

52. Bakkar, "Qualitative Aspects," 25, 38–42; and informal conversations with students and their parents. See also Tadros, "Hitting the Books," 16.

53. Zaki, "Guidelines for Improving," 113, 119. On European influence in Tunisia, see Obdeijn, "Enseignement de l'histoire dans la Tunisie moderne," 50–52. This situation was true for early nineteenth-century secular textbooks. See Szyliowicz, *Education and Modernization in the Middle East*, 105; and Aroian, "Nationalization of Arabic and Islamic Education," 56.

54. In 1954 the Ministry of Education created a "High Committee for Textbooks," after which came out a new secondary school textbook elaborated by Husayn and others. See MOE, Husayn et al., *Fusul mukhtara min kutub*.

55. In the early 1990s the Ministry of Education established a National Center for Curriculum and Instructional Materials Development. See Tadros, "Hitting the Books," 16.

56. Gonzalez-Quijano, "Politiques culturelles," 105.

57. 'Awad, quoted in Gonzalez-Quijano, "Politiques culturelles," 106.

58. On state publishing monopoly, see Gonzalez-Quijano, "Politiques culturelles," 106, 107.

59. On '59 textbooks and exam, see Buhayri, *Ta'rikh Misr*, 184–85; and see table 2.1.

60. On Pharaonism, see Tadros, "Hitting the Books"; and El-Din, "Egypt National Report."

61. Published between 1995 and 1999 (academic year 1995–96 to 1999–2000).

62. MOE, *Al-Dirasat al-ijtima'iyya* (Social Studies), fourth-year primary (1998–99), 39.

63. Nasser's *Philosophy of the Revolution* inspired the 1959 fourth-year elementary textbook, according to Buhayri, *Ta'rikh Misr*, 173.

64. See MOE, *Al-Dirasat al-ijtima'iyya* (Social Studies), fifth-year primary (1996–97), which contains thirty-four pages on history: Pharaonic (six pages), Islamic (ten pages), contemporary (eighteen pages). See also, within the nine pages on the 1952 Revolution, MOE, *Al-Dirasat al-ijtima'iyya* (Social Studies), third-year preparatory (2009–10), 80–81.

65. Rodinson, "Préface," in Carré, *Enseignement islamique*, xi–xii.

66. MOE, *Al-Dirasat al-ijtima'iyya* (Social Studies), third-year preparatory (1998–99), 64.

67. Ibid.

68. Buhayri, *Ta'rikh Misr*, 4.

69. Only 4 percent of students enrolled in preparatory schools attend private schools, and 1 percent experimental schools. Private tutoring by governmental teachers is illegal but widely practiced. Lloyd et al., "Impact of Educational Quality," 450.

70. 'Asim Ahmad al-Disuqi (A. D.), interview by author, Cairo, 2 July 1997. Born in 1939, Disuqi was a historian at the University of Cairo at the time of the interview.

71. UNESCO education statistics for 1999 offer inflated rates, with a 100 percent

gross enrollment in primary education—and a high apparent intake of 90 percent—while estimating the average school term in 1993 at 10.3 years, 11.2 for males and 9.3 for females (see UNESCO, *1999 Statistical Yearbook*, "Primary and Secondary Education," table II-9, p. II-369; and "Primary Education: Selected Indicators," table II-11, p. II-423). In the table listing primary education selected indicators, there is no data after 1985 for the cohort reaching the fifth or final year of primary school, nor any rate after 1970—with the exception of 1993—for school term expectancy. Illiteracy rate percentages for population aged fifteen and over, and between fifteen and twenty-four, are given as follows: 1980: 60.7 (Male 46.3/Female 75.3)/48.2 (35.8/61.5); 1985: 56.8 (42.9/70.9)/43; 1990: 52.9 (39.7/66.4)/38.7 (29.1/49.1); 1995: 48.9 (36.5/61.5)/34.5 (26.2/43.3); 2000: 44.7 (33.4/56.3)/30.4 (23.6/37.7). See UNESCO, *1999 Statistical Yearbook*, table II-11, p. II-423. For the first time in 2006, the Egyptian census took into account dropout numbers for cohorts age 6 to 18. See Egypt State Information Service (SIS) at https://www.sis.gov.eg/En/story.aspx?sid=9 (accessed 25 October 2012).

72. Di-Capua, "Jabarti of the 20th Century," 429.
73. Jamal Kamal, "We Are All Port Said!" *Ruz al-Yusuf*, 19 November 1956, 18–19.
74. Z. A. interview, 4 May 2000, Cairo.
75. See Taher, *Aunt Safiya*, 105.
76. *Al-Sha'b*, 5 October 1989, 1.
77. McDonald, "Exhibitions of Power," 9.
78. Luke, *Museum Politics*.
79. Bakkar, "Qualitative Aspects of Egyptian Social Studies Textbooks," 37.
80. Cooper and Stoler, *Tensions of Empire*.
81. See Buhayri, *Ta'rikh Misr*, 173–74.
82. Ezzat, "Revolution Revisited," 6.
83. On mass media, see Alleaume, "L'Égypte et son histoire," 15.

Part II. Burn, Edmund, Burn

1. Savage, *Allenby of Armageddon*, 351. Savage influenced generations of Allenby biographers, including Gardner, *Allenby*.
2. See Savage, *Allenby of Armageddon*, 306.
3. Edmund Allenby (1861–1936) served in South Africa and France during World War I, after which he was sent to Palestine.
4. Ahmad 'Awad (A. A.), interview by author, Port Said, 31 October 2002. Born in 1927 in Port Said, the late Ahmad 'Awad was a barber and poet.
5. Captain Ghazali (C. G.), interview by author, Port Said, 12 May 2002. Born in 1928 in Suez, Ghazali is a wrestling coach, poet, a playwright, choir director, painter, and calligrapher. He fought in 1948, 1956, 1967, and during the War of Attrition. Also see Mahmoud Bakr and Khaled el-Ghamri, "Simsimiya Stories," *Al-Ahram Weekly* 401 (October 29–November 4, 1998), http://weekly.ahram.org.eg/1998/401/people.htm (accessed 18 October 2012).

6. Kamal 'Id (K. I.), interview by author, Port Said, 12 May 2002. Born ca. 1932.

7. "Ophir at Port Said," *Times*, 13 April 1901, 4.

8. "Latest Intelligence: The War in Egypt," Reuter's Telegrams, *Times*, 21 August 1882, 3.

9. "Raid on Port Said," *Times*, 22 May 1916, 8; and Douin, *L'attaque du canal de Suez*, 60, 76–77.

10. "10,000 at Port Said Hail Mussolini's Sons on Ship," *New York Times*, 28 August 1935, 1.

11. "Wafdist Petition Refused," *Times*, 23 July 1930, 14; and "Anti-missionary Agitation," *Times*, 24 June 1933, 11.

12. "Egyptians Back Indonesians," *Washington Post*, 10 August 1947, 5.

13. See Idris, *City of Love and Ashes*.

14. 'Abd al-Rahim Gharib al-Banna (A. B.), interview by author, Ismailia, 1 November 2002. Born in 1923 in Ismailia, the late al-Banna was a worker.

15. Adam Morrow, "A Handful of Limbies Still Moulder Along the Canal Despite a Gubernatorial Decree," *Cairo Times*, 11–17 May 2000, 10.

16. A. B. interview, Ismailia, 1 November 2002.

17. This represented a large sum for the average wage earner. See "Hate Figure Festival Called Off in Egypt," press release, Agence France-Presse, 4 May 2002.

18. "New Reviews," *Sunday Times*, 7 May 2002, section 5, 10.

19. "Hate Figure Festival Called Off."

20. "Expansion of Natural Gas Networks," 24 March 1997, Middle East News Items. Available at Info-Prod Research Strategic Business Information Database, http://web.lexis-nexis.com/hottopics/lnacademic (accessed 18 October 2012).

21. *Al-Ahram Weekly*, issue no. 480, 4–10 May 2000.

22. Michel Lussault, *Images de la ville et politiques urbaines*, quoted in Bruyas, "Aménagement de la ville de Port Said," 143.

23. Carey, "Customs Confusion," 21; Khattab, "The Tale of a City"; and Shahine, "Under Siege."

24. See *Al-Kabtan* (The Captain) (1997) by Sayyid Sa'id. Set within the 1948 Palestinian exodus, *Al-Kabtan* depicts the rebellion of a colorful character against the pro-British governor of Port Said.

25. K. I. interview, Port Said, 12 May 2002.

26. On paradigmatic similarity, see Portelli, *The Battle of Valle Giulia*, 32.

Chapter 3. When Edmund Allenby Became al-Limby

1. See Cattaui, *L'Egypte*, 362, 364–65.

2. *Le Monde*, 28 July 1956, 2.

3. Kyle, *Suez*, 522. Also see Modelski, *Port Said Revisited*, 62. Modelski reports in her memoirs that both the French and the British tactlessly wrapped the statue with their national flags.

4. See Cattaui, *L'Egypte*, 363; and Mountjoy, "The Suez Canal at Mid-Century," 164–65.

5. De Sérionne, quoted in Cattaui, *L'Egypte*, 364.

6. Kipling, *Light that Failed*, 43. On literary inventions, see Modelski, *Port Said Revisited*, 49–54.

7. As seen in Tilmisani's film *Al-Suq al-sawda*. See Armbrust, "Egyptian Cinema On Stage and Off," 81.

8. *Le Monde*, 28 July 1956, 2. The 1936 treaty established the repartition of land forces around Ismailia and air forces to the southeast of Suez. A small contingent stayed in Port Said and Suez until World War II. See Aglietti, *Il Canale di Suez ed i Rapporti Anglo-Egiziano*, 106–7, 111–12.

9. *Le Monde*, 28 July 1956, 2.

10. The Compagnie administered Ismailia and Port-Tewfik's municipalities. See Saint Victor, *Le Canal de Suez*, 269–70.

11. In the 1950s the council included sixteen Frenchmen, nine Britons, five Egyptians, one Dutchman, and one American. See Baud, *L'Egypte* (1956), 229–30.

12. Until 1937 only 3 percent of industrial establishments employed more than ten workers. See Beinin and Lockman, *Workers on the Nile*, 41, 37.

13. This includes the residential quarters of Port Fouad built for foreigners in 1925. See Baud, *L'Egypte* (1956), 220, 222. On World War I and World War II labor migration, see Sibai, "Slums Family Life," 8. Peace caused shortages in employment. Foreign population estimates are hard to evaluate. They reflect juridical status but not necessarily nationality. The 1917 census counted 73,052 Egyptians and 18,038 foreigners on the Canal Zone. See Cattaui, *L'Egypte*, 375.

14. For the 1960 census, see Sibai, "Slums Family Life," 8, 15. For 2000 and 2009 population estimates, see Central Agency for Public Mobilization and Statistics (CAPMAS), "Estimates of Midyear Population by Governorate (2000–2009)," Statistical Yearbook 2011, table 2.5, at http://www.capmas.gov.eg/pdf/static/2-5.pdf (accessed 19 October 2012).

15. Suez was established in the fifteenth century. It bloomed as a large transit harbor to Asia and South Africa in the 1950s. See Baud, *L'Egypte* (1956), 220, 236–37.

16. Beinin and Lockman, *Workers on the Nile*, 36.

17. Ilbert, *Alexandrie, 1830–1930*, 2:662, 728.

18. The local folk music group Tanbura built upon that heritage.

19. Savage, *Allenby of Armageddon*, 294.

20. Communal tensions appear in many incidents. See "The Jewish Colony of Port Said Have Addressed a Petition" (*Times*, 13 May 1892, 5), according to which Greeks accused Jews of ritual slaughter.

21. 'Abd al-Rahim Gharib al-Banna's father and maternal uncle were card players.

22. Savage, *Allenby of Armageddon*; Wavell, *Allenby, A Study in Greatness*; and Gardner, *Allenby*. Field Marshal Archibald Wavell (1883–1950), who fought in the Second Boer War and served in France and India, assisted Allenby in Palestine. See Wavell's autobiography, *The Good Soldier*.

23. Yeçilbursa, *Baghdad Pact*.

24. "British Truck Ambushed in Suez; 2 Killed," *Chicago Daily Tribune*, 21 November

1951, 11; "Sabotage in Port Said," *Times*, 24 November 1951, 6; "Report Roads in Suez Wired to Behead Britons," *Chicago Daily Tribune*, 27 November 1951, 8; and "Signs of Change at Port Said," *Times*, 4 February 1952, 3.

25. A. B. interview, Ismailia, 1 November 2002. On Indian colonial police and administration, see Fawaz et al., *Modernity and Culture*, 10.

26. In 1965 the town was divided into four formal administrative sectors: al-Sharq, al-'Arab, al-Manakh, and al-Mina. Adjoining the Egyptian working-class neighborhood of al-'Arab, Al-Sharq roughly corresponded to al-Afranj, populated by Egyptian and foreign elites. Al-Manakh, destroyed in 1956, was commonly known as the "Masakin" because of its social housing and included the partially torn down 'Izab area. Al-Mina encompassed parts of the 'Arab and qabuti districts, near Lake Manzala; it was inhabited by fishermen and included the formerly British ("Golf") barracks transformed into homeless housing in the 1960s. See Al-Sibai, "Slums Family Life," 6.

27. Mona 'Awad (M. A.), interview by author, Port Said, 13 October 2002. Born ca. 1960 in Port Said, and daughter of poet Ahmad 'Awad, Mona 'Awad is a homemaker.

28. Cohen, *Masquerade Politics*.

29. Ibid., ix.

30. Ibid., 1.

31. Bakhtin, *Rabelais and His World*, 9.

32. Favret-Saada, *Les mots, la mort, les choses*, 133.

33. See Scott, *Domination and the Arts of Resistance*.

34. Hobsbawm and Ranger, *Invention of Tradition*, 1–2.

35. Ibid., 2.

36. A. A. interview, Port Said, 13 May 2002.

37. Some Ismailis contend that the custom originated from their city.

38. Lane, *An Account of the Manners*, 495. On Lane's life, see Starkey and Starkey, *Travellers in Egypt*, 233–53.

39. A notable exception is Shukr's "Shamm al-Nasim fi Bur Sa'id."

40. Klunzinger, *Upper Egypt*. Blackman's description (*Fellahin of Upper Egypt*, 261–62) indicates that he read Lane and witnessed the festival from afar. See also the folkloric account of British secret police officer Joseph W. McPherson in *Moulids of Egypt*, 4–5.

41. The burning of the Judas existed in Greece and Sicily and is similar to al-Limby. See Megas, *Greek Calendar Customs*, 110.

42. On historical Nawruz, see Shoshan, *Popular Culture in Medieval Cairo*, 49; and Sanders, *Ritual, Politics, and the City in Fatimid Cairo*, 83–98.

43. Rifaud, *Voyage en Egypte en Nubie*; Murray, "Nawruz, or the Coptic New Year"; Klunzinger, *Upper Egypt*; and Leeder, *Modern Sons of the Pharaohs*. Shoshan suggests that Leeder may have copied Klunziger. Leeder's narrative structure indeed mimics Klunzinger's and validates Shoshan's suggestion. Murray only mentions in passing Klunzinger's reference to effigy burning ("Nawruz," 80). On Rifaud, see Reid, *Whose Pharaohs?* 70, 72.

44. See Klunzinger, *Upper Egypt*, ix. A German physician who spent eight years in

Egypt (1860s–ca. 1875), Klunzinger seems most informed. He is critical of Lane's ignorance of rural life.

45. See Murray, "Nawruz, or the Coptic New Year," 81.

46. As Murray suggests, citing Kluzinger, with regard to Nawruz rural effigy burnings. Kluzinger recounted a three-day celebration of Nawruz in Upper Egypt, followed by the effigy burning of a mock king. See Murray, "Nawruz, or the Coptic New Year," 81. On rural practices, see also Blackman, *Fellahin of Upper Egypt*, 262.

47. Villagers continue to this day to come to the Canal cities during Shamm al-Nasim.

48. A. A. interview, Port Said, 31 October 2002.

49. A. A.'s family came from Damietta, A. B. and M.'s families (see n61 to chapter 1) from Upper Egypt. On rural migration, see Beinin and Lockman, *Workers on the Nile*, 26. Shukr overestimates the migration from neighboring governorates (see "Shamm al-nasim," 143–44).

50. C. G. interview, Port Said, 12 May 2002.

51. Shukr ("Shamm al-Nasim," 138) sees the origins of the Limby in the *'arusat al-khamasin* and rural customs.

52. A. A. interview, Port Said, 31 October 2002.

53. Turner, quoted in Mukerji and Schudson, *Rethinking Popular Culture*, 23.

54. Ibid.

55. A. B. interview, Ismailia, 1 November 2002.

56. See Doss and Barsoum, "Allenby, l'éxutoire," 24. This source inaccurately states that Allenby was commissioner in 1917. In a 4 August 2003 e-mail to the author, Doss explained that she interviewed the Khudayr brothers as well as people on the street. The article is thus based on vernacular stories.

57. Savage, *Allenby of Armageddon*, 307.

58. Ibid., 175.

59. By contrast, it is hard to elude the heroic depiction of Allenby, played by Jack Hawkins in David Lean's Hollywood epic *Lawrence of Arabia* (United States, 1962).

60. Mansfield, *British in Egypt*, 215.

61. Savage, *Allenby of Armageddon*, 180.

62. See Mansfield, *British in Egypt*, 215: "The new [1917] law was issued on the authority of the army and was [connected with] military security.... The fellahin were angered because they felt they had done nothing to provoke this action."

63. Ibid.

64. 'Ulawya and Shuman, "Al-Nass al-shi'ri" (Poetic Expression), 209.

65. On peasants' reluctance to volunteer, see Mansfield, *British in Egypt*, 215. Young (*Egypt*, 210) gives higher estimates than Mansfield: some 8,500 men "were being recruited for the Mesopotamian Labour Corps," and some 10,000 for France. The camel transport service of the Syrian campaign "of considerable hardship, often under fire, was work for which Egyptians alone were competent." Both Mansfield's 1971 book and Young's 1927 work embrace racial stereotypes.

66. Mansfield, *British in Egypt*, 215–16.

67. British apologists point to Egyptian profits. Others denounce British exclusion of inflation in their calculations. Most profits went to "big and medium landowners" and "garrison towns." See Mansfield, *British in Egypt*, 215–16; and Young, *Egypt*, 212.

68. For estimates of troop numbers in Egypt, see Hughes, *Allenby and British Strategy*, 150: late 1919, 128,000 troops; in 1920, 100,000 troops; in 1921, 20,000 troops.

69. Leeder, *Modern Sons*, 5–6.

70. Savage, *Allenby of Armageddon*, 180.

71. On corvée, see al-Sayyid-Marsot, *Short History of Modern Egypt*, 80.

72. See Brown, *Peasant Politics in Modern Egypt*, 195, 197, 198. See also 'Abd al-Wahid, *Al-Tatawwurat al-ijtima'iyya fi al-rif al-misri*; and Salim, *Misr fi al-harb al-'alamiyya al-ula*.

73. Quoted in Hughes, *Allenby and British Strategy*, 142.

74. C. G. interview, Port Said, 12 May 2002.

75. K. I. interview, Port Said, 12 May 2002.

76. See Beinin and Lockman, *Workers on the Nile*, 107–9.

77. Ibid., 108–10. Also see Shukr, "Shamm al-Nasim," 148. Such alliances contradict narratives that portray Egyptian foreign relations in antagonistic terms and the coalheavers' strike as an Egyptian nationalist protest.

78. See Sammy Ketz, "Netanyahu Burned at the Stake at Egypt's 'Festival against Injustice,'" Agence France-Presse press release, 28 April 1997. Ketz relates the effigy burning to a 1919 demonstration in Port Said that left seven dead and 17 wounded. Also see Hassan, "King of Spring."

79. Mas'ud Shuman (M. S.), interview by author, Port Said, 12 May 2002. Born in 1966, Shuman is a folklorist, anthropologist, and poet and is married to a Port Saidi.

80. My emphasis. Police Report (Cairo), 31 July 1919, quoted in Booth, "Colloquial Arabic Poetry," 424. Booth documents the nationalist use of oral stanzaic colloquial rhymes (*zajal*).

81. Wavell, *Allenby: A Study in Greatness*, 127. See also Gardner, *Allenby*, 253.

82. Shukr, "Shamm al-Nasim," 128.

83. So contends Shukr in "Shamm al-Nasim," 129. My calculations confirm this statement. Mulid al-Nabi celebrates the Prophet Muhammad's birthday (12 Rabi' of the Islamic calendar).

84. Hagg Yusif (H. Y.), interview by author, Port Said, 15 April 2001. Born in 1929. C. G. (interview, Port Said, 12 May 2002) added that it happened in the neighborhood of Salim Zaki.

85. The incident involved a group of French sailors who were beaten up while getting out of a car that passed near a crowd of young people in the "native quarters." Letter from M. Forcioli to Mr. Henri Gaillard, Minister of France in Egypt, 16 June 1920, CADN, Consulate/Port Said, 602/484.

86. The approach of Allenby "flag-waggers" was greeted by opposing "B.B.L." flags, signaling "Bully's Bull's Loose." See Savage, *Allenby of Armageddon*, 246.

87. See Doss and Barsoum, "Allenby, l'éxutoire," 24. This article situates the incident in 1917. Built on oral testimonies, it contains many inaccuracies.

88. Shukr, "Shamm al-Nasim," 128–29.
89. A. B. interview, Ismailia, 1 November 2003.
90. A. A. interview, Port Said, 31 October 2002.
91. Scott, *Domination and the Arts of Resistance*, 37.

Chapter 4. Port Said, Martyr City

1. M. S. interview, Port Said, 12 May 2002; and Hamdi, Folklore Studies researcher, Cairo, informal conversation, 8 May 2002.
2. See "British Quietly Give Suez Base to Egypt after 74-year Stay," *New York Times*, 14 June 1956, 1; and "Last British Soldier Quits Suez Canal Zone," *Los Angeles Times*, 14 June 1956, 18.
3. K. I. interview, Port Said, 12 May 2002; and other informal interviewees, such as Hamdi, Cairo, 8 May 2002.
4. K. I. interview, Port Said, 12 May 2002.
5. Cohen, *Masquerade Politics*, 128.
6. The term *fida'iyyin* here means resistance, resistance fighter, combatant. A U.S. reporter told the same story in 1969. He added that Moorhouse was caught tearing down posters of Nasser. Love, *Suez*, 657.
7. Inaccuracies are indicative of the teller's "dreams, and desires beneath them." Portelli, *Death of Luigi Trastulli*, 2.
8. Zaki, *Ruz al-Yusuf*, 5 November 1956, 6. Compare the Zaki caricature with Salah Jahin's page 7 illustration in the same issue of *Ruz al-Yusuf* of a British plane flying over the masculine and proletarian spirit of the Egyptian people.
9. Robert Doty, "Port Said Hostile as Exodus Nears," *New York Times*, 8 December 1956, 1.
10. A. B. interview, Ismailia, 1 November 2003.
11. There is no trace of "William" in British records of the 1956 War, but there is a Major Williams of Civil Affairs, wounded on 8 December by a "grenade thrown into his car." Confidential note prepared by Gen. Stockwell regarding the disappearance of Moorhouse, 24 December 1956, PRO, WO 258/136.
12. H. Y. interview, Port Said, 15 April 2001.
13. See "Bomb Injures British Officer in Latest Incident in Port Said," *New York Times*, 14 December 1956, 3.
14. A very young nurse who read about Mahran's story in the news met and married him; "she was [his] eyes." The love story is real. Most people view Mahran as a national hero in Port Said. Muhammad Mahran, interview by author, 23 January 2012, Port Said. Born in 1938. Mahran's blindness is no invention, yet there is no evidence as to his claims. Dia al-Din Hasan al-Qadi, a local history-teller, records a Hollywood-like tale of heroism that, like his pompous annals, mixes history and fiction. See al-Qadi, *Al-Atlas al-tarikhi*, 185.
15. The story generated a British theater play in 1957. A former lieutenant colonel and

British military chronicler wrote the most complete journalistic (although apologetic) account based on interviews with the British military and media. See Barker, *Suez*, 179–80. Love claimed in 1969 that fifth-grade Egyptian textbooks had featured the Moorhouse story since 1959. Love, *Suez*, 656.

16. I did not find any written evidence, yet this idea prevails in oral accounts. It passes for fact in 'Ulawya and Shuman, "Al-Nass al-shi'ri," 223–24.

17. Love, *Suez*, 657; and Barker, *Suez*, 179. The press adopted the latter story. See "Egyptians Kidnap, Slay Briton," *Chicago Daily Tribune*, 12 September 1956, 1.

18. See "Egypt Underground Says Kidnapped Briton Slain," *Christian Science Monitor*, 12 December 1956, 8; "Egyptians Kidnap a British Officer: Act Follows Arrest of Eight Arabs in Port Said Area," *New York Times*, 2 December 1956, 12; and Telegram No.1869, from UKDEL New York to Berne and UKSU, 31 December 1956, PRO, WO 258/136.

19. The prime minister received three telegrams on 17 December 1956. In one of them Major Thurnber warned, "Pull out of Port Said and leave young Moorhouse and a million votes behind you. Churchill wouldn't leave him." *Omnibus*, 28 December 1956, PRO, FO 371/119274, JE 1614/3.

20. *Christian Science Monitor*, 12 December 1956, 8.

21. Report, from W. H. Curtis, "Confidential note prepared by Gen. Stockwell regarding the disappearance of Moorhouse," 24 December 1956, PRO, WO 258/136.

22. Telegram confidential No.2899, 25 December 1956, PRO, FO 371/119 274, JE 16141. Investigations, however, continued until 31 December, even though by as early as 29 December the British had lost hope. See Telegram confidential No.1852, 29 December 1956, PRO, FO, 371/119274.

23. Deciphered telegram No.1869, from UKDEL New York to Berne and UKSU, 31 December 1956, PRO, WO 258/136.

24. "Port Said Death House Museum," *Times*, 3 December 1956, 12.

25. Most Cairenes did not know Mansur. See reference to Mansur in fourth-year preparatory social studies textbook, UAR, *Al-Dirasat al-itima'iyya* (1998–99), 40.

26. Directed by 'Izz al-Din Dhulfiqar.

27. Directed by Kamal al-Shaykh and starring Fatin Hamama and 'Umar Sharif.

28. Wassef, *Egypte: Cent ans de cinéma*, 29. Kamal Ramzi cites eight films related to the Suez War; see Gordon, "*Nasser 56/Cairo 96*," 179. See also Shohat, "Egypt: Cinema and Revolution," 30.

29. Armbrust, "Manly Men on a National Stage," 263–64.

30. According to Armbrust, the "project was one of the first large-scale experiments in government subsidized filmmaking in Egypt." Ibid., 263.

31. Ibid.

32. Song translation by author and Zaynab 'Ali. The Tanbura dates back to 1989 and borrows from the musical repertoire of *simsimiyya* music found in the Canal cities. Song cited in al-Wardani, "Al-Tanbura allati takhtaf al-ruh" (The Tanbura that Stirs the Soul), 21; and briefly mentioned in 'Ulawya and Shuman, "Al-Nass al-shi'ri," 224.

33. On Seymour, see Warren, *Encyclopedia of 20th Century Photography*, 1409.

34. Leonard Leddington, "No Peace yet at Port Said Despite Cease-Fire Pledge," *Washington Times*; and *Times Herald*, 8 November 1956, 9A.

35. Secret telegram No.1303, from UKDEL New York to FO, FO (secret) and Whitehall (secret) distribution, 19 November 1956, PRO, FO 371/1199274. According to this telegram, Hammarskjöld, the Swedish secretary-general of the United Nations (1953–61), "admitted that he did not know whether the troubles in Port Said were self-generated or were directed from Cairo."

36. Shaw, *Eden, Suez, and the Mass Media*. Shaw does not expose inconsistencies and mystifications. See also Love, *Suez*, 409, 529; and James, *Nasser at War*.

37. Herbert "gave the above information in strictest confidence and it should not, therefore, be quoted back either to him or to anybody else." See Priority secret telegram No.1462, from Mr. Middleton to FO, 23 December 1956, PRO, FO 371/119 274, JE 1094/396.

38. Herbert, *Damage and Casualties in Port Said*, 28. December '56 confidential report to Parliament cited in n37.

39. Emergency confidential No.PA/886, from Mr. Murray to FO, 23 November 1956, PRO, FO 371/118911. Egyptians claimed 12,000 civilian deaths in the early stages of the war. Shaw (*Eden, Suez and the Mass Media*, 84, 179) cites "as many as 1,500 Egyptian soldiers and civilians . . . killed and wounded." Love (*Suez*, 636) cites between 2,000 and 3,000 Egyptian deaths. Both Shaw and Love used news estimates. On average, Western sources, such as Herbert, cite 750–1,000 Egyptian deaths. Anglo-French casualties (see Kyle, *Suez*, 502–3) amounted to 23–33 deaths and 121 wounded.

40. Report, from J.K.J. Frost, Office of the Paymaster-General, to Lord Privy Seal, "Damage at Port Said," 30 November 1956, PRO, FO 371/118 920, JE 1094/384, 1–3.

41. Herbert, *Damage and Casualties in Port Said*, 28.

42. Ibid., 9–10.

43. Love, *Suez*, 596.

44. *Ruz al-Yusuf*, 12 November 1956, 23. See also Barker, *Suez*, 178. A French diplomatic note (neither dated nor authored) reports a poster in Arabic and English indicating: "Death to those who collaborate with murderers." Manuscript note, CADN, Suez vice-consulate/Port Said, 298/74.

45. Report, from Murray to FO, "Verbatim Text of General Stockwell's letter to General Burns of December 15," 12 December 1956, PRO, FO 371/118 920, JE 1094/396, 2–3.

46. *Ruz al-Yusuf*, 19 November 1956, 14–15.

47. Zahdi, *Ruz al-Yusuf*, 5 November 1956, 11.

48. Secret telegram No.1303, from UKDEL New York to FO, FO (secret) and Whitehall (secret) distribution, 19 November 1956, PRO, FO 371/1199274.

49. Report, from J.K.J. Frost, Office of the Paymaster-General, to Lord Privy Seal, "Damage at Port Said," 30 November 1956, PRO, FO 371/118 920, JE 1094/384, 3. The French agreed. Expressing his "regrets" about recent official underestimates ("a hundred victims") of casualties, yet acknowledging that 75 percent of the 1,500–2000 Egyptian casualties were dead, a French diplomat blamed Nasser's recklessness. Telegram No. MT 2/AL, Andre Brenac to chief-commander of French Operational Forces (CCFFO), 12 November 1956, CADN, Suez vice-consulate/Port Said, 298/75.

50. Shehada, *Die Suezkrise von 1956*, 321.

51. Barker, *Suez*, 140, 147, 150, 165. The Foreign Office advised counterpropaganda agencies to advertise that "in accordance to Nasser's instructions civilians including children were armed. Many Egyptian soldiers wore civilian galabiyehs over their uniforms" and sniping "led to house to house fighting with consequent damage to property and loss of life." See Diplomatic correspondence to British High Commission (UK HC) India, PRO, FO 371/118911. Also see Note No.25557, from FO to Murray, 19 November 1956, PRO, FO 371/118911. This note recommends publishing "photographs of undamaged parts of Port Said" as well as using "fake Egyptian propaganda" in order to "discredit the rest of the propaganda." On the use of fake propaganda, see Confidential note, UKDEL New York to FO, FO (secret) and Whitehall (secret) distribution, 21 November 1956, PRO, FO 371/118911.

52. Hussein, *Drawings by School Children of Port Said*, 5.

53. "Gang Seizes British Aide in Port Said," *Washington Times-Herald*, 12 December 1956, A5; and UAR, *'Id al-Nasr* (Victory Day), 56.

54. Communication, from Jacques Roux to MAE, "Discours du Président Nasser le 21 décembre à Port-Saïd," 28 December 1965, CADN, French embassy in Egypt (Ambassade EG), 22/Fêtes, 1–2.

55. Telegram No.1345/AL, from Jacques Roux to MAE, "10ème anniversaire de la bataille de Port-Saïd," 28 December 1966, CADN (Ambassade EG), 22/Fêtes, 1.

56. See "Chou Honors Egyptians Killed in 1956 Fighting," *Washington Post*, 18 December 1963, A16; "Nikita Scores 'Imperialism' in the Middle East," *Chicago Tribune*, 20 May 1964, A10; and Telegram No.1345/AL, from Jacques Roux to MAE, 28 December 1966, "10ème anniversaire de la bataille de Port-Saïd," CADN, Ambassade EG, 22/Fêtes, 1.

57. Zayyat's *The Open Door* was originally published in 1960 as *Al-Bab al-maftuh* and turned into a movie by Wahid Farid in 1963.

58. H. Y. interview, Port Said, 15 April 2001.

59. K. I. interview, Port Said, 12 May 2002.

60. Ibid.

61. Ramadan, *Umm Kulthum*.

62. Six of the seven songs Umm Kulthum released in 1956 were patriotic; see the Web site "Umm Kulthum: The Star of the East, the Diva of Arabic Song," http://almashriq.hiof.no/egypt/700/780/umKoulthoum/ (accessed 21 October 2012).

63. Western historiography validates Egyptian claims that the British wanted to oust Nasser from power; see Louis and Owen, *Suez 1956*. See also Love, *Suez*, 396.

64. See Hewedy, "Nasser and the Crisis of 1956," 171: A former lieutenant-colonel wrote some thirty years later that "millions of people in cities, villages, schools, and factories joined [Nasser] to resist invasion. Thousands of small arms were distributed without registration throughout the country."

65. See Mahfuz, *Autumn Quail*, 133. The British jammed the Egyptian radio on 16 November (Barker, *Suez*, 178). Herbert's report (*Damage and Casualties in Port Said*, 10) is contradictory.

66. Special feature "Know Your Weapons," in *Ruz al-Yusuf*, 12 November 1956, 22.

67. Armbrust, "Manly Men on a National Stage," 248.

68. See an illustration by an unidentified author showing a female resistance fighter, in military uniform, cutting electric wires with an axe, in *Ruz al-Yusuf*, 12 November 1956, 23.

69. *Ruz al-Yusuf*, 12 November 1956, 23. See also "Those Who Survived," *Ruz al-Yusuf*, 19 November 1956.

70. Museum artifacts are not all dated. Most Nasserian paintings are from the early 1960s.

71. See special feature "Know Your Weapons," in *Ruz al-Yusuf*, 12 November 1956, 23.

72. Mahfuz, *Autumn Quail*, 133.

73. See special feature "Know Your Weapons," in *Ruz al-Yusuf*, 12 November 1956, 23.

74. Hewedy, "Nasser and the Crisis of 1956," 161.

75. See Marilyn Booth's introduction to Zayyat, *Open Door*, ix.

76. Kilpatrick, "The Egyptian Novel from Zaynab to the Canvas," 252.

77. Zayyat, *Open Door*, 362.

78. "'Hit him! Give it to him!' . . . A heavy rock in the hand of a young woman sailed at the head of a parachutist as he tried to get his balance. He fell to the ground, his head shattered" (Zayyat, *Open Door*, 347). Zayyat's depiction is also in contrast with the "matronly, manly, or defeminized" deprecating images of political women by males in 1920s–30s Egypt, as discussed by Baron, *Egypt as a Woman*, 185. On Communardes, see Gullikson, *Unruly Women of Paris*, 183–90.

79. Armbrust, "Manly Men on a National Stage," 249.

80. See Idris, *City of Love and Ashes*.

81. See Marilyn Booth's introduction to Zayyat, *Open Door*, xxiv. In Shahin's film, Salah al-Din's right hand is a Copt.

82. The role of Jamila Bu Hirad (1935–) was tailored for the Egyptian actress and producer Magda al-Sabbahi (1931–). The film was produced shortly after Jamila's arrest in 1957.

83. The main characters speak in Cairene dialect, and the peasants have a sort of Upper Egyptian accent.

84. A doctor fights in the secret resistance in *Bur Sa'id* while an Algerian bey (first mistaken for a collaborator) supports the Front de Libération Nationale in *Jamila*. The people are first suspicious of the wealthy but soon accept them.

85. As described in the film, historic National Liberation Front leader Muhammad Larbi Bin M'Hidi (1923–57) was arrested and then assassinated by the French military while in custody. His execution was disguised as a suicide.

86. Secret documents on Jamila's torture are smuggled out and publicized by the Egyptian media. In all these films and their U.S. and European counterparts, emotional fulfillment is subordinate to national liberation and female self-realization to male political awakening.

87. Meital, "Egyptian Perspectives on the Suez War," 203.

88. K. I. interview, Port Said, 12 May 2002.

89. For example, Barker, *Suez*, 19; and Louis and Owen, *Suez 1956*.

90. A. A. interview, Port Said, 31 October 2002.
91. Ahmed, *Border Passage*, 172.
92. Picasso Gallery exhibit, 25 September to 25 October 2011, Cairo.
93. Z. A. interview, Cairo, 27 April 2000.
94. Raf. A. interview, Cairo, 2 May 2001.
95. A. A. interview, Port Said, 5 May 2002.
96. The composition and organization of the troupe reveals its grassroots origins. Some, however, criticize it for its commercialization because it received foreign funding.
97. M. S. interview, Port Said, 12 May 2002.

Chapter 5. The End of History

1. A. B. interview, Ismailia, 1 November 2002.
2. K. I. interview, Port Said, 12 May 2002.
3. A. A. interview, Port Said, 31 October 2002.
4. A 1979 pamphlet (without page numbers and printed for foreign consumption) echoed this message of peace with the following words: "On June 5, 1975, President Sadat, motivated by his genuine awareness of the changes that have come over world politics and world economy, declared the reopening of the Suez Canal and this brave resolution was considered by the whole world as a sincere step heading for peace and aiming at alleviating the world economic crisis." See ARE, *Canal in 4 Years*.
5. 'Umar al-Faruq (O.F.), interview by author, Cairo, 27 June 2000. In English. Al-Faruq is a translator.
6. Lt.-Gen. Hugh Charles Stockwell (1903–86) was the head of the British forces and of the Allied Task Force in 1956.
7. N. H. interview, Cairo, 23 March 2000.
8. Fa'iq Rida (F. R.), interview by author, Cairo, 22 March 2000. Born in 1935, in Alexandria, Rida is a retired lawyer.
9. A. B. interview, Ismailia, 12 December 2002.
10. Modelski, *Port Said Revisited*, 62.
11. N. H. interview, Cairo, 23 March 2000. Egyptian accounts do not differentiate between French and British behaviors, whereas the British and French blame each other. Compare Zwang, *Chirurgien du contingent*, 47; and Barker, *Suez*, 170.
12. N. H. interview, Cairo, 23 March 2000; and Bisati, *Houses behind the Trees*.
13. Bisati, *Houses behind the Trees*, 57–58.
14. Ibid., 39.
15. The Seven-Day War did not survive, while the Six-Day War (the June War in Egypt) endured. See Barker, *Suez*.
16. Telegram No.644/AL, Jacques Roux to MAE, "Le conflit militaire israélo arabe de l'ouverture des hostilités au cessez-le-feu (5–9 juin)," 23 June 1967, CADN, Ambassade EG/Cairo, 323/III, 3.
17. Z. A. interview, Cairo, 4 May 2000.

18. "Hastily, in the night between the 8th and the 9th, teams from the Socialist Union proceeded to take off the banderoles ... the slogans, that became derisory, such as 'we will meet in Tel-Aviv,' or 'Victory is ours.'" See Telegram No.644/AL, Jacques Roux to MAE, "Le conflit militaire israélo arabe de l'ouverture des hostilités au cessez-le-feu (5–9 juin)," 23 June 1967, CADN, Ambassade EG/Cairo, 323/III, 6.

19. Z. A. interview, Cairo, 4 May 2000.

20. Director Tawfiq Salih initiated the wave of such films in 1968 with *Al-Mutamarridun* (The Rebels). Husayn Kamal followed, also in 1968, with *Shay' min al-khawf* (A Bit of Fear) and Kamal al-Shaykh in 1969 with *Miramar*.

21. In Badrakhan's film, Su'ad Husni plays a political activist tortured and raped in prison. The film voyeuristically portrays the violence of the Nasserian state.

22. A theory upheld by Haykal in *1967: Al-Infijar*.

23. "The film, along with the entire Nagm/Imam repertoire of songs eventually came to represent the [grassroots and popular left-wing] movement that emerged" after 1970 and that was critical both of Sadat's right-wing policies and of Nasser's failures. See Khouri, *Arab National Project*, 97.

24. Cited in 'Ulawya and Shuman, "Al-Nass al-shi'ri," 224.

25. Barker, *Suez*, 178.

26. Benjamin, *La Revolución*.

27. Ibid., 73.

28. A. B. interview, Ismailia, 1 November 2003.

29. N. H. interview, Cairo, 23 March 2000.

30. A. B. interview, Ismailia, 1 November 2003.

31. Report No. 85 drafted 21 June 1967, from Jacques Charreyron, General Consul of France in Cairo, to Jacques Roux, French Ambassador, "Voyage dans la Zone du Canal," 23 June 1967, CADN, Ambassade EG, 323/III, 5.

32. A. A. interview, Port Said, 13 May 2002

33. N. H. interview, Cairo, 23 March 2000.

34. "Egypt Says at Least 200 Civilians Died in Port Said Air Raids," *Times*, 25 October 1973, 9. A 1971 French diplomatic report estimated the number of refugees from the Canal Zone at six hundred thousand, the destruction of the city of Suez at 40 percent, and the number of (mostly rural) people who stayed in the Suez area at fifty thousand. See Report No. 177/AL, Puaux to Schumann, "Suez, ville morte," 5 February 1971, CADN, Ambassade EG, 323/III.

35. A. A. interview, Port Said, 13 May 2002.

36. A. B. interview, Ismailia, 1 November 2003.

37. A. A. (interview, Port Said, 13 May 2002) claimed that this help was sufficient, but the dispersion of family members suggests otherwise, as do diplomatic records. A French report thus indicates the insufficiency of state indemnities for ordinary citizens (LE3 per month) at the exclusion of Canal employees and the "miserable conditions in the camps." See Telegram No.433/AL, Pierre Susini to Michel Debré, MAE, "Du problème des réfugiés égyptiens de la zone du Canal," 4 April 1969, CADN, Ambassade EG, 323/III.

38. A. B. interview, Ismailia, 1 November 2003.

39. Bisati, *Houses behind the Trees*, 45–47.

40. Telegram confidential No. 71, Bergus (Cairo) to SECSTATE, DEPSTATE (Washington), SITREP 10–17 July 1967, 7/18/67, NARA, DEPSTATE Documents, RG 59/Box 2552.

41. Telegram confidential No. 236, Bergus (Cairo) to SECSTATE, DEPSTATE (Washington), SITREP 5–11 August 1967, 8/12/67, NARA, RG 59/Box 2552, 2.

42. Telegram confidential No. 179, Bergus (Cairo) to SECSTATE, DEPSTATE (Washington), SITREP 27 July–4 August 1967, 8/5/67, NARA, RG 59/Box 2552, 1.

43. Telegram confidential No. 236, Bergus (Cairo) to SECSTATE, DEPSTATE (Washington), SITREP 5–11 August 1967, 8/12/67, NARA, RG 59/Box 2552.

44. "Egypt Gears Up to Open Suez Canal," *Chicago Tribune*, 1 June 1975, B17.

45. On the other hand, Sa'id Marzuq's first film, *Zawjati wa-al-kalb* (*My Wife and the Dog*, 1971), shows his predilection for an apolitical and lighter cinematic genre.

46. Such paradox may be considered in relation to Yusif Shahin's 1971 *Al-Ikhtiyar* (The Choice), and Abu Sayf's *Hammam al-Malatili* (Malatily Bathhouse).

47. Modelski, *Port Said Revisited*, 191–92; and Christopher Wren, "Duty Free Zone Is Boon to Port Said—And Smuggling," *New York Times*, 19 April 1978, A3.

48. A. B. interview, Ismailia, 1 November 2003.

49. Ibid.

50. Ibid.

51. UAR, "Al-'Id al-qawmi li-muhafazat al-Suwis, 22 mars 1967," 8.

52. "Iftar ma'ana" (Break the Fast with Us), Egyptian television broadcast, channel 9, 15 November 2002.

53. The theater performance was written and directed by 'Ali Salim in 1968, during the first year of the War of Attrition. Allen, "Egyptian Drama after the Revolution," 106–7.

54. N. H. interview, Cairo, 23 March 2000.

55. F. R., informal conversation with author, Cairo, 1 February 2000.

56. A. B. interview, Ismailia, 1 November 2003.

57. *Al-Ahram* celebrated the opening of the Canal in 1975 with a special historical series (titled "From the Foundation of the Canal to Present Economic Stakes") that lasted a few days, until 6 June 1975. See "Laylat Isma'il wa-Ujini 'ala-al-qana" (Night of Isma'il and Eugénie on the Canal), *Al-Ahram*, 1 June 1975, 4–5; "Al-Nar 'ala-al-qana" (Fire on the Canal), *Al-Ahram*, 2 June 1975, 4–5; "Al-Siyasa hawla-al-qana" (Politics regarding the Canal), *Al-Ahram*, 3 June 1975: 4–5; and "1500 miliun jinih khsaratha Misr . . ." (1500 Million Pounds That Egypt Lost), *Al-Ahram*, 4 June 1975, 4–5. Also see "Egypt Gears up to Open Suez Canal," *Chicago Tribune*, 1 June 1975, B17, and "Suez Canal Cities Spread toward Renewal," *Christian Science Monitor*, 27 December 1976, 14.

58. UAR, *Canal in 4 Years*.

59. See "Suez Canal Cities Spread toward Renewal," *Christian Science Monitor*, 27 December 1976, 14; and "60 Nations Interested in Port Said Free Trade Zone Plan," *Los Angeles Times*, 20 December 1965, B13.

60. "Suez Canal Cities Spread toward Renewal," *Christian Science Monitor*, 27 December 1976, 14.

61. Christopher Wren, "Duty Free Zone Is Boon to Port Said—And Smuggling," *New York Times*, 19 April 1978, A3.

62. Goldschmidt, *Biographical Dictionary of Modern Egypt*, 221. Fixed assets in "land, buildings, and equipment increased in value from LE16.5 million [in 1972] to a stunning 1,990 [in 1981]." Beattie, *Egypt during the Nasser Years*, 151–52.

63. A. B. interview, Ismailia, 1 November 2003.

64. Christopher Wren, "Duty-Free Zone Is Boon to Port Said—And Smuggling," *New York Times*, 19 April 1978, A3.

65. Ralph Schaffer, "Egyptians Do 'Pilgrimage' to a Duty-Free Zone," *Christian Science Monitor*, 18 October 1979, 11.

66. C. G. interview, Port Said, 12 May 2002.

67. Beattie, *Egypt during the Nasser Years*, 151–53.

68. C. G. interview, Port Said, 12 May 2002.

69. "Suez Canal Cities Spread toward Renewal," *Christian Science Monitor*, 27 December 1976, 14.

Part III. St. Mary, Mother of Egypt

1. Voile, *Les coptes d'Égypte*, 51–52.

2. See ibid., 56–59.

3. On the growing influence of laymen in religious life, see Skovgaard-Petersen, *Defining Islam for the Egyptian State*, 155–56.

4. Turner and Turner, *Image and Pilgrimage in Christian Culture*, 202. On *communitas*, see ibid., 250.

5. Perry and Echeverría, *Under the Heel of Mary*, 193.

6. Ibid., 2.

Chapter 6. The Science of Miracles

1. Meinardus, *Coptic Saints*, 6; and Masry, *Introduction to the Coptic Church*, 49.

2. Telegram confidential No.476/Cairo No.2386, from Bergus, USINT (Cairo), to SECSTATE, DEPSTATE (Washington), SITREP 3–9 May 1968, "Apparition of Virgin Mary, first reported in Church Cairo Suburb April 2, formally confirmed by Pope Kyrollos May 4," 5/11/68, NARA, RG 59/Box 2553.

3. See Nil's late 1970s Catholic narrative, *Les apparitions de la Vierge*, 73.

4. The chief photographer of *Al-Ahram*, Wajih Risq Matta, ensured that the photograph had not been falsified. See Zaki, *Our Lord's Mother Visits Egypt*, 23–26; and Nil, *Les apparitions de la Vierge*, 133.

5. For example, *Egyptian Gazette*, 11 April 1969.

6. To my knowledge, the term "visitation" rarely appears in 1968 news, but it is common after the 1980s.

7. On the pilgrimage to the Church, consider Viaud's, *Les pélerinages Coptes en Egypte*,

35; Meinardus, *Coptic Saints*, 75; and Shafik's 1998 film, *Umm al-Nur wa-banatiha* (The Mother of Light and Her Daughters), which is a thoughtful reflection on the Coptic Church, women, traditionalism, and the isolation of Coptic communities.

8. Hilmi, *Al-'Adhra tazur Misr* (The Virgin Visits Egypt), 54.

9. *Al-Ahram*, 5 May 1968, 1; and Hilmi, *Al-'Adhra tazur Misr*, 54.

10. Gayed, *Apparition of the Virgin*, 54.

11. In a telegram, U.S. Intelligence officer Bergus notes: "Working press waited many hours for official statement." See Telegram confidential No. 2500, from Bergus, USINT (Cairo), to SECSTATE, SITREP 17–23 May 1968, 5/25/68, NARA, RG 59/2553, 3. See also Nil, *Les apparitions*, 109–10.

12. Voile, *Les coptes d'Égypte*, 88.

13. *Al-Ahram*, 6 May 1968, 5.

14. Hilmi, *Al-'Adhra tazur Misr*, 46, 179. Hilmi's testimony is distinctly inspired by contemporary clerical publications.

15. In premodern visions, the Virgin characteristically asked the seer to build her a shrine. See Turner and Turner, *Image and Pilgrimage*, 209.

16. See Gayed, *Apparition of the Virgin*, 9; Nil, *Les apparitions de la Vierge*, 108; Rehab Saad, "A Place of Pilgrimage," *Al-Ahram Weekly*, 28 June–4 July 2001, 17; Swann, *Great Apparitions of Mary*, 206; and Ruggles, *Apparition Shrines*, 161.

17. *Al-Ahram*, 4 May 1968, 4. Other periodicals are less political, such as *Ruz al-Yusuf*. Its 13 May 1968 issue on the Marian apparition speaks lyrically of religious devotion but ends with a discussion of paranormal phenomena. The 20 May issue recounts Bernadette Soubirous' story but also depicts Western sexual liberation as excessive.

18. *Al-Ahram*, 5 May 1968, 3.

19. *Al-Musawwar*, 10 May 1968, 26–27.

20. *Al-Ahram*, 5 May 1968, 3. Hilmi (*Al-'Adhra tazur Misr*, 50) reports thirteen witnesses: seven (male) Muslims, three (male) church officials, and three (male) Christians (one physician, one lawyer, and one of unknown profession).

21. 'Izzat al-Sa'dani report, *Al-Ahram*, 7 May 1968, 1.

22. Hilmi, *Al-'Adhra tazur Misr*, 47.

23. 'Izzat al-Sa'dani, *Al-Ahram*, 7 May 1968, 3.

24. Ibid.

25. Ibid.

26. *Al-Ahram*, 6 May 1968, 3.

27. Ibid.

28. On divine communication, see Schwebel, *Apparitions, Healings, and Weeping Madonnas*, 121.

29. *Al-Ahram*, 5 May 1968, 1.

30. Ibid.

31. Qaradawi, *Dars al-nakba al-thaniya, li madha inhazamna wa kayfa nantasir* (The Lesson of the Second Disaster, Why We Were Defeated, How We Shall Overcome).

32. Skovgaard-Petersen, *Defining Islam*, 194.

33. Haddad, "Islamists and the 'Problem of Israel,'" 274.
34. Zeghal, "Nasser et les Oulémas d'al-Azhar," 111.
35. See Heymann and Abitbol, *L'historiographie israélienne aujourd'hui*, 22.
36. *Al-Ahram*, 5 May 1968, 1. Nil's rendition of Gregorius' words (*Les apparitions de la Vierge*, 130) is rather different from the original, as he translates "God" as "Jesus-God."
37. Barraclough, *Christian World*, 310; and Rey, *Our Lady of Class Struggle*, 109.
38. Boff, quoted in Rey, *Our Lady of Class Struggle*, 110.
39. Dabashi and Chelkowski, *Staging a Revolution*.
40. Boff, quoted in Rey, *Our Lady of Class Struggle*, 109.
41. There is little evidence of the pope's reluctance to politicize the event. See John Iskander, "Here Today, Gone Tomorrow," *Cairo Times*, 12–18 October 2000, 18; and Thomas Brady, *New York Times*, 5 May 1968. On papal reluctance, see Meinardus, *Two Thousand Years*, 118.
42. See Nil, *Les apparitions de la Vierge*, 9. The Catholic Church, after the Lourdes vision, similarly organized a Bureau de constatations médicales. On pilgrimage, see Martin, *Roses, Fountains, and Gold*, 11.
43. As a result of his position, 'Azm was expelled from the philosophy department at the American University in Beirut. See 'Azm, "Islam and the Science-Religion Debates in Modern Times," 286.
44. See 'Azm, *Naqd al-fikr al-dini* (Critique of Religious Thought), 100.
45. On the Egyptianization of Jeanne d'Arc, see Booth, "Egyptian Lives," cited in Armbrust, "Manly Men on a National Stage," 249.
46. 'Abid, quoted in 'Azm, *Naqd al-fikr al-dini*, 97.
47. Vivier, "Coptes orthodoxes d'Egypte," 41. Emphasis added.
48. See Kolenkow, "Talking through the Saints," n109.
49. On other churches, see Martin, *Roses, Fountains, and Gold*, 13.
50. Cannuyer, *Les Coptes*, 161.
51. See John Iskander, "Here Today, Gone Tomorrow," *Cairo Times*, 12–18 October 2000, 17–18.
52. Gruber, "Monastery as the Nexus of Coptic Cosmology," 71.
53. See Van Doorn-Harder, "Discovering New Roles," 93.
54. Turner and Turner, *Image and Pilgrimage*, 203.
55. Van Doorn-Harder, "Discovering New Roles," 95.
56. Ibid., 94.
57. Vivier, "Coptes orthodoxes d'Egypte," 55; and Van Doorn-Harder, "Discovering New Roles," 94.
58. The "belief that a saint's body will not decay is of relatively recent origin and may have been adopted from Western or Byzantine Churches." Meinardus, *Coptic Saints*, 65.
59. On Islamic legal opinions, see Kupferschmidt, "Reformist and Militant Islam in Urban and Rural Egypt," 406.
60. Van Doorn-Harder, "Kyrillos VI," 240.
61. Ibid., 238.

62. Formal hagiographical booklets were published by his nephew, F. Mansur, right after his death. In 1962 the future Pope Shanuda III (1923–2012) became bishop of the newly created Ministry of Religious Education. See Voile, *Les coptes d'Égypte*, 189, 200, 206.

63. See, for instance, Mayeur-Jaouen, "The Coptic Mouleds," 226; Van Doorn-Harder and Vogt, *Between Desert and City*, 12; Immerzeel, "Coptic Art," 283–84. See also Butrus, *Zuhurat wa mu'jizat wa iqtidar*.

64. On religious commercialization, see, for example, Mayeur-Jaouen, "Coptic Mouleds," 226; and Vivier, "Coptes orthodoxes d'Egypte," 55.

65. Kaufmann, *Consuming Visions*, 1, 4, 5.

66. See Albert-Llorca, *Les Vierges miraculeuses*; and Bowman, "Nationalizing the Sacred," 445, 450.

67. Sadiq, *Al-Watani*, 14 June 1981, 1, 4. Sadiq later reported on the 1986 apparition and sat on its investigation committee. On state involvement in religious tourism, see Voile, *Les coptes d'Égypte*, 231.

68. Quranic verses and patriotic declarations preface this self-published pamphlet, which offers news articles and religious and medical documents but rarely mentions sources. See Hilmi, *Al-'Adhra tazur Misr*, 2001.

69. Van Doorn-Harder, "Kyrillos VI," 239.

70. Voile, *Les coptes d'Égypte*, 236.

71. Hilmi, *Al-'Adhra tazur Misr*, 32. On Gregorius, see Voile, *Les coptes d'Égypte*, 60. On Kyrillus' first hagiography, see Voile, *Les coptes*, 276.

72. *Al-Ahram*, 6 May 1968. Emphasis added.

73. Ibid.

74. On Catholic investigations, see Swann, *Great Apparitions of Mary*, 11.

75. *Al-Ahram*, 6 May 1968.

76. Swann, *Great Apparitions of Mary*, 13.

77. Jeanne d'Arc's interrogators also used tradition and spiritual and canon law as a means of evaluation: "It was suspicious, they thought, that the supposed saints visited, kissed, and embraced her frequently for no good reason" (Christian, *Apparitions* 191). On evil and divine work in medieval European Christianity, see Le Goff, *L'imaginaire médiéval*, 293.

78. *Al-Ahram*, 5 May 1968. See late nineteenth-century Irish "scrupulous" methods in Cusack, *Apparition of the Blessed Virgin*, 18–19.

79. On monastic spirituality, see Farag, *Sociological and Moral Studies*, 6–7.

80. On Catholic revivalism, see Turner and Turner, *Image and Pilgrimage*, 208. On Catholic dogma, see Rey, *Our Lady of Class Struggle*, 85–122.

81. Turner and Turner, *Image and Pilgrimage*, 203.

82. Meinardus, *Coptic Saints*, 9.

83. On Catholic missionaries, see Voile, *Les coptes d'Égypte*, 218.

84. On spirituality and female empowerment, see Jansen, "Visions of Mary in the Middle East," 148–51.

85. Meinardus, *Coptic Saints*, 7–9.
86. On religious consumerism, see Armbrust, "Synchronizing Watches," 207–26; and Starrett, "Political Economy of Religious Commodities in Cairo," 51–68.
87. Hasan al-Fidawi and Samih Husan, "Al-'Adhra' Mariam," *Ruz al-Yusuf*, 8 January 2010, 42.
88. *Al-Ahram*, 5 May 1968, 3.
89. Guirguis, *An Armenian Artist in Ottoman Egypt*, 9, 18, 27, 30, 92. See also Sadek and Sadek, *L'incarnation de la lumière*.
90. Crain, "Reimaging Identity," 135, 136.
91. On neoclassicist influence, see Immerzeel, "Coptic Art," 283–84.
92. *Al-Ahram*, 5 May 1968, 3.
93. *Al-Ahram*, 6 May 1968, 5.
94. For instance, *Zuhurat al-'Adhra' khilala-al-qarn al-'ashrin* (Apparitions of the Virgin in the Twentieth Century). Presenting the Church's stamp of approval and the outward appearance of an Egyptian product, this videotape is in fact a dubbed, bootlegged copy of a North American film that does not bear mention of the original title and date of production. See also the newer and more sophisticated DVD documentary film *'Adhra' al-Zaytun* (The Virgin of Zaytun), produced by Kamal Matar for the 2008 anniversary of the apparition and copyrighted by the Church of Zaytun.
95. See Spicer and Hamilton, "Defining the Holy," 1–2; and Moore, *Selling God*.
96. To paraphrase Le Goff, *L'imaginaire médiéval*, 24.
97. To borrow the musing of Lefebvre, *Le temps des méprises*, 16.
98. See Gayed, *Apparition of the Virgin*, 14.
99. See Shoshan, *Popular Culture in Medieval Cairo*, 20. On recuperations of the vision, see Meinardus, *Coptic Saints*, 5; and Hall, *Mary, Mother and Warrior*.

Chapter 7. Globalizing the Virgin, Nationalizing Religion

1. See Nil, *Les apparitions de la Vierge*, 79.
2. Illustration by Jamal Kamal, "Egypt Will Rise Again," *Ruz al-Yusuf*, 10 June 1968, 18–19.
3. See *Ruz al-Yusuf*, 3 May 1990, 66. Voile mentions a resurgence of miracles after 1968 but ends her survey in 1970 (*Les coptes d'Égypte*, 238).
4. The Coptic press writes of visitations going back either to early Christianity or to 1968. See Butrus, *Zuhurat wa mu'jizat wa iqtidar*, 75–77. This work does not mention Munufiyya, but it was published in 1998. See also Meinardus, *Two Thousand Years*, 116–17.
5. Informal conversation with R., a thirty-year-old Copt and computer engineer, Cairo, 16 March 2002. On Shantana al-Hajar, see Meinardus, *Two Thousand Years*, 117.
6. The Virgin "appeared to thousands of people ... and not in any place.... She also distinguished Herself by the miracles performed under Her auspices to many ... Muslims and Christians ... without distinction" (Pope Shanuda, quoted in Butrus, *Tajaliyyat wa mu'jizat*, 54).

7. Perry and Echeverría, *Under the Heel of Mary*, 2.

8. See Butrus, *Tajaliyyat wa mu'jizat*. This booklet, sold in Coptic churches, offers anonymous testimonials of miracles and visions. Perry and Echeverría (*Under the Heel of Mary* 154, 311–13) argue that Marian cultism developed simultaneously with challenges to Catholic theology and authority. Hoping to convert the Eastern Church to Rome, the Catholic Church launched a Marian jubilee in 1987 that culminated in 2000. On conversions, see Guirguis, *Conversions religieuses et mutations politiques*.

9. Butrus, *Tajaliyyat wa mu'jizat*, 10–11.

10. See Perry and Echeverria, *Under the Heel of Mary*, 154. In 2000 Pope John Paul II declared: "Given the relativism and subjectivism that contaminate a large part of contemporary culture, bishops are called to defend and promote the doctrinal unity of their faithful." See "John Paul II Entrusts Third Millennium to Mary," online at http://www.ewtn.com/entrustment/News/entrust1.htm (accessed 15 July 2010).

11. Pope Shanuda, quoted in Butrus, *Tajaliyyat wa mu'jizat*, 54.

12. See 'Abd al-Fattah, *Al-Hala al-diniyya* (The Religious Situation), 93.

13. In 1980 the pope cancelled Easter celebrations in protest. See Watson, *Among the Copts*, 96.

14. 'Azm, *Naqd al-fikr al-dini*, 111.

15. The Islamist paper *Al-Ahrar* has been the main propagator of religious defamation. The independent *Sawt al-Umma* called 2010 the year of religious conflicts. See 'Antar 'Abd al-Latif, "2010 'amm al-futun al-ta'ifiyya" (2010: Year of Confessional Dissents), *Sawt al-Umma*, 25 December 2009, 5. This issue considers all kinds of religious conflicts.

16. See *Al-Masri al-Yawm*, 20 December 2009, 3; 25 December 2009, 1; and 26 December 2009, 3.

17. Kolenkow, "Talking through the Saints," 100.

18. See Gayed, "The Apparitions of Virgin Mary at Zeitoun Church, Egypt, with Real Photos," online at http://www.zeitun-eg.org/stmaridx.htm (accessed 18 July 2010). Gayed (d. 1996) was Pope Shanuda's brother. Also see Gayed, *Apparition of the Virgin*, 37, 39–41, 45. A first clash in Alexandria in March 1972 followed the distribution of pamphlets claiming that the pope was planning to convert Muslims. A church was then burnt in a Khanka village in November. See Ramses Farah, *Religious Strife in Egypt*, 2, 4, 10.

19. Official statistics estimated the community at 10 percent of the population of 35 million in 1973, half of the Church's estimate. See Nelson, "The Virgin of Zeitun," 10. Copts remain the largest Christian community (4.2 million) in the Middle East. See Grégoire Delhaye, "Les racines du dynamisme de la diaspora copte" in *EchoGéo*, Sur le vif 2008, posted online 22 August 2008, http://echogeo.revues.org/6963 (accessed 5 July 2009).

20. See Meinardus, *Two Thousand Years*, 116.

21. According to an ecclesiastically approved Holy Bible Web Site (http://www.zeitun-eg.org/), the apparitions started in 1983 and were sanctioned in 1987 (accessed 10 July 2009).

22. On Latin American indigenization of the Virgin, see Hall, *Mary, Mother and Warrior*. On the appropriation of shrines by Christian and Muslim Palestinians, see Bowman, "Nationalizing the Sacred," 431–60. On St. Michael, see Meinardus, *Two Thousand Years*, 117.

23. See Father Gregorius, "Zuhur al-'adhra fi Zaytun fi 2 min Abril 1968" (The Visit of the Virgin in Zaytun on 2 April 1968), *Al-Watani*, 30 March 2008.

24. Vivier, "Coptes orthodoxes d'Egypte," 50. On Marian theology, see Pelikan, *Mary through the Centuries*, 8–21.

25. The evidence points to 300–400 CE; see Valensi, *La Fuite en Egypte*, 99, 112.

26. See Vivier, "Coptes orthodoxes d'Égypte," 49–50.

27. See Ministry of Education, *Suwwar min al-tarikh al-masri* (Images of Egyptian History), fifth-year elementary (1955), 125; and MOE, *Dirasat wa suwwar min al-tarikh al-qawmi* (Lessons and Images of the National History), fifth-year elementary (1963), 80.

28. Nil, "Les apparitions de la Vierge," 73. The religious literature abounds in prophecies announcing the '68 visitation. See, for example, Finnestad, "Apparitions, Icons, and Photos," 7–34.

29. Vivier, "Coptes orthodoxes d'Egypte," 50. It would be interesting to know the exact amount of the revenue such relations engender.

30. See Taher, *Aunt Safiyya and the Monastery*, 126.

31. Remarks based on aforementioned events and published in the national press in 1968, 1986, 1990, 1997, 2000, 2009.

32. Shanuda, undated statement quoted in Butrus, *Tajaliyyat wa mu'jizat*, 54.

33. In witchcraft, the announcer suggests paranormal or supernatural phenomena, thus allowing the bewitched to shift from positivist to supernatural modes of explanation and resolutions of hardships. See Favret-Saada, *Les mots, la mort, les sorts*.

34. *Musawwar*, 10 May 1968, 28–29.

35. Rehab Saad, "A Place of Pilgrimage," *Al-Ahram Weekly*, 28 June–4 July 2001, 17.

36. See *Akhir Sa'a*, 20 December 2000, 8. The picture of the fully embodied Virgin in 2000 was, similarly, taken by a "simple human being" who "did not wish to make declarations," "a Muslim woman," "a friend" who did "not want any trouble." *Akhir Sa'a* investigated the "first picture in the world of the Virgin." In 2009–10 people took pictures with their cell phones. The events were televised.

37. Perry and Echeverría, *Under the Heel of Mary*, 76.

38. *Akhir Sa'a*, 20 December 2000, 8.

39. See for example Nil, *Les apparitions de la Vierge*, 1980.

40. *Akhir Sa'a*, 20 December 2000, 8. This is the first mention I found of the Virgin's Palestinian features. By contrast, Nil's testimonies, as well as press reports, purport that St. Mary's features were blurry. *Musawwar* offered a special supplement on 17 May 1968 with artistic representations of the Virgin entitled: "The Virgin has Oriental Palestinian features, not European ones" (np).

41. *Akhir Sa'a*, 20 December 2000, 8.

42. See the Holy Bible Web Site (Our Lady of Zeitun online) http://www.zeitun-eg.org (accessed 10 July 2009).

43. Published in *Al-Watani*, 12 December 2000.

44. See the medieval European debate on evidence in Christian, *Apparitions*, 190–93.

45. Pope Shanuda, 4 November 2000, quoted in *Akhir Sa'a*, 20 December 2000, 11.

46. *Al-Watani*, 27 December 2009, 1.

47. Victor Salama, "Ihtifal bi-al-'id al-arba'in li-sayyidat al-'adhra bi-al-Zaytun; Qadasat al-Baba Shanuda yazur kanisat al-tajalli fi 31 mars" (Celebration of the Fortieth Anniversary of the Apparition of the Virgin in Zaytun; His Holiness the Pope Shanuda Visits the Church of the Apparition on 31 March), March 2008, no. 2410, *Al-Watani* online, http://www.wataninet.com/ArticleDetails.aspx?A=17890 (accessed 22 July 2010).

48. To the best of my knowledge, festivities started on 31 March. Daily and weekly periodicals published between 30 March and 1–2 April—as well as in the week preceding and following celebrations—yield meager results. *Ruz al-Yusuf*, *Sabah al-Khayr*, *Akhir Sa'a*, *Al-Musawwar*, *Al-Ahram*, *Al-Jumhuriyya*, *Al-Akhbar*, *Al-Usbu'*, *Nahdat Masr*, *Uktubir*, and the sensationalist *Akhbar al-Hawadith al-'Arabiyya* did not mention the events.

49. 'Amru Bayumi, "Shanuda yahdar ihtifalat zuhur al-'adhra' fi Zaytun wa tajaddud al-jadal bayna al-urthuduks wa-al-injiliyin hawla qadisiyyat Maryam" (Shanuda Attends the Celebrations of the Visit of the Virgin; Renewal of the Controversy between the Orthodox and the Anglican Church about the Holy Virgin), *Al-Masri al-Yawm*, 30 March 2008. Available at http://www.almasryalyoum.com (accessed 19 July 2009). *Al-Masri al-Yawm* is an independent Cairo daily paper competing with *Al-Ahram*.

50. Salah al-Laithi, *Ruz al-Yusuf*, 13 May 1968, 18.

51. Sherine Nasr, "Cause for Celebration," *Al-Ahram Weekly*, 3–9 April 2008, no. 891, http://weekly.ahram.org.eg/2008/891/eg6.htm (accessed 11 May 2010).

52. This poorly written online article seems to have been written a day after the commemoration. See *Al-Qahira*, 1 April 2008.

53. "Zahirat al-'adhra' fi al-Zaytun fi 2 min abril 1968" (Apparition of the Virgin Mary in Zaytun on 2 April 1968), *Al-Watani*, 30 March 2008, http://www.wataninet.com/ArticleDetails.aspx?A=NUMBER (accessed 10 June 2008).

54. Ibid.

55. See Sa'dani, *Al-Ahram*, 7 May 1968, 3; *Al-Musawwar*, 10 May 1968, 26–27; and *Al-Ahram Weekly*, 3–9 April 2008.

56. *Al-Watani*, 30 March 2008.

57. See *Masri al-Yawm*, 30 March 2008.

58. Victor Salama and Nader Shukri, "Holy Virgin Appears at Warraq, Giza," *Al-Watani*, English, http://www.wataninet.com/ArticleDetails.aspx?A=25345 (accessed 3 August 2011).

59. Ibid.

60. Raf'at 'Adli (Raf. A.) (b. 1940 in Asyut) interview by author, Cairo, 2 May 2000.

61. Ibid.

62. Ibid.

63. Valensi, *La Fuite en Egypte*, 225–26; and Bowman, "Nationalizing the Sacred,"

431–60. One finds similar devotional "crisscrossing" in Mexico. See Turner and Turner, *Image and Pilgrimage*, 202. See also Meinardus, *Coptic Saints*, 69.

64. Raf. A. interview, Cairo, 2 May 2000.

65. *Umm al-Nur wa-banatiha*, dir. Shafik; and Taher, *Aunt Safiyya and the Monastery*.

66. Taher, *Aunt Safiyya and the Monastery*, 20.

67. Raf. A. interview, Cairo, 2 May 2000.

68. *Umm al-Nur wa-banatiha*, dir. Shafik.

69. To paraphrase Barraclough with regard to social and religious organizations (*Christian World* 299).

70. See Nelson, "The Virgin of Zeitun," 10; and Pennington, "The Copts in Modern Egypt," 161.

71. In the late nineteenth century, 45 percent of all civil servants were Christian, according to Pennington, "The Copts in Modern Egypt," 160. See also Smith, "Egyptian Copts," 69–70.

72. The association between non-Muslim and foreign interests structures modern sectarian semantics. Capitulations were abolished between 1937 and 1949. See Aghion and Feldman, *Les Actes de Montreux*. On 1929 citizenship law and naturalization, see Beinin, *Dispersion of the Egyptian Jewry*, 37–38, 40, and Smith, "Egyptian Copts," 71–72.

73. Ibrahim et al., *Copts of Egypt*, 16.

74. After 1967 Nasser publicly praised Christian soldiers' patriotism in response to the Muslim Brotherhood's defamation. Nelson does not identify among sources of hostility but cites a "series of incidents [in] Alexandria, Mansoura and Damanhour" ("Virgin of Zeitun" 10). See also Mayeur-Jaouen, "La religion populaire," 121, 126.

75. Ramses Farah, *Religious Strife in Egypt*, 2; and Pennington, "Copts in Modern Egypt," 165.

76. Sami Sharaf, "Abu Bakr jamma'a al-Qur'an 'maktuba' wa 'Abd al-Nasir jamma'a al-Qur'an masmu'an" (Abu Bakr Collected the 'Written' Qur'an and 'Abd al-Nasser Collected the 'Oral' Qur'an), *Al-Musawwar*, 28 September 2011, 31.

77. "There is a hidden hand. That's a personal conviction, because after the event, a picture of the raped girl circulated on mobiles" (Egyptian Minister of Culture, quoted in Asma Nasar, "Faruq Husni, 'The Occurrence of Sectarian Strife Is an International Plot,'" *Ruz al-Yusuf*, 22 January 2010, 24).

78. Ramses Farah, *Religious Strife in Egypt*, 4; Pennington, "Copts in Modern Egypt," 163; and Ibrahim et al., *Copts of Egypt*, 16.

79. On Sadat's introduction of Islamic law, see Ramses Farah, *Religious Strife in Egypt*, 1, 3, 5, 38.

80. Makdisi, *Culture of Sectarianism*, 164–65.

81. Ibid., 36.

82. Beinin, *Dispersion of the Egyptian Jewry*, 40.

83. *Mutamasirun* were long-time "assimilated" residents from Italy, Greece, Malta, Syria, and so on, who retained ties with their countries of origin.

84. Raf. A. interview, Cairo, 2 May 2000.

Conclusion: "What Revolution?!"

1. Huda 'Abd al-Nasir, "Jamal 'Abd al-Nasir fi muwajahat al-sahafa" (Jamal 'Abd al-Nasser Faces the Press), *Al-Ahram*, 13 January 2012, 7.
2. See Reza, "Endless Emergency," 538.
3. Ibid., 544.
4. Ibid., 540.
5. Nasir, "Jamal 'Abd al-Nasir," *Al-Ahram*, 13 January 2012, 7.
6. See James, *Nasser at War*.
7. DaMatta, *Carnivals, Rogues, and Heroes*, 34.
8. Raf. A. interview, Cairo, 2 May 2000.

Bibliography

Archival Collections

Archives Nationales, Ministère des Affaires Etrangères, Paris.
Archives Nationales, Centre des Archives Diplomatiques, Nantes.
Archives Nationales, Centre des Archives du Monde du Travail, Roubaix; Private Archives of the Compagnie Maritime du Canal de Suez.
Centre d'Études et de Documentation Économique Juridique et Sociale, Cairo.
Mathaf Wizarat al-Ta'lim wa-l-Tarbiyya (Education Museum and Documents Library, Ministry of Education), Cairo; Al-Wahda al-Arshifiyya: Al-Jughrafiyya wa-al-Ta'rikh (Archival Series: History and Geography). Al-Majmu'a al-Wathiqiyya: Muqararat al-Ta'rikh (Documentary Collection: History Curricula).
National Archives of the United Kingdom, British Public Record Office, Kew Richmond; Foreign Office Documents; War Office Documents.
United States National Archives and Records Administration, College Park, Department of State Documents, RG, 59.

Textbooks

Ministry of Education, Egypt, Taha Husayn, 'Ali al-Bajawi, and 'Abd al-Salam Harun Ibrahim al-Abyari. *Fusul mukhtara min kutub al-ta'rikh li-al-sana al-ula al-thanawiyya* (Selected Texts from History Books for the First Year of Secondary School). Cairo: Wizarat al-Tarbiyya wa-al-Ta'lim, 1955.

Ministry of Education, Egypt, Mustafa 'Abd al-Rahim and Ibrahim Namir Sayf al-Din. *Qisas wa muhadithat sahla min tarikh Misr al-qadim* (Simple Stories and Events from the History of Ancient Egypt). Al-Sana al-thalitha ibtida'i wa-al-khamisa al-awwaliyya (Third primary and fifth elementary level). Cairo: Wizarat al-Ma'arif al-'Umumiyya, 1949.

Ministry of Education, United Arab Republic. *Al-Dirasat al-ijtima'iyya* (Social Studies). Al-Saff al-khamis ibtida'i (Fifth-year primary). Cairo: Wizarat al-Tarbiyya wa-al-Ta'lim, 1996–97.

———. *Al-Dirasat al-ijtima'iyya* (Social Studies). Al-Saff al-rabi' ibtida'i (Fourth-year primary). Cairo: Wizarat al-Tarbiyya wa-al-Ta'lim, 1998–99.

———. *Al-Dirasat al-ijtima'iyya* (Social Studies). *Jughrafiyya al-'alam wa dirasat fi tarikh Misr al-hadith* (World Geography and Historical Studies in Modern Egypt). Al-Saff al-thalith i'dadi (Third-year preparatory). Cairo: Wizarat al-Tarbiyya wa-al-Ta'lim, 1998–99.

———. *Al-Dirasat al-ijtima'iyya* (Social Studies). *Jughrafiyya al-watan al-'arabi wa ma'alim al-ta'rikh al-islami* (Geography of the Arab Homeland and Islamic History Instruction). Al-Saff al-thani i'dadi (Second-year preparatory). Cairo: Wizarat al-Tarbiyya wa-al-Ta'lim, 1999–2000.

———. *Al-Dirasat al-ijtima'iyya* (Social Studies). *Jughrafiyyat al-'alam wa ta'rikh Misr al-hadith* (World Geography and History of Modern Egypt). Al-Saff al-thalith i'dadi (Third-year preparatory). Cairo: Wizarat al-Tarbiyya wa-al-Ta'lim, 2009–2010.

———. *Al-Dirasat al-ijtima'iyya* (Social Studies). *Watanna al-'arabi* (Our Arab Homeland). *Zawahir tabi'iyya wa hadara islamiyya* (Environment and Islamic Civilization). Al-Saff al-thalith i'dadi (Second-year preparatory). Cairo: Matabi' Markaz Tadrib al-Shurta, 2009–2010.

———. *Al-Dirasat al-ijtima'iyya* (Social Studies). *Zawahir tabi'iyya wa hadara misriyya* (Environment and Egyptian Civilization). Al-Saff al-awwal i'dadi (First-year preparatory). Cairo: Wizarat al-Tarbiyya wa-al-Ta'lim, 2009–2010.

———. *Al-Ta'rikh li-l-thanawiyya al-'amma* (History for the General Secondary Level). Cairo: Wizarat al-Tarbiyya wa-al-Ta'lim, 1997–98.

———. *Dirasat wa suwwar min al-tarikh al-qawmi* (Lessons and Images of the National History). Al-Sana al-khamisa ibtida'i (Fifth-year elementary). Cairo: Wizarat al-Tarbiyya wa-al-Ta'lim, 1963.

———. *Suwwar min al-tarikh al-masri* (Images of Egyptian History). Al-Sana al-khamisa ibtida'i (Fifth-year elementary). Cairo: Wizarat al-Tarbiyya wa-al-Ta'lim, 1955.

Ministry of Education, United Arab Republic, 'Abd al-Karim, Ahmad 'Izzat, and Abu Futuh Radwan. *Tarikh al-watan al-'arabi fi-al-'asr al-hadith* (History of the Arab Homeland in the Modern Era). Al-Sana al-thalitha i'dadi (Third-year preparatory). Cairo: Wizarat al-Tarbiyya wa-al-Ta'lim, 1959.

Ministry of Education, United Arab Republic, 'Abd al-Karim, Ahmad 'Izzat, Abu-al-Futuh Radwan, and 'Abd al-Hamid al-Batrik. *Tarikh Misr al-watan al-'arabi fi-al-'asr al-hadith* (History of Egypt: The Arab Homeland in the Modern Era). Al-Sana al-rabi'a i'dadi (Fourth-year preparatory). Cairo: Wizarat al-Tarbiyya wa-al-Ta'lim, 1954.

Ministry of Education, United Arab Republic, Yusif Yusif Khalil et al. *Tabaqan li-al-manahij al-mawhida bayna Misr wa-al-Sudan wa Libya* (Application of the Unified Curricula Between Egypt, the Sudan, and Libya). Al-Sana al-thalitha ibtida'i (Third-year elementary). Cairo: Wizarat al-Tarbiyya wa-al-Ta'lim, 1971.

Other Sources

'Abd al-Fattah, Nabil, ed. *Al-Hala al-diniyya fi Misr* (The Religious Situation in Egypt). Cairo: Markaz al-Dirasat al-Siyasiyya wa-al-Istratijiyya, 1995.

'Abd al-Fattah, Nabil, 'Abd al-Wahid, Fatima 'Ilm al-Din. *Al-Tatawwurat al-ijtima'iyya fi-al-rif al-misri* (Social Developments in Rural Egypt). Cairo: Al-Hay'a al-Misriyya al-'Amma li-l-Kitab, 1984.

Abdalla, Ahmad. *The Student Movement and National Politics in Egypt, 1923–1973*. London: Al-Saqi Books, 1985.

Abdel-Malek, Anouar. *Egypte, Société militaire*. Paris: Editions du Seuil, 1962.

Abécassis, Frédéric. "Une certaine idée de la nation: Le collège de la Sainte Famille et l'Egypte nassérienne (1949–1962)." D.E.A. diss., Université d'Aix-Marseille, 1991.

———. "L'enseignement étranger en Egypte et les élites locales, 1920–1960: Francophonie et identités nationales." Ph.D. diss., Université d'Aix-Marseille, 2000.

Aclimandos, Tawfik. "Louis 'Awad (1915–1990), un philosophe iconoclaste." *Egypte-Monde Arabe* 2 (1990): 165–66.

Aghion, Raoul, and I. R. Feldman. *Les actes de Montreux: abolition des capitulations en Egypte, annotés d'après les procès-verbaux officiels des séances et les notes personnelles des auteurs*. Courtrai: Jos. Vermaut; Paris: A. Pedone, 1937.

Aglietti, Bruno. *Il canale di Suez ed i rapporti anglo-egiziano. Contente in appendice i testi dei principali trattati concernenti il canale di Suez e l'Egitto*. Florence: Casa Editrice Del Dott, 1939.

Ahl al-qimma (The People at the Top). Film. Directed by 'Ali Badrakhan. Egypt, 1981.

Ahmad, Layla. *A Border Passage*. London: Penguin Books, 1999.

Albert-Llorca, Marlène. *Les Vierges miraculeuses: Légendes et rituels*. Paris: Gallimard, 2002.

Alleaume, Ghislaine. "L'Égypte et son histoire: Actualité et controverses." *Bulletin du CEDEJ* 20, no. 2 (1986): 9–78.

Allen, Roger. "Egyptian Drama after the Revolution." *Edebiyat* 4, no. 1 (1979): 97–134.

Amin, Sajeda, and Cynthia B. Lloyd. *Women's Lives and Rapid Fertility Decline*. Population Council Working Papers, no 117. New York: Population Council, 1998.

Ard al-salam (The Land of Peace). Film. Directed by Kamal al-Shaykh. Egypt, 1957.

Armbrust, Walter. "Egyptian Cinema On Stage and Off." In *Off Stage/On Display: Intimacy and Ethnography in the Age of Public Culture*, edited by Andrew Shryock, 69–98. Stanford, Calif.: Stanford University Press, 2002.

———. "Manly Men on a National Stage (and the Women Who Make Them Stars)." In *Histories of the Modern Middle East: New Directions*, edited by Israel Gershoni, Hakan Erdem, and Ursula Woköck, 247–75. London: Lynne Rienner Publishers, 2002.

———. *Mass Culture and Modernism in Egypt*. Cambridge, UK: Cambridge University Press, 1996.

———, ed. *Mass Mediations: New Approaches to Popular Culture in the Middle East and Beyond*. Berkeley: University of California Press, 2000.

———. "Synchronizing Watches: The State, the Consumer, and Sacred Time in Ramadan Television." In *Religion, Media, and the Public Sphere*, edited by Birgit Meyer and Annalies Moors, 207–26. Bloomington: Indiana University Press, 2005.

———. "Terrorism and Kabab: A Capraesque View of Modern Egypt." In *Images of Enchantment: Visual and Performing Arts in the Middle East*, edited by Sherifa Zuhur, 283–99. Cairo: American University in Cairo Press, 1998.

Aroian, Lois A. "The Nationalization of Arabic and Islamic Education in Egypt: Dar al-'Ulum and al-Azhar." Cairo Papers in Social Science 6, monograph 4. Cairo: American University in Cairo Press, 1983.

'Asfur, al- (The Sparrow). Film. Directed by Yusif Shahin. Egypt, 1972.

'Awad, Luwis. "Bonnes feuilles." *Egypte/Monde Arabe* 2 (2nd trim. 1990): 168.

———. *The Literature of Ideas in Egypt*. Atlanta, Ga.: Scholars Press, 1986.

'Azima, al- (Determination). Film. Directed by Kamal Salim. Egypt, 1939.

'Azm, Sadiq Jalal, al-. "Islam and the Science-Religion Debates in Modern Times." *European Review* 15, no. 3 (2007): 283–97.

———. *Naqd al-fikr al-dini* (Critique of Religious Thought). Beirut: Dar al-Tali'a, 1969.

'Azra' al-Zaytun. DVD Film. Directed by Ra'uf Tadrus. Optimum Media Egypt, 2008.

Badran, Margot. *Feminists, Islam, and Nation: Gender and the Making of Modern Egypt*. Princeton, N.J.: Princeton University Press, 1995.

Bahloul, Joëlle. *The Architecture of Memory: A Jewish Muslim Household in Colonial Algeria, 1937–1962*. Cambridge, UK: Cambridge University Press, 1996.

Baghdadi, 'Abd al-Latif. *Dhubbat yunyu yatakallamuna* (The June Officers Speak Out). Cairo: Al-Manar al-Jadid, 1989.

Bakhtin, Mikhail M. *The Dialogic Imagination*. Austin: University of Texas Press, 1984.

———. *Rabelais and His World*. Bloomington: Indiana University Press, 1965.

———. *Speech Genres and Other Late Essays*. Translated from the Russian by V. W. McGee. Austin: University of Texas Press, 1986.

Bakkar, Nadia Ahmed. "Qualitative Aspects of Egyptian Social Studies Textbooks." Ph.D. diss., University of Illinois at Urbana-Champaign, 1985.

Barker, A. J. *Suez: The Seven Day War*. New York: Frederick A. Praeger, 1965.

Baron, Beth. *Egypt as a Woman. Nationalism, Gender, and Politics*. Berkeley: University of California Press, 2005.

Barraclough, Geoffrey, ed. *The Christian World: A Social and Cultural History*. New York: Harry N. Abrams, 1981.

The Battle of Algiers. Film. Directed by Gillo Pontecorvo. Algeria, 1965.

Baud, Marcelle. *L'Égypte. Les guides bleus*. Paris: Librairie Hachette, 1950.

———. *L'Égypte. Les guides bleus*. Paris: Librairie Hachette, 1956.

Baz, Shahida El-. "Méthodes d'assimilation passive et d'affaiblissement de l'esprit critique du système d'enseignement en Egypte." *Dimensions sociales de l'enseignement en Egypte*. Dossier du CEDEJ 3, 225–38. Cairo: CEDEJ, 1980.

Beattie, Kirk. *Egypt during the Nasser Years*. Boulder: University of Colorado Press, 1994.

Beinin, Joel. *The Dispersion of the Egyptian Jewry: Culture, Politics, and the Formation of a Modern Diaspora*. Berkeley: University of California Press, 1998.

Beinin, Joel, and Zackary Lockman. *Workers on the Nile: Nationalism, Communism, Islam, and the Egyptian Working Class, 1882–1954*. Princeton, N.J.: Princeton University Press, 1987.

Belli, Mériam. "Le 'moment 1967': De la colère, des illusions, et de la phase finale de la lutte." *Egypte/Monde Arabe* 4–5 (2000/2, 2001/1): 41–55.

Benjamin, Thomas. *La Revolución: Mexico's Great Revolution as Memory, Myth, and History*. Austin: University of Texas Press, 2000.

Bergson, Henri. *Matière et mémoire: Essai sur la relation du corps à l'esprit*. 1896. Reprint, Paris: Félix Alcan, 1912.

———. *Mémoire et vie*. Texts selected by Gilles Deleuze. Paris: Presses Universitaires de France, 1968.

Bhabha, Homi K., ed. *Nation and Narration*. London: Routledge, 1990.

Bidaya wa-l-nihaya, al-. (The Beginning and the End). Film. Directed by Salah Abu Sayf. Egypt, 1959.

Bisati, Muhammad al-. *Houses behind the Trees*. Translated by Denys Johnson-Davies. Austin: University of Texas Press, 1998. Originally published as *Buyut wara' al-ashjar*. Cairo: Dar al-Hilal, 1993.

Blackman, Winifred S. *The Fellahin of Upper Egypt: Their Religious Society and Industrious Life To-day with Specific Reference to Survivals from Ancient Times*. London: George Harrap, 1927.

Bloch, Marc. *Apologie pour l'histoire ou métier d'historien*. Paris: Colin, 1974.

Blunt, Wilfred Scaven. *Secret History of the Occupation of Egypt, Being a Personal Narrative of Events*. 1922. Reprint, New York: Howard Fertig, 1967.

Boaz, Shoshan. *Popular Culture in Medieval Cairo*. Cambridge, UK: Cambridge University Press, 1993.

Boff, Leonardo. *The Maternal Face of God: The Feminine and Its Religious Expressions*. San Francisco: Harper and Row, 1987.

Boktor, Amir. *School and Society in the Valley of the Nile*. Cairo: Elias' Modern Press, 1936.

Booth, Marilyn. "Colloquial Arabic Poetry, Politics, and the Press in Modern Egypt." *International Journal of Middle East Studies* 24, no. 3 (1992): 419–40.

———. "The Egyptian Lives of Jeanne d'Arc." In *Remaking Women: Feminism and Modernity in the Middle East*, edited by Lila Abu-Lughod, 171–211. Princeton: Princeton University Press, 1998.

Bourdieu, Pierre, and Jean-Claude Passeron. *La reproduction: Eléments pour une théorie du système d'enseignement*. Paris: Editions de Minuit, 1970.

Bowman, Glenn. "Nationalizing the Sacred: Shrines and Shifting Identities in the Israeli Occupied Territories." *Man* 28, no. 3 (September 1993): 431–60.

Brown, Nathan J. *Peasant Politics in Modern Egypt: The Struggle against the State*. New Haven, Conn.: Yale University Press, 1990.

Bruyas, Frédérique. "Aménagement de la ville de Port Saïd: Le point de vue de l'architecte. Images idéales, méthode et déconstruction du rêve." *Egypte/Monde Arabe*, no.23 (1995): 131–68.

Buhayri, Zaki al-. *Ta'rikh Misr al-hadith wa-l-mu'asir fi al-muqararat al-madrasiyya al-misriyya bayna-l-ihtilal wa-l-istiqlal* (History of Modern and Contemporary Egypt in Egyptian School Curricula: Between Occupation and Independence). Cairo: Dar Nahdat al-Sharq, 1996.

Burguière, André. "L'historiographie des origines de la France: Genèse d'un imaginaire national." *Annales* 58, no. 1 (2003): 41–62.

Bur Sa'id (Port Said). Film. Directed by 'Izz al-Din Dhulfiqar, 1957.

Butrus, Yusif. *Tajaliyyat wa mu'jizat Umm al-Nur* (Visitations and Miracles of the Mother of Light). Cairo: Matba'at al-Misriyyin, 1998.

———. *Zuhurat wa mu'jizat wa iqtidar walidat Allah wa Yusif al-Najjar* (Visitations, Miracles, and Power of the Mother of God and Joseph the Carpenter). Cairo: Matba'at al-Misriyyin, 2001.

Cannuyer, Christian. *Les Coptes*. Belgique: Editions Brepols, 1990.

———. "Deux grands papes de notre temps: Cyrille VI (d1971) et Chenouda III, patriarches coptes d'Alexandrie." *Solidarité-Orient* 199 (1996): 1–14.

Carey, Glen. "Customs Confusion: New Year's Tariff Changes Prompt Demonstrations in Port

Said and Questions about Egypt's Commitment to the WTO." *Cairo Times,* 10–16 January 2002, 21.

Carré, Olivier. *Enseignement islamique et idéal socialiste: analyse conceptuelle des manuels d'instruction musulmane en Égypte.* Beirut: Dar el-Machreq, 1974.

———. *La légitimation islamique des socialismes arabes: Analyse combinatoire des manuels scolaires égyptiens, syriens, et irakiens.* Paris: Presse de la Fondation Nationale des Sciences Politiques, 1979.

Carroll, Michael P. *The Cult of the Virgin Mary: Psychological Origins.* Princeton, N.J.: Princeton University Press, 1986.

Carruthers, Mary. *The Book of Memory: A Study of Memory in Medieval Culture.* New York: Cambridge University Press, 1990.

Cattaui, Joseph Pasha, ed. *L'Egypte: Aperçu historique et géographique, gouvernement et institutions, vie économique et sociale.* Cairo: Institut Français d'Archéologie Orientale, 1926.

Chalcraft, John T. *The Striking Cabbies of Cairo and Other Stories: Crafts and Guilds in Egypt.* Albany: State University of New York Press, 2005.

Christian, William. *Apparitions in Late and Medieval Renaissance Spain.* Princeton, N.J.: Princeton University Press, 1981.

Clancy-Smith, Julia. *Mediterraneans: North Africa and Europe in an Age of Migration, c. 1800–1900.* Berkeley: University of California Press, 2011.

———. *Rebel and Saint: Muslim Notables, Populist Protest, Colonial Encounters (Algeria and Tunisia, 1800–1904).* Berkeley: University of California Press, 1994.

Clayton, Mary. *The Cult of the Virgin Mary in Anglo-Saxon England.* Cambridge, UK: Cambridge University Press, 1990.

Cochran, Judith. *Education in Egypt.* London: Croom Helm, 1986.

Cohen, Abner. *Masquerade Politics: Explorations in the Structure of Urban Cultural Movements.* Berkeley: University of California Press, 1993.

Cole, Juan. *Colonialism and Revolution in the Middle East: Social and Cultural Origins of Egypt's Urabi Movement.* Princeton, N.J.: Princeton University Press, 1993.

Connerton, Paul. *How Societies Remember.* Cambridge, UK: Cambridge University Press, 1989.

Cooper, Frederick. *Colonialism in Question: Theory, Knowledge, History.* Berkeley: University of California Press, 2005.

Cooper, Frederick, and Ann Laura Stoler, eds. *Tensions of Empire: Colonial Cultures in a Bourgeois World.* Berkeley: University of California Press, 1997.

Coudougnan, Gérard. *Enseignement de l'histoire pré-Islamique en Egypte de 1952 à 1984 d'après les manuels scolaires.* Dossiers du CEDEJ. Cairo: Centre d'Études et de Documentation Economiques Juridiques et Sociales, 1985.

Crabbs, Jack A. *The Writing of History in Nineteenth Century Egypt: A Study in National Transformation.* Cairo: American University in Cairo Press, 1984.

Crain, Mary M. "Reimaging Identity, Cultural Production and Locality under Transnationalism: Performances of *San Juan* in the Ecuadorean Andes." In *Recasting Ritual: Performance, Media, Identity,* edited by Felicia Hughes-Freeland and Mary M. Crain, 137–62. London: Routledge, 1998.

Cromer, Earl of. *Modern Egypt,* vol. 1. New York: Macmillan Company, 1908.

Crubellier, Maurice. *L'école républicaine, 1870–1940: Esquisse d'une histoire culturelle*. Paris: Editions Christians, 1993.
Cusack, Mary Francis. *The Apparition of the Blessed Virgin*. New York: Lynch, Cole, and Muhan, 1880.
Dabashi, Hamid, and Peter Chelkowski. *Staging a Revolution: The Art of Persuasion in the Islamic Republic of Iran*. New York: New York University Press, 1999.
Dakhlia, Jocelyn. *L'oubli de la cité: La mémoire collective à l'épreuve du linéage dans le Jérid tunisien*. Paris: La Découverte, 1990.
DaMatta, Roberto. *Carnivals, Rogues, and Heroes: An Interpretation of the Brazilian Dilemma*. Translated by John Drury. 1979. Reprint, Notre Dame: University of Notre Dame Press, 1991.
Danielson, Virginia. "Performance, Political Identity, and Memory: Umm Kulthum and Jamal Abd al-Nasser." In *Images of Enchantment: Visual and Performing Arts in the Middle East*, edited by Sherifa Zuhur, 109–22. Cairo: American University in Cairo Press, 1998.
———. *The Voice of Egypt: Umm Kulthum's Arab Song and Egyptian Society in the Twentieth Century*. Chicago: University of Chicago Press, 1997.
Dening, Greg. *The Death of William Gooch: A History's Anthropology*. Honolulu: University of Hawai'i Press, 1995.
Dessouki, Sami H. *Suez Canal: Changing World*. London: Heinemann, 1982.
Di-Capua, Yoav. "Jabarti of the 20th Century: The National Epic of 'Abd al-Rahman al-Rafi'i and Other Egyptian Stories." *International Journal of Middle East Studies* 36 (2004): 429–50.
Din, Nadia Gamal El-. "Egypt National Report: Education for All 2000 Assessment." UNESCO, October 1999, http://www.unesco.org/wef/countryreports/egypt/contents.html (accessed 14 July 2005).
Doss, Amira, and Magda Barsoum, "Allenby, l'éxutoire," *Ahram Hebdo*, 1–7 May 2002, 24.
Douin, Georges. *L'attaque du canal de Suez*. Paris: Librairie Delagrave, 1922.
Drioton Etienne, and Jacques Vandier. *L'Egypte: Des origines à la conquête d'Alexandre*. Paris: Presses Universitaires de France, 1962.
Dubisch, Jill. *In a Different Place: Pilgrimage, Gender, and Politics at a Greek Island Shrine*. Princeton, N.J.: Princeton University Press, 1995.
Duby, Georges. *Les trois ordres ou l'imaginaire du féodalisme*. Paris: Gallimard, 1978.
During, Simon. *Modern Enchantments: The Cultural Power of Secular Magic*. Cambridge, Mass.: Harvard University Press, 2002.
Egypt Tourism Department. *Guide Book for Tourism*. Cairo: Al-Maaref Press, 1947.
Ezzat, Dina. "A Revolution Revisited: What Do Celebrations of 23 July Mean to Today's Egyptians?" *Al-Ahram Weekly*, no. 753 (28 July–3 August 2005): 6.
Fahmy, Khaled. *All the Pasha's Men: Mehmed Ali, His Army, and the Making of Modern Egypt*. Cairo: University of Cairo Press, 2003.
Faksh, Mahmud A. "The Consequences of the Introduction and Spread of Modern Education: Education and National Integration in Egypt." *Middle East Studies* 16, no. 2 (1980): 42–55.
———. "Education and Elite Recruitment: An Analysis of Egypt's Post-1952 Political Elite." *Comparative Education Review* 20, no. 2 (1976): 140–50.
Farag, Iman. "Analyse de presse: L'enseignement en question, enjeux d'un débat." *Egypte/Monde Arabe*, nos. 18–19 (1994): 241–329.

———. "La construction sociale d'une éducation nationale: Enjeux politiques et trajectoires éducatives (Egypte–première moitie du XXème siècle)." Ph.D. diss., Ecole des Hautes études en sciences sociales, 1999.

———. "Enjeux éducatifs et réforme sociale." In *Entre réforme sociale et mouvement national. Identité et modernisation en Egypte, 1882–1962*, edited by Alain Roussillon, 191–213. Cairo: CEDEJ, 1995.

———. "Isma'il al-Qabbani et la mesure de l'intelligence." *Egypte/Monde Arabe*, nos. 18–19 (1994): 55–67.

———. "Les manuels d'histoire égyptiens: Genèse et imposition d'une norme." *Genèse* 44 (2001): 4–29.

———. "L'Université égyptienne: Enjeux et modes de mobilisation." *Maghreb-Machrek*, no. 127 (1990): 65–83.

Farag, Farag Rofail. *Sociological and Moral Studies in the Field of Coptic Monasticism*. Leiden: E. J. Brill, 1964.

Fargues, Philippe. "Note sur la diffusion de l'instruction scolaire d'après les recensements égyptiens." *Egypte/Monde Arabe*, nos. 18–19 (1994): 115–34.

Favret-Saada, Jeanne. *Les mots, la mort, les sorts*. Paris: Gallimard, 1977.

Fawaz, Leila Tarazi, C. A. Bayly, and Robert Ilbert, eds. *Modernity and Culture: From the Mediterranean to the Indian Ocean*. New York: Columbia University Press, 2002.

Fawzi, Muhammad. *Harb al-thalath sanawat* (The Three-Year War). Cairo: Dar al-Mustaqbal al-'Arabi, 1980.

Fergany, Nader. "L'éducation féminine en Egypte: Éléments pour un bilan." *Études du Monde Arabe*, nos. 18–19 (1994): 101–13.

Ferro, Marc. *Comment on raconte l'histoire aux enfants à travers le monde*. Paris: Payot, 1983.

Finnestad, Raghnild Bjerre. "Apparitions, Icons, and Photos: A Study of Modern Coptic Visions of the Holy World." *Temenos: Studies in Comparative Religion* 30 (1994): 7–34.

Frisch, Michael. *A Shared Authority: Essays on the Craft and Meaning of Oral and Public History*. Albany: State University of New York Press, 1990.

Furet, François, and Jacques Ozouf, eds. *Lire et écrire: L'alphabétisation des Français de Calvin à Jules Ferry*. Paris: Les Editions de Minuit, 1977.

Fussel, Paul. *The Great War and Modern Memory*. London: Oxford University Press, 1975.

Galt, Russell. *The Effects of Centralization on Education in Egypt*. Cairo: Department of Education, American University at Cairo, 1936.

Garcia-Arenal, Mercedes, and Gerard Wiegers. *A Man of Three Worlds: Samuel Pallache, a Moroccan Jew in Protestant Europe*. Baltimore: Johns Hopkins University Press, 2007.

Gardner, Brian. *Allenby*. London: Cassell, 1965.

Gawhary, Karim el-. "'Nothing More to Lose': Landowners, Tenants, and Economic Liberalization in Egypt." *Middle East Research and Information Project* 204, no. 27 (1997): 41–42.

Gayed, Hegomenos Boutros. *The Apparition of the Virgin Mary at Zeitoun*. Cairo: Anba Rueis Press Coptic Patriarchate, 1985.

Gershoni, Israel, Hakan Erdem, and Ursula Woköck, eds. *Histories of the Modern Middle East: New Directions*. London: Lynne Rienner Publishers, 2002.

Gershoni, Israel, and James Jankowski. *Redefining the Egyptian Nation, 1930–1945*. Cambridge, UK: Cambridge University Press, 1995.

Ghosh, Amitav. *In an Antique Land*. New York: Vintage Books, 1992.
Gillis, John R., ed. *Commemorations: The Politics of National Identity*. Princeton, N.J.: Princeton University Press, 1994.
Goldschmidt, Arthur. *Biographical Dictionary of Modern Egypt*. Boulder, Colo.: Lynne Rienner Publishers, 2000.
Gonzalez-Quijano, Yves. *Les gens du livre*. Paris: Editions du Centre National de Recherche Scientifique, 1998.
———. "Politiques culturelles et industrie du livre en Egypte." *Maghreb-Machrek* 127 (1990): 104–20.
Gordon, Joel. *Nasser's Blessed Movement: Egypt's Free Officers and the July Revolution*. New York: Oxford University Press, 1992.
———. "Nasser 56/Cairo 96: Reimaging Egypt's Lost Community." In *Mass Mediations: New Approaches to Popular Culture in the Middle East and Beyond*, edited by Walter Armbrust, 161–81. Berkeley: University of California Press, 2000.
———. *Revolutionary Melodrama: Popular Film and Civic Identity in Nasser's Egypt*. Chicago: Middle East Documentary Press, 2002.
———. "Secular and Religious Memory in Egypt: Recalling Nasserist Civics." *Muslim World* 87, no. 2 (1997): 94–110.
Gruber, Mark Francis. "The Monastery as the Nexus of Coptic Cosmology." In *Between Desert and City: The Coptic Orthodox Church*, edited by Nelly Van Doorn-Harder and Kari Vogt, 66–83. Oslo: Novus forlag, Instituttet for Sammenlignende Kulturforskning, 1997.
Guirguis, Laure, ed. *Conversions religieuses et mutations politiques: Tares et avatars du communautarisme Égyptien*. Paris: Editions Non Lieu, 2008.
Guirguis, Magdi. *An Armenian Artist in Ottoman Egypt: Yuhanna al-Armani and His Coptic Icons*. Cairo: American University in Cairo Press, 2008.
Gullikson, Gay L. *Unruly Women of Paris: Images of the Commune*. Ithaca, N.Y.: Cornell University Press, 1996.
Haddad, Yvonne. "Islamists and the 'Problem of Israel': The 1967 Awakening." *Middle East Journal* 46, no. 2 (Spring 1992): 266–85.
Halbwachs, Maurice. *Les cadres sociaux de la mémoire*. Paris: Librairie Félix Alcan, 1925.
———. *La mémoire collective*. 1968. Reprint, Paris: Albin Michel, 1997.
———. *La mémoire collective chez les musiciens*. Paris: Librairie Félix Alcan, 1939. Originally published in *Revue Philosophique* (March–April 1939): 139–65.
Hall, Linda B. *Mary, Mother and Warrior: The Virgin in Spain and the Americas*. Austin: University of Texas Press, 2004.
Hammam al-Malatili (The Malatily Bathhouse). Film. Directed by Salah Abu Sayf. Egypt, 1973.
Hammoudi, Abdellah. *La victime et ses masques: essais sur le sacrifice et la mascarade au Maghreb*. Paris: Editions du Seuil, 1988.
Handler, Richard. "Is 'Identity' a Useful Cross-Cultural Concept?" In *Commemorations: The Politics of National Identity*, edited by John R. Gillis, 27–40. Princeton, N.J.: Princeton University Press, 1994.
Haram, al- (The Sin). Film. Directed by Henri Barakat. Egypt, 1965.

Harby, Moh. Khairy, and Moh. el-Hadi Afifi, eds. *Education in Modern Egypt.* Cairo: Ministry of Education, Documentation Center for Education, 1958.

Hasanayn, Muhammad Samir. *Ta'rikh wa nizam al-ta'lim fi Misr* (History and System of Education in Egypt). Tanta: Dar Khalifa li-al-Tiba'a, 1997.

Hassan, Fayza. "The King of Spring." *Al-Ahram Weekly*, no. 48 (15–21 April 1999).

Hassan, Muhammad Hassan. "Choix culturels et orientations éducatives en Egypte, 1923–1952." *Egypte/Monde Arabe*, nos. 18–19 (1994): 17–37.

Haykal, Muhammad Hasanayn. *1967: Al-Infijar. Harb al-thalathin sana* (1967: The Explosion. The Thirty-Year War). Cairo: Dar al-Ahram, 1990.

Herbert, Edwin Savory. *Damage and Casualties in Port Said. Report by Sir Edwin Herbert on His Investigation into the Effects of the Military Action in October and November, 1956. Presented by the Minister of Defense to Parliament by Command of Her Majesty.* London: Her Majesty's Stationery Service, 1956.

Herrera, Linda. *Scenes of Schooling: Inside a Girls' School in Cairo.* Cairo Papers in Social Science 15, monograph 1. Cairo: American University in Cairo Press, 1992.

Hewedy, Amin. "Nasser and the Crisis of 1956." In *Suez 1956: The Crisis and Its Consequences*, edited by William Roger Louis and Roger Owen, 161–72. Oxford: Clarendon Press, 1989.

Heymann, Florence, and Michel Abitbol, eds. *L'historiographie israélienne aujourd'hui.* Paris: Editions du Centre National de la Recherche Scientifique, 1998.

Heyworth-Dunne, James. *An Introduction to the History of Education in Egypt.* London: Luzac and Co., 1939.

Hilmi, Isma'il. *Al-'Adhra tazur Misr* (The Virgin Visits Egypt). 1996. Reprint, Cairo: al-Tawfiq li-l-Nashar, al-Hay'a al-'Amma li-l-Kitab, 2001.

Hobsbawm, Eric, and Terence Ranger, eds. *The Invention of Tradition.* Cambridge, UK: Cambridge University Press, 1983.

Hughes, Matthew. *Allenby and British Strategy in the Middle East, 1917–1919.* London: Frank Cass, 1999.

Hughes-Freeland, Felicia, and Mary M. Crain, eds. *Recasting Ritual: Performance, Media, Identity.* London: Routledge, 1999.

Husayn, Taha. *Al-Ayyam* (The Days). Cairo: Dar al-Ma'arif, 1962.

———. *Mustaqbal al-thaqafa fi Misr.* 1938. Reprint, Cairo: Matba'at al-Ma'arif, 1944. Translated by Sidney Glazer as *The Future of Culture in Egypt.* Ann Arbor: American Council of Learned Societies, 1954.

Hussein, Kamal Eldin, ed. *Drawings by School Children of Port Said on the Fight for the Defense of the City.* Rome: Académie Egyptienne, 1958.

Ibrahim, Saad Eddin, Marilyn R. I. Tadros, Mohammed Anwar El-Fiki, and Soliman Shafik Soliman. *The Copts of Egypt.* Minority Rights Group International Report. Cairo: Ibn Khaldoun Center for Development Studies, 1996. http://www.unhcr.org/refworld/pdfid/469cbf8ed.pdf.

Idris, Yusif. *City of Love and Ashes.* Translated by Neil R. Hewison. Cairo: American University in Cairo Press, 1999. Originally published as *Qisat Hubb.* Cairo: Dar al-Kitab al-'Arabi, 1967.

Ikhtiyar, al- (The Choice). Film. Directed by Yusif Shahin. Egypt, 1971.

Ilbert, Robert. *Alexandrie, 1830–1930: Histoire d'une communauté citadine.* 2 vols. Cairo: Institut Français d'Archéologie Orientale, 1996.

Immerzeel, Mat. "Coptic Art." In *Between Desert and City: The Coptic Orthodox Church Today*, edited by Nelly Van Doorn-Harder and Kari Vogt, 275–88. Oslo: Novus forlag, Instituttet for Sammenlignende Kulturforskning, 1997.
Ireton, François. "La lettre et le chiffre: Le processus d'alphabétisation en Egypte durant la période nassérienne." *Peuples Méditerranéens* (Special Issue: Nasser—25 ans), nos. 74–75 (1996): 147–73.
Irhab wa-al-kabab, al- (Terrorism and Kebab). Film. Directed by Sharif 'Arafa. Egypt, 1993.
James, Laura M. *Nasser at War: Arab Images of the Enemy*. New York: Palgrave Macmillan, 2006.
Jamila Bu Hirad (Djamila the Algerian). Film. Directed by Yusif Shahin. Egypt, 1958.
Jansen, Willy. "Visions of Mary in the Middle East: Gender and the Power of a Symbol." In *Gender, Religion and Change in the Middle East: Two Hundred Years of History*, edited by Inger Marie Okkenhaug and Inglvild Flaskerud, 137–54. Oxford: Berg, 2005.
Joutard, Pierre. *La légende des camisards: Une sensibilité au passé*. Paris: Editions Gallimard, 1977.
Kabtan, al- (The Captain). Film. Directed by Sayyid Sa'id. Egypt, 1997.
Karnak, al- (Karnak). Film. Directed by Ali Badrakhan. Egypt, 1975.
Karnouk, Liliane. *Contemporary Egyptian Art*. Cairo: American University in Cairo Press, 1995.
———. *Modern Egyptian Art: The Emergence of a National Style*. Cairo: American University in Cairo Press, 1988.
Kaufmann, Suzanne. *Consuming Visions: Mass Culture and the Lourdes Shrine*. Ithaca, N.Y.: Cornell University Press, 2005.
Kerr, Malcom. *The Arab Cold War, 1958–1964: A Study in Ideology and Politics*. London: Oxford University Press, 1965.
Khater, Akram F. *Inventing Home: Emigration, Gender, and the Middle Class in Lebanon, 1870–1920*. Berkeley: University of California Press, 2001.
Khattab, Azza. "The Tale of a City," *Egypt Today*, March 2002.
Khawf, al- (The Fear). Film. Directed by Sa'id Marzuq. Egypt, 1973.
Khouri, Malek. *The Arab National Project in Youssef Chahine's Cinema*. Cairo: American University in Cairo Press, 2010.
Kilpatrick, Hilary. "The Egyptian Novel from Zaynab to the Canvas." In *Modern Arabic Literature*, edited by M. M. Badawi, 223–69. Cambridge, UK: Cambridge University Press, 1992.
Kipling, Rudyard. *The Light That Failed*. New York/Boston: H. M. Caldwell Company, 1899.
Klunzinger, Carl Benjamin. *Upper Egypt: Its People and Its Products: A Descriptive Account of the Manners, Customs, Superstitions, and Occupations of the People of the Nile Valley, the Desert, and the Red Sea Coast, with Sketches of the Natural History and Geology*. Introduction by Dr. Schweinfurth. London: Blackie and Son, 1878.
Kolenkow, Anitra Bingham. "Talking through the Saints." In *Between Desert and City: The Coptic Orthodox Church Today*, edited by Nelly Van Doorn-Harder and Kari Vogt, 99–110. Oslo: Novus forlag, Instituttet for Sammenlignende Kulturforskning, 1997.
Krämer, Gudrun. *Jews in Modern Egypt, 1914–1952*. Seattle: University of Washington Press, 1989.
Kupferschmidt, Uri M. "Reformist and Militant Islam in Urban and Rural Egypt." *Middle East Studies* 23, no. 4 (October 1987): 403–18.

Kyle, Keith. *Suez*. New York: St. Martin's Press, 1991.
La waqt li-l-hubb (No Time for Love). Film. Directed by Salah Abu Sayf. Egypt, 1963.
LaDuke, Betty. "Egyptian Painter Inji Efflatoun: The Merging of Art, Feminism, and Politics." *NWSA Journal* 47, no. 3 (Spring 1989): 474–93.
Landsberg, Alison. *Prosthetic Memory: The Transformation of American Remembrance in the Age of Mass Culture*. New York: Columbia University Press, 2004.
Lane Edward W. *An Account of the Manners and Customs of the Modern Egyptians*. 1896. Reprint, London: Darf Publishers, 1986.
Lashin (Lachine, the People's Hope). Film. Directed by Fritz Kramp. Egypt, 1939.
Lavabre, Marie-Claire. "Usages du passé, usages de la mémoire." *Revue Française de science politique* 44, no. 3 (1994): 480–93.
Leeder, S. H. *Modern Sons of the Pharaohs: A Study of the Manners and Customs of the Copts of Egypt*. London: Hodder and Stoughton, 1918.
Lefebvre, Henri. *La production de l'espace*. Paris: Editions Anthropos, 1974.
———. *Le temps des méprises*. Paris: Stock, 1975.
Le Goff, Jacques. *Histoire et mémoire*. Paris: Gallimard, 1988.
———. *L'imaginaire médiéval*. Paris: Gallimard, 1985.
Le Goff, Jacques, and Pierre Nora, eds. *Faire de l'histoire*. Paris: Gallimard, 1974.
Lefebvre, Henri. *La production de l'espace*. Paris: Editions Anthropos, 1974.
Lemke, Wolf-Dieter. *Maḥmūd Šaltūt (1893–1963) und die Reform der Azhar: Untersuchungen zu Erneuerungsbestrebungen im Ägyptisch-Islamischen Erziehungssystem*. Frankfurt: Verlag Peter D. Lang, 1980.
Lloyd, Cynthia B., Sahar el Tawila, Wesley H. Clark, and Barbara S. Mensch. "The Impact of Educational Quality on School Exit in Egypt." *Comparative Education Review* 47, no. 4 (2003): 444–67.
Loraux, Nicole. "Pour quel consensus?" *Le genre humain* 18 (1988): 9–23.
Louis, William Roger, and Roger Owen, eds. *Suez 1956: The Crisis and Its Consequences*. Oxford: Clarendon Press, 1989.
Love, Kenneth. *Suez: The Twice Fought War*. London: McGraw-Hill, 1969.
Lowenthal, David. "For the Motion." In *Key Debates in Anthropology*, edited by Tim Ingold, 206–12. London: Routledge, 1996.
Luke, Timothy W. *Museum Politics: Power Plays at the Exhibition*. Minneapolis: University of Minnesota Press, 2002.
Lury, Celia. *Prosthetic Culture: Photography, Memory, and Identity*. New York: Routledge, 1998.
MacAloon, John J., ed. *Rite, Drama, Festival, Spectacle: Rehearsals Toward a Theory of Cultural Performance*. Philadelphia: Institute for the Study of Human Issues, 1984.
Mahfuz, Najib. *Adrift on the Nile*. Translated by Frances Liardet. Cairo: University of Cairo Press, 1993. Originally published as *Tharthara fawqa al-Nil*. Cairo: Maktabat Misr, 1965.
———. *Autumn Quail*. Translated by Roger Allen. Cairo: American University in Cairo Press, 1985. Originally published as *Al-Summan wa-al-kharif*. Cairo: Maktabat Misr, 1964.
Makdisi, Ussama. *The Culture of Sectarianism: Community, History, and Violence in Nineteenth-Century Ottoman Lebanon*. Berkeley: University of California Press, 2000.

Mansfield, Peter. *The British in Egypt*. 1971. Reprint, New York: Holt, Rinehart, and Winston, 1972.
Martin, John. *Roses, Fountains, and Gold: The Virgin Mary in History, Art, and Apparition*. San Francisco: Ignatius Press, 1998.
Masry, Iris Habib al-. *Introduction to the Coptic Church*. Cairo: Dar al-'Alam al-'Arabi, 1977.
Matsuda, Matt. *The Memory of the Modern*. New York: Oxford University Press, 1996.
Mauss, Marcel. *Sociologie et anthropologie*. Paris: Presses Universitaires de France, 1950.
Mayer, Thomas. *The Changing Past: Egyptian Historiography of the Urabi Revolt, 1882–1983*. Gainesville: University Presses of Florida, 1988.
Mayeur-Jaouen, Catherine. "The Coptic Mouleds: Evolution of the Traditional Pilgrimages." In *Between Desert and City: The Coptic Orthodox Church Today*, edited by Nelly Van Doorn-Harder and Kari Vogt, 212–29. Oslo: Novus forlag, Instituttet for Sammenlignende Kulturforskning, 1997.
———. "La religion populaire copte à l'heure du renouveau." *Chrétiens et sociétés, XVI–XX siècles* 4 (1997): 5–29.
McDonald, Sharon. "Exhibitions of Power and Powers of Exhibitions." In *The Politics of Display: Museums, Science, Culture*, edited by Sharon McDonald, 1–21. London: Routledge, 1998.
McPherson, Joseph W. *The Moulids of Egypt* (Egyptian Saints-Days). Cairo: Ptd. N. M. Press, 1941.
Megas, George A. *Greek Calendar Customs*. Athens: Gertrud S. Christou and Son, 1958.
Meinardus, Otto F. A. *Coptic Saints and Pilgrimages*. Cairo: American University in Cairo Press, 2002.
———. *Patriarchen unter Nasser und Sadat*. Hamburg: Deutsches Orient Institut, 1998.
———. *Two Thousand Years of Coptic Christianity*. Cairo: American University in Cairo Press, 1999.
Meital, Yoram. "Egyptian Perspectives on the Suez War." In *The 1956 War: Collusion and Rivalry in the Middle East*, edited by David Tal, 195–207. London: Frank Cass, 2001.
Melton, James van Horn. *Absolutism and the Eighteenth-Century Origins of Compulsory Schooling in Prussia and Austria*. Cambridge, UK: Cambridge University Press, 1988.
Messick, Brinkley. *The Calligraphic State: Textual Domination and History in a Muslim Society*. Berkeley: University of California Press, 1993.
Messiri, Sawsan, el-. *Ibn al-Balad: A Concept of Egyptian Identity*. Leiden: E. J. Brill, 1978.
Miramar (Miramar). Film. Directed by Kamal al-Shaykh. Egypt, 1969.
Mitchell, Timothy. *Colonizing Egypt*. 1988. Reprint, Berkeley: University of California Press, 1991.
———. *Rule of Experts: Egypt, Techno-Politics, Modernity*. Berkeley: University of California Press, 2002.
Modelski, Sylvia. *Port Said Revisited*. Washington, D.C.: Faros, 2000.
Moore, Laurence R. *Selling God: American Religion in the Marketplace of Culture*. New York: Oxford University Press, 1995.
Moreh, Smuel, trans. *Napoleon in Egypt: Al Jabarti's Chronicle of the French Occupation, 1798*. Princeton, N.J.: Markus Wiener Publishing, 1993.
Mountjoy, Alan B. "The Suez Canal at Mid-Century." *Economic Geography* 34, no. 2 (1958): 155–67.

Mukerji, Chandra, and Michael Schudson, eds. *Rethinking Popular Culture: Contemporary Perspective in Cultural Studies*. Berkeley: University of California Press, 1991.
Murray, Margaret A. "The King of All the Nobles." *Ancient Egypt* (1924): 96–97.
———. "Nawruz, or the Coptic New Year." *Ancient Egypt* (1921): 79–81.
Mutamarridun, al- (The Rebels). Film. Directed by Tawfiq Salih. Egypt, 1968.
Nasim, Sulayman. *Ta'rikh al-tarbiyya al-qibtiyya* (History of Coptic Education). Cairo: Dar al-Karnak li-al-Nashr wa-al-Tab' wa-al-Tawzi', 1963.
Nasir Salah al-Din, al- (Saladin). Film. Directed by Yusif Shahin. Egypt, 1963.
Nasser, Jamal 'Abd el-. *Egypt's Liberation: The Philosophy of the Revolution*. Translated by Dorothy Thompson. Washington, D.C.: Public Affairs Press, 1955. Originally published as *Falsafat al-thawra, bi-qalam Jamal 'Abd al-Nasir*. Cairo: Dar al-Ma'arif, 1954.
Nelson, Cynthia. "Religious Experience, Sacred Symbols, and the Social Reality: An Illustration from Egypt." *Humaniora Islamica* 2 (1974): 253–66.
———. "Self, Spirit Possession and World View: An Illustration from Egypt." *International Journal of Social Psychiatry* 17, no. 3 (1971): 194–209.
———. "Stress, Religious Experience and Mental Health." *Catalyst* (1972): 48–57.
———. "The Virgin of Zeitun." *Worldview* 16, no. 9 (1973): 5–11.
Nil, Michel (pseud.). *Les apparitions de la Très Sainte Vierge Marie en Egypte, 1968–1969*. Paris: Téqui, 1980.
Nispen tot Sevenaer, Christian van. "Changes in Relations between Copts and Muslims (1952–1994) in the Light of the Historical Experience." In *Between Desert and City: The Coptic Orthodox Church Today*, edited by Nelly Van Doorn-Harder and Kari Vogt, 22–34. Oslo: Novus forlag, Instituttet for Sammenlignende Kulturforskning, 1997.
Nora, Pierre. "Between Memory and History: *Les Lieux de Mémoire*." Translated by Marc Roudebush. Introduced and edited by Natalie Zemon Davis and Randolph Starn. *Representations* 26 (Spring 1989): 7–25.
———, ed. *Les lieux de mémoire*. 3 vols. Paris: Gallimard, 1984–92. Translated by Arthur Goldhammer as *Realms of Memory*. New York: Columbia University Press, 1996.
Obdeijn, Herman. "Enseignement de l'histoire dans la Tunisie moderne, 1881–1970." Ph.D. Diss., Katholieke Universiteit te Nijmegen, 1975.
Orsi, Robert Anthony. *The Madonna of 115th Street: Faith and Community in Italian Harlem, 1880–1950*. New Haven, Conn.: Yale University Press, 1985.
Ory, Pascal. *Une nation pour mémoire: 1889, 1939, 1989, trois jubilés révolutionnaires*. Paris: Presse de la Fondation Nationale de Sciences Politiques, 1992.
Ozouf, Mona. *L'école de la France: Essais sur la Révolution, l'utopie et l'enseignement*. Paris: Gallimard, 1984.
Pamuk, Orhan. *Istanbul: Memories and the City*. New York: Knopf, 2005.
Pelikan, Jaroslav. *Mary through the Centuries: Her Place in the History of Culture*. New Haven, Conn.: Yale University Press, 1996.
Pennington, J. D. "The Copts in Modern Egypt." *Middle Eastern Studies* 18, no. 2 (April 1982): 158–79.
Perry, Nicolas, and Loreto Echeverría. *Under the Heel of Mary*. London: Routledge, 1988.
Pignol, Armand. "50 ans d'histoire de la radio et de la télévision en Egypte, 1934–1984." *Bulletin du CEDEJ* 21 (1987): 17–36.

Platt, Raye R., and Mohammed Bahy Hefny. *Egypt: A Compendium*. New York: American Geographical Society, 1958.
Podeh, Elie, and Onn Winckler, eds. *Rethinking Nasserism: Revolution and Historical Memory in Modern Egypt*. Gainesville: University Press of Florida, 2004.
Portelli, Alessandro. *The Battle of Valle Giulia: Oral History and the Art of Dialogue*. Madison: University of Wisconsin Press, 1997.
———. *The Death of Luigi Trastulli and Other Stories: Form and Meaning in Oral History*. Albany: State University of New York Press, 1991.
Principio y Fin (The Beginning and the End). Film. Directed by Arturo Ripstein. Mexico, 1993.
Qadi, Dia al-Din Hasan al-, ed. *Al-Atlas al-tarikhi li-butulat sha'b Bur Sa'id 'amm 1956* (Historical Atlas of the Heroes of Port Said's People in the Year 1956). Port Said: Muhafizat Bur Sa'id, Lajnat al-tarikh wa-al-turath, 1997.
Qaradawi, Yusuf al-. *Dars al-Nakba al-Thaniya, li madha 'inhazamna wa kayfa nantasir* (Lesson from the Second Disaster: Why We Were Defeated and How We Shall Triumph). Cairo: Maktaba Wahba, 1987.
Qilsh, Kamal, ed. *Arba'un 'amman 'ala al-'idwan, Bur Sa'id . . . ayyam al-muqawma* (Forty Years Since the Attack, Port Said . . . During the Resistance). Cairo: Kitab al-Ahali, 1997.
Ramadan, 'Abd al-'Azim. *Tahtim al-aliha: Qissat harb yunyu 1967* (The Destruction of the Idols: Stories of the June 1967 War). Cairo: Maktabat Madbuli, 1986.
Ramadan, Sa'd Sami. *Umm Kulthum: Sawt fi-tarikh umma* (Umm Kulthum: Voice in the History of a Nation). Beirut: al-Sharika al-'Alamiyya li-al-Kitab, 1997.
Ramses Farah, Nadia. *Religious Strife in Egypt: Crisis and Ideological Conflict in the Seventies*. Cairo: American University in Cairo Press, 1986.
Rappaport, Joanne. *The Politics of Memory*. New York: Cambridge University Press, 1990.
Rawi, Salah al-. "Al-thaqafa al-sha'biyya . . . wa-al-muqawma—tamhid ula" (Popular Culture . . . and the Resistance—Preliminaries). In *Thaqafat al-muqawma. Dirasat wa-buhuth* (Culture of the Resistance. Studies and Research), vol. 1, *Mu'tamar udaba' Misr fi-al-aqalim* (Conference of Egypt's Regional Authors), 11th meeting, edited by Husayn Mahran, 125–72. Cairo: Al-Hay'a al-'Amma li Qusur al-Thaqafa, 1996.
Reid, Donald M. *Cairo University and the Making of Modern Egypt*. Cairo: American University in Cairo Press, 1990.
———. *Whose Pharaohs? Archaeology, Museums, and Egyptian National Identity from Napoleon to World War I*. Berkeley: University of California Press, 2002.
Rey, Terry. *Our Lady of Class Struggle: The Cult of the Virgin Mary in Haiti*. Trenton, N.J.: Africa World Press, 1999.
Reymond, Paul. *Le port de Port-Saïd: Mémoires de la Société d'Études Historiques et Géographiques de l'Isthme de Suez*, vol. 1. Cairo: Imprimerie du Scribe Egyptien, 1950.
Reza, Sadiq. "Endless Emergency: The Case of Egypt." *New Criminal Law Review* 10, no. 4 (Fall 2007): 532–53.
Rifaey, Tonia. "An Illustration of the Transitional Period in Egypt during 1919–1924: Political Cartoons in Egypt's Revolutionary History." Master's thesis, American University in Cairo, 1997.

Rifaud, J. J. *Tableau de l'Egypte, de la Nubie et des lieux circonvoisins ou Itinéraire à l'usage des voyageurs qui visitent ces contrées*. Paris: Chez Treuttel et Würtz Libraires, 1830.

———. *Voyage en Egypte en Nubie et lieux circonvoisins depuis 1805 jusqu'en 1827*. Paris: Treuttel et Würtz Libraires, 1830.

Riou, Edouard M. *Itinéraire de l'Isthme*. Paris: Aux Bureaux de l'Illustration, 1869.

Roudometof, Victor. *Collective Memory, National Identity, and Ethnic Conflict: Greece, Bulgaria, and the Macedonian Question*. London: Praeger, 2002.

Rousso, Henry. *Le syndrôme de Vichy de 1944 à nos jours*. Paris: Editions du Seuil, 1987.

Rudd qalbi (My Heart's Return). Film. Directed by 'Izz al-Din Dhulfiqar. Egypt, 1957.

Ruggles, Robin. *Apparition Shrines: Places of Pilgrimage and Prayer*. Boston: Pauline Books, 2000.

Russel, Thomas W. *Egyptian Service, 1902–1946*. London: John Murray, 1949.

Ryzova, Lucie. "I Am a Whore but I Will Be a Good Mother: On the Production and Consumption of the Female Body in Modern Egypt." *Arab Studies Journal* 13, no. 1 (Spring 2005): 80–123.

Saad, Reem. "Les deux passés des paysans de Nasser: Mémoire politique et vie quotidienne dans un village d'Egypte." *Peuples Méditerranéens* (Special Issue: *Nasser—25 ans*), nos. 74–75 (1996): 259–79.

———. "The Nation in the Village: War and Migration in Narratives of Egyptian Peasants." In *Twenty Years of Development in Egypt (1977–1997)*, part 2. Cairo Papers in Social Science 21, monograph 4. Cairo: American University in Cairo Press, 1998.

———. "Peasants' Perceptions of Recent Egyptian History." Ph.D. diss., University of Oxford, St Anne's College, 1994.

———. *Social History of an Agrarian Reform Community in Egypt*. Cairo: American University in Cairo Press, 1989.

———. "The Two Pasts of Nasser's Peasants: Political Memories and Everyday Life in an Egyptian Village." In *History and the Present*, edited by Partha Chatterjee and Anjan Ghosh, 183–208. New Delhi: Permanent Black, 2002.

Saad el-Din, Mursi, ed. *Gazbia Sirry, Lust for Color*. Cairo: American University in Cairo Press, 1998.

Sadek, Ashraf, and Bernadette Sadek. *L'incarnation de la lumière: Le renouveau copte à travers l'oeuvre d'Isaac Fanous*. Limoges: Le Monde Copte, 2000.

Saint Victor, Guillaume de. *Le Canal de Suez*. Paris: Librairie du Receuil Sirey, 1934.

Salim, Latifa Muhammad. *Misr fi-al-harb al-'alamiyya al-ula* (Egypt during the First World War). Cairo: al-Hay'a al-Misriyya al-'Amma li-al-Kitab, 1984.

Sanders, Paula. *Ritual, Politics, and the City in Fatimid Cairo*. New York: State University of New York Press, 1994.

Savage, Raymond. *Allenby of Armageddon: A Record of the Career and Campaigns of Field Marshal Viscount Allenby, GCB, GCMG*. London: Hodder and Stoughton, 1925.

Sayyid Abdalla, Abd al-Hamid al-. "Improving the Teaching of Social Studies in Egyptian Secondary Schools." Ph.D. diss., Columbia University, 1955.

Sayyid-Marsot, Afaf Lutfi, al-. *A Short History of Modern Egypt*. Cambridge, UK: Cambridge University Press, 1985.

Sayyid Bulti al- (Mister Fish). Film. Directed by Tawfik Salih. Egypt, 1969.

Schwebel, Lisa. *Apparitions, Healings, and Weeping Madonnas: Christianity and the Paranormal*. New York: Paulist Press, 2004.
Scott, James C. *Domination and the Arts of Resistance: Hidden Transcripts*. New Haven, Conn.: Yale University Press, 1990.
Shafik, Viola. *Arab Cinema: History and Cultural Identity*. Cairo: American University in Cairo Press, 1998.
Shahine, Gihan. "Under Siege." *al-Ahram Weekly*, 10–16 January 2002.
Shamir, Shimon, ed. *The Jews of Egypt: A Mediterranean Society in Modern Times*. Boulder, Colo.: Westview Press, 1987.
Sharaf, al- (The Honor). Film. Directed by Muhammad Sha'ban. Egypt, 1998.
Shaw, Tony. *Eden, Suez and the Mass Media: Propaganda and Persuasion during the Suez Crisis*. New York: Tauris Academic Studies, 1996.
Shay, Anthony. *Choreographic Politics: State Folk Dance Companies, Representation and Power*. Middletown, Conn.: Wesleyan University Press, 2002.
Shay' min al-khawf (A Bit of Fear). Film. Directed by Husayn Kamal. Egypt, 1969.
Shehada, Hazem. *Die Suezkrise von 1956 unter besonderer Berücksichtigung der Ägyptischen Darstellung*. Saarbrücken-Scheidt: Dadder, 1992.
Shemm, Paul Christopher. "Resistance and Popular Culture in Egypt." Master's thesis, University of Texas at Austin, 1998.
Shohat, Ella. "Egypt: Cinema and Revolution." *Critical Arts* 2, no. 4 (1983): 22–32.
Shoshan, Boaz. *Popular Culture in Medieval Cairo*. Cambridge, UK: Cambridge University Press, 1993.
Shryock, Andrew. *Nationalism and the Genealogical Imagination: Oral History and Textual Authority in Tribal Jordan*. Berkeley: University of California Press, 1997.
———, ed. *Off Stage/On Display: Intimacy and Ethnography in the Age of Public Culture*. Palo Alto, Calif.: Stanford University Press, 2002.
Shukr, 'Aysha. "Shamm al-nasim fi Bur Sa'id. Dirasa madaniyya fi Bur Sa'id" (Shamm al-Nasim in Port Said: Urban Study of Port Said). Ph.D. diss., University of 'Ayn al-Shams, Cairo, n.d.
Sibai, Shawqi al-. "Slums Family Life: A Study of Three Dwellings in the City of Port Said." Master's thesis, American University in Cairo, 1965.
Sika, Nadine M. *Educational Reform in Egyptian Primary Schools Since the 1990s: A Study of Political Values and Behavior of Sixth Grade Students*. Lewiston, N.Y.: Edwin Mellen Press, 2010.
Sigin Abu Za'bal (Prisoner of Abu Zaabal). Film. Directed by Niazi Mustafa. Egypt, 1957.
Skovgaard-Petersen, Jacob. *Defining Islam for the Egyptian State: Muftis and Fatwas of the Dar al-Ifta*. Leiden: Brill, 1997.
Smith, Charles. "The Egyptian Copts: Nationalism, Ethnicity, and Definition of Identity for a Religious Minority." In *Nationalism and Minority Identities in Islamic Societies*, edited by Maya Shatzmiller, 58–84. Montreal: McGill-Queen's University Press, 2005.
Somekh, Sasson. "The Suez War in Arabic Literature." In *The Suez-Sinai Crisis, 1956*, edited by Selwyn Ilan Troen and Moshe Shemesh, 172–79. London: Frank Cass, 1990.
Spence, Jonathan D. *The Memory Palace of Matteo Ricci*. New York: Viking Penguin, 1984.
———. *Treason by the Book*. New York: Viking, 2001.

Spicer, Andrew, and Sarah Hamilton. "Defining the Holy: The Delineation of Sacred Space." In *Defining the Holy: Sacred Space in Medieval and Early Modern Europe*, edited by Andrew Spicer and Sarah Hamilton, 1–26. Hants, UK: Ashgate, 2005.
Starkey, Paul, and Janet Starkey. *Travellers in Egypt*. London: I. B. Tauris, 1998.
Starrett, Gregory. "The Political Economy of Religious Commodities in Cairo." *American Anthropologist* 97, no. 1 (1995): 51–68.
——. *Putting Islam to Work: Education, Politics, and Religious Transformation in Egypt*. Comparative Studies on Muslim Societies 25. Berkeley: University of California Press, 1998.
Stoler, Ann L. *Carnal Knowledge and Imperial Power: Race and the Intimate in Colonial Rule*. Berkeley: University of California Press, 2002.
Suq al-sawda, al- (Black Market). Film. Directed by Kamal al-Tilmisani. Egypt, 1945.
Swann, Ingo. *The Great Apparitions of Mary: An Examination of Twenty-two Supranormal Appearances*. New York: Crossroad Publishing Company, 1996.
Swedenburg, Ted. *Memories of Revolt: The 1936–1939 Rebellion and the Palestinian National Past*. Minneapolis: University of Minnesota Press, 1995.
Szyliowicz, Joseph S. *Education and Modernization in the Middle East*. Ithaca, N.Y.: Cornell University Press, 1973.
Tadros, Mariz. "Hitting the Books." *al-Ahram Weekly*, 13–19 September 2001, 16.
Tahir, Bahaa'. *Aunt Safiyya and the Monastery: A Novel*. Translated by Barbara Romaine. Berkeley: University of California Press, 1996. Originally published as *Khalti Safiya wa-al-dayr*. Cairo: Dar al-Hilal, 1991.
Tak, Herman. *South Italian Festivals: A Local History of Ritual and Change*. Amsterdam: Amsterdam University Press, 2000.
Taussig, Michael. *Mimesis and Alterity: A Particular History of the Senses*. New York: Routledge, 1993.
Thomas, Keith. *Religion and the Decline of Magic*. New York: Charles Scribner's Sons, 1971.
Thoraval, Yves. *Regards sur le cinéma Égyptien, 1895–1975*. 1977. Reprint, Paris: L'Harmattan, 1996.
Troen, Selwyn Ilan, and Moshe Shemesh, eds. *The Suez-Sinai Crisis, 1956: Retrospective and Reappraisal*. London: Frank Cass, 1990.
Turner, Victor W. *Drama, Fields, and Metaphors: Symbolic Action in Human Society*. Ithaca, N.Y.: Cornell University Press, 1974.
Turner, Victor, and Edith L. B. Turner. *Image and Pilgrimage in Christian Culture*. New York: Columbia University Press, 1978.
'Ulawya, Qasim Mus'ad, and Mas'ud Shuman. "Al-Nass al-shi'ri al-sha'bi fi mantiqat al-qana wa hiss al-muqawma" (Popular Poetic Expression in the Region of the Canal and the Voice of the Revolution). In *Thaqafat al-muqawma. Dirasat wa-buhuth* (Culture of the Resistance: Studies and Research), vol. 1, Mu'tamar udaba' Misr fi-al-aqalim (Conference of Egypt's Regional Authors), 11th meeting, edited by Husayn Mahran, 197–290. Cairo: Al-Hay'a al-'Amma li Qusur al-Thaqafa, 1996.
Umm al-Nur wa-banatiha (The Mother of Light and Her Daughters). Film. Directed by Viola Shafik. Egypt, 1998.
UNESCO. *1982 Statistical Yearbook (Arab Member States)*. UK: UNESCO, 1983.
——. *1996 Statistical Yearbook*. UK: UNESCO, 1997.
——. *1999 Statistical Yearbook*. UK: UNESCO, 2000.

UNICEF. "Early Marriage: Child Spouses." *Innocenti Digest*, no. 7 (March 2001). http://www.unicef-irc.org/publications/pdf/digest7e.pdf (accessed 23 February 2012).

United Arab Republic. "Address by President Jamal Abdel Nasser at the Great Popular Rally at Gumhuria Square on the Occasion of the Celebrations of the Thirteenth Anniversary of the Revolution, July 22, 1965." In *Speeches by President Jamal Abdel Nasser on the Occasion of the Thirteenth Anniversary of the Revolution*. Cairo: UAR Information Department, 1965.

———. "Address by President Jamal Abdel Nasser at the Great Popular Rally Held in Suez on the Occasion of Its National Day. March 22nd, 1966." Cairo: Maslahat al-Isti'lamat, 1966.

———. *The Canal in 4 Years: 5 June 1975–5 June 1979*. Cairo: UAR Public Relations/Suez Canal Authority. June 1979.

———. *The Egyptian Revolution in Three Years, 1952–1955*. Cairo: Maslahat al-Isti'lamat, 1955.

———. *'Id al-nasr* (Victory Day). Cairo: UAR Information Department, 1964.

———. "Al-'Id al-qawmi li-muhafazat al-Suwis, 22 mars 1967" (National Day at the Governorate of Suez, 22 March 1967). Cairo: Wizara al-Ishara al-Qawmi, Maslahat al-Isti'lamat, 1967.

———. *La Victoire de Port Saïd/ Victory of Port Said*. Illustrated by Gamal Kotb. Cairo: UAR Information Department, 23 December 1962.

'Uways, Sayyid. *L'histoire que je porte sur mon dos*. Translated by Nashwa al-Azhari, Gilbert Delanoue, and Alain Roussillon. Cairo: CEDEJ, 1989. Originally published as *Al-Ta'rikh alladhi ahmiluhu 'ala dahri*, 3 vols. Cairo: Dar al-Hilal, 1985.

Valensi, Lucette. *Fables de la mémoire: La glorieuse bataille des trois rois*. Paris: Editions du Seuil, 1992.

———. *La Fuite en Egypte*. Paris: Editions du Seuil, 2002.

Van Doorn-Harder, Nelly. "Discovering New Roles: Coptic Nuns and Church Revival." In *Between Desert and City: The Coptic Orthodox Church Today*, edited by Nelly Van Doorn-Harder and Kari Vogt, 83–98. Oslo: Novus forlag, Instituttet for Sammenlignende Kulturforskning, 1997.

———. "Kyrillos VI (1902–1971): Planner, Patriarch and Saint." In *Between Desert and City: The Coptic Orthodox Church Today*, edited by Nelly Van Doorn-Harder and Kari Vogt, 230–42. Oslo: Novus forlag, Instituttet for Sammenlignende Kulturforskning, 1997.

Van Doorn-Harder, Nelly, and Kari Vogt, eds. *Between Desert and City: The Coptic Orthodox Church Today*. Oslo: Novus forlag: Instituttet for Sammenlignende Kulturforskning, 1997.

Viaud, Gérard. *Les pélerinages Coptes en Egypte*. Cairo: Institut Français d'Archéologie Orientale, 1979.

Vitalis, Robert. "American Ambassador in Technicolor and Cinemascope: Hollywood and Revolution on the Nile." In *Mass Mediations: New Approaches to Popular Culture in the Middle East and Beyond*, edited by Walter Armbrust 269–91. Berkeley: University of California Press, 2000.

Vivier, Anne-Sophie. "Coptes orthodoxes d'Egypte: Discours et pratiques identitaires." Master's thesis, Université de Paris X, 2000.

Voile, Brigitte. *Les coptes d'Égypte sous Nasser: Sainteté, miracles, apparitions*. Paris: CNRS Éditions, 2004.

Wahba, Magdi. *Cultural Policy in Egypt*. UNESCO Studies and Documents in Cultural Politics. Paris: Presses Universitaires de France, 1972.

Wardani, Mahmud al-. "Al-Tanbura allati takhtaf al-ruh" (The Tanbura That Stirs the Soul), *Akhbar al-Adab*, no. 477, (September 2002), 21.

Warren, Lynne, ed. *Encyclopedia of 20th Century Photography*. New York: Routledge, 2006.
Wassef, Magda, ed. *Égypte: Cent ans de cinéma*. Paris: Institut du Monde Arabe, 1995.
Waterbury, John. *The Egypt of Nasser and Sadat: The Political Economy of Two Regimes*. Princeton, N.J.: Princeton University Press, 1983.
Watson, John H. *Among the Copts*. Brighton, UK: Sussex Academic Press, 2002.
Wavell, Archibald Percival, Earl of. *Allenby: A Study in Greatness*. Vol. 1 of *The Biography of Field-Marshal Viscount Allenby of Megiddo and Felixstowe*. New York: Oxford University Press, 1940.
———. *Allenby in Egypt*. Vol. 2 of *The Biography of Field-Marshal Viscount Allenby of Megiddo and Felixstowe*. London: George G. Harrap and Co., 1943.
———. *The Good Soldier*. London: Macmillan, 1948.
Weinstein, Rodolph, and Rudolph M. Bell. *Saints and Society: The Two Worlds and Western Christendom, 1000–1700*. Chicago: University of Chicago Press, 1982.
Wickham, Carrie Rosefsky. *Mobilizing Islam: Religion, Activism, and Political Change in Egypt*. New York: Columbia University Press, 2002.
Williamson, Bill. *Education and Social Change in Egypt and Turkey: A Study in Historical Sociology*. London: Macmillan, 1987.
Winter, Jay, and Emmanuel Sullivan, eds. *War and Remembrance in the Twentieth Century*. Cambridge, UK: Cambridge University Press, 1999.
Yeçilbursa, Behçet Kemal. *The Baghdad Pact: Anglo-American Defence Policies in the Middle East, 1950–1959*. New York: Frank Cass, 2005.
Young, George. *Egypt*. London: E. Benn Ltd., 1927.
Zaki, Pearl. *Our Lord's Mother Visits Egypt in 1968*. Cairo: Dar el Alam el Arabi, 1977.
Zaki, Saad Yassa. "Guidelines for Improving the Preparation and Selection of Textbooks for Primary Schools in the United Arab Republic." Ph.D. diss., Columbia University, 1968.
Zawjati wa-al-kalb (My Wife and the Dog). Film. Directed by Sa'id Marzuq. Egypt, 1971.
Zayyat, Latifa al-. *The Open Door*. Translated by Marilyn Booth. Cairo: American University in Cairo Press, 2000. Originally published as *Al-Bab al-maftuh*, 1960. Reprint, Cairo: al-Hay'a al-Misriyya al-'Amma li-l-Kitab, 1989.
Zeghal, Malika. "Nasser et les Oulémas d'al-Azhar: La réinvention d'une mémoire politique." *Peuples Méditerranéens* (Special Issue: *Nasser—25 ans*), nos. 74–75 (1996): 101–18.
Zemon Davis, Natalie, and Randolph Starn. "Introduction." In "Memory and Counter-Memory: Special Issue," *Representations* 26 (Spring 1989): 1–6.
Zuhur, Sherifa, ed. *Colors of Enchantment: Theater, Dance, Music, and the Visual Arts of the Middle East*. Cairo: American University in Cairo Press, 2001.
———, ed. *Images of Enchantment: Visual and Performing Arts in the Middle East*. Cairo: American University in Cairo Press, 1998.
Zuhurat al-'Adhra khilala al-qarn al-'ashrin (The Visits of the Virgin during the Twentieth Century). Film. Kanisat al-qadis al-'azim al-anba Shanuda al-athariyya bi Misr al-qadima, bi Dayr Abi Sayfayn (The Church of H.H. the Great Pope Shanuda of the Apostolic Church of Egypt, Old Cairo). N.p., n.d.
Zwang, Gérard. *Chirurgien du contingent: Suez—Algérie, mai 1956-octobre 1958*. Unité Mixte de Recherche 5609 du Centre National de la Recherche Scientifique. Montpellier: Université Paul Valéry, 2000.

Index

Page numbers in italics refer to illustrations

'Abbas, Ra'uf, 42, 46
'Abd al-Nasir, Jamal. *See* Nasser
Abitbol, Michel, 174
Abu Sayf, Salah, 127–28, 153
Abu Shadi, 'Ali, 82
'Adli, Raf'at, 132–33, 209–10, 211, 214–15, 223–24
Aflatun, Inji, 36, 40
Agencies. *See* Egyptian vernacular politics, agencies, historical perceptions
Ahl al-qimma (Badrakhan), 158–59
Ahmad, Layla, 30, 55, 130
'Ajati, 'Abd al-Hamid al-, 15–16
Akhir Sa'a, 194, 204
Al-Afranji, 88, 100
Al-Ahali, 207
Al-Ahram, 169; apparition reported by, 167, 170–73, 195, 207, 208, 256n17, 256n20; Gregorius confides in, 175
Al-'Arab, 79, 88, 101, 128
Al-'Asfur (Shahin), 146
Al-Azhar, 20, 31, 33, 43, 165, 174, 179, 213; Shaykh al-Azhar, 174
Al-'Azima (Salim), 20, 27
Al-Bidaya wa-l-nihaya (Abu Sayf), 27
Alexandria, 87
Algerian Front of National Liberation, 129
'Ali, Mehmet, 51
Al-Irhab wa-l-kabab ('Arafa), 33, 234n82
Al-Karnak (Badrakhan), 146, 253n21, 253n23
Al-Khawf (Marzuq), 153, 154
"Allahu Akbar," 34, 234n84
Alleaume, Ghislaine, 73
Allenby, Edmund, 13, 122; departure of, 99–100, 103; effigy burning of, 76–79, 88–95, 97, 100, 103–4, 107, 109; foretold death of, 76–79; as

High Commissioner, 98; mission of, 95–98, 245n56, 245n59; as Moorhouse, 109; in Palestine campaign, 76. *See also* Al-Limby; Burn, Edmund, Burn
Al-Limby, 2, 13, 76–78; Allenby as, 85–104, 105–6; comeback of, 158; discontinuation of, 136; Eden as, 86, 106–7, 118; Moorhouse as, 109, 134–35; transformation of, 155, 160. *See also* Allenby, Edmund; haraq al-Limby; Limby Spring festival
Al-Masri al-Yawm, 207
Al-Musawwar, 167
Al-Qahira News, 207
Al-Watani, 169, 170, 181, 195, 204, 207, 208
Ambivalence, of utterances, 139, 146
Amiriyya, 16. *See also* Education, governmental
Anachronistic state of being, 54–58
Anglo-Egyptian Treaty, 86, 87, 243n8
Anticolonialism, 35, 56, 60, 67, 80, 106, 116, 135, 177
Apostolic Coptic Church, 196
Apparitions: of Shubra, 177; of Virgin Mary, 193–95, 199, 204, 259n6; of Warraq, 209; of Zaytun, 166–69, 171–72, 176–78, 181–82, 185, 190, 192–93, 195–201, 203–4, 207–9
Arabic education, 19, 21, 55–56
Arab-Islamic nationalism, 57, 212
Arab-Israeli conflict, 4, 70, 84
Arabization, 56
Arab nationalism, 8, 34, 56, 164
Arab socialism, 32, 51, 57–59
Arab Socialist Union (ASU), 48, 176, 181, 212
Arab Spring, 14, 215
'Arafa, Sharif, 33
Archangel Michael. *See* St. Michael
'Arif, 'Abd al-Salam, 120

Armani, Yuhanna al-, 187
Armbrust, Walter, 20, 26, 114, 124
Assassination, of Sadat, 200
ASU. *See* Arab Socialist Union
Asyut: apparition of St. Mary at, 206–7; University of, 19
Atatürk, Mustafa Kemal, 58
'Atawa, Faruq, 189
Athanasius, 168, 170
'Awad, Ahmad: Bandung barbershop of, 77, 92, 129, 133, 150; interview with, 90–93, 102–3, 129–30, 137–38, 216; remembrances of, 129–30, 216
'Awad, Luwis, 19, 59, 230n2
'Awad, Mona, 244n27
Awwali, 16, 20, 230n5. *See also* Education, elementary instruction
Ayyubi, Salah al-Din al-, 15–17, 49, 124
'Azir, Riyad Najib, 169
'Azm, Sadiq Jalal al-, 176–77, 198, 257n43

Badrakhan, 'Ali, 146, 158
Bakhtin, Mikhail, 3, 9, 11
Bambuti, 138
Banna, 'Abd al-Rahim Gharib al-: accounts of, 81, 88, 95, 136, 148–49, 151–52, 154; interview with, 101–2, 105, 141, 151, 155, 157, 159
Banning, of Limby Spring festival, 81–84, 94, 108, 134
Baring, Evelyn (Earl of Cromer), 96, 229n2, 238n21
Basic Education, 16, 20, 23, 24, 47, 50
Battle of Algiers (Pontecorvo), 47, 128–29
Battle of Port Said, 80, 88, 115, 120–28, 147, 149
Battle of the Canal, 80, 88
Benjamin, Thomas, 38
Bergus, Donald, 153, 254nn40–43, 255n2, 256n11
Bint al-balad, 38, 39
Bisati, Muhammad al-, 143–44, 151, 152
Black, gray, and other creative dialectics, 116–21, 249n44
Bloch, Marc, 5, 227n13
Boff, Leonardo, 175
Bombing: of Port Said, 139, 141–42, 149, 252n11; of Suez, 139, 142, 149–50, 153, 253n34
Books: about Suez War, 126–27. *See also* Textbooks
Bread, freedom, and social justice, 217–19
British: colonial occupation, 53, 54, 64, 77, 86, 96; in Port Said, 77, 80, 84–104, 134; in Suez War, 105–35
British Protectorate, 76, 86
Broadcast, of Nasser, 58, 239n47
Bully's Bull, 94–103. *See also* Allenby
Burn, Edmund, Burn, 75–84
Burning Eden, 106–7
Burrows, Larry, 117
Bur Sa'id (Dhulfiqar), 113–14, 124, 128, 235n84, 251n84
Buyut wara' al-ashjar (Bisati), 143–44, 151, 152

Cadres de la mémoire (Halbwachs), 6
Cafavy, Constantine, 87
Cairene institutions, 75
Cairo, 1–2, 152–54
Canal cities, 77, 81, 87, 98–99, 144, 158–60, 163, 248n32
Canal Zone, 80, 87, 136, 149, 243n13, 253n34
Casualties, of Suez War, 117–18, 119, 249n39, 249n49
Catholicism, 184–86, 196–97, 200; Copts and, 188, 206, 208
Celebrations: Evacuation Day, 106; Limby Spring festival, 2, 13, 76–81, 84, 89–94, 105, 107, 136, 160
Celebrities, Suez War involvement of, 123
Center of Earth, Port Said as, 80–81
Centralization, of state power, 54, 165
Christianity, 13, 97, 175, 177, 198, 200, 201
Christians, 200, 204, 206, 207, 212, 263n71, 263n74; Muslims and, 197, 208, 209–11, 214
Chronotopia, 5, 10, 94
Church: Apostolic Coptic, 182, 185, 196; St. Michael's, 168. *See also specific churches*
Church Committee of Investigation, 169, 171, 183–84, 196, 203, 206
Church of St. Damiana at Shubra, 182, 193, 199–200
Church of St. Marc bombing, 199
Church of St. Mary, at Zaytun, 167, 169–70, 181
Cinema, 25–26, 106, 130, 135, 147, 232n38, 232n40, 232n43. *See also* Films
Citadel, 70–71, 83
Citizenship, 14, 23, 48, 58, 71, 213–14
Civic education, 49–50, 237n3
Civilians, in Suez Canal, 121, 150–55, 253n34, 253n37

Clifford, James, 5
Coeducation, 31–32
Collectivity: memory and, 5–9, 72, 83, 227n4, 228n21, 228n24, 229n40; nation and, 7, 49, 113, 228n29
Colonial: ideology, 53, 96; order, 78, 87–89, 94, 101–2, 106, 107; troops, 80, 87, 88
Colonialism, 54, 56, 103, 116, 126, 130, 137–38
Commission of Inquiry. *See* Church Committee of Investigation
Communion of saints, 179, 257n58
Communitarian cohesion, 79, 88, 103–4
Communitarian unity, 195, 209
Communitas, 166, 178, 206
Community: in Coptic Church, 165, 197, 199, 201, 260n19; historical utterance and, 164; nation and, 79, 104, 164, 192–93; nation-state and, 163; in Port Said, 89–91, 114
Compagnie Universelle du Canal Maritime de Suez, 85, 86, 88, 98, 106, 149, 243nn11–12
Compulsory education, 46. *See also* Education, compulsory
Conflict, 11, 12, 49, 79, 87, 94, 100, 104, 157, 164, 178, 196
Conscript march (1967 War), 142–43
Construction, in Port Said, 158
Coptic Canon Law, 180
Coptic Church, 13, 191; adaptation of, 165; Apostolic, 196; community in, 165, 197, 199, 201, 260n19; in Egypt, 200; "Flight of the Holy Family," 200–201; income of, 181–82; political activism of, 164, 178, 213; religious trends of, 185, 187–88, 197; Virgin Mary and, 200–201
Coptic Institute of Higher Studies, 183
Coptic-Islamic-Pharaonic story, 100–103
Coptic Mariological piety, 170, 186
Coptic Mariology, 187, 206
Coptic martyrdom, 197–98
Coptic Orthodox patriarch, 173, 182
Coptic publications, 193, 200, 259n4
Copts, Muslims and, 177, 213
Cromer, Earl of. *See* Baring, Evelyn
Cult: of saints, 179, 185; of Virgin Mary, 166, 185, 196, 198. *See also* Mariophany
Cultural distinctness, 163
Cultural productions, 3
Cultural Revolution, 20, 49
Culture economy, 35

Curricular homogenization, 30, 49, 54, 55, 56, 239n33
Curriculum, in schoolhouse, 50, 65–66, 238nn5–6

Dakhlia, Jocelyn, 7
Damages: in Port Said, 139; in Suez War, 118. *See also* Bombing, of Port Said
Dar al-'Ulum, 31
Dayan, Moshe, 136–37
Death: of Kyrillus VI, 192; of memory, 7; of Nasser, 138, 154, 161, 192
Decolonization, 4, 56
De Gaulle, Charles, 4, 110
Democratic society, Free Officers and, 14, 51
Dening, Greg, 10
Dhat (Ibrahim), 161
Dialectics. *See* Black, gray, and other creative dialectics
Di-Capua, Yoav, 69
Discourse, intrachristian, 196
Discursive strategies, 193–95
Districts, of Port Said, 88–89, 244n26
Disuqi, 'Asim Ahmad al-, 68
Divine sapience, 188–90
Doves and clouds, 168–73
Durrell, Lawrence, 87
Duty-free zones, of Port Said, 155, 158

Eden, Anthony, 86, 107, 111, 115, 118, 122
Education, 15–17, 230n15, 231nn14–15; Arabic, 55–56; basic, 47; civic, 49–50, 237n3; coeducation, 31–32; compulsory, 15–16, 19, 22, 24, 46, 236n110, 237n3, 238n5; current system of, 47–48; elementary instruction, 20–23, 231nn21–22; enrollment increase for, 45; expenditures for, 43, 236n110; female, 28–33, 35–36, 39, 45, 47–48, 71, 231n19, 233n57, 233n63, 233n67; Free Officers and, 56; governmental, 16, 20, 30; history instruction levels in, 22; literacy and, 28; Nasserian schoolhouse, 17, 19, 20, 50–51, 55, 71; primary, 16, 19, 21; private, 47, 56–57, 237n124; school fee, 25; social inclusion in, 20; statistics about, 68, 240n71; student enrollment, 29; textbooks, 21–23, 231n17, 231n19, 231n22, 237n128; tuition-free, 16, 17, 19–21, 23, 28, 221; of 'Uthman, 21, 24–25, 68, 231n16. *See also specific universities*

Education policies: after 1952 Revolution, 19, 23, 28, 33, 44, 49, 58, 64, 71, 105; before 1952 Revolution, 20, 23, 30, 32, 34, 69; of Sadat, 33, 59, 64, 69, 72

Educational institutions reformation, 20, 31, 33, 35, 48, 165

Educative Nasserism, 28, 44, 236n117

Effigy burning, 246nn85–87; of Allenby, 76–79, 88–95, 97, 100, 103–4, 107, 109; making of, 108; during Shamm al-Nasim, 12, 76, 82, 90, 95, 103, 107, 115

Egalitarianism, 11, 14, 24, 43–44, 48, 71, 220–21, 224

Egypt: "Flight of the Holy Family" to, 200–201; as homogenous nation, 214; Mother of, 163–91, 200

Egyptian autonomy, 4

Egyptianization, 56–58, 59, 257n45

Egyptian nationalism, 54–55

Egyptian vernacular politics, agencies, historical perceptions: through 1950s–1960s history, 3, 4, 76; through cultural productions, 3

Elementary instruction, 20–23, 231nn21–22

Employment pledge, 33

Empowerment, of women, 185–86

Enlightenment, 64–67, 70

Enrollment: increase in, 45; student, 29

Epistemology, 197, 260n10

Ethnicity, political legitimacy and, 53

Ethnonationalism, 51–52

Ethnoracial concepts, of identity, 53

European nationals, in Port Said, 81, 86, 103–4

Evacuation, of Port Said, 136, 138, 140, 151, 252n4

Evacuation Day celebrations, 106

Expenditures, for education, 43, 236n110

Faith, Virgin Mary and, 188

Faksh, Mahmud A., 56, 58

Familiarity, of saints, 179

Fargues, Philippe, 30

Farid, Muhammad, 19, 52

Faruq, Muhammad, 204, 261n36

Faruq monarchy, 16, 20, 26, 30, 32, 44, 49, 212, 214, 218, 224

Fatiha, 'Abd al-Hamid, 68

Favret-Saada, Jeanne, 7

Fellah (pl. Fellahin), 15, 24, 27, 30, 38, 44, 55, 92–93, 119, 126, 150

Female primary schooling, 28–32, 47, 233n63, 233n67

Ferry, Jules, 49

Fida'iyyin, 109, 119, 124, 127, 149, 247n6. *See also* Resistance, popular

Films, 25–26, 124, 127–28, 232n38, 232n40, 232n43, 251n85. *See also* Cinema

"Flight of the Holy Family": to Egypt, 200–201; Route of, 201; secularization of, 201; tourism and, 201

Foreign schools, 57–58, 231n19, 239n33

Fortieth anniversary, of Zaytun, 199, 200, 207, 262n48

Freedom, 217–19

Free Officers, 44, 48, 54, 106, 128, 148, 212; Committee of, 123; democratic ideals supported by, 14, 51, 71; education and, 56; legacy of, 70, 217, 219; military courts of, 219; Nasser's founding of, 64, 69; power of, 26–27; reforms of, 51; repression conducted by, 34, 40, 67, 131, 146, 147, 221; secular schooling established by, 12, 41, 51; Taha Husayn and, 19; women and, 28, 30, 35–36. *See also* Education, female; Women

French Guizotian education ideal, 51

The Future of Education (Husayn), 23

Garb, of Virgin Mary, 205

Gayed, Boutros, 199, 260n18

German raid, of Port Said, 80

Ghazali, Captain, 78, 97, 100, 134, 160–61

Girls from Bahary (Sa'id), 39

Girodet, Anne-Louis, 54

Giza, church of al-Warraq at, 199

Giza Mariophany, 199, 203, 207, 209

Globalization, of Virgin Mary, 192–215; apparitions, 193–95, 199, 204, 259n6; Coptic sacred space and, 200; discursive strategies of, 193–95; "Flight of the Holy Family," 200–201; modern identities, monosemy of, 207–12; narration of, 203–6; 1968–1986: An Incurable Darkness, 195–98; peace, love, penitence, 206–7; St. Michael, 200–202; validation of, 203–6

Gospel of St. Matthew, 201

Governor, of Port Said, 138–39

Gregorius, Abba, 175, 183, 187, 188, 207, 208

Halbwachs, Maurice, 3, 4, 6

Hammam al-Malatili (Abu Sayf), 153

Handler, Richard, 5
Hara, 20, 78, 161
Haraq al-Limby, 13, 76, 78, 90, 92, 105
Harb, Tal'at, 20
Haykal, Muhammad Hasanayn, 199
Head of state, Nasser as, 53–54
Hegemonic processes, 164–65
Hegemony: ideological, 165; of state institutions, 50, 51, 72, 83, 165
Herbert, Edwin, 117, 118
High Commissioner, Allenby as, 98
Hijra, 116, 149–55
Historical lies, 50
Historical perceptions. *See* Egyptian vernacular politics, agencies, historical perceptions
Historical representations, 3–6, 12, 28, 48–50, 69, 72, 100, 106, 124
Historical themes, in textbooks, 62–63
Historical utterances, 9–10, 144, 179, 229n40; of '56 moment, 129; of 1950s-1960s, 14, 163–64; about '67 events, 148
Historiography: British, 116; Middle East, 4, 49, 52–54
History: curriculum of, 65–66; institutional, 70; instruction levels for, 22; of 1950s–1960s, 3, 4, 76
History-making, 2–3
Hobsbawm, Eric, 7, 90
Homogenization-curricular, 30, 49, 54, 55, 56, 213, 239n33
Homogenous nation, Egyptian society as, 54–55, 213–14, 222
Hong Kong of the West, Port Said as, 157–60, 254n57
House of 'Ali, 53. *See also* Ottoman
Husayn, Taha, 43, 230n4, 231n7; as Minister of Education, 19, 23–24, 232n27; tuition-free secondary education instituted by, 19; University of Alexandria founded by, 19
Husni, Nabila, 31, 45, 139–40, 141–42, 149, 150, 233n66

Ibrahim, Sun'allah, 161
Iconographical tradition, of Virgin Mary, 185, 186, 187
'Id, Kamal, 78–79, 98, 107, 121–23, 129, 136
'Id al-Nasr, 120, 121
Ideals, subversion of, 219–20

Identity: ethnoracial concepts of, 53; scholarship on, 5–7
Ideological hegemony, 165
Ideology, 27, 45, 51, 56, 58–59, 69, 70, 83, 211, 213, 221
Idris, Yusuf, 127
Immaculata of the Miraculous Medallion, 185, 197, 205
Incurable otherness, 1–14
Incurable past, 4–5
Indigenization: of saints, 200, 201; of Virgin Mary, 201
Infitah, 59, 67, 133, 158, 160–61
Institutional hegemony, 50, 165
Institutional history, 10, 51, 70, 126, 133, 144, 147
Institutional utterances, 133, 144
The Invention of Tradition (Hobsbawm, Ranger), 7
Islamic scriptures, 50
Islamic university of al-Azhar, 20, 31, 33, 48. *See also* al-Azhar
Ismailia, 86, 88, 124, 154; alteration of, 163; *hijra* in, 151; Limby festival in, 160, 161; Muslim Brotherhood in, 106; Open Door Policy in, 81; Shamm al-Nasim festival in, 76, 90; war in, 139, 141, 149
Israel, 4, 22, 61, 70, 94, 146, 154; bombing by, 141–42, 145, 149, 153, 252n11; loudspeakers of, 149; peace with, 157; Port Said occupied by, 107, 136, 139–40, 149; religious trends of, 174
Isthmus urban societies, cultural distinctness of, 78, 115, 116, 144, 163, 222

Jacobinic principles, 218
Jamila (Shahin), 124, 128, 251n86
January Revolution, 216
Jerusalem, 177
Jews, 128, 154, 175, 196
July Revolution, 16, 32, 61, 64, 67, 80, 131, 212
June War, 136, 140, 141, 143, 149, 156, 158, 161, 164

Kamal, Jamal, 69, 192
Kamil, Mustafa, 19, 52, 68
Das Kapital (Marx), 57
Kennedy, John F., 4, 130
Khalil, Tawfiq, patron of St. Mary's church, 170
Khaliq, 'Ali 'Abd al-, 156
Khan Yunus, 95
Khedivial age, 55

Khedivial state, 53. *See also* Ottoman
Khedivial textbook, 51
Khrushchev, Nikita, 120
Khudayr family, 108, 112–13, 160
Kidnapping, of Moorhouse, 109–16, 247n15, 248n22
Kipling, Rudyard, 86
Kolenkow, Anitra B., 178
Kuttab: to *makatib*, 41–43, 236n108; punishment at, 37
Kyrillus VI (Cyril VI), 183; death of, 192; healing by, 178; politics of, 190; as pope, 167; veneration of, 179, 180–81, 182, 258n62

Labib, Sonia, 172, 183
Lacy, Brig. John H. S., 106
Lane, Edward, 91, 244n40
Language schools, 58
Law No. 210 of 1953, 23
Laythi, Salah al-, 207
Leeder, S. H., 96–97
Legacy: of Free Officers, 70, 217, 219; of Nasser, 130–31, 143, 212–15, 219–20
Lesseps, Ferdinand de, 85, 126, 242n3
Liberal Constitutional Party, 23
Les lieux de mémoire (Nora), 7, 228n32
Limby Spring festival: banning of, 81–84, 134; effigy burning at, 76–79, 88–95, 97, 100, 103–4, 107, 109; in Ismailia, 160, 161; as merry celebration, 134; nationalist interpretation of, 105; in 1960s, 136; in Port Said, 2, 76–79, 81–84, 88–95, 97, 100, 103–4; revitalization of, 107, 160–62
Literacy, 20, 28, 30, 47, 222, 232n27, 233n57
Literary critic, Bakhtin as, 3, 9, 11
Literature, of Mariophany, 196–97
Longing, belonging and, 223–24
Lourdes, 181, 185

Madrasa, 41, 235n105
Mahfuz, Najib, 123
Mahmud, Sa'id, 39
Mahran, Muhammad, 110–11, 112, 123, 247n14
Maktab, 16. *See also Kuttab*
Malraux, André, 58
Ma'mun, Hasan, 174
Manhouse, 108
Mansur, Fawzi, 183

Mansur, Nabil, 113
Marcelle, 184–85, 258n77
March 30 Program Speech, 168, 170
Marian event, 13, 14, 166, 169, 177, 186, 193–95
Marian veneration, 198
Mariophany: as divisive topic, 198; Giza, 199, 203, 207, 209; literature of, 196–97; motifs and structure of, 203–4, 261n33; narratives of, 203–4; in national press, 202; publicity of, 200, 201; utterances of, 190–91, 192, 196, 207, 209; at Zaytun, 8, 168, 170, 171, 173, 174, 178, 182, 185, 187, 190–91, 192, 203, 208
Martyr City, Port Said as, 80, 105–35
Marx, Karl, 57
Marzuq, Sa'id, 153, 154
Maspero, massacre of, 215, 218
Masquerade politics, 17, 89
Mass-market, 13, 158, 161, 216; religious commodities and, 165, 181, 185–86, 188, 190, 200, 206, 216, 222, 259n86
Mass media, 12, 13, 25, 48, 71, 73, 126, 148, 198, 218
Mat'al, Zaki 'Abd al-, 34; on Nasser, 131–32; on National Charter, 57–58; on 1967 war, 144–46; testimony of, 146–47
Mater Dolorosa, 186
Media, mass. *See* Mass media
Mediterranean Expeditionary Force, 95
Mehmet 'Ali dynasty, 214. *See also* Ottoman
La mémoire collective (Halbwachs), 6–7, 228n24
Memory: collectivity and, 5–9; death of, 7; national collective, 83; scholarship on, 8, 11
Memory-politics, 16, 48, 59, 64, 67, 72, 75, 83, 112–13, 131
Mexican Revolution, 38, 148
Middle East historiography, 4, 49, 52–54
Military courts, of Free Officers, 219
Military leadership, 69
Military legacy, of Free Officers, 70
Military museums, 70–71
Military presence, in Port Said, 80, 86, 97
Ministry of Education: Husayn as, 19, 23–24, 232n27; museum of, 39; reorganization of, 59; textbooks and, 67, 72, 240nn54–55
Ministry of Tourism, 168
Miracles: endorsement of, 176; Jerusalem liberation as, 177; poetics of, 178–82, 197; during Sadat's years, 198–200; science of, 167–91; stories of, 199

Misr al-awwal, 157
Mission, of Allenby, 95–98, 245n56, 245n59
Mitchell, Timothy, 50
Mnemosyne, 8
Modern identities, monosemy of, 207–12
Modernization, of 1950s–1960s, 35, 84, 164, 211, 223
Monarchy overthrow, 51, 105, 148
Monopolization, of Virgin Mary, 200
Monosemy, of modern identities, 207–12
Moorhouse, Anthony Gerard, 135; kidnapping of, 109–16, 247n15, 248n22; museum of, 110, 112, 113
Mother of Egypt, 163–91, 200
Mother of God, 198
Mother of Light, 168–69, 169, 176, 189
Motifs and structure, of Mariophany, 203–4, 261n33
Mubarak, Muhammad Husni, 13, 33, 59, 64, 72, 83
Muhammad, 108
Muhammad 'Ali Street, 101–2
Muhammad Mahmud Street, 218
Mulhouse, 108
Mulid al-Nabi, 100
Multiparty parliamentary system, 165
Munaqiba combatant, 125
Murray, Sir Archibald, 95–96
Musa, Constantine, 189
Museum: of Education, 35, 35, 39; Military, 70–71; of Moorhouse, 110, 112, 113; October War, 70, 83
Muslim Brotherhood, 106, 212, 214, 220
Muslims, 128; Christians and, 197, 208, 209–11, 214; Copts and, 177; at Giza church, 199; hostility of, 165; Mariophany narratives and, 203–4; Nasser and, 213; publications of, 182; saints and, 179, 198
Mutamasirun, 214

Nabil al-Mansur Street, 108
Najib, Muhammad, 23
Naksa, 138, 144, 146, 147, 156, 170, 174, 175. *See also* 1967 War
Narration, of Globalization, of Virgin Mary, 203–6
Narratives, 229n42; of Mariophany, 203–4; polyphonic, 9–10; polysemic, 9; of visitations, 193–95
Nasikh, Ibrahim al-, 187
Nasir, Huda 'Abd al-, 217
Nasser, Jamal 'Abd al-, 44, 54–55, 77, 130; broad-cast of, 58, 239n47; Cultural Revolution and, 20, 49; death of, 138, 154, 161, 192; downfall of, 129; employment pledge of, 33; Free Officers founded by, 64, 69; as head of state, 53–54; Islam and, 41, 51, 57, 131, 213, 214; legacy of, 130–31, 143, 146, 212–15, 219–20; March 30 Program Speech of, 168, 170; nationalizations under, 32; policies of, 4, 9, 33, 34, 40–41, 56, 72, 126; popularity of, 106; press conference of, 144; textbooks and, 60–61, 64, 67, 119, 201; years of, 11–13, 120, 216–17, 217. *See also* Nationalization
Nasser 56 (Fadil), 130
Nasserian Arab Socialist Union, 48, 145, 148, 176, 181, 212. *See also* ASU
Nasserian pledge, 221–23
Nasserian schoolhouse, 17, 19, 20, 50–51, 55, 71
Nasserism, 30, 33, 36, 43; educative, 28, 44, 236n117
Nation: collectivity and, 7, 17, 228n29; community and, 10, 49, 75, 164, 192, 201, 222
National Charter, 51, 57
National collective memory, 83
Nationalism: Arab, 8, 26, 34, 56, 58, 64, 126, 131–32, 164, 212; Egyptian, 54–55; scholarship on, 7; secular, 212. *See also* Ethnonationalism
Nationalist interpretation, of Limby spring festival, 105, 108
Nationalists, 53, 214
Nationalization: under Free Officers, 56; under Nasser, 32, 46, 56, 129; of schooling, 51, 55–56; of Suez Canal, 39, 58, 61, 106, 110, 115, 139, 147; of Virgin Mary, 192, 200
National press, Mariophany in, 202
National unity, 11, 133, 156, 164, 178, 183, 195, 197
Nation-state: community and, 55, 57, 163; memory-politics of, 75
New order, 34–41; anachronistic state of being in, 54–58; castle of clay, 58–64; culture economy in, 25, 35; past rewritten in, 35, 51, 58, 69; revolution, rectification, enlightenment, 64–67, 70; schooling reforms in, 49–74; useful lessons, 67–71; women in, 35, 35–37. *See also* Women
Nijm, Ahmad Fu'ad, 79, 146
1919 Revolution, 98, 246n78
1950s–1960s: history of, 3, 4, 76; modernization of, 35, 84, 164, 211, 223; schooling reforms in, 49–74; utterances of, 75, 84

1952 Revolution, 44, 51, 68, 148; education policies after, 19, 23, 28, 33, 64, 71, 105; education policies before, 23, 56, 69; intelligentsia and, 36, 40, 48, 230n2; in textbooks, 22, 60, 61, 64, 67–70
1956 events, 105–7, 129. *See also* Suez War
1956 War, 106, 109–10, 140, 144, 147–48
1960s, Limby Spring festival in, 136
1961 Reform Law, 32, 46, 51, 57, 59, 127, 165, 234n76
1967 War, 13, 61, 76, 135, 136, 138, 140, 141, 143–46, 148–49, 153–55, 156, 158, 161, 164, 196
1968–1986: An Incurable Darkness, 195–98
1973 War, 137, 155. *See also* October War
Nonalignment movement, 4, 129–30
Nora, Pierre, 3, 7

October War, 76, 138, 143, 144, 155, 156
October War Museum, 70, 83
One-party system, 165
Open Door policy, of Sadat, 81. *See also* Infitah
The Open Door (Zayyat), 121, 126–28, 250n57
Orozco, José Clemente, 38
Orthodoxy, radicalism and, 176
Ottoman rule, nationalist reinvention of, 51, 53, 55, 238n18, 238n27
Our Lady of the Palestine Liberation Organization, 173–78
Our Lady of Zaytun, 168

Palestine campaign, of Allenby, 76
Palestinian features, of Virgin Mary, 205, 261n40
Palestinian Maidens, 185–88
Palestinian resistance, 83–84, 109, 162, 168
Pan-Arabism, 4, 34, 60, 131, 161
Papal miracles, 180–81
Paradigm, of schoolhouse, as matrix of the nation, 49
Pasha, Khalil Ibrahim, 170
Patriotic love, during Suez War, 126, 134–35
Peace, 36, 61, 70, 76, 138, 155, 157, 162; with Israel, 70, 113, 157; love, penitence, and, 206–7
Peasant. *See* Fellah
Performances, 10, 33–34, 69, 75, 94, 171
Phenomenon, of Virgin Mary, 167, 176, 183, 184, 188
Philosophy of the Revolution (Nasser), 55, 64, 173, 179, 191
Photographs, of Suez War, 117
Podeh, Elie, 11

Poetics, of miracles, 178–82
Policies: of Nasser, 4, 9, 33, 34, 40–41, 56, 72, 126; of Sadat, Open Door, 81. *See also* Education policies; Infitah
Political activism, of Coptic Church, 164, 178, 213
Political legitimacy, ethnicity and, 53
Politicization, of religion, 164, 174, 207, 213
Politics: of Kyrillus VI, 176, 190; masquerade, 89; sectarian, 212, 213. *See also* Egyptian vernacular politics, agencies, historical perceptions; Memory-politics, of nation-state; Secular politics downfall
Polyphonic narratives, 5, 9–10
Polysemic narratives, 9, 94
Pontecorvo, Gillo, 128, 129
Pope, Kyrillus VI as, 167
Popular revolution, 38, 51, 218
Population, of Port Said, 86–87, 91, 243nn12–15
Portelli, Alessandro, 3, 5, 10, 109
Port Said, 2–3, 40, 45; alteration of, 163; battle of, 80, 88, 115, 120–28, 147, 149; British in, 77, 80, 84–104, 134; celebrations in, 77, 81, 82, 105–8, 134, 161; as center of Earth, 80–81; community in, 90–91; construction in, 158; districts of, 88–89, 244n26; duty-free zones of, 155, 158; evacuation of, 136, 138, 140, 151, 252n4; foreign nationals departing of, 81, 135, 214; German raid of, 80; governor of, 138–39; as Hong Kong of the West, 157–60, 254n57; Israeli bombing of, 141–42, 252n11; Israeli loudspeakers in, 149; Israeli occupation of, 136, 139–40, 149; Limby Spring festival in, 2, 76–79, 81–84, 88–95, 97, 100, 103–4; as Martyr City, 80, 105–35; military presence in, 80, 86, 97; population of, 86–87, 91, 243nn12–15; prosperity of, 159–60; repopulation of, 157; strategic importance of, 85; temporary shelters after exodus from, 151–52; trafficking in, 158; war damages in, 139; workers in, 87–88, 90–93, 96, 97, 245n65. *See also* Bombing; Damages; Suez War
Port Tewfik, 86
Present: is everything, 75–104; schooling reforms in, 50–54
Presira, 170, 199
Press conference, of Nasser, 144
Primary education, 16, 19, 21
Primary schooling, female, 28–32, 47, 233n63, 233n67

Prince of Wales, 80
Private lessons, 46, 47, 237n124
Private schools, 47, 56, 57, 68, 239n38, 240n69
Propaganda, 113–14, 116–21, 123–24, 145–48
Prosperity, of Port Said, 159–60
Publications: Coptic, 193, 200, 259n4; Islamic, 182
Public utterances, 11, 84, 104, 108, 135, 143, 144, 146
Pugnatoribus, 174
Punishment at kuttab, 37, 41, 42

Qabbani, Isma'il al-, 19
Qalyubiyya, 68–69
Qaradawi, Yusuf al-, 174
Queen's son-in-law, 109, 111–16

Racialization, of religion, 213–14
Radicalism, orthodoxy and, 176
Rafi'i, 'Abd al-Rahman al-, 69, 72, 148
Rakha, Muhammad, 39
Ramadan, 156, 161
Rami, 193–95
Ranger, Terence, 7
Ranke, Leopold von, 5
Recruitment, of youth, 152–53
Rectification, 64–67
"Red" revolutionary Virgin, 195–96
Reforms, of Free Officers, 51
Reinforcement, of state power, 165
Religion: politicization of, 164; racialization of, 213
Religious burning ceremonies, 92–93, 244n41, 244n243, 245n46
Religious commodities, 165, 181, 185–86, 188, 190, 200, 206, 216, 222, 259n86
Religious distinctions, 164, 213, 222
Religious literate scripturalism, 13, 198, 211, 222
Religious trends: of Coptic Church, 185, 187–88, 197; of Israel, 174
Remembrance, 3, 6, 7, 9, 25, 75, 155; of 'Awad, 129–30, 216; scholarship on, 7
Repopulation, of Port Said, 157
Republican ideology, 14, 17, 71, 213–14, 221
Resistance: popular, 2, 11, 13, 40, 53, 61–63, 65, 69, 77, 80, 84, 87, 88, 106, 110, 114, 116, 119, 121, 124, 126, 152; social, 13, 219
Revision, of textbooks, 50–51, 59
Revolution, 64–67, 216. *See also specific revolutions*
Revolutionary Command Council, 123
Revolutionary socialization, 58

Rida, Fa'iq, 140–41, 157
Riou, Edouard M., 85
Rivera, Diego, 38
Roman Catholicism, 196, 197, 206
Roux, Jacques, 144, 145
Rudd qalbi (Dhulfiqar), 26, 27
Ruiz, Antonio Machado, 1
Ruz al-Yusuf, 11, 119, 124, 128, 187, 192, 207

Saad, Reem, 11
Sabir, Umm, 172
Sacred, 7, 13, 184–85, 188, 201, 228n32; commodification of, 190–91
Sadat, Anwar al-: assassination of, 200; education policies of, 33, 47, 59, 64, 69, 72; as Nasser's successor, 138; October War and, 156–57; Open Door policy of, 81; visions stopped under, 198–200
Sadiq, Mus'ad, 181, 258n67
Saint-Exupéry, Antoine de, 58
Saints: communion of, 179, 257n58; cults of, 179, 185; familiarity with, 179; indigenization of, 200, 201; Muslims and, 179, 198; nationalization of, 200. *See also* St. Mary; St. Michael
Salim, Kamal, 20
Savage, Raymond, 76, 87, 97, 100, 243n22
SCAF. *See* Supreme Council of the Armed Forces
Scholarship: on identity, 7; on memory, 8; on nationalism, 7; on remembrance, 7
School: fee of, 25; foreign, 57–58; language, 58; private, 56, 68, 239n38, 240n69; tuition of, 21, 24, 25. *See also* Education; Nasserian schoolhouse
Schoolgirls, 40
Schoolhouse, 71–72; class performance in, 68; curriculum in, 50, 65–66, 238nn5–6; as matrix of the nation, 49; Nasserian, 17, 19, 20, 50–51, 55, 71; nationalization of, 51
Schooling, secular, 12, 41, 51
Schooling reforms: historical lies, 50; historical representations, 49–50; in 1950s–1960s, 49–74; in the present, 50–54
Science, of miracles, 167–91
Scientific Study on the Truth of the Apparition of the Virgin at her Church of Zaytun, 177
Scott, James, 103
Sectarian conflict, 164, 196, 207–9, 213
Sectarian politics, 212–14

Secularization, of "Flight of the Holy Family," 201
Secular nationalism, 128, 131, 212, 222
Secular politics downfall, 164, 174
Secular schooling, 12, 23, 30, 35, 39, 41, 51, 56
Seers, 8, 179, 202, 204–5
Sérionne, Charles de, 86
Seymour, David "Chim," 117
Shafik, Viola, 211
Shahin, Yusif, 127–28, 146
Shaltut, Mahmud, 179
Shamm al-Nasim: celebrations of, 91, 99, 100, 106; effigy burning during, 12, 76, 82, 90, 95, 103, 107, 115
Shanuda, Zaki, 169, 183, 195, 196
Shanuda III, 180, 203, 206
Sharqiyya, 200
Shubra, 203
Shukr, 'Aysha, 100
Shuman, Mas'ud, 96, 134
Siba'i, Mahmud al-, 172
Sirri, Jadhbiyya, 36–38, 39
Six-Day War, 154, 155, 156–57. *See also* June War; 1967 War
Sniping, during Suez War, 119, 250n51
Social cohesion, 7, 78, 88, 104, 164, 198
Social control, 33, 35, 59, 164
Social dislocation, 164
Social inclusion, in education, 16, 20, 32, 43, 48
Socialization, revolutionary, 58
Socialization policies, of Nasser, 34, 56
Social justice, 217–19
Social studies, 49, 50–51, 58, 239n50
Spence, Jonathan, 167
State power: centralization of, 165; reinforcement of, 165
Statistics, about education, 68, 240n71
St. Mary: Arab government protection of, 177; at Asyut, 206–7; church of, at Zaytun, 167, 170, 181; as Mother of Egypt, 163–91. *See also* Virgin Mary
St. Michael, 200–202, 261n22; church of, at Shubra, 168
Stockwell, Hugh Charles, 139
Strategic importance, of Port Said, 85
Student enrollment, 29, 33, 45, 46
Suez Canal, 76, 85, 106; civilians in, 121, 150–55, 253n34, 253n37; conflict in, 12, 80, 96; lore about, 114–15; nationalization of, 39, 110, 139;
propaganda films about, 113–14. *See also* Port Said
Suez Canal Company, 88
Suez War, 76, 80, 86; black, gray, and other creative dialectics, 116–21, 249n44; books written about, 126–27; British historiography of, 116; British in, 105–35; casualties of, 117–18, 119, 249n39, 249n49; celebrities involved in, 123; damages in, 118; patriotic love during, 126, 134–35; photographs of, 117; propaganda used in, 116–21, 123–24, 147; sniping during, 119, 250n51; women in, 124–26, 251n68; youth during, 119–20
Supreme Council of the Armed Forces (SCAF), 219
Surur, Najib, 79

Taha, 'Amm, 52–53
Tahir, 'Adil, 181
Tahrir Square, 14, 15, 33, 171, 218
Tanbura musicians, 115–16, 133–34
The Teacher (Sirri), 36
Television, 25, 33, 146, 234n83
Temporary shelters, in Egypt, 152
Terre des Hommes (Saint-Exupéry), 58
Terrorism, Zionist, 177
Testimony: of Mat'al, 146–47; of 'Uthman, Taha Sa'ad, 41, 52–53; about Virgin Mary, 166, 170, 179, 182, 183
Textbooks, 21–23, 231m22, 231n17, 231n19, 237n128; civic education and, 49–50, 237n3; guidelines for, 59; historical themes in, 62–63; history curriculum in, 65–66; ideology and, 58–59; imposition of, 57; Islamic scriptures in, 50; Khedivial, 51; during Mubarak years, 64; during Nasser years, 60–61, 64, 67, 119, 201; production of, 51; publishing of, 59; revision of, 50–51, 59; during Sadat years, 64; social studies in, 49, 50–51, 58, 239n50; women and, 50
Thabat, Mina, 204
Thawra, 148. *See also* Revolution
Theological uniformity cultural myths, 211
Third Republic, 28, 43, 49
Tourism, "Flight of the Holy Family" and, 201
Trafficking, in Port Said, 158
Tsirkas, Stratis, 87
Tuition-free secondary education, 16, 19, 23
Turkish descent, 55, 238n27

Turkish-Ottoman oppression, 51
Turner, Victor, 94
Turner, Victor and Edith, 166, 186

'Ubur, 155, 156, 158
Ughniyya 'ala-l-mammar ('Abd al-Khaliq), 156
'Ulawyah, Q. M., 96
Umm al-Nur wa-banatiha (Shafik), 211
"Umm Kulthum" (Fatima Ibrahim al-Biltaji), 36, 123, 216
University of Alexandria, 19
University of Asyut, 19
University of 'Ayn al-Shams, 19
University of Cairo, 43, 45, 46
University of Mansura, 19
'Urabi, Colonel Ahmad, 44, 52, 53, 236n113
'Uthman, Taha Sa'ad, 1, 2, 7, 21, 24, 25, 42, 53, 68, 227n1; education of, 21, 68, 231n16; interview with, 24–25, 41–42, 52; testimony of, 41, 52–53
'Uthman, 'Uthman Ahmad, 159
Utterances: ambivalence of, 139, 146; historical, 9; institutional, 133; Mariophany, 190–91, 192, 196, 207, 209; of 1950s–60s, 75, 84; public, 143, 144, 146; vernacular, 75; Zaytun, 185, 192. *See also* Historical utterances
'Uways, Muhammad Hamid, 38, 69–70, 235n94

Validation, of Globalization, of Virgin Mary, 203–6
Vanguard of the People, 51
Veneration: of Kyrillus VI, 179, 180–81, *181*, 182, 258n62; Marian, 198
Vernacular utterances, 75
Virgin Mary: apparitions, 170, 193–95, 199, 204, 259n6; blue-eyed, 185–88; Coptic Church and, 200–201; cult of, 196; doves and clouds and, 168–73; faith and, 188; garb of, 205; iconographical tradition of, 185, 186, *186*, 187; indigenization of, 201; Jewish acts condemned by, 175, 196; monopolization of, 200; nationalization of, 192; Palestinian features of, 205, 261n40; phenomenon of, 167, 176, 183, 184, 188; representations of, 185; testimony about, 166, 170, 179, 182, 183; visions of, 170; visitations of, 193–95, 204–5; women's empowerment and, 185–86; at Zaytun, 7, 8, 13, 164, 166, 167–71, *169*,

178, 183, 188–90, 192–93, 197, 203, 208, 259n94. *See also* Globalization, of Virgin Mary; St. Mary
Virgin of Guadalupe, 200
Virgin of Peace, 196
Visions, of Virgin Mary, 170
Visitation: narratives of, 193–95; of Virgin Mary, 193–95, 204–5

Wafd party, 16, 17, 19, 43, 87
War, 138–49; fabrications of, 145, 253n18; in Ismailia, 139, 141, 149. *See also specific wars*
War of Attrition, 81, 138, 143, 150, 154, 171
Warraq apparition, at Giza, 199, 203, 207, 209
Williams, James, 110, 112
Winckler, Onn, 11
Women: empowerment of, 33, 185–86; as fighters, 70, 114, 119, 121, 124, 125, 127; Free Officers and, 36; in New order, 35, 35–37; patriarchal nationalism and, 124; in Suez War, 124–26, 251n68; textbooks and, 50, 237n128
Workers, in Port Said, 87–88, 90–93, 96, 97, 245n65
World War I, 13, 54, 80, 98, 104
World War II, 4, 13, 80, 86, 87, 92, 106

Yasif, Sa'di, 129
Years, of Nasser, 11–13
Youstous of Saint Anthony, 178
Youth: recruitment of, 119, 120, 147, 152–53; during Suez War, 119–20
Yusif, Hagg, 99–100, 109, 110, 114–15, 121

Zaghlul, Sa'd, 56, 80
Zahira, 105
Zaynab, Sayyida, 210
Zaytun, 177; Church of, 169, *169*, 171; fortieth anniversary of, 199, 200, 207, 262n48; Mariophany at, 8, 168, 170, 171, 173, 174, 178, 182, 185, 187, 190–91, 192, 203, 208; Our Lady of, 168; utterances of, 185, 192; Virgin Mary at, 7, 8, 13, 164, 166, 167–71, *169*, 178, 183, 188–90, 192–93, 197, 203, 208, 259n94
Zayyat, Latifa al-, 121, 126–27, 251n78
Zayyid, Sa'd, 172
Zionist terrorism, 177

Mériam N. Belli is associate professor of history at the University of Iowa.

www.ingramcontent.com/pod-product-compliance
Lightning Source LLC
Chambersburg PA
CBHW021850230426
43671CB00006B/333